Edward R. Tufte
Nara

Visual Explanations

Images and Quantities, Evidence and Narrative

Graphics Press · *Cheshire, Connecticut*

PUBLISHED BY GRAPHICS PRESS LLC
POST OFFICE BOX 430, CHESHIRE, CONNECTICUT 06410

ISBN: 9798842789023 Paperback.

Printed in the United States of America *Seventh printing, with revisions, June 2005*

Introduction

ASSESSMENTS of change, dynamics, and cause and effect are at the heart of thinking and explanation. To understand is to know *what cause provokes what effect, by what means, at what rate.* How then is such knowledge to be represented?

This book describes design strategies—the proper arrangement in space and time of images, words, and numbers—for presenting information about motion, process, mechanism, cause and effect. These strategies are found again and again in portrayals of explanations, quite independent of the particular substantive content or technology of display.

And we also enter the cognitive paradise of explanation, a sparkling and exuberant world, intensely relevant to the design of information. Those who discover an explanation are often those who construct its representation. Thus we see Robert Burton in 1633 designing the title page of *The Anatomy of Melancholy* so as to reflect the book's elaborate argument (as did Hobbes in *Leviathan*); Christiaan Huygens in 1659 not only detecting the rings of Saturn but also luminously picturing his discoveries; John Snow in 1854 finding the evidence needed to end an epidemic and skillfully presenting that evidence; Richard Feynman developing space-time diagrams for quantum electrodynamics and also reasoning about the displays of evidence involved in the disastrous decision to launch the space shuttle Challenger; magicians for centuries contriving illusions about cause and effect and then in turn explaining techniques of illusion production; Ad Reinhardt presenting exquisitely subtle colors in his work and also teaching about styles of modern art with perceptive and droll cartoons. All these quick-witted creators and discoverers demonstrate methods by which to represent, describe, illustrate, and, indeed, construct knowledge.

Many of our examples suggest that clarity and excellence in thinking is very much like clarity and excellence in the display of data. When principles of design replicate principles of thought, the act of arranging information becomes an act of insight.

The first part of this book examines the logic of depicting quantitative evidence. What principles should inform our designs for showing data? Where do those principles come from? How can the integrity of quantitative descriptions be maintained in the face of complex and animated representations of data? What are the standards for evaluating visual evidence, especially for making decisions and reaching conclusions?

The second part considers design strategies, often for the arrangement of images as narrative. Here the issues are more visual—and lyrical—than quantitative. The idea is to make designs that enhance the richness, complexity, resolution, dimensionality, and clarity of the content. By extending the visual capacities of paper, video, and computer screen, we are able to extend the depth of our own knowledge and experience. And so this part of the book reports on architectures of comparison and narrative: parallelism, multiples, confections.

Several of the illustrations have been edited and redrawn (as noted in the citations) in order to repair battered originals, to make new color separations, and to improve the design. Primary sources—the themes for my variations—are always indicated.

My three books on information design stand in the following relation:

> *The Visual Display of Quantitative Information* is about *pictures of numbers*, how to depict data and enforce statistical honesty.
>
> *Envisioning Information* is about *pictures of nouns* (maps and aerial photographs, for example, consist of a great many nouns lying on the ground). *Envisioning* also deals with visual strategies for design: color, layering, and interaction effects.
>
> *Visual Explanations* is about *pictures of verbs*, the representation of mechanism and motion, of process and dynamics, of causes and effects, of explanation and narrative. Since such displays are often used to reach conclusions and make decisions, there is a special concern with the integrity of the content and the design.

These books are meant to be self-exemplifying: the objects themselves embody the ideas written about. Enchanted by the elegant and precise beauty of the best displays of information, and also inspired by the idea of self-exemplification, I have come to write, design, and publish the three books myself.

Acknowledgments

I am thankful for access to these libraries and galleries: Bibliothèque Royale Albert, Brussels; Rosgartenmuseum, Constance; The British Library, London; National Gallery of Art, and Hirshhorn Museum and Sculpture Garden, Washington, DC; William Andrews Clark Memorial Library, Los Angeles; and, at Yale University, the Art and Architecture Library, Geology Library, Medical Historical Library, Social Science Library, Sterling Memorial Library, and Interlibrary Loan. Even more helpful were dealers in rare books: Jonathan Hill, Richard Lan, Charles B. Wood III, and the auction houses Sotheby's and Christie's.

In this complex project, many have provided advice and assistance during the past six years. I remember gratefully:

For ideas and examples, Sam Antupit, Juliane Brand, David Cameron, Matthew Carter, William Cleveland, Morris Cohen, Nicholas Cox, Hanna Demetz, Inge Druckrey, Elisabeth Fairman, Alvan Feinstein, Creighton Gilbert, Christopher Hailey, Joanna Hitchcock, Ray Hyman, Patrick Lynch, David Morrison, David Pendlebury, Johnstone Quinan, Eric Roberts, Steven Smith, Suzanne Tatian, and Virginia Tufte. Frederick Lighthall of the University of Chicago wrote a very helpful letter about the decision to launch the space shuttle Challenger.

For providing the Babar drawing, the gracious Laurent de Brunhoff and Phyllis Rose. For explaining his unique cyclogram, Cosmonaut Georgi Grechko. For two scientific illustrations, Patricia Wynne. For translations, Dmitry Krasny, Simon Varey, and Craig Williams.

For photography, Bob Adelman, Michael Arsenault, Paul Harris, Roger Kelso, and R. J. Phil. For helping with my efforts at underwater photography, Michael Bonini and Patricia Kobrin of New England Diving, and the staff at Fisheye of Cayman in Grand Cayman, British West Indies.

For design assistance, Bonnie Scranton, Weilin Wu, John Connolly, and Dmitry Krasny. For typesetting in Monotype Bembo, Michael and Winifred Bixler; for advice on design, Howard I. Gralla.

For managing Graphics Press with special care, Karen Bass, Elaine Lau, Elaine Morse, Kathy Orlando, Carolyn Williams, Kate Bigwood, Cynthia Bill, Onslo Carrington, Real Masse, Katherine McDonnell, and Peter Taylor.

Most of all, these wonderful colleagues contributed directly to making this book: Jamy Ian Swiss, a professional magician and lecturer, is co-author of chapter 3 on explaining magic. Bonnie Scranton, now at *Newsweek*, helped to design many of the original images shown here, including the rainbow map, history of modern painting, and museum interface. Colleen Bushell of the National Center for Supercomputing Applications at the University of Illinois produced the animation of a thunderstorm. Seth Powsner of the Yale University Medical School is co-author of our work (first published in *The Lancet*) on displays for monitoring the care and condition of medical patients.

Cheshire, Connecticut

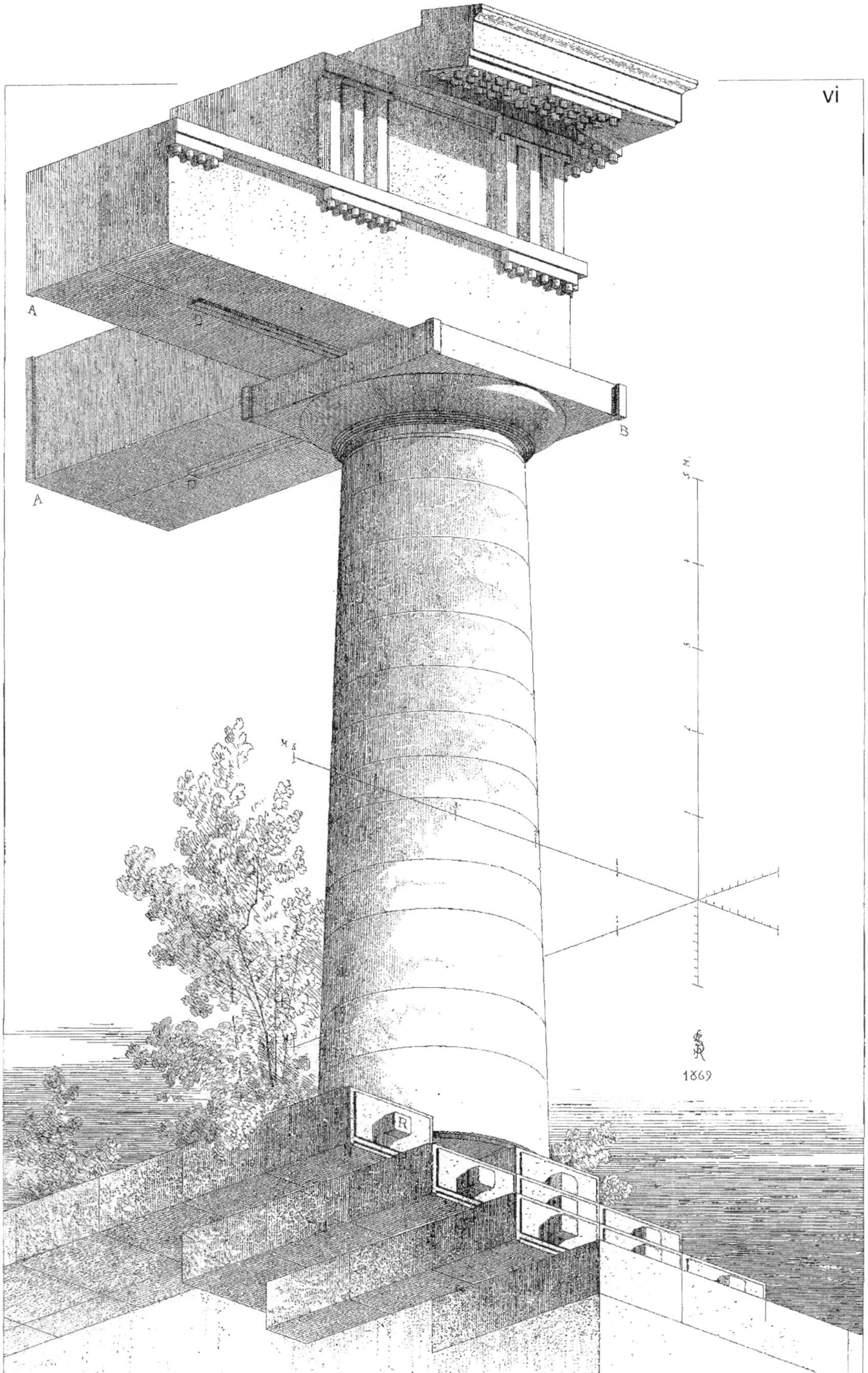

DESSINE PAR A CHOISY

GRAVE PAR H. SAUVESTRE

1 Images and Quantities

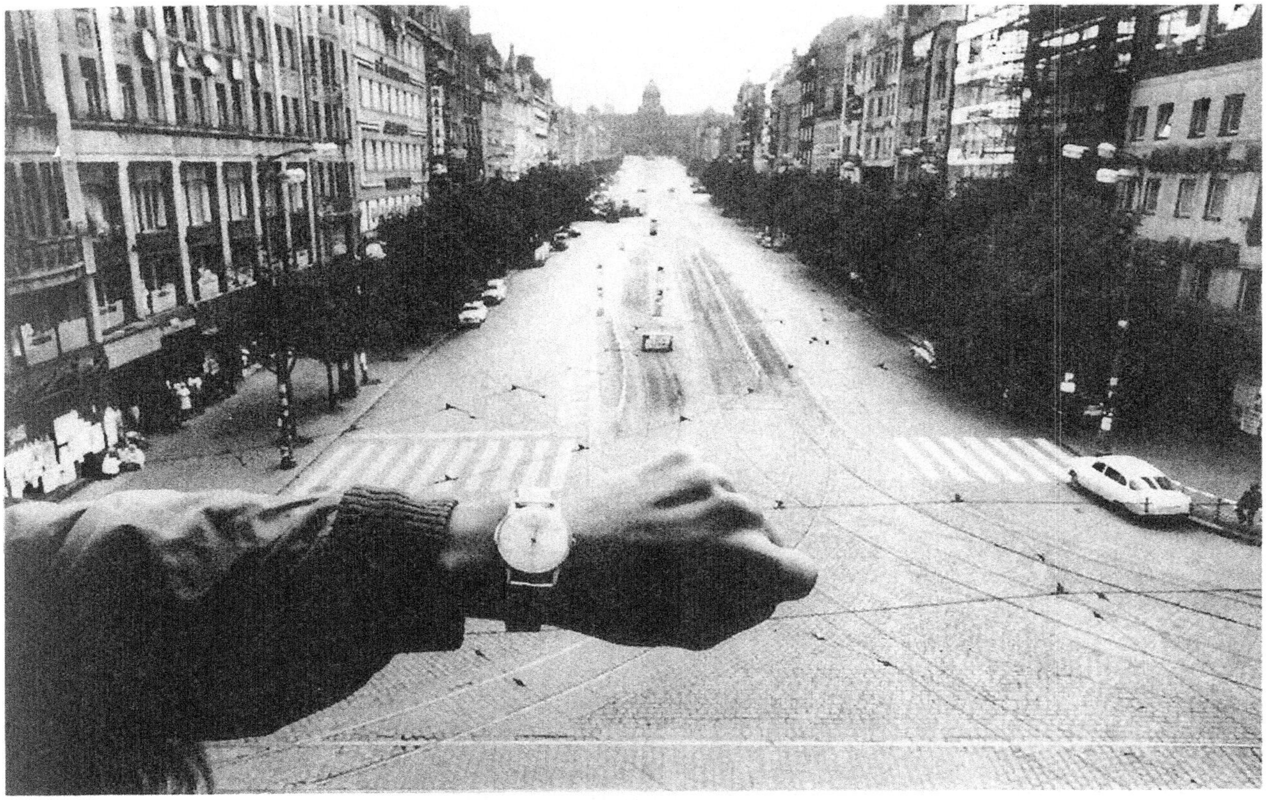

Josef Koudelka, *The Urge to See*, Prague, August 22, 1968.

OUR thinking is filled with assessments of quantity, an approximate or exact sense of number, amount, size, scale. In scientific work, both order-of-magnitude reasoning and precise measurements are pervasive. How are such quantities represented in visual expressions of ideas, experience, evidence? How are moving images, photographs, diagrams, maps, and charts to be scaled and labeled? And what makes images quantitatively eloquent?

VISUAL techniques for depicting quantities include *direct labels* (for example, the numerically labeled grids of statistical graphics, or, at left, dimensional tripods in architectural drawings); *encodings* (color scales); and *self-representing scales* (objects of known size appearing in an image). Using all these methods, Josef Koudelka's haunting and vehement photograph, *The Urge to See*, testifies to the empty streets during the 1968 Soviet invasion of Czechoslovakia that ended the Prague Spring of democratic reform. In the foreground, a watch documents the hour (*direct label*), as the shadows and gray light hint at the time of day (*encoding*), while in the distance Soviet tanks surround the national museum (*self-representing scales*, as many familiar objects in perspective demarcate the street and the photographer's location).

Auguste Choisy, *L'art de bâtir chez les romains* (Paris, 1873), plate XXIII, Segeste.

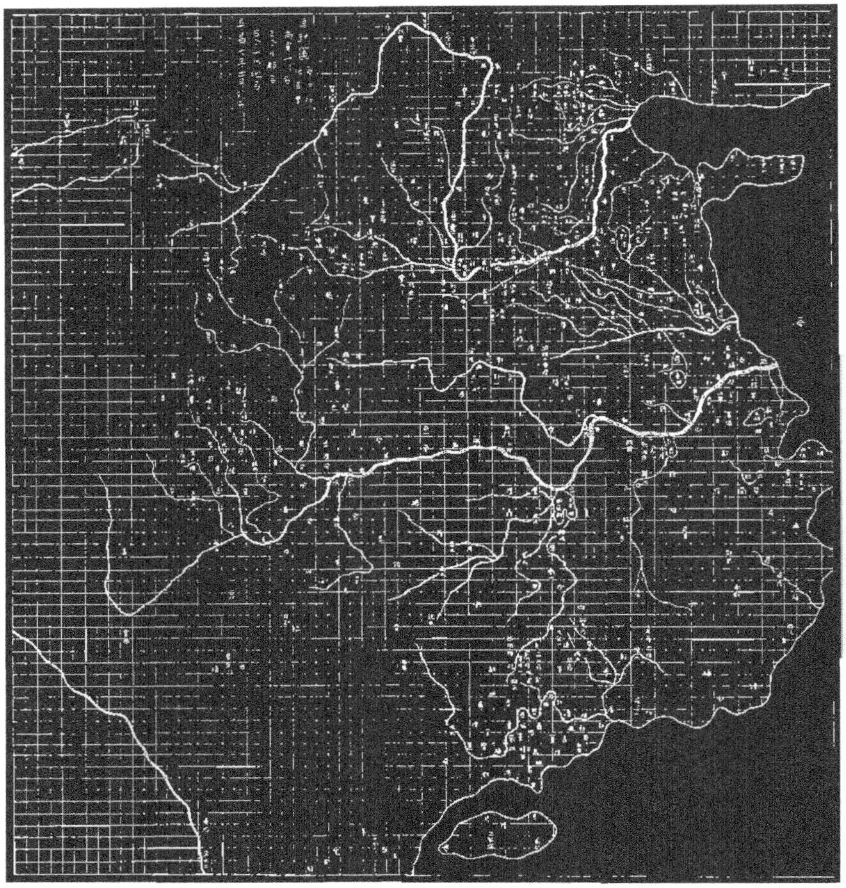

The original stone engraving is 32 by 31 in or 80 by 79 cm; redrawn from Edouard Chavannes, "Les Deux Plus Anciens Spécimens de la Cartographie Chinoise," *Bulletin de l'École Française de l'Extrême Orient*, 3 (1903), pp. 214–247, Carte B.

MAPS express quantities visually by location (two-dimensional addresses of latitude and longitude) and by areal extent (surface coverage). Some 900 years ago a fully scaled map was engraved in stone by precocious Chinese cartographers. The *Yu ji tu* or the Map of the Tracks of Yu is

> . . . the most remarkable cartographic work of its age in any culture, carved in stone in +1137 but probably dating from before +1100. . . . The coastal outline is relatively firm and the precision of the network of river systems extraordinary. . . . Anyone who compares this map with the contemporary productions of European religious cosmography cannot but be amazed at the extent to which Chinese geography was at that time ahead of the West. . . . There was nothing like it in Europe till the Escorial MS. map of about +1550.[1]

A note on the stone indicates that each grid square represents 100 *li*, a scale of map to world of approximately 1 to 4,500,000.

Despite their quantifying scales and grids, maps resemble miniature pictorial representations of the physical world. To depict relations between *any* measured quantities, however, requires replacing the map's natural spatial scales with abstract scales of measurement not based on geographic analogy. To go from maps of existing scenery to graphs of newly measured and collated data was an enormous conceptual step. Embodied in the very first maps were all the ideas necessary for making

[1] Joseph Needham, *Science and Civilization in China, volume 3: Mathematics and the Sciences of the Heavens and the Earth* (Cambridge, 1959), pp. 547–549. See also Cao Wanru, *et al.*, eds., *Zhongguo gudai ditu ji* [*Atlas of Ancient Chinese Maps*] (Beijing, 1990); and Cordell D. K. Yee, "Reinterpreting Traditional Chinese Geographical Maps," in J. B. Harley and David Woodward, eds., *The History of Cartography, volume 2, book 2: Cartography in the Traditional East and Southeast Asian Societies* (Chicago, 1994), pp. 47–50.

statistical graphics—quantified measures of locations of nouns in two-dimensional space—and yet it took 5,000 years to change the name of the coordinates from *west-east* and *north-south* to empirically measured variables *X* and *Y*. The even longer history of art took a similar course: the naturalistic coordinate system of painted cave-wall and canvas was first dislocated by Cubism's fractured images from multiple viewpoints and then eventually abandoned altogether in 20th-century abstract painting, as the two dimensions of the canvas no longer referred to worldly scenery but only to themselves.

One of the earliest visual representations of statistical data was drawn in 1644 by Michael Florent van Langren, a Flemish astronomer to the Spanish court. Appropriately enough for statistics, this graph shows 12 diverse estimates of the distance between Toledo and Rome. Measured in degrees longitude, the scale locates Toledo, the historic Spanish city portrayed in El Greco's *View of Toledo*, at the prime meridian of 0°. All the longitudes are too large, perhaps a result of underestimating

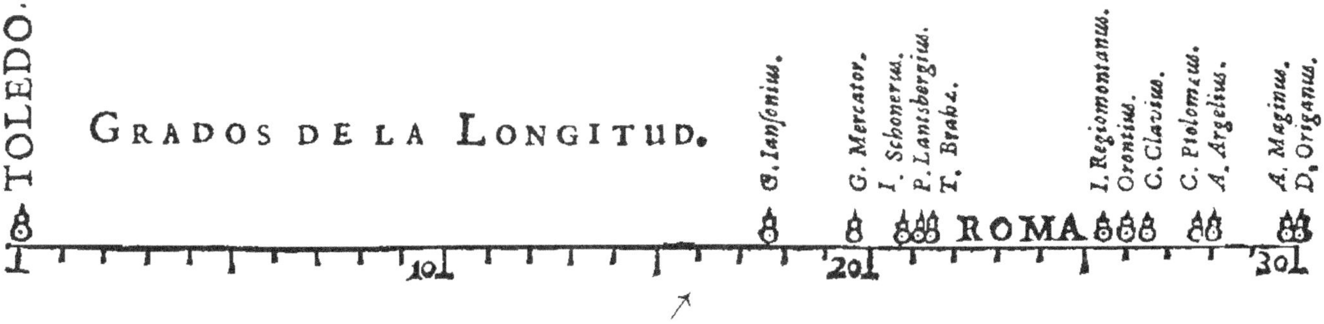

the earth's circumference. The correct distance is 16° 30′. Combining nouns with numbers, the chart cites the astronomers and cartographers making the estimates—Jansson, Mercator, Schoener, Lansberge, Brahe, Regiomontanus, Ptolemy, and others. On Langren's scale, the broadly inexact position of Rome, sprawled out 22° to 25° from Toledo, places it far east of its actual location and well across the Adriatic Sea into western Greece. A one-dimensional map of data, the chart is remarkably advanced for its time, spatially arranging (rather than merely recording in a table) various estimates of the same quantity. Furthermore, the data are distributed in relation to a putatively true value. Langren's chart appears to be the earliest display of a distribution of common measurements; and it is my candidate for the first statistical graphic ever.[2]

Michael Florent van Langren, *La Verdadera Longitud por Mar y Tierra* (Antwerp, 1644), p. 3. The purpose of the graph was to advance Langren's own method for the determination of longitude because of "... the existence of such enormous errors, as can be seen from the line, which shows the different distances that the greatest astronomers and geographers put between Rome and Toledo ..."

By 1765, two-dimensional space was liberated from pictorially-based scales. J. H. Lambert described a *general* graphical grid (no more analogies to maps) for depicting systematic relations between measured quantities:

> We have in general two variable quantities, x, y, which will be collated with one another by observation, so that we can determine for each value of x, which may be considered as an abscissa, the corresponding ordinate y. Were the experiments or observations completely accurate, these ordinates would give a number of points

[2] On the history of statistical graphics, see H. Gray Funkhouser, "Historical Development of the Graphical Representation of Statistical Data," *Osiris*, 3 (November 1937), 269–404; and James R. Beniger and Dorothy L. Robyn, "Quantitative Graphics in Statistics: A Brief History," *American Statistician*, 32 (February 1978), pp. 1–11.

> through which a straight or curved line should be drawn. But as this is not so, the line deviates to a greater or lesser extent from the observational points. It must therefore be drawn in such a way that it comes as near as possible to its true position and goes, as it were, through the middle of the given points.[3]

Modern scientific graphics were now in place; the two-dimensional plane was quantified, available for any measured data. Used with fitted models, graphics could describe and characterize relations between variables—thus displaying the essential evidence necessary for establishing cause and effect.

[3] Johann Heinrich Lambert, *Beyträge zum Gebrauche der Mathematik und deren Anwendung* (Berlin, 1765), as quoted in Laura Tilling, "Early Experimental Graphs," *British Journal for the History of Science*, 8 (1975), pp. 204–205.

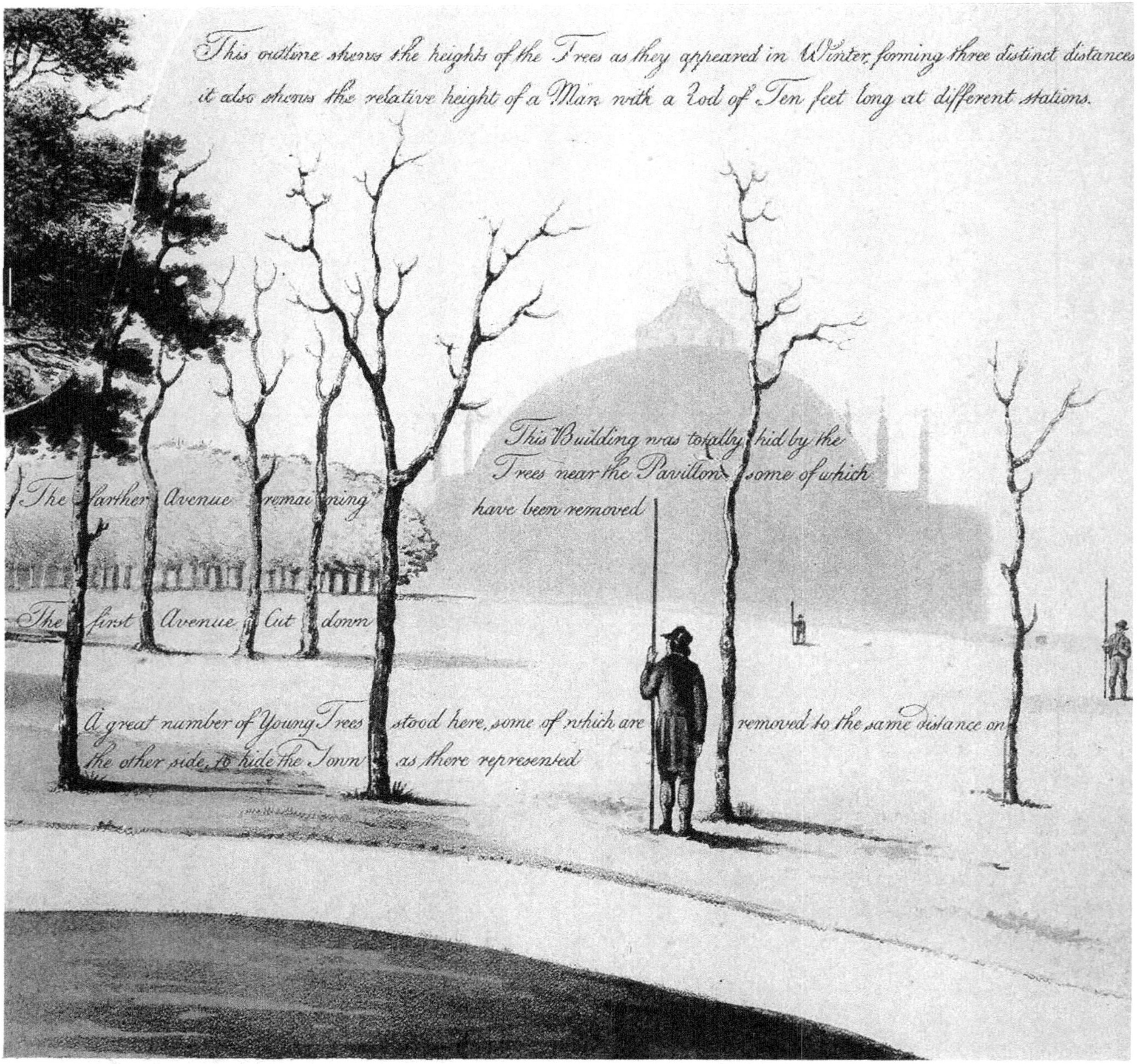

Humphry Repton, *Designs for the Pavillon at Brighton* (London, 1808), pp. 40–41, detail, redrawn.

> through which a straight or curved line should be drawn. But as this is not so, the line deviates to a greater or lesser extent from the observational points. It must therefore be drawn in such a way that it comes as near as possible to its true position and goes, as it were, through the middle of the given points.[3]

Modern scientific graphics were now in place; the two-dimensional plane was quantified, available for any measured data. Used with fitted models, graphics could describe and characterize relations between variables—thus displaying the essential evidence necessary for establishing cause and effect.

[3] Johann Heinrich Lambert, *Beyträge zum Gebrauche der Mathematik und deren Anwendung* (Berlin, 1765), as quoted in Laura Tilling, "Early Experimental Graphs," *British Journal for the History of Science*, 8 (1975), pp. 204–205.

Humphry Repton, *Designs for the Pavillon at Brighton* (London, 1808), pp. 40–41, detail, redrawn.

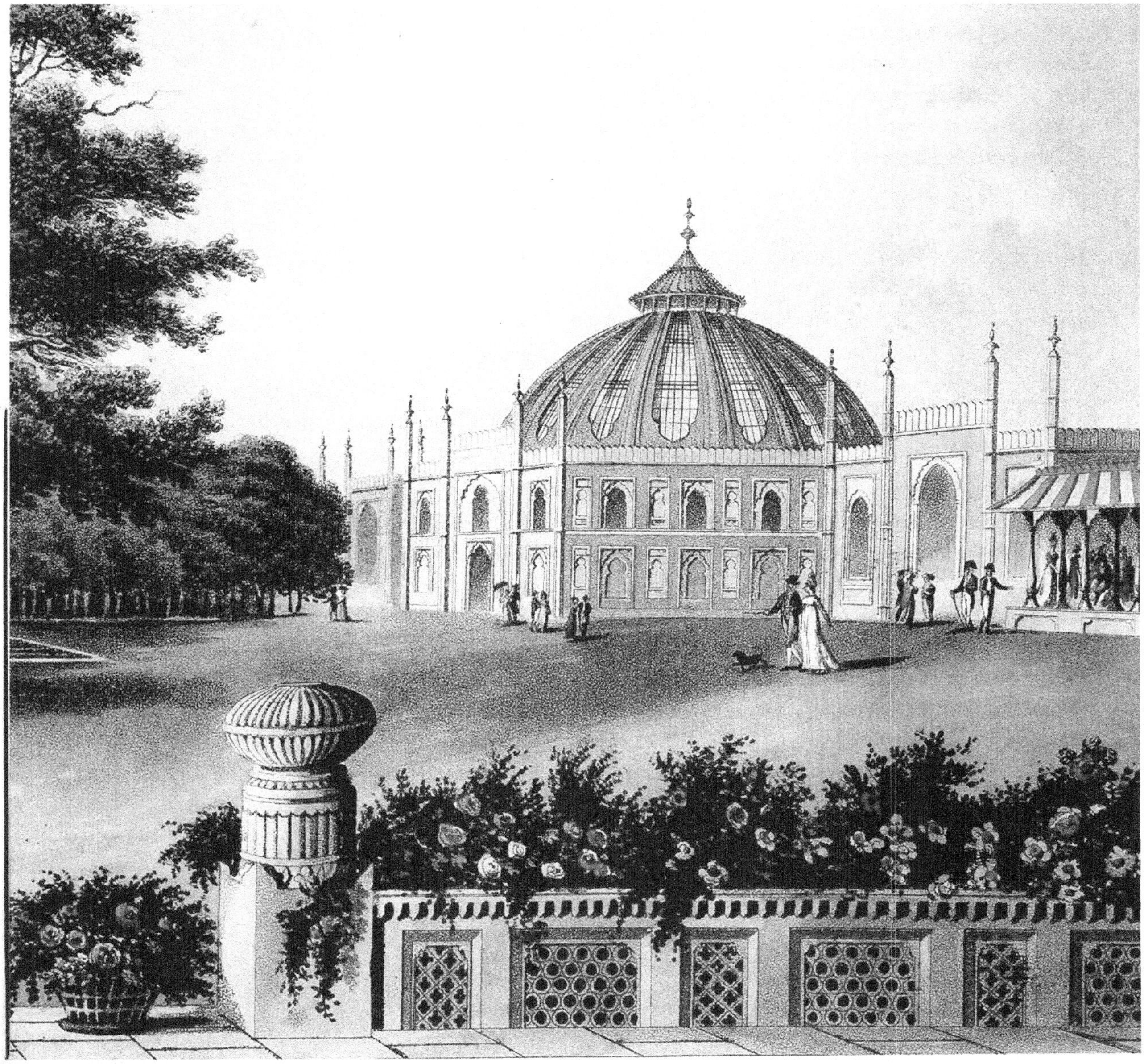

NOT a great many substantive problems, however, are exclusively two-dimensional. Indeed, the world is generally multivariate. For centuries, the profound, central issue in depicting information has been how to represent three or more dimensions of data on the two-dimensional display surfaces of walls, stone, canvas, paper, and, recently, computer screens. Of course, this is something that architects and painters (using perspective) and animators (using perspective and motion) have done for a long time.

Humphry Repton, the British landscape architect, quantified the perspective drawing at left by placing three people with ten-foot poles around the grounds shown on the *before* flap. To explain the scaling, which combines the methods of self-representation and direct labels, words are integrated into the image: "This . . . shews the heights of the Trees as they appeared in Winter, forming three distinct distances; it also shews the relative height of a Man with a Rod of Ten feet long at different stations." These markers are necessary, since the perspective drawing itself reads ambiguously with regard to the sizes of objects in the background.[4] When the distances are reconstructed, however, it is clear that the pole-person in the deep background of the *before* flap is too small compared with the scaling of the *after* drawing.

Repton's shift in scaling dramatizes the visual consequences of his plans. In the *before* flap on top, the Brighton pavilion appears hidden, isolated, distant—impressions intensified by the tiny person and by the over-writing on the shadowy building. When the flap is raised to reveal the proposed redesign, the space between us and the pavilion has now become intimate and comfortable, filled with well-dressed visitors (giants, compared with the drab Lilliputian pole-people). A lush garden and patio dominate the foreground. Strolling in an area previously occupied by the miniature pole-person of *before*, an animated *after* couple walk a dog (which would be immense if seen in *before* space). Repton overreached in several other *before/after* comparisons, exaggerating the impact of his proposed improvements. In the plan at left, the designs of the flap, the pole-people, and the integrated text are all ingenious and delightful—but the integrity of the work is compromised by persistent visual cheating.

Sometimes images can be quantified in vivid and memorable ways, here in the photograph at right by a ladder-person. Lift the flap at lower right to reveal a self-representing scale for the vast *Mural with Blue Brushstroke* (68 by 32 ft, or 21 by 10 m). Roy Lichtenstein, the artist, stands atop the ladder!

Published photographs of works of art often fail to indicate a sense of the *sizes* of the original objects. Scholarly writings usually report the dimensions of the original; the scalings of published reproductions, however, vary capriciously in amount of reduction or enlargement. In practice, the sizes of reproduced images depend almost entirely on

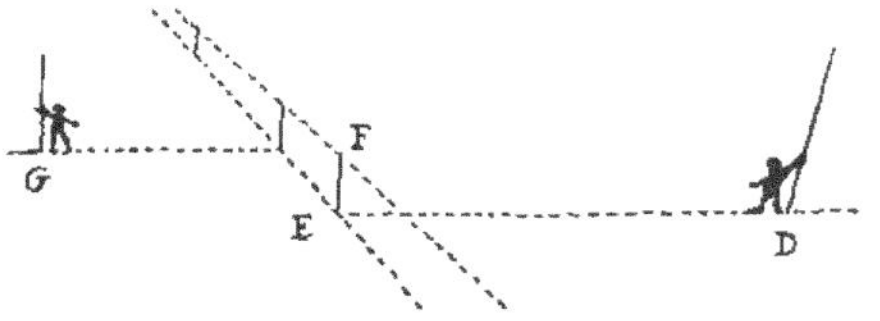

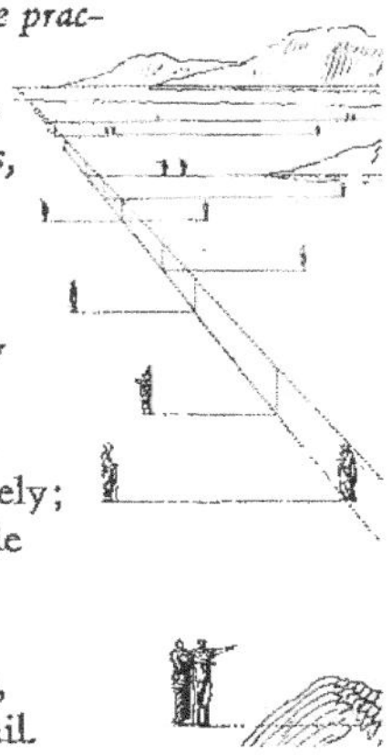

[4] As early as 1642, pole-people were active in scaling recession for landscapes; above, Jean Dubreuil, *La perspective pratique nécessaire à tous peintres, graveurs, sculpteurs, architectes, orfevres, brodeurs, tapissiers et autres se servant du dessein* (Paris, 1642), plate 126, detail. A few years before Repton, Valenciennes deployed toga-people perspectively; at right, Pierre Henri de Valenciennes, *Élémens de perspective pratique à l'usage des artistes* (Paris, 1800), plate xxxv, detail.

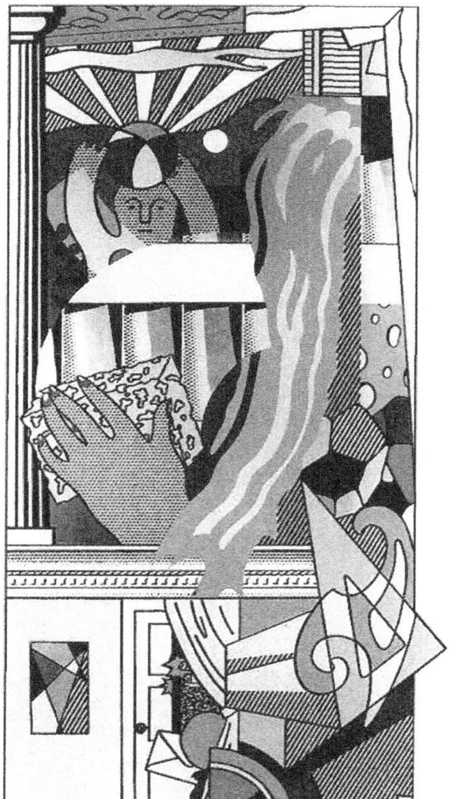

Photograph by Bob Adelman; originally published in *Roy Lichtenstein: Mural with Blue Brushstroke*, essay by Calvin Tomkins, with photographs and interview by Bob Adelman (New York, 1988), p. 127.

convenience of fit into the grid layout of a page or computer screen. Although the physical scope of a work of art is not always a relevant variable, for some works—Lichtenstein's mural, Monet's water lilies (paintings with areas of 250 square feet or 23 square meters), colossal statues of *David* or the People's Heroic Leader, posters, delicate and precious miniatures, postage stamps, typography—their size is surely an expressive factor.[5] How then can tiny, irregularly scaled reproductions tell us about measure, magnitude, presence, absolute or relative size?

Partial visual knowledge about size of a work can be conveyed by maintaining a consistent relative scale throughout an entire set of reproduced images, similar to a photograph showing a group of objects at a constant scale relative to one another, at least after adjusting for the effects of perspective. It is as if the objects to be reproduced were photographed all at once in a gallery: for example, the historic

[5] On size and scale, see Meyer Schapiro, "On Some Problems in the Semiotics of Visual Art: Field and Vehicle in Image-Signs [1969]," in *Theory and Philosophy of Art: Style, Artist, and Society: Selected Papers* (New York, 1994), pp. 22–26.

Herbert Matter, *Thirteen Photographs: Alberto Giacometti and Sculptures* (Hamden, 1978). Redrawn. Norman Ives and Sewell Sillman, the publishers, printed only 56 copies of this exquisite portfolio.

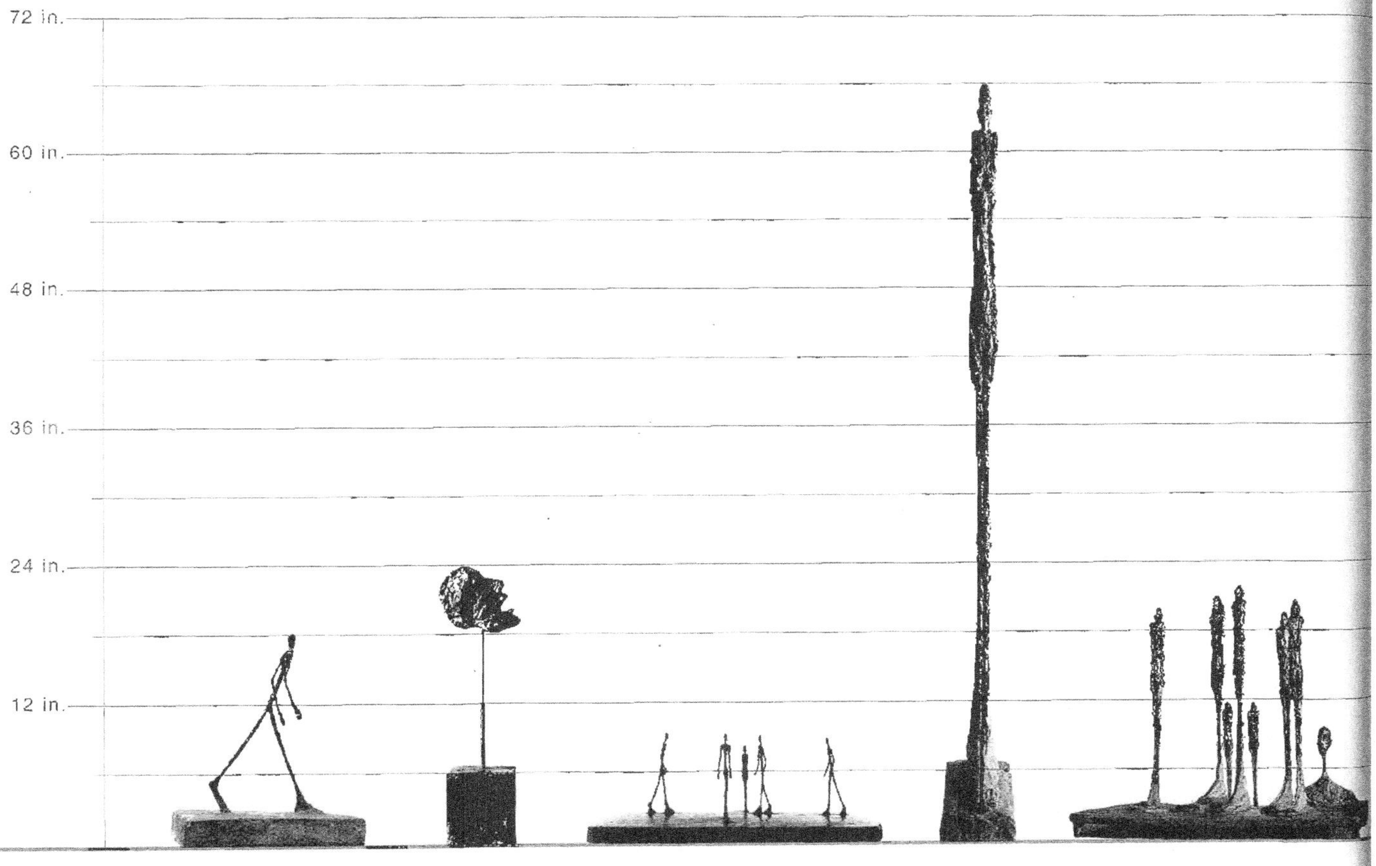

1
Alberto Giacometti, 1965

2
Man Walking (Homme qui Marche). 1950
Bronze, 18¼" h.

3
Head of a Man on a Rod (Tête sur Tige). 1947
Bronze, 24" h.

4
City Square (La Place). 1948
Bronze, 24¾" long

5
Standing Woman (Femme Debout) 1948
Bronze, 66" h.

6
Seven Figures and a Head (The Forest) (7 Figures et 1 Tête (La Forêt)). 1950
Painted Bronze, 22" h.

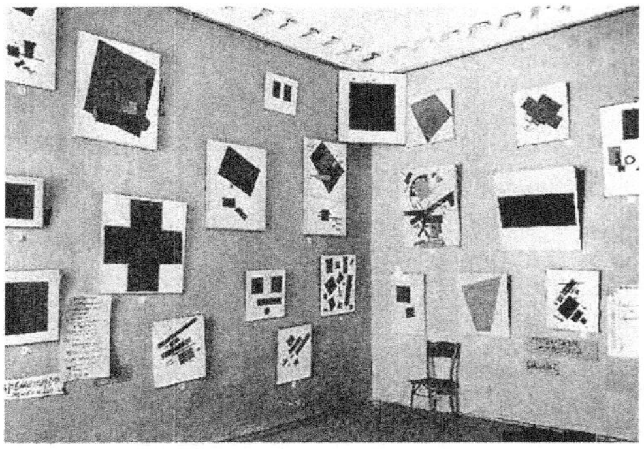

photograph at right of Malevich's 1915 Petrograd "0–10" exhibition of Suprematist paintings, which are of course scaled relative to each other and to the known size of the chair in the corner.

A constant scale factor is used below in this visual table of contents for Herbert Matter's portfolio of photographs of Alberto Giacometti's sculptures. Each sculpture is measured and scaled on a common grid in an extraordinary gallery of images. (This design is also helpful for field guides to birds, fish, plants, and the like.) Titles, dates, and dimensions are shown, with front and side views for items 7, 8, 9. At far lower left, the blank first entry refers to a portrait of Giacometti, whose head is self-scaling and need not be placed on a grid. Designed by Herbert Matter, the original published sheet is large, 20 by 48 inches, or 51 by 123 cm. On that sheet, the sculptures are depicted at 19% of their actual size; here, they are all at 7% of actual size, small but comparable.

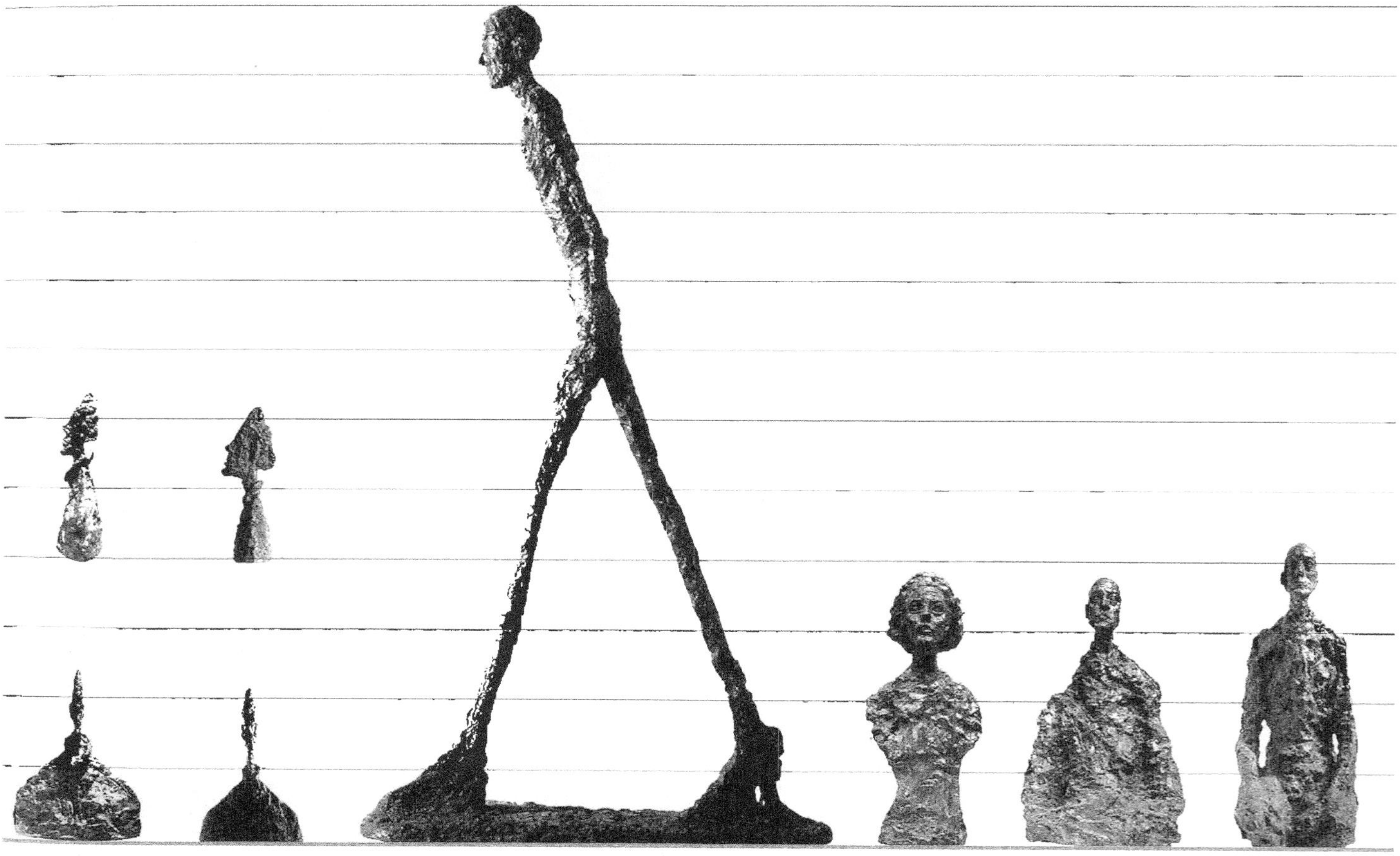

7
Diego in a jacket
(Diego au Blouson).
1953
Bronze, 14" h.

8 & 9
Bust of Diego
(Buste de Diego).
1954
Bronze, 13 1/4" h.

10
Walking Man I (Homme qui Marche I.).
1959-1960
Bronze, 72" h.

11
Bust of Annette VIII
(Buste d'Annette VIII).
1962
Bronze, 23 1/4" h.

12
Bust of Elie Lotar
(Buste d'Elie Lotar).
1965
Bronze, 22 3/4" h.

13
Elie Lotar
(Elie Lotar).
1965
Bronze, 25 3/4" h.

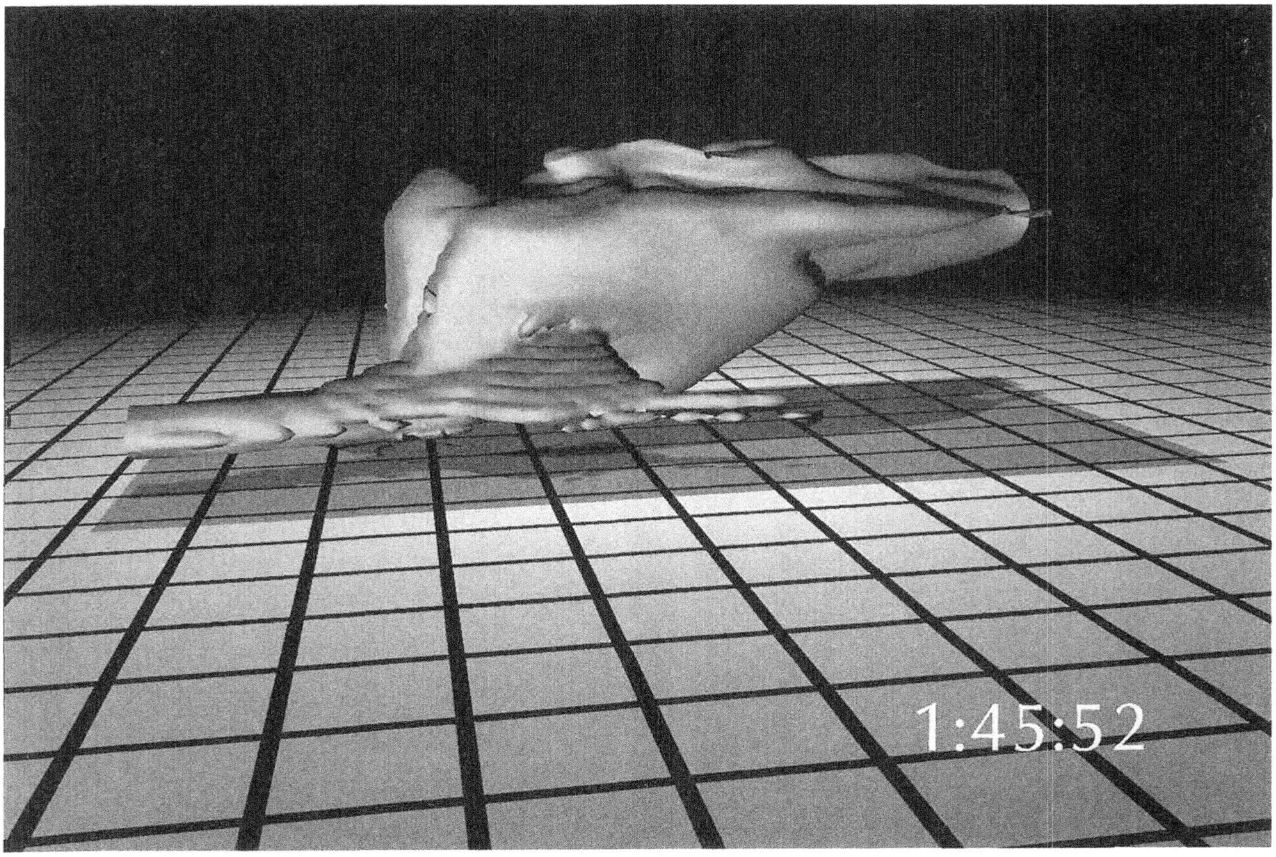

THE dequantification characteristic of art reproductions is also seen in scientific and technical imaging. Shown above is a video frame from a numerical model simulating a thunderstorm. Based on nine time-dependent partial differential equations as well as data gathered during a severe storm in Oklahoma and Texas, this supercomputer animation begins with a small cumulus cloud that grows into a fully developed storm. The five-minute movie describes a storm lasting two hours and twenty minutes, as indicated by the conspicuous time-stamp at lower right. Beneath the cloud, a rectangle delineates a two-dimensional projection of the computational domain. Near the ground, the cloud is trimmed away, revealing the grid and creating a sense of movement of the storm against the grid plane.

Image from the videotape "Study of a Numerically Modeled Severe Storm," National Center for Supercomputing Applications, University of Illinois at Urbana-Champaign, described in Robert B. Wilhelmson, Brian F. Jewett, Louis J. Wicker, Matthew Arrott, Colleen B. Bushell, Mark Bajuk, Jeffrey Thingvold, and Jeffery B. Yost, "A Study of the Evolution of a Numerically Modeled Severe Storm," *International Journal of Supercomputer Applications*, 4 (Summer 1990), pp. 20–36.

This is a classic of scientific visualization. Nevertheless, a redesign can improve the animation's context, precision, and visual character.

How big is that cloud? What direction is it moving? What are the dimensions of the grid? These fundamentals of scale, orientation, and labels—for centuries routine in maps and statistical graphics—are often missing in the colorful images emanating from computer visualizations. In one scholarly compilation (19 articles, 43 authors)

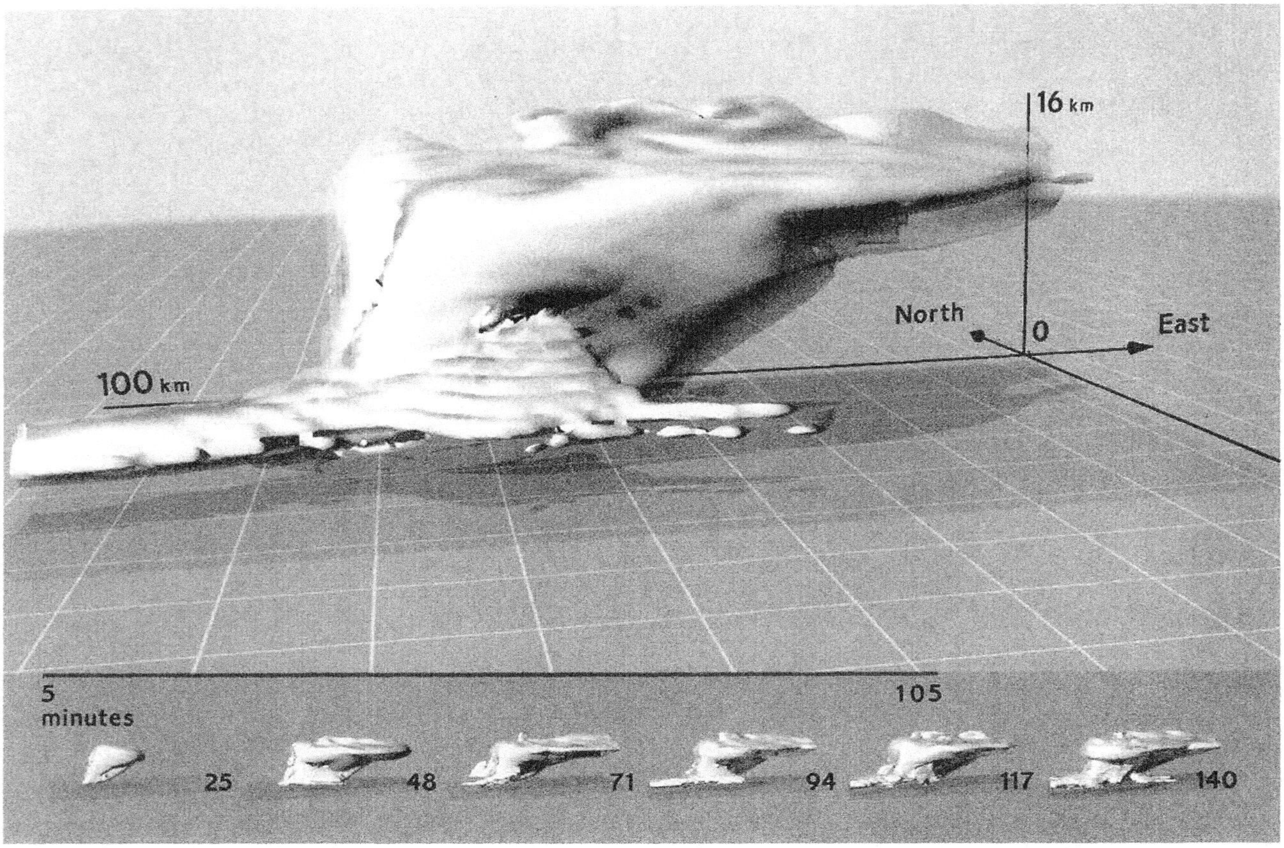

of supercomputer scientific animations, 65% of the 134 color images published had *no scales or labeled dimensions at all* and 22% had partial labels or scales. Only 13% had complete labels and scales.[6]

Restoring quantitative order, my redesign above locates the storm within a three-dimensional tripod of scales and directional arrows. Six small clouds depict a still-land history of the storm and also serve as three-dimensional tick marks for the red time-line, which flows left to right as time passes. The small, still, spatial sequence of images provides a context for the large, moving, temporal sequence above.

Despite the forceful perspective, the original image (left page) is informationally flat. Every element—clock, grid, rectangular domain, cloud, shadow, the brooding School-of-Caravaggio background—is intense and contrasty. In the original, the dominant visual effect (more than half of the pixels) is the orthodontic grid, which lacks quantified scales. The grid resembles the tiled *pavimento* patterns of Renaissance paintings that exaggerate perspective recession and appear in the most improbable circumstances: "... the stable at Bethlehem often boasts a decorative floor, and Saint John finds a small area of tiled paving to stand on in the wilderness."[7] Perhaps an excess of enthusiasm for trendy

Redesigned animation by Edward Tufte and Colleen B. Bushell, with assistance of Matthew Arrott, Polly Baker, and Michael McNeill; scientific data from Robert B. Wilhelmson, Brian F. Jewett, Crystal Shaw, and Louis J. Wicker (Department of Atmospheric Sciences and the National Center for Supercomputing Applications, University of Illinois at Urbana-Champaign); original visualization by Matthew Arrott, Mark Bajuk, Colleen B. Bushell, Jeffrey Thingvold, Jeffery B. Yost, National Center for Supercomputing Applications, University of Illinois at Urbana-Champaign.

[6] Gregory M. Nielson, Bruce Shriver, and Lawrence J. Rosenblum, eds., *Visualization in Scientific Computing* (Los Alamitos, California, 1990). Similarly dismal rates of dequantification were found in 12 other recent compilations of "scientific" visualizations.

[7] Lawrence Wright, *Perspective in Perspective* (London, 1983), p. 82.

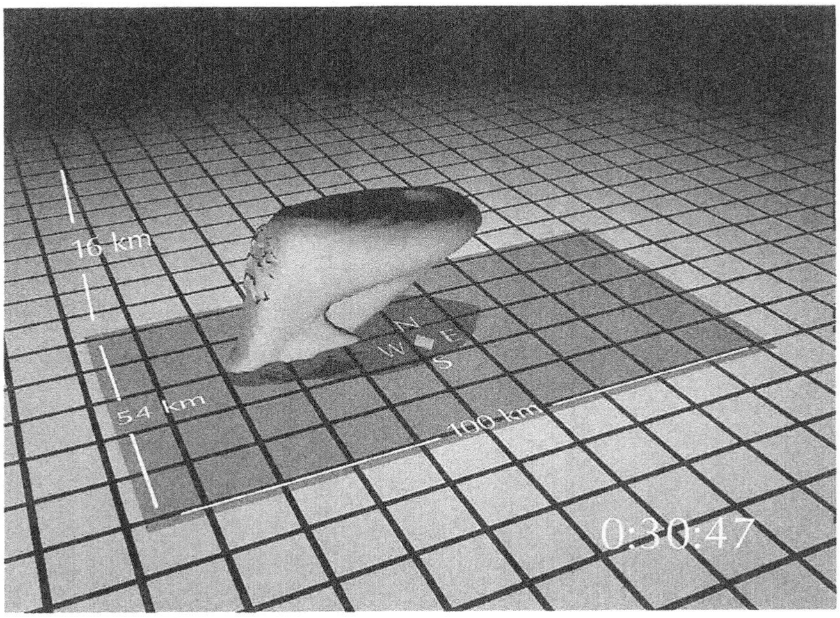

Image from the videotape "Study of a Numerically Modeled Severe Storm," National Center for Supercomputing Applications, University of Illinois at Urbana-Champaign, described in Robert B. Wilhelmson, Brian F. Jewett, Louis J. Wicker, Matthew Arrott, Colleen B. Bushell, Mark Bajuk, Jeffrey Thingvold, and Jeffery B. Yost, "A Study of the Evolution of a Numerically Modeled Severe Storm," *International Journal of Supercomputer Applications*, 4 (Summer 1990), pp. 20–36.

new technologies of three-dimensional display—perspective drawing in the 1500s and supercomputer animations in the 1990s—led to these over-exuberant tiles and grids that disrupt the unity of pictorial content. In this stable at Bethlehem, complete with ox and donkey, the tiles are merely inappropriate and unintentionally humorous; for the storm, however, the tremendous grid aggrandizes geometric perspective.[8]

[8] Describing another tiled stable (with walls of receding stone blocks), James Elkins writes: "In Fernando Gallego's *Nativity*, done in the last third of the fifteenth century, the box outshines the Child himself, and all but the most important figures are kept out in order to emphasize its geometric perfection. The chinks are drawn as dark lines, probably in imitation of a preparatory drawing, and their occlusions and jointings are done with as much care, and with more authority, than the divine drama." James Elkins, *The Poetics of Perspective* (Ithaca, New York, 1994), p. 121. Another stable with a tile grid is the Nativity panel by Michael Pacher, *St. Wolfgang Altarpiece* (1471–1481), Church of St. Wolfgang, Austria.

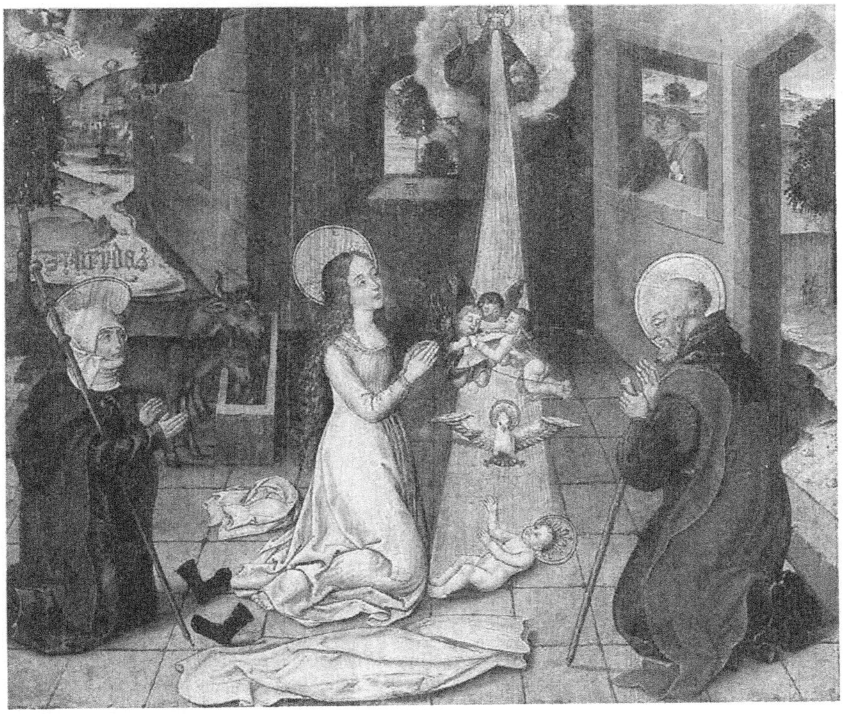

Rudolf Stahel, *Geburt Christi* (Constance, 1522), 30 by 36 in or 77 by 92 cm. The attribution to Stahel is uncertain.

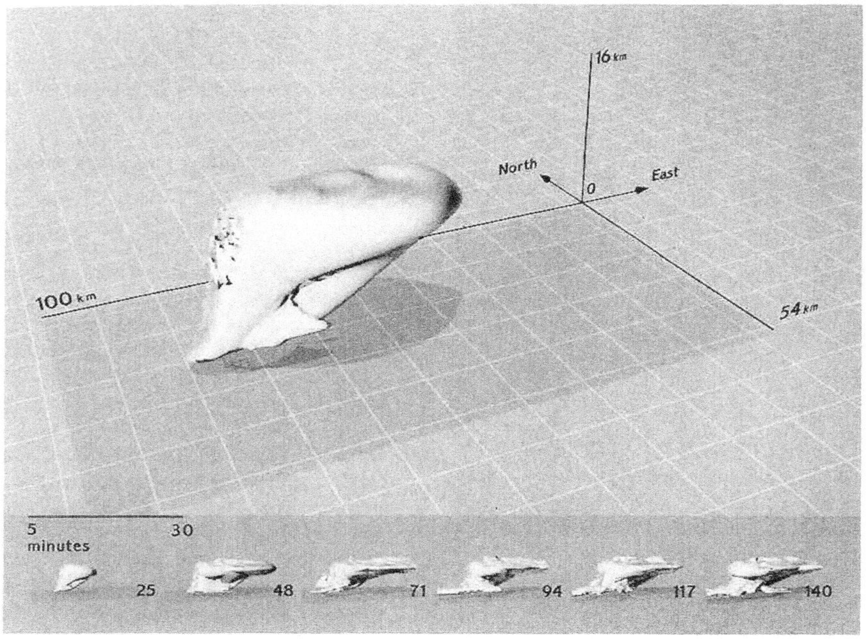

Redesigned animation by Edward Tufte and Colleen B. Bushell, with assistance of Matthew Arrott, Polly Baker, and Michael McNeill; scientific data from Robert B. Wilhelmson, Brian F. Jewett, Crystal Shaw, and Louis J. Wicker (Department of Atmospheric Sciences and the National Center for Supercomputing Applications, University of Illinois at Urbana-Champaign); original visualization by Matthew Arrott, Mark Bajuk, Colleen B. Bushell, Jeffrey Thingvold, Jeffery B. Yost, National Center for Supercomputing Applications, University of Illinois at Urbana-Champaign.

Besides the grid, two other layers of information lie beneath the cloud: a rectangular computational domain and the animation shadow. In cartoons, it is the animation shadow that gets Mickey and Minnie Mouse off the ground visually when they jump up. In this computer scene, one of the several simulated light sources is always above the moving cloud, casting a shadow beneath. Metaphors used in design of scientific visualizations include stages, lights, cameras, movies, cartoons, and, regrettably, television. These enterprises are not distinguished by their commitment to quantitative evidence; better guides for design are excellent maps and statistical graphics.

The original design at far upper left briefly quantifies the storm, as measurement scales and compass directions appear for only 14 seconds (in a grand total of 315 seconds of animation) before vanishing. In the redesign above, the omnipresent tripod might eventually attract attention to an unusual scale: the vertical dimension up into the air is multiplied two-fold compared with the scales down on the ground. Stretching the vertical sometimes helps to depict natural scenes, but such shifts in scaling should be persistently made clear to viewers.

More generally, when scientific images become dequantified, the language of analysis may drift toward credulous descriptions of form, pattern, and configuration—rather than answers to the questions *How many? How often? Where? How much? At what rate?*[9]

Extravagant dequantification is seen in a video flyover of the planet Venus, cooked up from radar data collected during the 1992 Magellan space probe. The vivid animation takes viewers on a rollercoaster tour of steep canyons and soaring mountains, sharply silhouetted against

[9] Ironically, one of the first and best visualizations, the movie *Powers of Ten* made by Charles and Ray Eames, deals entirely with the subject of quantity. And an excellent book allows still-land comparisons with the movie; see Philip Morrison, Phylis Morrison, and The Office of Charles and Ray Eames, *Powers of Ten* (New York, 1982). See also a delightful videotape by Wayne Lytle, *The Dangers of Glitziness and Other Visualization Faux Pas* (Cornell Theory Center, 1993); and Al Globus and Eric Raible, "Fourteen Ways to Say Nothing with Scientific Visualization," *Computer* (July 1994), pp. 86–88.

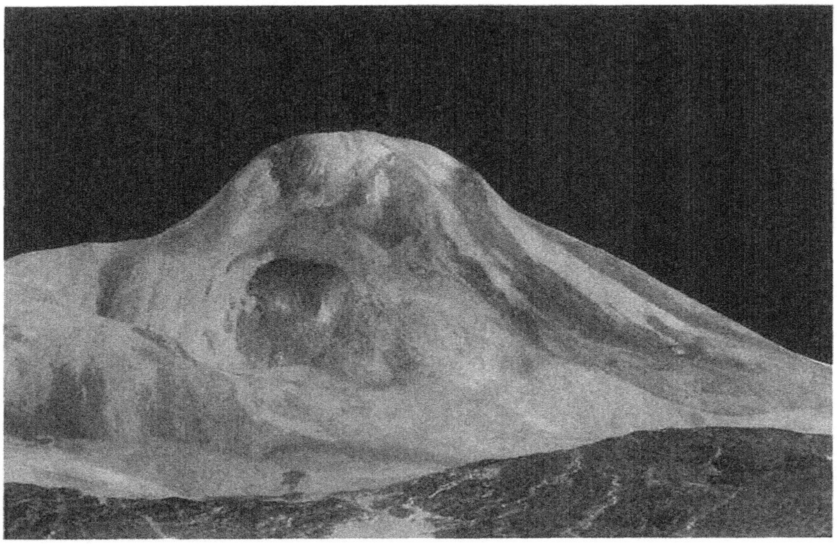

a dark sky. The excitement, however, results from an exaggeration of the vertical scale by 22.5 times! Terrific television but lousy science. David Morrison, the distinguished planetary researcher, had enough:

> This is a call for the formation of a Flat Venus Society. In the face of a media blitz that conveys the impression that Venus is characterized by soaring mountains and deep canyons, a dedicated group is needed to promote the fact that our sister planet is mostly flat, rolling plains.
>
> The beautiful and widely publicized "three-dimensional images" and video "fly-overs" of Venus released by NASA and the Magellan Project at the Jet Propulsion Laboratory all have a vertical exaggeration of 22.5 to 1. This distortion greatly exceeds that normally used even by geologists. . . .
>
> But the reality is different. Take for example, the large shield volcanos of Venus that are usually featured in these videos. They have heights of up to 5 km and widths of several hundred kilometers. It doesn't take a rocket scientist to calculate that the mean slopes are no more than 3°. Yet the public thinks they are precipitous peaks with near-vertical walls rising into a black sky. (A *black* sky? On *Venus*?)
>
> There are a few steep slopes on Venus, and they are important. On the edges of the Ishtar highlands, slopes can approach the angle of repose, providing startling evidence that this plateau is maintained by currently active tectonic forces. But who can tell from the released images?[10]

When such large scaling multipliers are used, viewers might well be shown a Repton-style *before/after* comparison, the natural (flat Venus) and stretched scales (hyped Venus). Otherwise our knowledge is surely imprisoned by the arbitrary technology of image processing and display, just as Matthew Paris, some 750 years ago, was constrained to produce this conspicuously squarish map of Britain. A note on the map, drawn around 1250, explains the distortion: "The whole island should have been longer if only the page had permitted."[11] At least Paris made a clear announcement of the scaling situation right there on his map.

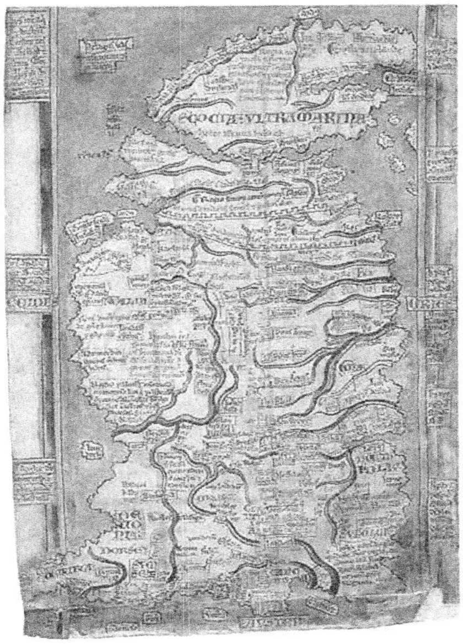

[10] David Morrison, "Forum: Flat Venus Society Organizes," *EOS* 73 (March 3, 1992); see also Ellen R. Stofan, "Reply," *ibid.* For another critique ("a cartoon volcano") of these images of Venus as made available on a computer network, see Clifford Stoll, *Silicon Snake Oil* (New York, 1995), pp. 83–84. The downloaded images contain no mention of the hyped vertical, and the *sole* documentation is "8000-meter-high Maat Mons on Venus, from NASA's Magellan Spacecraft, courtesy of Jet Propulsion Lab." Large vertical multiples appropriately show mountainous relief in maps depicting entire planets; however, these are *still-land overview* maps, not flyovers close to the surface. In the video of Venus, intense closeness and brisk motion make for a strong impression of height in perspective; a vertical multiplier is not needed to show terrain. In contrast, on still-land globes and maps of the world, mountains without vertical enhancement would be invisible relative to vast latitudinal and longitudinal scales. Finally, hiding a 22.5-fold exaggeration leads to serious errors: a textbook now claims this image of Venus is "how the surface would look to the human eye." Robert Wilson, *Astronomy Through the Ages* (Princeton, 1997), plate 18.

[11] P. D. A. Harvey, "Local and Regional Cartography in Medieval Europe," in J. B. Harley and David Woodward, eds., *The History of Cartography, volume 1: Cartography in Prehistoric, Ancient, and Medieval Europe and the Mediterranean* (Chicago, 1987), p. 496.

Enthusiasts, partisans, and liars have long tinkered with graphical evidence by dequantifying images, selecting and hyping advantageous visual effects, distorting data. Recently, inexpensive computing and ingenious techniques for image processing have provided endless new opportunities for mischief. Arbitrary, transient, one-sided, fractured, undocumented materials have become the great predicament of image making and processing. How are we to assess the integrity of visual evidence? What ethical standards are to be observed in the production of such images?[12] One way to enforce some standard of truth-telling is to insist that the innocent, unprocessed, natural image be shown along with the manipulated image, and, further, that the manipulators and their methods be identified. If images are to be credible, their source and history must be documented. And, if an image is to serve as serious evidence, a more rigorous accounting should reveal the overall pool of images from which the displayed image was selected.

[12] The issues raised by image processing are discussed in William J. Mitchell, *The Reconfigured Eye: Visual Truth in the Post-Photographic Era* (Cambridge, Massachusetts, 1992).

FINALLY, despite the chronic dangers of misrepresentation, appropriate re-expressions or transforms of scales are among the most powerful strategies for exploring data. And in both two- and three-dimensional design, it is often useful to see images and objects at approximately an order of magnitude smaller and larger than actual size.

For example, consider this helpful rescaling, a solution (developed by William Cleveland) to the problem of the aspect ratio in statistical displays. The graph at right shows the number of sunspots by year, 1749 to 1924, moving along in the well-known 11-year cycle. But there is much more in these data than simply rhythms and shapes. Cleveland's good idea is to choose an aspect ratio that centers the absolute values of the slopes of selected line segments on 45°, a technique implemented by iterative computing. Applying this method to the sunspot data yields the graph at lower right, which reveals that cycles tend to rise rapidly and decline slowly, a behavior strongest for cycles with sharp peaks, less strong for medium peaks, and absent for cycles with small peaks.[13] From the original spiky mass of data, fresh and subtle information about quantities emerges with a radiant clarity in the rescaled image.

Number of sunspots each year, 1749–1924

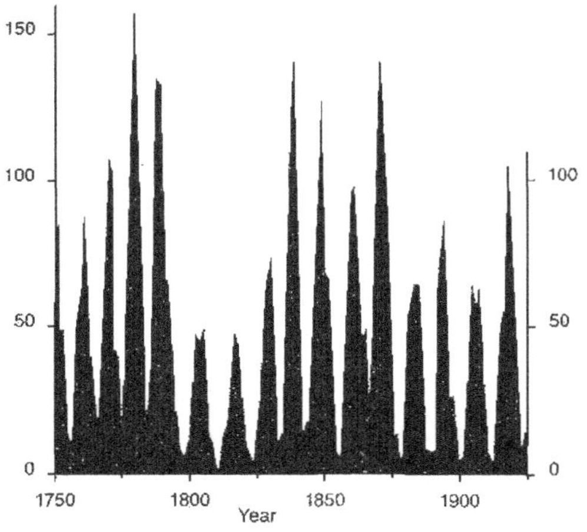

Number of sunspots each year, 1749–1924

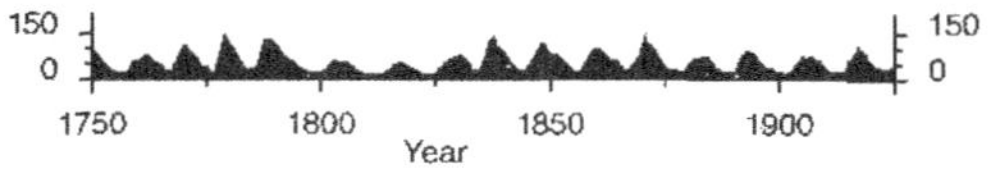

[13] William S. Cleveland, *The Elements of Graphing Data* (Murray Hill, New Jersey, revised edition, 1994), pp. 66–79. Redrawn.

Although we often hear that data speak for themselves, their voices can be soft and sly.

Frederick Mosteller, Stephen E. Fienberg, and Robert E. K. Rourke, *Beginning Statistics with Data Analysis* (Reading, Massachusetts, 1983), p. 234.

Negligent speech doth not only discredit the person of the Speaker, but it discrediteth the opinion of his reason and judgment; it discrediteth the force and uniformity of the matter, and substance.

Ben Jonson, *Timber: or, Discoveries* (London, 1641), first printed in the Folio of 1640, *The Workes . . .*, p. 122 of the section beginning with *Horace his Art of Poetry*.

MTI ASSESSMENT OF TEMPERATURE CONCERN ON SRM-25 (51L) LAUNCH

- 0 CALCULATIONS SHOW THAT SRM-25 O-RINGS WILL BE 20° COLDER THAN SRM-15 O-RINGS
- 0 TEMPERATURE DATA NOT CONCLUSIVE ON PREDICTING PRIMARY O-RING BLOW-BY
- 0 ENGINEERING ASSESSMENT IS THAT:
  - 0 COLDER O-RINGS WILL HAVE INCREASED EFFECTIVE DUROMETER ("HARDER")
  - 0 "HARDER" O-RINGS WILL TAKE LONGER TO "SEAT"
    - 0 MORE GAS MAY PASS PRIMARY O-RING BEFORE THE PRIMARY SEAL SEATS (RELATIVE TO SRM-15)
      - 0 DEMONSTRATED SEALING THRESHOLD IS 3 TIMES GREATER THAN 0.038" EROSION EXPERIENCED ON SRM-15
  - 0 IF THE PRIMARY SEAL DOES NOT SEAT, THE SECONDARY SEAL WILL SEAT
    - 0 PRESSURE WILL GET TO SECONDARY SEAL BEFORE THE METAL PARTS ROTATE
      - 0 O-RING PRESSURE LEAK CHECK PLACES SECONDARY SEAL IN OUTBOARD POSITION WHICH MINIMIZES SEALING TIME
- 0 MTI RECOMMENDS STS-51L LAUNCH PROCEED ON 28 JANUARY 1986
  - 0 SRM-25 WILL NOT BE SIGNIFICANTLY DIFFERENT FROM SRM-15

Joe C. Kilminster

JOE C. KILMINSTER, VICE PRESIDENT
SPACE BOOSTER PROGRAMS

MORTON THIOKOL INC.
Wasatch Division

INFORMATION ON THIS PAGE WAS PREPARED TO SUPPORT AN ORAL PRESENTATION AND CANNOT BE CONSIDERED COMPLETE WITHOUT THE ORAL DISCUSSION

The final approval and rationale for the launch of the space shuttle Challenger, faxed by the rocket-maker to NASA the night before the launch. The rocket blew up 12 hours later as a result of cold temperatures.

2 Visual and Statistical Thinking: Displays of Evidence for Making Decisions

WHEN we reason about quantitative evidence, certain methods for displaying and analyzing data are better than others. Superior methods are more likely to produce truthful, credible, and precise findings. The difference between an excellent analysis and a faulty one can sometimes have momentous consequences.

This chapter examines the statistical and graphical reasoning used in making two life-and-death decisions: how to stop a cholera epidemic in London during September 1854; and whether to launch the space shuttle Challenger on January 28, 1986. By creating statistical graphics that revealed the data, Dr. John Snow was able to discover the cause of the epidemic and bring it to an end. In contrast, by fooling around with displays that obscured the data, those who decided to launch the space shuttle got it wrong, terribly wrong. For both cases, the consequences resulted directly from the *quality* of methods used in displaying and assessing quantitative evidence.

The Cholera Epidemic in London, 1854

In a classic of medical detective work, *On the Mode of Communication of Cholera,*[1] John Snow described—with an eloquent and precise language of evidence, number, comparison—the severe epidemic:

> The most terrible outbreak of cholera which ever occurred in this kingdom, is probably that which took place in Broad Street, Golden Square, and adjoining streets, a few weeks ago. Within two hundred and fifty yards of the spot where Cambridge Street joins Broad Street, there were upwards of five hundred fatal attacks of cholera in ten days. The mortality in this limited area probably equals any that was ever caused in this country, even by the plague; and it was much more sudden, as the greater number of cases terminated in a few hours. The mortality would undoubtedly have been much greater had it not been for the flight of the population. Persons in furnished lodgings left first, then other lodgers went away, leaving their furniture to be sent for. . . . Many houses were closed altogether owing to the death of the proprietors; and, in a great number of instances, the tradesmen who remained had sent away their families; so that in less than six days from the commencement of the outbreak, the most afflicted streets were deserted by more than three-quarters of their inhabitants.[2]

[1] John Snow, *On the Mode of Communication of Cholera* (London, 1855). An acute disease of the small intestine, with severe watery diarrhea, vomiting, and rapid dehydration, cholera has a fatality rate of 50 percent or more when untreated. With the rehydration therapy developed in the 1960s, mortality can be reduced to less than one percent. Epidemics still occur in poor countries, as the bacterium *Vibrio cholerae* is distributed mainly by water and food contaminated with sewage. See Dhiman Barua and William B. Greenough III, eds., *Cholera* (New York, 1992); and S. N. De, *Cholera: Its Pathology and Pathogenesis* (Edinburgh, 1961).

[2] Snow, *Cholera*, p. 38. See also *Report on the Cholera Outbreak in the Parish of St. James's, Westminster, during the Autumn of 1854*, presented to the Vestry by The Cholera Inquiry Committee (London, 1855); and H. Harold Scott, *Some Notable Epidemics* (London, 1934).

Cholera broke out in the Broad Street area of central London on the evening of August 31, 1854. John Snow, who had investigated earlier epidemics, suspected that the water from a community pump-well at Broad and Cambridge Streets was contaminated. Testing the water from the well on the evening of September 3, Snow saw no suspicious impurities, and thus he hesitated to come to a conclusion. This absence of evidence, however, was not evidence of absence:

> Further inquiry . . . showed me that there was no other circumstance or agent common to the circumscribed locality in which this sudden increase of cholera occurred, and not extending beyond it, except the water of the above mentioned pump. I found, moreover, that the water varied, during the next two days, in the amount of organic impurity, visible to the naked eye, on close inspection, in the form of small white, flocculent [loosely clustered] particles. . . .[3]

From the General Register Office, Snow obtained a list of 83 deaths from cholera. When plotted on a map, these data showed a close link between cholera and the Broad Street pump. Persistent house-by-house, case-by-case detective work had yielded quite detailed evidence about a possible cause-effect relationship, as Snow made a kind of streetcorner correlation:

> On proceeding to the spot, I found that nearly all of the deaths had taken place within a short distance of the pump. There were only ten deaths in houses situated decidedly nearer to another street pump. In five of these cases the families of the deceased persons informed me that they always sent to the pump in Broad Street, as they preferred the water to that of the pump which was nearer. In three other cases, the deceased were children who went to school near the pump in Broad Street. Two of them were known to drink the water; and the parents of the third think it probable that it did so. The other two deaths, beyond the district which this pump supplies, represent only the amount of mortality from cholera that was occurring before the irruption took place.
>
> With regard to the deaths occurring in the locality belonging to the pump, there were sixty-one instances in which I was informed that the deceased persons used to drink the pump-water from Broad Street, either constantly or occasionally. In six instances I could get no information, owing to the death or departure of every one connected with the deceased individuals; and in six cases I was informed that the deceased persons did not drink the pump-water before their illness.[4]

Thus the theory implicating the particular pump was confirmed by the observed covariation: in this area of London, there were few occurrences of cholera exceeding the normal low level, except among those people who drank water from the Broad Street pump. It was now time to act; after all, the reason we seek causal explanations is in order to *intervene*, to govern the cause so as to govern the effect: "Policy-thinking is and must be causality-thinking."[5] Snow described his findings to the authorities responsible for the community water supply, the Board of Guardians of St. James's Parish, on the evening of September 7, 1854. The Board ordered that the pump-handle on the Broad Street well be removed immediately. The epidemic soon ended.

[3] Snow, *Cholera*, p. 39. A few weeks after the epidemic, Snow reported his results in a first-person narrative, more like a laboratory notebook or a personal journal than a modern research paper with its pristine, reconstructed science. Recent research has found additional complexities in the story of John Snow; see Howard Brody, *et al.*, "Map-Making and Myth-Making in Broad Street: The London Cholera Epidemic, 1854," *The Lancet* 356 (July 1, 2000), 64–68.

[4] Snow, *Cholera*, pp. 39–40.

[5] Robert A. Dahl, "Cause and Effect in the Study of Politics," in Daniel Lerner, ed., *Cause and Effect* (New York, 1965), p. 88. Wold writes "A frequent situation is that description serves to maintain some *modus vivendi* (the control of an established production process, the tolerance of a limited number of epidemic cases), whereas explanation serves the purpose of *reform* (raising the agricultural yield, reducing the mortality rates, improving a production process). In other words, description is employed as an aid in the human *adjustment* to conditions, while explanation is a vehicle for ascendancy over the environment." Herman Wold, "Causal Inference from Observational Data," *Journal of the Royal Statistical Society*, A, 119 (1956), p. 29.

Moreover, the result of this intervention (a before/after experiment of sorts) was consistent with the idea that cholera was transmitted by impure water. Snow's explanation replaced previously held beliefs that cholera spread through the air or by some other means. In those times many years before the discovery of bacteria, one fantastic theory speculated that cholera vaporously rose out of the burying grounds of plague victims from two centuries earlier.[6] In 1886 the discovery of the bacterium *Vibrio cholerae* confirmed Snow's theory. He is still celebrated for establishing the mode of cholera transmission *and* consequently the method of prevention: keep drinking water, food, and hands clear of infected sewage. Today at the old site of the Broad Street pump there stands a public house (a bar) named after John Snow, where one can presumably drink more safely than 140 years ago.

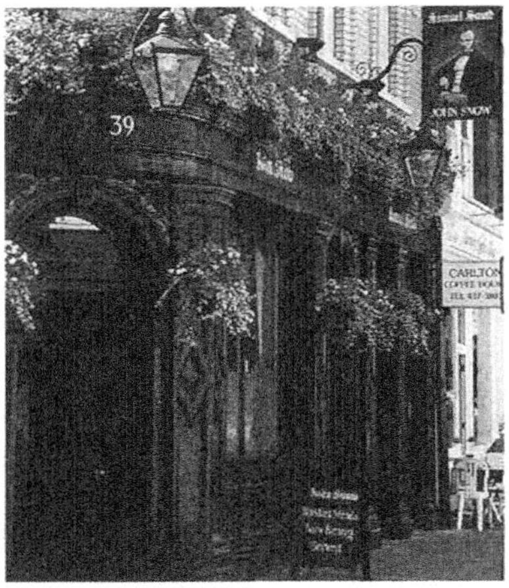

WHY was the centuries-old mystery of cholera finally solved? Most importantly, Snow had a *good idea*—a causal theory about how the disease spread—that guided the gathering and assessment of evidence. This theory developed from medical analysis and empirical observation; by mapping earlier epidemics, Snow detected a link between different water supplies and varying rates of cholera (to the consternation of private water companies who anonymously denounced Snow's work). By the 1854 epidemic, then, the intellectual framework was in place, and the problem of how cholera spread was ripe for solution.[7]

Along with a good idea and a timely problem, there was a *good method*. Snow's scientific detective work exhibits a shrewd intelligence about evidence, a clear logic of data display and analysis:

1. *Placing the data in an appropriate context for assessing cause and effect.* The original data listed the victims' names and described their circumstances, all in order by date of death. Such a stack of death certificates naturally lends itself to time-series displays, chronologies of the epidemic as shown below. *But descriptive narration is not causal explanation;* the passage of time is a poor explanatory variable, practically useless in discovering a strategy of how to intervene and stop the epidemic.

[6] H. Harold Scott, *Some Notable Epidemics* (London, 1934), pp. 3–4.

[7] Scientists are not "admired for failing in the attempt to solve problems that lie beyond [their] competence. . . . If politics is the art of the possible, research is surely the art of the soluble. Both are immensely practical-minded affairs. . . . The art of research [is] the art of making difficult problems soluble by devising means of getting at them. Certainly good scientists study the most important problems they think they can solve. It is, after all, their professional business to solve problems, not merely to grapple with them. The spectacle of a scientist locked in combat with the forces of ignorance is not an inspiring one if, in the outcome, the scientist is routed. That is why so many of the most important biological problems have not yet appeared on the agenda of practical research." Peter Medawar, *Pluto's Republic* (New York, 1984), pp. 253–254; 2–3.

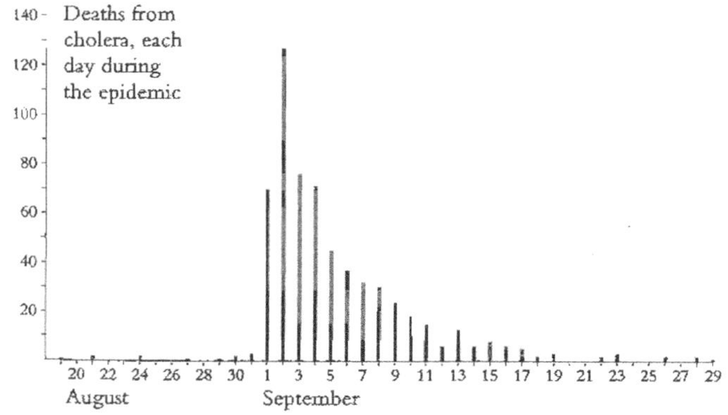

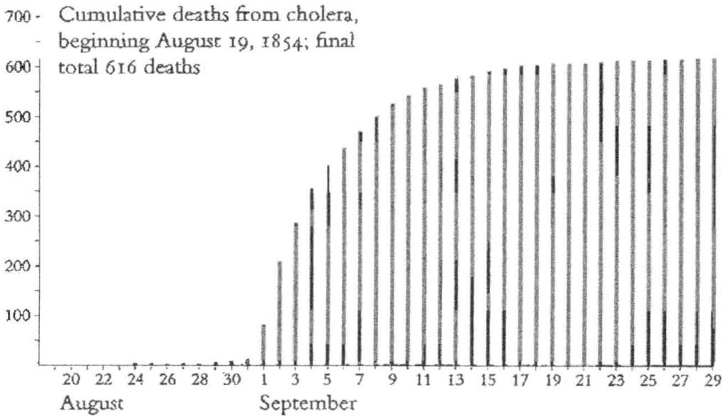

Instead of plotting a time-series, which would simply report each day's bad news, Snow constructed a graphical display that provided direct and powerful testimony about a possible cause-effect relationship. Recasting the original data from their one-dimensional temporal ordering into a two-dimensional spatial comparison, Snow marked deaths from cholera (▬) on this map, along with locations of the area's 13 community water pump-wells (◉). The notorious well is located amid an intense cluster of deaths, near the D in BROAD STREET. This map reveals a strong association between cholera and proximity to the Broad Street pump, in a context of simultaneous comparison with other local water sources and the surrounding neighborhoods without cholera.

2\. *Making quantitative comparisons.* The deep, fundamental question in statistical analysis is *Compared with what?* Therefore, investigating the experiences of the victims of cholera is only part of the search for credible evidence; to understand fully the cause of the epidemic also requires an analysis of those who *escaped* the disease. With great clarity, the map presented several intriguing clues for comparisons between the living and the dead, clues strikingly visible at a brewery and a workhouse (tinted yellow here). Snow wrote in his report:

> There is a brewery in Broad Street, near to the pump, and on perceiving that no brewer's men were registered as having died of cholera, I called on Mr. Huggins, the proprietor. He informed me that there were above seventy workmen employed in the brewery, and that none of them had suffered from cholera—at least in severe form—only two having been indisposed, and that not seriously, at the time the disease prevailed. The men are allowed a certain quantity of malt liquor, and Mr. Huggins believes they do not drink water at all; and he is quite certain that the workmen never obtained water from the pump in the street. There is a deep well in the brewery, in addition to the New River water. (p. 42)

Saved by the beer! And at a nearby workhouse, the circumstances of non-victims of the epidemic provided important and credible evidence about the cause of the disease, as well as a quantitative calculation of an expected rate of cholera compared with the actual observed rate:

> The Workhouse in Poland Street is more than three-fourths surrounded by houses in which deaths from cholera occurred, yet out of five-hundred-thirty-five inmates only five died of cholera, the other deaths which took place being those of persons admitted after they were attacked. The workhouse has a pump-well on the premises, in addition to the supply from the Grand Junction Water Works, and the inmates never sent to Broad Street for water. If the mortality in the workhouse had been equal to that in the streets immediately surrounding it on three sides, upwards of one hundred persons would have died. (p. 42)

Such clear, lucid reasoning may seem commonsensical, obvious, insufficiently technical. Yet we will soon see a tragic instance, the decision to launch the space shuttle, when this straightforward logic of statistical (and visual) comparison was abandoned by many engineers, managers, and government officials.

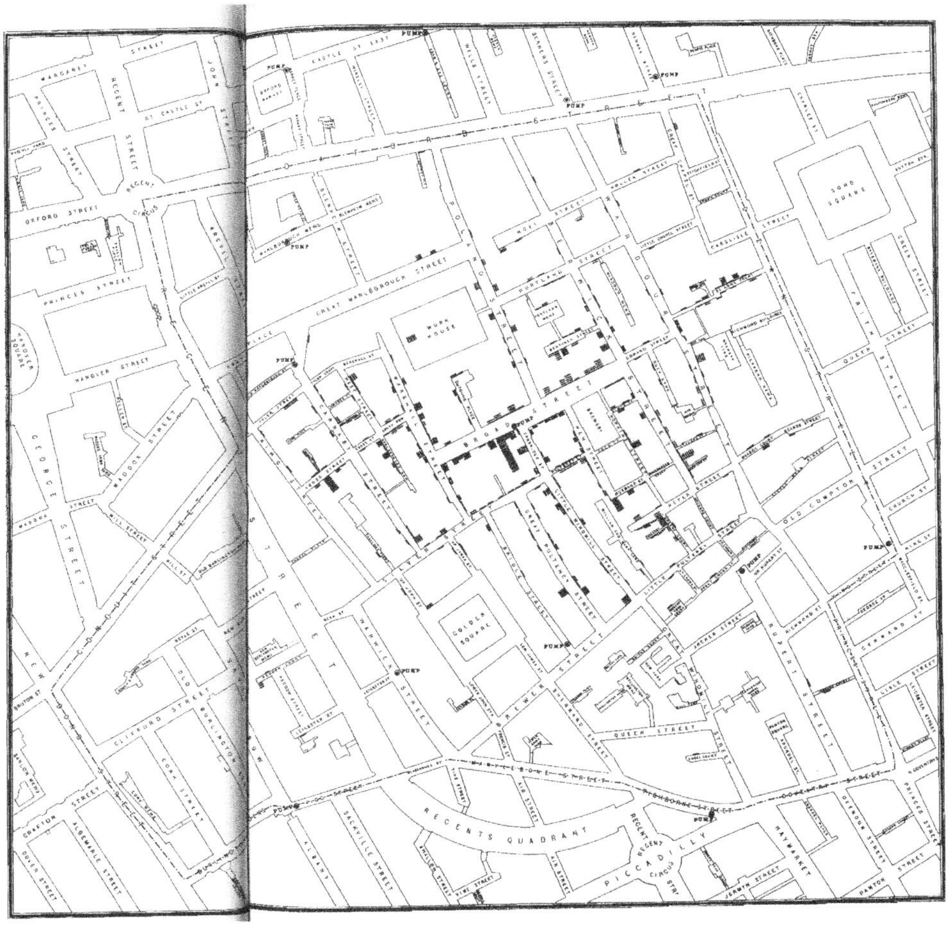

3. *Considering alternative explanations and contrary cases.* Sometimes it can be difficult for researchers—who both report *and* advocate their findings—to face up to threats to their conclusions, such as alternative explanations and contrary cases. Nonetheless, the credibility of a report is enhanced by a careful assessment of *all* relevant evidence, not just the evidence overtly consistent with explanations advanced by the report. The point is to get it right, not to win the case, not to sweep under the rug all the assorted puzzles and inconsistencies that frequently occur in collections of data.[8]

Both Snow's map and the time-sequence of deaths show several apparently contradictory instances, a number of deaths from cholera with no obvious link to the Broad Street pump. And yet . . .

> In some of the instances, where the deaths are scattered a little further from the rest on the map, the malady was probably contracted at a nearer point to the pump. A cabinet-maker who resided on Noel Street [some distance from Broad Street] worked in Broad Street. . . . A little girl, who died in Ham Yard, and another who died in Angel Court, Great Windmill Street, went to the school in Dufour's Place, Broad Street, and were in the habit of drinking the pump-water. . . .[9]

In a particularly unfortunate episode, one London resident made a special effort to obtain Broad Street well-water, a delicacy of taste with a side-effect that unwittingly cost two lives. Snow's report is one of careful description and precise logic:

> Dr. Fraser also first called my attention to the following circumstances, which are perhaps the most conclusive of all in proving the connexion between the Broad Street pump and the outbreak of cholera. In the 'Weekly Return of Births and Deaths' of September 9th, the following death is recorded: 'At West End, on 2nd September, the widow of a percussion-cap maker, aged 59 years, diarrhea two hours, *cholera epidemica* sixteen hours.' I was informed by this lady's son that she had not been in the neighbourhood of Broad Street for many months. A cart went from Broad Street to West End every day, and it was the custom to take out a large bottle of the water from the pump in Broad Street, as she preferred it. The water was taken on Thursday, 31st August, and she drank of it in the evening, and also on Friday. She was seized with cholera on the evening of the latter day, and died on Saturday. . . . A niece, who was on a visit to this lady, also drank of the water; she returned to her residence, in a high and healthy part of Islington, was attacked with cholera, and died also. There was no cholera at the time, either at West End or in the neighbourhood where the niece died.[10]

Although at first glance these deaths appear unrelated to the Broad Street pump, they are, upon examination, strong evidence pointing to that well. There is here a clarity and undeniability to the link between cholera and the Broad Street pump; only such a link can account for what would otherwise be a mystery, this seemingly random and unusual occurrence of cholera. And the saintly Snow, unlike some researchers, gives full credit to the person, Dr. Fraser, who actually found this crucial case.

[8] The distinction between science and advocacy is poignantly posed when statisticians serve as consultants and witnesses for lawyers. See Paul Meier, "Damned Liars and Expert Witnesses," and Franklin M. Fisher, "Statisticians, Econometricians, and Adversary Proceedings," *Journal of the American Statistical Association*, 81 (1986), pp. 269–276 and 277–286.

[9] Snow, *Cholera*, p. 47.

[10] Snow, *Cholera*, pp. 44–45.

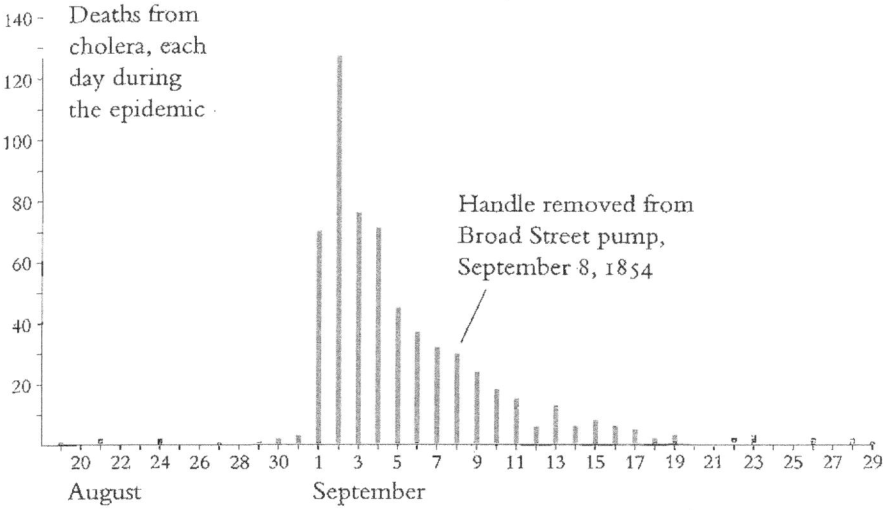

Data source: plotted from the table in Snow, *Cholera*, p. 49.

Ironically, the most famous aspect of Snow's work is also the most uncertain part of his evidence: it is not at all clear that the removal of the handle of the Broad Street pump had much to do with ending the epidemic. As shown by this time-series above, the epidemic was already in rapid decline by the time the handle was removed. Yet, in many retellings of the story of the epidemic, the pump-handle removal is *the* decisive event, the unmistakable symbol of Snow's contribution. Here is the dramatic account of Benjamin Ward Richardson:

> On the evening of Thursday, September 7th, the vestrymen of St. James's were sitting in solemn consultation on the causes of the [cholera epidemic]. They might well be solemn, for such a panic possibly never existed in London since the days of the great plague. People fled from their homes as from instant death, leaving behind them, in their haste, all the mere matter which before they valued most. While, then, the vestrymen were in solemn deliberation, they were called to consider a new suggestion. A stranger had asked, in modest speech, for a brief hearing. Dr. Snow, the stranger in question, was admitted and in few words explained his view of the 'head and front of the offending.' He had fixed his attention on the Broad Street pump as the source and centre of the calamity. He advised removal of the pump-handle as the grand prescription. The vestry was incredulous, but had the good sense to carry out the advice. The pump-handle was removed, and the plague was stayed.[11]

Note the final sentence, a declaration of cause and effect.[12] Modern epidemiologists, however, are somewhat skeptical about the evidence that links the removal of the pump handle directly to the epidemic's end. Nonetheless, the decisive point is that John Snow got it all exactly right:

> John Snow, in the seminal act of modern public health epidemiology, performed an intervention that was non-randomized, that was appraised with historical controls, and that had major ambiguities in the equivocal time relationship between his removal of the handle of the Broad Street pump and the end of the associated epidemic of cholera—but he correctly demonstrated that the disease was transmitted through water, not air.[13]

[11] Benjamin W. Richardson, "The Life of John Snow, M.D.," foreword to John Snow, *On Chloroform and Other Anaesthetics: Their Action and Administration* (London, 1858), pp. xx–xxi.

[12] Another example of the causal claim: "On September 8, at Snow's urgent request, the handle of the Broad Street pump was removed and the incidence of new cases ceased almost at once," E. W. Gilbert, "Pioneer Maps of Health and Disease in England," *The Geographical Journal*, 124 (1958), p. 174. Gilbert's assertion was repeated in Edward R. Tufte, *The Visual Display of Quantitative Information* (Cheshire, Connecticut, 1983), p. 24.

[13] Alvan R. Feinstein, *Clinical Epidemiology: The Architecture of Clinical Research* (Philadelphia, 1985), pp. 409–410. And A. Bradford Hill ["Snow—An Appreciation," *Proceedings of the Royal Society of Medicine*, 48 (1955), p. 1010] writes: "Though conceivably there might have been a second peak in the curve, and though almost certainly some more deaths would have occurred if the pump handle had remained in situ, it is clear that the end of the epidemic was not dramatically determined by its removal."

At a minimum, removing the pump-handle prevented a recurrence of cholera. Snow recognized several difficulties in evaluating the effect of his intervention; since most people living in central London had fled, the disease ran out of possible victims—which happened simultaneously with shutting down the infected water supply.[14] The case against the Broad Street pump, however, was based on a diversity of additional evidence: the cholera map, studies of unusual instances, comparisons of the living and dead with their consumption of well-water, and an idea about a mechanism of contamination (a nearby underground sewer had probably leaked into the infected well). Also, the finding that cholera was carried by water—a life-saving scientific discovery that showed how to intervene and prevent the spread of cholera—derived not only from study of the Broad Street epidemic but also from Snow's mappings of several other cholera outbreaks in relation to the purity of community water supplies.

[14] "There is no doubt that the mortality was much diminished, as I said before, by the flight of the population, which commenced soon after the outbreak; but the attacks had so far diminished before the use of the water was stopped, that it is impossible to decide whether the well still contained the cholera poison in an active state, or whether, from some cause, the water had become free from it." Snow, *Cholera*, pp. 51–52.

4. *Assessment of possible errors in the numbers reported in graphics.* Snow's analysis attends to the sources and consequences of errors in gathering the data. In particular, the credibility of the cholera map grows out of supplemental details in the text—as image, word, and number combine to present the evidence and make the argument. Detailed comments on possible errors annotate both the map and the table, reassuring readers about the care and integrity of the statistical detective work that produced the data graphics:

> The deaths which occurred during this fatal outbreak of cholera are indicated in the accompanying map, as far as I could ascertain them. There are necessarily some deficiencies, for in a few of the instances of persons who died in the hospitals after their removal from the neighbourhood of Broad Street, the number of the house from which they had been removed was not registered. The address of those who died after their removal to St. James's Workhouse was not registered; and I was only able to obtain it, in a part of the cases, on application at the Master's Office, for many of the persons were too ill, when admitted, to give any account of themselves. In the case also of some of the workpeople and others who contracted the cholera in this neighbourhood, and died in different parts of London, the precise house from which they had removed is not stated in the return of deaths. I have heard of some persons who died in the country shortly after removing from the neighbourhood of Broad Street; and there must, no doubt, be several cases of this kind that I have not heard of. Indeed, the full extent of the calamity will probably never be known. The deficiencies I have mentioned, however, probably do not detract from the correctness of the map as a diagram of the topography of the outbreak; for, if the locality of the few additional cases could be ascertained, they would probably be distributed over the district of the outbreak in the same proportion as the large number which are known.[15]

> The deaths in the above table [the time-series of daily deaths] are compiled from the sources mentioned above in describing the map; but some deaths which were omitted from the map on account of the number of the house not being known, are included in the table. . . .[16]

[15] Snow, *Cholera*, pp. 45–46.

[16] Snow, *Cholera*, p. 50.

Snow drew a *dot map*, marking each individual death. This design has statistical costs and benefits: death *rates* are not shown, and such maps may become cluttered with excessive detail; on the other hand, the sometimes deceptive effects of aggregation are avoided. And of course dot maps aid in the identification and analysis of individual cases, evidence essential to Snow's argument.

The big problem is that dot maps fail to take into account the number of people living in an area and at risk to get a disease: "an area of the map may be free of cases merely because it is not populated."[17] Snow's map does not fully answer the question *Compared with what?* For example, if the population as a whole in central London had been distributed just as the deaths were, then the cholera map would have merely repeated the unimportant fact that more people lived near the Broad Street pump than elsewhere. This was not the case; the entire area shown on the map—with and without cholera—was thickly populated. Still, Snow's dot map does not assess varying densities of population in the area around the pump. Ideally, the cholera data should be displayed on both a dot and a rate map, with population-based rates calculated for rather small and homogeneous geographic units. In the text of his report, however, Snow did present rates for a few different areas surrounding the pump.

[17] Brian MacMahon and Thomas F. Pugh, *Epidemiology: Principles and Methods* (Boston, 1970), p. 150.

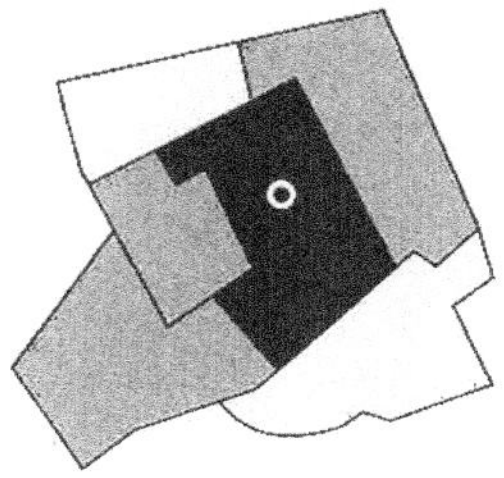

In this aggregation of individual deaths into six areas, the greatest number is concentrated at the Broad Street pump.

Aggregations by area can sometimes mask and even distort the true story of the data. For two of the three examples at right, constructed by Mark Monmonier from Snow's individual-level data, the intense cluster around the Broad Street pump entirely vanishes in the process of geographically aggregating the data (the greater the number of cholera deaths, the darker the area).[18]

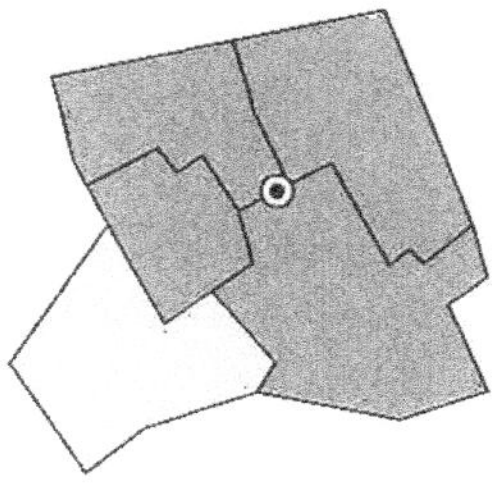

Using different geographic subdivisions, the cholera numbers are nearly the same in four of the five areas.

In describing the discovery of how cholera is transmitted, various histories of medicine discuss the famous map and Snow's analysis. The cholera map, as Snow drew it, is difficult to reproduce on a single page; the full size of the original is awkward (a square, 40 cm or 16 inches on the side), and if reduced in size, the cholera symbols become murky and the type too small. Some facsimile editions of *On the Mode of Communication of Cholera* have given up, reprinting only Snow's text and not the crucial visual evidence of the map. Redrawings of the map for textbooks in medicine and in geography fail to reproduce key elements of Snow's original. The workhouse and brewery, those essential compared-with-what cases, are left unlabeled and unidentified, showing up only as mysterious cholera-free zones close to the infected well. Standards of quality may slip when it comes to visual displays; imprecise and undocumented work that would be unacceptable for words or tables of data too often shows up in graphics. Since it is *all* evidence—regardless of the method of presentation—the highest standards of statistical integrity and statistical thinking should apply to *every* data representation, including visual displays.

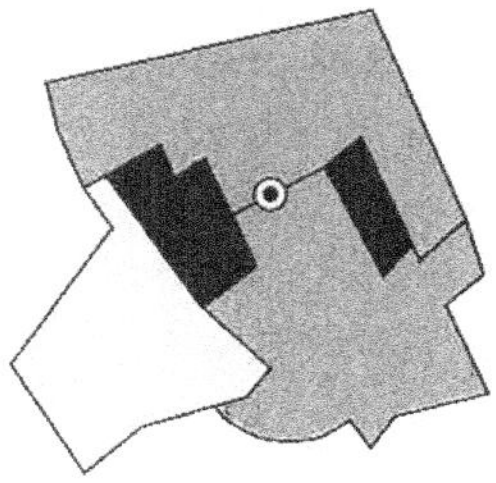

In this aggregation of the deaths, the two areas with the most deaths do not even include the infected pump!

[18] Mark Monmonier, *How to Lie with Maps* (Chicago, 1991), pp. 142–143.

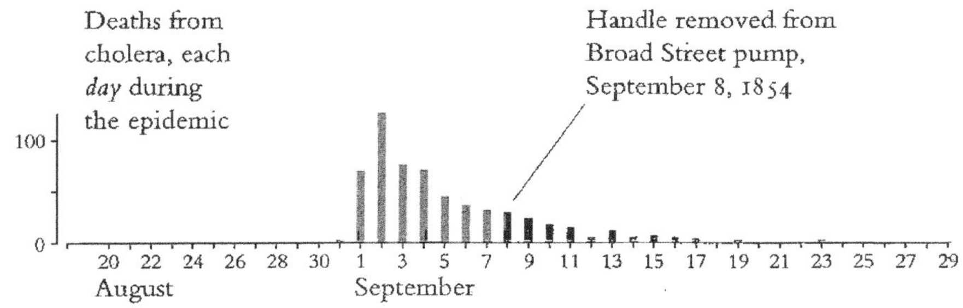

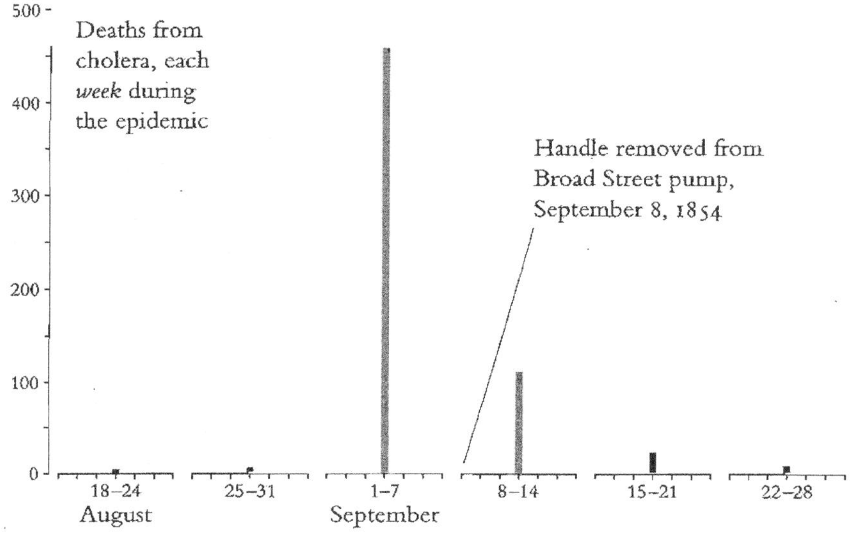

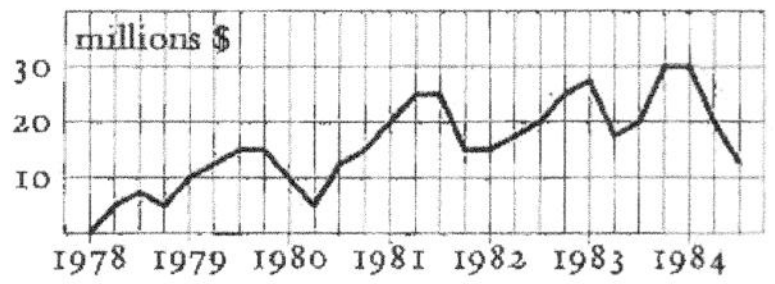

Above, this chart shows *quarterly* revenue data in a financial graphic for a legal case. Several dips in revenue are visible.

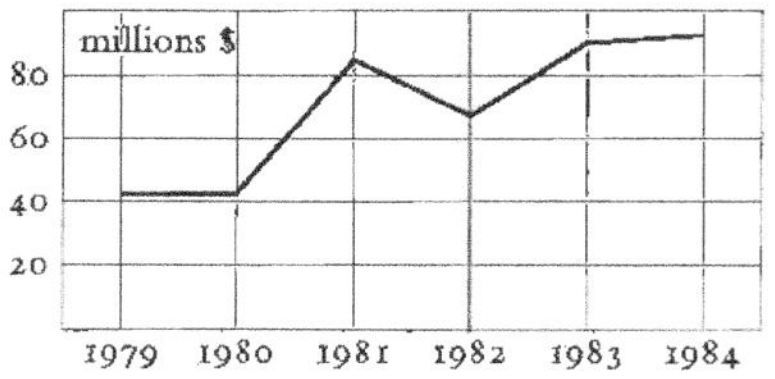

Aggregating the quarterly data into years, this chart above shows revenue by *fiscal year* (beginning July 1, ending June 30). Note the dip in 1982, the basis of a claim for damages.

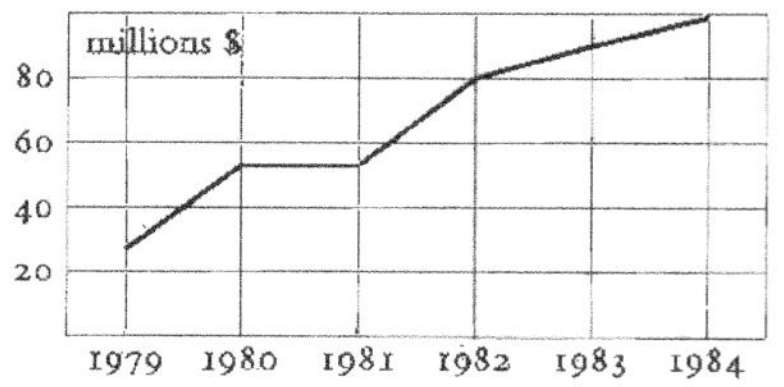

Shown above are the same quarterly revenue data added up into *calendar years*. The 1982 dip has vanished.

Aggregations over time may also mask relevant detail and generate misleading signals, similar to the problems of spatial aggregation in the three cholera maps. Shown at top is the familiar *daily* time-series of deaths from cholera, with its smooth decline in deaths unchanged by the removal of the pump-handle. When the daily data are added up into *weekly* intervals, however, a different picture emerges: the removal had the apparent consequence of reducing the weekly death toll from 458 to 112! But this result comes purely from the aggregation, for the daily data show no such effect.[19] Conveniently, the handle was removed in early morning of September 8; hence the plausible weekly intervals of September 1–7, 8–14, and so on. Imagine if we had read the story of John Snow as reported in the first few pages here, and if our account showed the weekly instead of daily deaths—then it would all appear perfectly convincing although quite misleading.

Some other weekly intervals would further aggravate the distortion. Since two or more days typically pass between consumption of the infected water and deaths from cholera, the removal date might properly be *lagged* in relation to the deaths (for example, by starting to count post-removal deaths on the 10th of September, 2 days *after* the pump

[19] Reading from the top, these clever examples reveal the effects of temporal aggregation in economic data; from Gregory Joseph, *Modern Visual Evidence* (New York, 1992), pp. A42–A43.

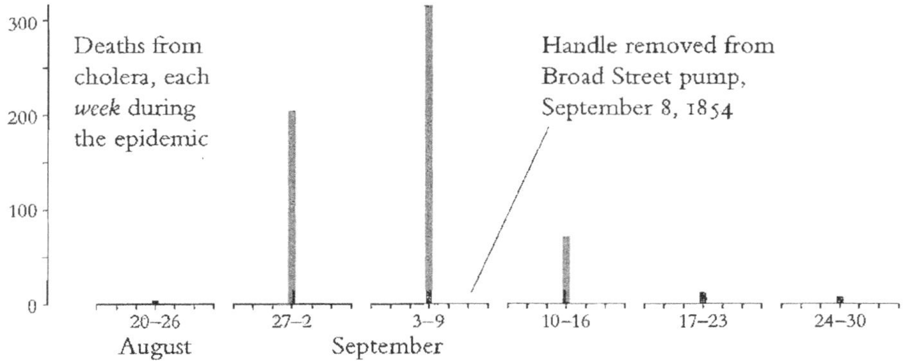

handle was taken off). These lagged weekly clusters are shown above. The pseudo-effect of handle removal is now even stronger: after three weeks of increasing deaths, the weekly toll plummets when the handle is gone. A change of merely two days in weekly intervals has radically shifted the shape of the data representation. As a comparison between the two weekly charts shows, the results depend on the arbitrary choice of time periods—a sign that we are seeing method not reality.

These conjectural weekly aggregations are as condensed as news reports; missing are only the decorative clichés of "info-graphics" (the language is as ghastly as the charts). At right is how pop journalism might depict Snow's work, complete with celebrity factoids, over-compressed data, and the isotype styling of those little coffins.

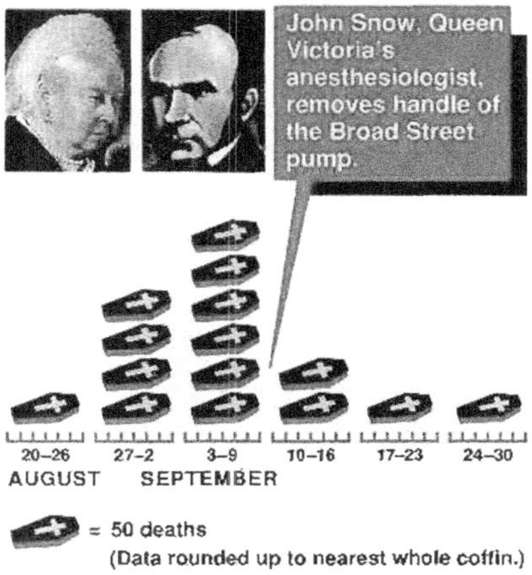

Time-series are exquisitely sensitive to choice of intervals and end points. Nonetheless, many aggregations are perfectly sensible, reducing the tedious redundancy and uninteresting complexity of large data files; for example, the *daily* data amalgamate times of death originally recorded to the hour and even minute. If in doubt, graph the detailed underlying data to assess the effects of aggregation.

A further difficulty arises, a result of fast computing. It is easy now to sort through thousands of plausible varieties of graphical and statistical aggregations—and then to select for publication only those findings strongly favorable to the point of view being advocated. Such searches are described as *data mining, multiplicity*, or *specification searching*.[20] Thus a prudent judge of evidence might well presume that those *graphs, tables, and calculations revealed in a presentation are the best of all possible results chosen expressly for advancing the advocate's case.*

EVEN in the face of issues raised by a modern statistical critique, it remains wonderfully true that John Snow did, after all, show exactly how cholera was transmitted and therefore prevented. In 1955, the *Proceedings of the Royal Society of Medicine* commemorated Snow's discovery. A renowned epidemiologist, Bradford Hill, wrote: "For close upon 100 years we have been free in this country from epidemic cholera, and it is a freedom which, basically, we owe to the logical thinking, acute observations and simple sums of Dr. John Snow."[21]

[20] John W. Tukey, "Some Thoughts on Clinical Trials, Especially Problems of Multiplicity," *Science*, 198 (1977), pp. 679–684; Edward E. Leamer, *Specification Searches: Ad Hoc Inference with Nonexperimental Data* (New York, 1978). On the other hand, "enough exploration must be done so that the results are shown to be relatively insensitive to plausible alternative specifications and data choices. Only in that way can the statistician protect himself or herself from the temptation to favor the client and from the ensuing cross-examination." Franklin M. Fisher, "Statisticians, Econometricians, and Adversary Proceedings," *Journal of the American Statistical Association*, 81 (1986), p. 279. Another reason to explore the data thoroughly is to find out what is going on! See John W. Tukey, *Exploratory Data Analysis* (Reading, Massachusetts, 1977).

[21] A. Bradford Hill, "Snow—An Appreciation," *Proceedings of the Royal Society of Medicine*, 48 (1955), p. 1012.

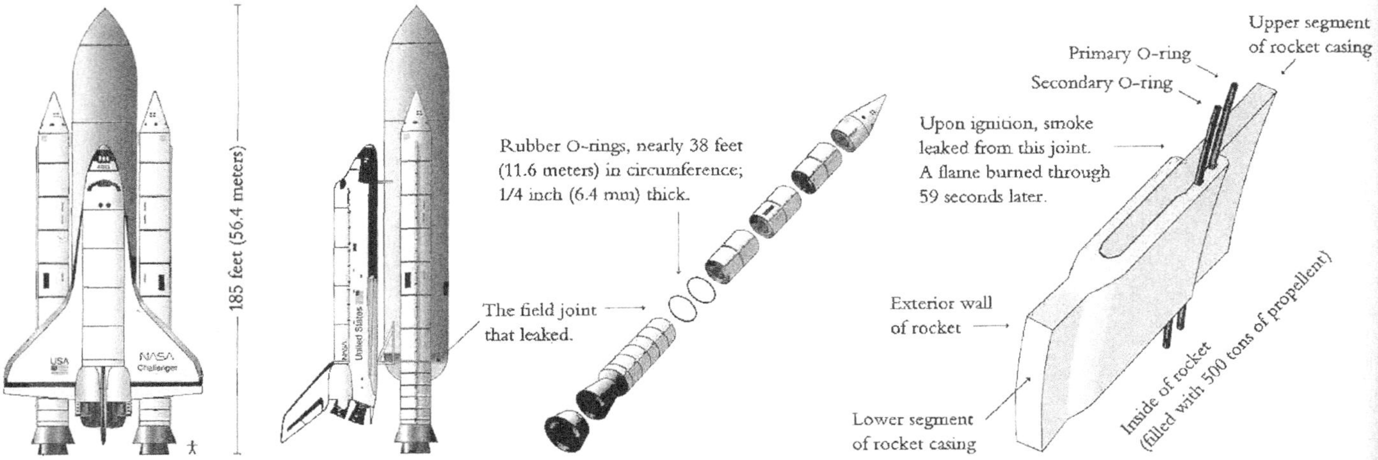

The shuttle consists of an *orbiter* (which carries the crew and has powerful engines in the back), a large liquid-fuel *tank* for the orbiter engines, and 2 solid-fuel *booster rockets* mounted on the sides of the central tank. Segments of the booster rockets are shipped to the launch site, where they are assembled to make the solid-fuel rockets. Where these segments mate, each joint is sealed by two rubber O-rings as shown above. In the case of the Challenger accident, one of these joints leaked, and a torch-like flame burned through the side of the booster rocket.

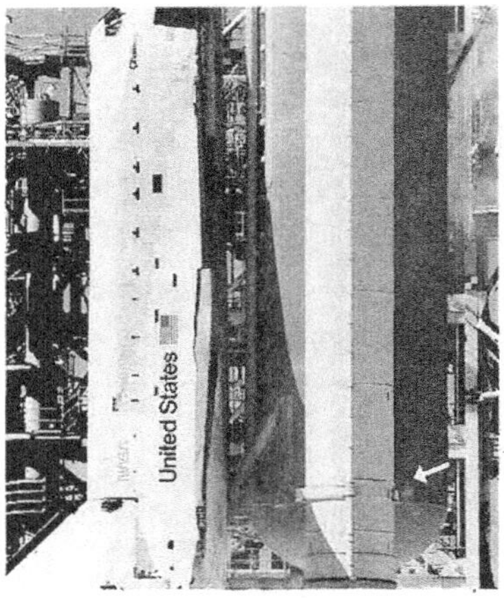

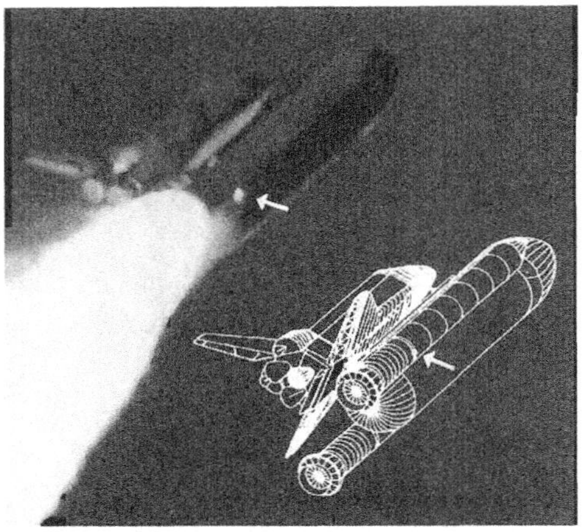

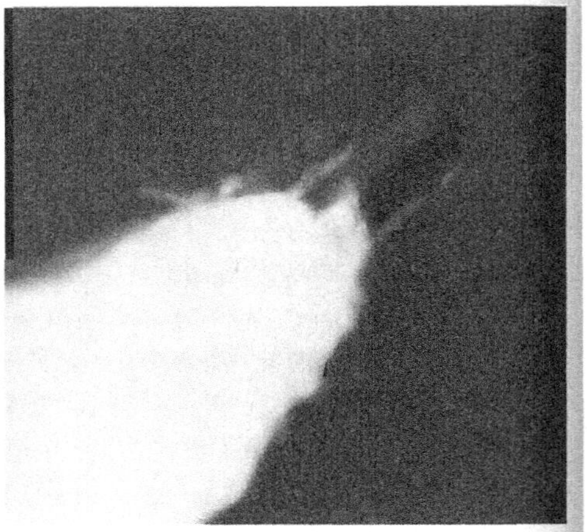

Less than 1 second after ignition, a puff of smoke appeared at the aft joint of the right booster, indicating that the O-rings burned through and failed to seal. At this point, all was lost.

On the launch pad, the leak lasted only about 2 seconds and then apparently was plugged by putty and insulation as the shuttle rose, flying through rather strong cross-winds. Then 58.788 seconds after ignition, when the Challenger was 6 miles up, a flicker of flame emerged from the leaky joint. Within seconds, the flame grew and engulfed the fuel tank (containing liquid hydrogen and liquid oxygen). That tank ruptured and exploded, destroying the shuttle.

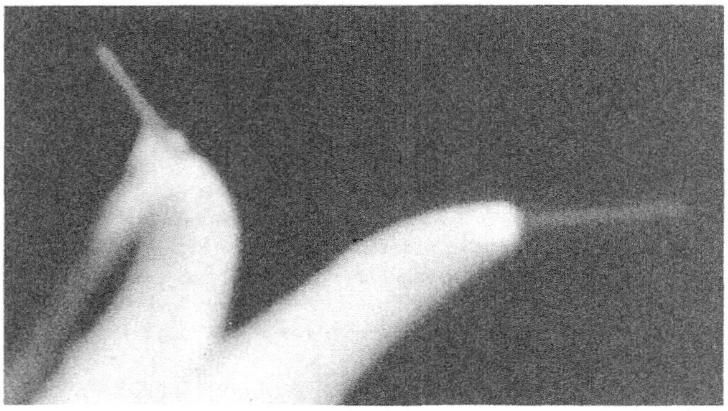

As the shuttle exploded and broke up at approximately 73 seconds after launch, the two booster rockets crisscrossed and continued flying wildly. The right booster, identifiable by its failure plume, is now to the left of its non-defective counterpart.

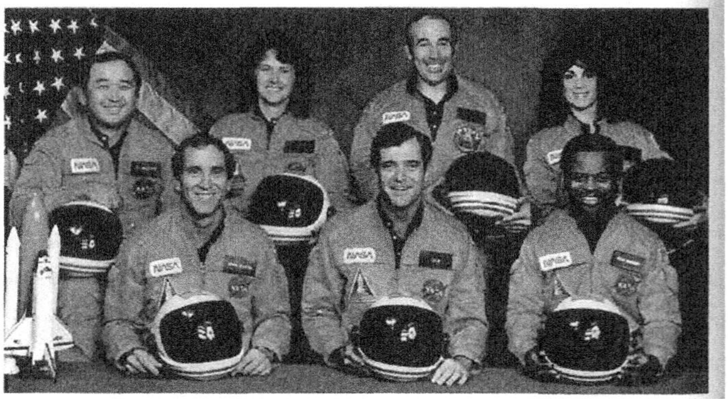

The flight crew of Challenger 51-L. Front row, left to right: Michael J. Smith, pilot; Francis R. (Dick) Scobee, commander; Ronald E. McNair. Back row: Ellison S. Onizuka, S. Christa McAuliffe, Gregory B. Jarvis, Judith A. Resnik.

The Decision to Launch the Space Shuttle Challenger

ON January 28, 1986, the space shuttle Challenger exploded and seven astronauts died because two rubber O-rings leaked.[22] These rings had lost their resiliency because the shuttle was launched on a very cold day. Ambient temperatures were in the low 30s and the O-rings themselves were much colder, less than 20°F.

One day before the flight, the predicted temperature for the launch was 26° to 29°. Concerned that the rings would not seal at such a cold temperature, the engineers who designed the rocket opposed launching Challenger the next day. Their misgivings derived from several sources: a history of O-ring damage during previous cool-weather launches of the shuttle, the physics of resiliency (which declines exponentially with cooling), and experimental data.[23] Presented in 13 charts, this evidence was faxed to NASA, the government agency responsible for the flight. A high-level NASA official responded that he was "appalled" by the recommendation not to launch and indicated that the rocket-maker, Morton Thiokol, should reconsider, even though this was Thiokol's only no-launch recommendation in 12 years.[24] Other NASA officials pointed out serious weaknesses in the charts. Reassessing the situation after these skeptical responses, the Thiokol managers changed their minds and decided that they now favored launching the next day. They said the evidence presented by the engineers was inconclusive, that cool temperatures were not linked to O-ring problems.[25]

Thus the *exact cause* of the accident was intensely debated during the evening before the launch. That is, for hours, the rocket engineers and managers considered the question: *Will the rubber O-rings fail catastrophically tomorrow because of the cold weather?* These discussions concluded at midnight with the decision to go ahead. That morning, the Challenger blew up 73 seconds after its rockets were ignited.

THE immediate cause of the accident—an O-ring failure—was quickly obvious (see the photographs at left). But what are the general causes, the lessons of the accident? And what is the meaning of Challenger? Here we encounter diverse and divergent interpretations, as the facts of the accident are reworked into moral narratives.[26] These allegories regularly advance claims for the special relevance of a distinct analytic approach or school of thought: if only the engineers and managers had the skills of field X, the argument implies, this terrible thing would not have happened. Or, further, the insights of X identify the deep causes of the failure. Thus, in management schools, the accident serves as a case study for reflections about groupthink, technical decision-making in the face of political pressure, and bureaucratic failures to communicate. For the authors of engineering textbooks and for the physicist Richard Feynman, the Challenger accident simply confirmed what they already

[22] My sources are the five-volume *Report of the Presidential Commission on the Space Shuttle Challenger Accident* (Washington, DC, 1986) hereafter cited as *PCSSCA*; Committee on Science and Technology, House of Representatives, *Investigation of the Challenger Accident* (Washington, DC, 1986); Richard P. Feynman, "*What Do You Care What Other People Think?" Further Adventures of a Curious Character* (New York, 1988); Richard S. Lewis, *Challenger: The Final Voyage* (New York, 1988); Frederick Lighthall, "Launching the Space Shuttle Challenger: Disciplinary Deficiencies in the Analysis of Engineering Data," *IEEE Transactions on Engineering Management*, 38 (February 1991), pp. 63–74; and Diane Vaughan, *The Challenger Launch Decision: Risky Technology, Culture, and Deviance at NASA* (Chicago, 1996). The text accompanying the images at left is based on *PCSSCA*, volume 1, pp. 6–9, 19–32, 52, 60. Illustrations of shuttle at upper left by Weilin Wu and Edward Tufte.

[23] *PCSSCA*, volume 1, pp. 82–113.

[24] *PCSSCA*, volume 1, p. 107.

[25] *PCSSCA*, volume 1, p. 108.

[26] Various interpretations of the accident include *PCSSCA*, which argues several views; James L. Adams, *Flying Buttresses, Entropy, and O-Rings: The World of an Engineer* (Cambridge, Massachusetts, 1991); Michael McConnell, *Challenger: A Major Malfunction* (New York, 1987); Committee on Shuttle Criticality Review and Hazard Analysis Audit, *Post-Challenger Evaluation of Space Shuttle Risk Assessment and Management* (Washington, DC, 1988); Siddhartha R. Dalal, Edward B. Fowlkes, and Bruce Hoadley, "Risk Analysis of the Space Shuttle: Pre-Challenger Prediction of Failure," *Journal of the American Statistical Association*, 84 (December 1989), pp. 945–957; Claus Jensen, *No Downlink* (New York, 1996); and, cited above in note 22, the House Committee Report, the thorough account of Vaughan, Feynman's book, and Lighthall's insightful article.

knew: awful consequences result when heroic engineers are ignored by villainous administrators. In the field of statistics, the accident is evoked to demonstrate the importance of risk assessment, data graphs, fitting models to data, and requiring students of engineering to attend classes in statistics. For sociologists, the accident is a symptom of structural history, bureaucracy, and conformity to organizational norms. Taken in small doses, the assorted interpretations of the launch decision are plausible and rarely mutually exclusive. But when *all* these accounts are considered together, the accident appears thoroughly overdetermined. It is hard to reconcile the sense of inevitable disaster embodied in the cumulated literature of post-accident hindsight with the experiences of the first 24 shuttle launches, which were distinctly successful.

REGARDLESS of the indirect cultural causes of the accident, there was a clear proximate cause: an inability to assess the link between cool temperature and O-ring damage on earlier flights. Such a pre-launch analysis would have revealed that this flight was at considerable risk.[27]

On the day before the launch of Challenger, the rocket engineers and managers needed a quick, smart *analysis* of evidence about the threat of cold to the O-rings, as well as an effective *presentation* of evidence in order to convince NASA officials not to launch. Engineers at Thiokol prepared 13 charts to make the case that the Challenger should *not* be launched the next day, given the forecast of very chilly weather.[28] Drawn up in a few hours, the charts were faxed to NASA and discussed in two long telephone conferences between Thiokol and NASA on the night before the launch. The charts were unconvincing; the arguments against the launch failed; the Challenger blew up.

These charts have weaknesses. First, the title-chart (at right, where "SRM" means Solid Rocket Motor), like the other displays, does not provide the *names* of the people who prepared the material. All too often, such documentation is absent from corporate and government reports. Public, named authorship indicates responsibility, both to the immediate audience and for the long-term record. Readers can follow up and communicate with a named source. Readers can also recall what they know about the author's reputation and credibility. And so even a title-chart, if it lacks appropriate documentation, might well provoke some doubts about the evidence to come.

The second chart (top right) goes directly to the immediate threat to the shuttle by showing the history of eroded O-rings on launches prior to the Challenger. This varying damage, some serious but none catastrophic, was found by examining the O-rings from rocket casings retrieved for re-use. Describing the historical distribution of the *effect* endangering the Challenger, the chart does not provide data about the possible *cause*, temperature. Another impediment to understanding is that the same rocket has three different names: a NASA number (61A LH),

[27] The commission investigating the accident concluded: "A careful analysis of the flight history of O-ring performance would have revealed the correlation of O-ring damage and low temperature. Neither NASA nor Thiokol carried out such an analysis; consequently, they were unprepared to properly evaluate the risks of launching the 51-L [Challenger] mission in conditions more extreme than they had encountered before." *PCSSCA*, volume I, p. 148. Similarly, "the decision to launch STS 51-L was based on a faulty engineering analysis of the SRM field joint seal behavior," House Committee on Science and Technology, *Investigation of the Challenger Accident*, p. 10. Lighthall, "Launching the Space Shuttle," reaches a similar conclusion.

[28] The 13 charts appear in *PCSSCA*, volume IV, pp. 664–673; also in Vaughan, *Challenger Launch Decision*, pp. 293–299.

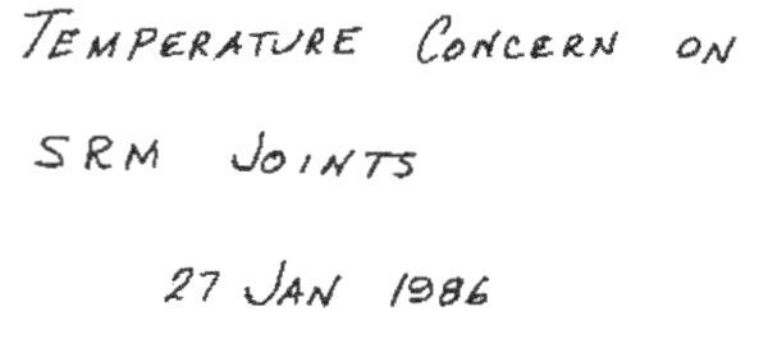

HISTORY OF O-RING DAMAGE ON SRM FIELD JOINTS

		Cross Sectional View			Top View		
	SRM No.	Erosion Depth (in.)	Perimeter Affected (deg)	Nominal Dia. (in.)	Length Of Max Erosion (in.)	Total Heat Affected Length (in.)	Clocking Location (deg)
61A LH Center Field**	22A	None	None	0.280	None	None	36°--66°
61A LH ~~CENTER~~ FIELD**	22A	NONE	NONE	0.280	NONE	NONE	338°-18°
51C LH Forward Field**	15A	0.010	154.0	0.280	4.25	5.25	163
51C RH Center Field (prim)***	15B	0.038	130.0	0.280	12.50	58.75	354
51C RH Center Field (sec)***	15B	None	45.0	0.280	None	29.50	354
41D RH Forward Field	13B	0.028	110.0	0.280	3.00	None	275
41C LH Aft Field*	11A	None	None	0.280	None	None	--
41B LH Forward Field	10A	0.040	217.0	0.280	3.00	14.50	351
STS-2 RH Aft Field	2B	0.053	116.0	0.280	--	--	90

*Hot gas path detected in putty. Indication of heat on O-ring, but no damage.
**Soot behind primary O-ring.
***Soot behind primary O-ring, heat affected secondary O-ring.

Clocking location of leak check port - 0 deg.

OTHER SRM-15 FIELD JOINTS HAD NO BLOWHOLES IN PUTTY AND NO SOOT NEAR OR BEYOND THE PRIMARY O-RING.

SRM-22 FORWARD FIELD JOINT HAD PUTTY PATH TO PRIMARY O-RING, BUT NO O-RING EROSION AND NO SOOT BLOWBY. OTHER SRM-22 FIELD JOINTS HAD NO BLOWHOLES IN PUTTY.

Thiokol's number (SRM no. 22A), and launch date (handwritten in the margin above). For O-ring damage, six types of description (erosion, soot, depth, location, extent, view) break the evidence up into stupefying fragments. An overall index summarizing the damage is needed. This chart quietly begins to define the scope of the analysis: a handful of previous flights that experienced O-ring problems.[29]

The next chart (below left) describes how erosion in the primary O-ring interacts with its back-up, the secondary O-ring. Then two drawings (below right) make an effective visual comparison to show how rotation of the field joint degrades the O-ring seal. This vital effect, however, is not linked to the potential cause; indeed, neither chart appraises the phenomena described in relation to temperature.

[29] This chart does not report an incident of field-joint erosion on STS 61-C, launched two weeks before the Challenger, data which appear to have been available prior to the Challenger prelaunch meeting (see *PCSSCA*, volume II, p. H-3). The damage chart is typewritten, indicating that it was prepared for an earlier presentation before being included in the final 13; handwritten charts were prepared the night before the Challenger was launched.

PRIMARY CONCERNS -

FIELD JOINT - HIGHEST CONCERN

- o EROSION PENETRATION OF PRIMARY SEAL REQUIRES RELIABLE SECONDARY SEAL FOR PRESSURE INTEGRITY
  - o IGNITION TRANSIENT - (0-600 MS)
    - o (0-170 MS) HIGH PROBABILITY OF RELIABLE SECONDARY SEAL
    - o (170-330 MS) REDUCED PROBABILITY OF RELIABLE SECONDARY SEAL
    - o (330-600 MS) HIGH PROBABILITY OF NO SECONDARY SEAL CAPABILITY
- o STEADY STATE - (600 MS - 2 MINUTES)
  - o IF EROSION PENETRATES PRIMARY O-RING SEAL - HIGH PROBABILITY OF NO SECONDARY SEAL CAPABILITY
    - o BENCH TESTING SHOWED O-RING NOT CAPABLE OF MAINTAINING CONTACT WITH METAL PARTS GAP OPENING RATE TO MEOP
    - o BENCH TESTING SHOWED CAPABILITY TO MAINTAIN O-RING CONTACT DURING INITIAL PHASE (0-170 MS) OF TRANSIENT

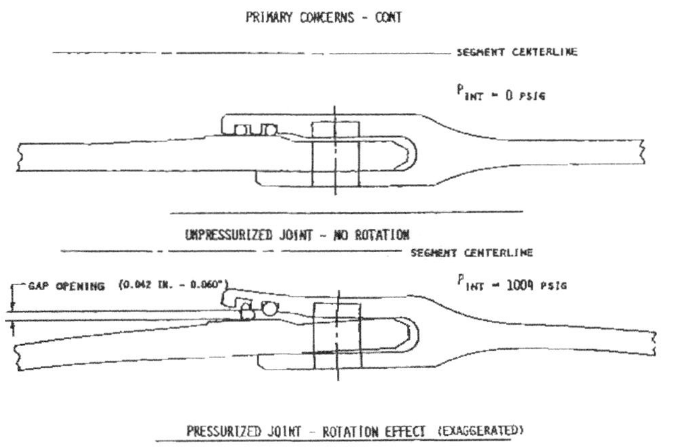

BLOW BY HISTORY

SRM-15 WORST BLOW-BY

- 2 CASE JOINTS (80°), (110°) ARC
- MUCH WORSE VISUALLY THAN SRM-22

SRM 22 BLOW-BY

- 2 CASE JOINTS (30-40°)

SRM-13A, 15, 16A, 18, 23A 24A

- NOZZLE BLOW-BY

HISTORY OF O-RING TEMPERATURES (DEGREES - F)

MOTOR	MBT	AMB	O-RING	WIND
DM-4	68	36	47	10 MPH
DM-2	76	45	52	10 MPH
QM-3	72.5	40	48	10 MPH
QM-4	76	48	51	10 MPH
SRM-15	52	64	53	10 MPH
SRM-22	77	78	75	10 MPH
SRM-25	55	26	29 27	10 MPH 25 MPH

Two charts further narrowed the evidence. Above left, "Blow-By History" mentions the two previous launches, SRM 15 and SRM 22, in which soot (blow-by) was detected in the field joints upon post-launch examination. This information, however, was already reported in the more detailed damage table that followed the title chart.[30] The bottom two lines refer to *nozzle* blow-by, an issue not relevant to launching the Challenger in cold weather.[31]

Although not shown in the blow-by chart, temperature is part of the analysis: SRM 15 had substantial O-ring damage and also was the coldest launch to date (at 53° on January 24, 1985, almost one year before the Challenger). This argument by analogy, made by those opposed to launching the Challenger the next morning, is reasonable, relevant, and weak. With only one case as evidence, it is usually quite difficult to make a credible statement about cause and effect.

If one case isn't enough, why not look at two? And so the parade of anecdotes continued. By linking the blow-by chart (above left) to the temperature chart (above right), those who favored launching the Challenger spotted a weakness in the argument. While it was true that the blow-by on SRM 15 was on a cool day, the blow-by on SRM 22 was on a *warm* day at a temperature of 75° (temperature chart, second column from the right). One engineer said, "We had blow-by on the hottest motor [rocket] and on the coldest motor.[32] The superlative "-est" is an extreme characterization of these thin data, since the total number of launches under consideration here is exactly *two*.

With its focus on blow-by rather than the more common erosion, the chart of blow-by history invited the rhetorically devastating—for those opposed to the launch—comparison of SRM 15 and SRM 22. In fact, as the blow-by chart suggests, the two flights profoundly differed: the 53° launch probably barely survived with significant *erosion* of the primary and secondary O-rings on both rockets as well as blow-by; whereas the 75° launch had no erosion and only blow-by.

[30] On the blow-by chart, the numbers 80°, 110°, 30°, and 40° refer to the *arc* covered by blow-by on the 360° of the field (called here the "case") joint.

[31] Following the blow-by chart were four displays, omitted here, that showed experimental and subscale test data on the O-rings. See *PCSSCA*, volume IV, pp. 664–673.

[32] Quoted in Vaughan, *Challenger Launch Decision*, pp. 296–297.

These charts *defined the database for the decision:* blow-by (not erosion) and temperature for two launches, SRM 15 and SRM 22. Limited measure of effect, wrong number of cases. Left out were the other 22 previous shuttle flights and their temperature variation and O-ring performance. A careful look at such evidence would have made the dangers of a cold launch clear. Displays of evidence implicitly but powerfully define the scope of the relevant, as presented data are selected from a larger pool of material. Like magicians, chartmakers reveal what they choose to reveal. That selection of data—whether partisan, hurried, haphazard, uninformed, thoughtful, wise—can make all the difference, determining the scope of the evidence and thereby setting the analytic agenda that leads to a particular decision.

For example, the temperature chart reports data for two developmental rocket motors (DM), two qualifying motors (QM), two actual launches with blow-by, and the Challenger (SRM 25) forecast.[33] These data are shown again at right. What a strange collation: the first 4 rockets were test motors that never left the ground. Missing are 92% of the temperature data, for 5 of the launches with erosion and 17 launches without erosion.

Depicting bits and pieces of data on blow-by and erosion, along with some peculiarly chosen temperatures, these charts set the stage for the unconvincing conclusions shown in two charts below. The major recommendation, "O-ring temp must be ≥ 53°F at launch," which was rejected, rightly implies that the Challenger could not be safely launched the next morning at 29°. Drawing a line at 53°, however, is a crudely empirical result based on a sample of size one. That anecdote was certainly not an auspicious case, because the 53° launch itself had considerable erosion. As Richard Feynman later wrote, "The O-rings of the solid rocket boosters were not designed to erode. Erosion was a clue that something was wrong. Erosion was not something from which safety could be inferred."[34]

[33] The table of temperature data, shown in full at left, is described as a "History of O-ring Temperatures." It is a highly selective history, leaving out nearly all the actual flight experience of the shuttle:

MOTOR	O-RING	
DM-4	47	Test rockets ignited on fixed horizontal platforms in Utah.
DM-2	52	
QM-3	48	
QM-4	51	
SRM-15	53	The only 2 shuttle launches (of 24) for which temperatures were shown in the 13 Challenger charts.
SRM-22	75	
SRM-25	29 27	Forecasted O-ring temperatures for the Challenger.

[34] Richard P. Feynman, "*What Do You Care What Other People Think?" Further Adventures of a Curious Character* (New York, 1988), p. 224; also in Feynman, "Appendix F: Personal Observations on the Reliability of the Shuttle," *PCSSCA*, volume II, p. F2. On the many problems with the proposed 53° temperature line, see Vaughan, *Challenger Launch Decision*, pp. 309–310.

CONCLUSIONS :

o TEMPERATURE OF O-RING IS NOT ONLY PARAMETER CONTROLLING BLOW-BY

SRM 15 WITH BLOW-BY HAD AN O-RING TEMP AT 53°F
SRM 22 WITH BLOW-BY HAD AN O-RING TEMP AT 75°F
FOUR DEVELOPMENT MOTORS WITH NO BLOW-BY WERE TESTED AT O-RING TEMP OF 47° TO 52°F

DEVELOPMENT MOTORS HAD PUTTY PACKING WHICH RESULTED IN BETTER PERFORMANCE

o AT ABOUT 50°F BLOW-BY COULD BE EXPERIENCED IN CASE JOINTS

o TEMP FOR SRM 25 ON 1-28-86 LAUNCH WILL BE 29°F 9 AM
38°F 2 PM

o HAVE NO DATA THAT WOULD INDICATE SRM 25 IS DIFFERENT THAN SRM 15 OTHER THAN TEMP

RECOMMENDATIONS :

o O-RING TEMP MUST BE ≥ 53°F AT LAUNCH

DEVELOPMENT MOTORS AT 47° TO 52°F WITH PUTTY PACKING HAD NO BLOW-BY
SRM 15 (THE BEST SIMULATION) WORKED AT 53°F

o PROJECT AMBIENT CONDITIONS (TEMP & WIND) TO DETERMINE LAUNCH TIME

The 13 charts failed to stop the launch. Yet, as it turned out, the chartmakers had reached the right conclusion. They had the correct theory and they were thinking causally, but they were not *displaying* causally. Unable to get a correlation between O-ring distress and temperature, those involved in the debate concluded that they didn't have enough data to quantify the effect of the cold.[35] The displayed data were very thin; no wonder NASA officials were so skeptical about the no-launch argument advanced by the 13 charts. For it was as if John Snow had ignored some areas with cholera and *all* the cholera-free areas and their water pumps as well. The flights without damage provide the statistical leverage necessary to understand the effects of temperature. *Numbers become evidence by being in relation to.*

[35] *PCSSCA*, volume IV, pp. 290, 791.

This data matrix shows the complete history of temperature and O-ring condition for all previous launches. Entries are ordered by the possible cause, temperature, from coolest to warmest launch. Data in red were exhibited at some point in the 13 pre-launch charts; and the data shown in black were not included. I have calculated an overall O-ring damage score for each launch.[36] The table reveals the link between O-ring distress and cool weather, with a concentration of problems on cool days compared with warm days:

[36] For each launch, the score on the damage index is the severity-weighted total number of incidents of O-ring erosion, heating, and blow-by. Data sources for the entire table: *PCSSCA*, volume II, pp. H1–H3, and volume IV, p. 664; and *Post-Challenger Evaluation of Space Shuttle Risk Assessment and Management*, pp. 135–136.

Flight	Date	Temperature °F	Erosion incidents	Blow-by incidents	Damage index	Comments
51-C	01.24.85	53°	3	2	11	Most erosion any flight; blow-by; back-up rings heated.
41-B	02.03.84	57°	1		4	Deep, extensive erosion.
61-C	01.12.86	58°	1		4	O-ring erosion on launch two weeks before Challenger.
41-C	04.06.84	63°	1		2	O-rings showed signs of heating, but no damage.
1	04.12.81	66°			0	Coolest (66°) launch without O-ring problems.
6	04.04.83	67°			0	
51-A	11.08.84	67°			0	
51-D	04.12.85	67°			0	
5	11.11.82	68°			0	
3	03.22.82	69°			0	
2	11.12.81	70°	1		4	Extent of erosion not fully known.
9	11.28.83	70°			0	
41-D	08.30.84	70°	1		4	
51-G	06.17.85	70°			0	
7	06.18.83	72°			0	
8	08.30.83	73°			0	
51-B	04.29.85	75°			0	
61-A	10.30.85	75°		2	4	No erosion. Soot found behind two primary O-rings.
51-I	08.27.85	76°			0	
61-B	11.26.85	76°			0	
41-G	10.05.84	78°			0	
51-J	10.03.85	79°			0	
4	06.27.82	80°			?	O-ring condition unknown; rocket casing lost at sea.
51-F	07.29.85	81°			0	

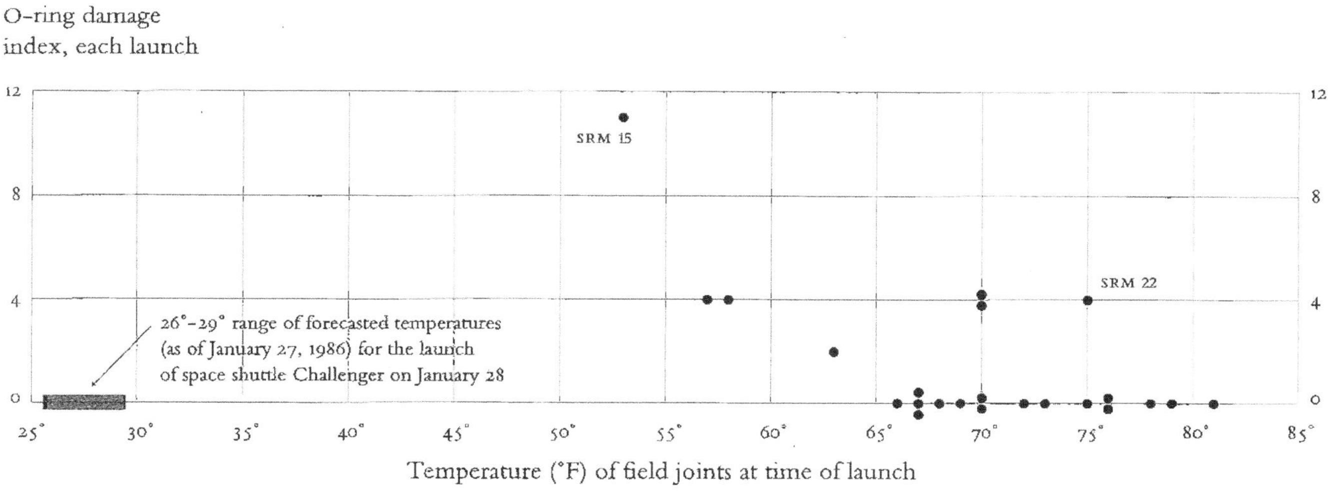

When assessing evidence, it is helpful to see a full data matrix, all observations for all variables, those private numbers from which the public displays are constructed. No telling what will turn up.

Above, a scatterplot shows the experience of all 24 launches prior to the Challenger. Like the table, the graph reveals the serious risks of a launch at 29°. Over the years, the O-rings had persistent problems at cooler temperatures: indeed, *every* launch below 66° resulted in damaged O-rings; on warmer days, only a few flights had erosion. In this graph, the temperature scale extends down to 29°, visually expressing the stupendous extrapolation beyond all previous experience that must be made in order to launch at 29°. The coolest flight without any O-ring damage was at 66°, some 37° warmer than predicted for the Challenger; the forecast of 29° is 5.7 standard deviations distant from the average temperature for previous launches. This launch was completely outside the engineering database accumulated in 24 previous flights.

IN the 13 charts prepared for making the decision to launch, there is a scandalous discrepancy between the intellectual tasks at hand and the images created to serve those tasks. As analytical graphics, the displays failed to reveal a risk that was in fact present. As presentation graphics, the displays failed to persuade government officials that a cold-weather launch might be dangerous. In designing those displays, the chartmakers didn't quite know what they were doing, and they were doing a lot of it.[37] We can be thankful that most data graphics are *not* inherently misleading or uncommunicative or difficult to design correctly.

The graphics of the cholera epidemic and shuttle, and many other examples,[38] suggest this conclusion: *there are right ways and wrong ways to show data; there are displays that reveal the truth and displays that do not.* And, if the matter is an important one, then getting the displays of evidence right or wrong can possibly have momentous consequences.

[37] Lighthall concluded: "Of the 13 charts circulated by Thiokol managers and engineers to the scattered teleconferees, six contained no tabled data about either O-ring temperature, O-ring blow-by, or O-ring damage (these were primarily outlines of arguments being made by the Thiokol engineers). Of the seven remaining charts containing data either on launch temperatures or O-ring anomaly, *six of them included data on either launch temperatures or O-ring anomaly but not both in relation to each other.*" Lighthall, "Launching the Space Shuttle Challenger," p. 65. See also note 27 above for the conclusions of the shuttle commission and the House Committee on Science and Technology.

[38] Edward R. Tufte, *The Visual Display of Quantitative Information* (Cheshire, Connecticut, 1983), pp. 13–77.

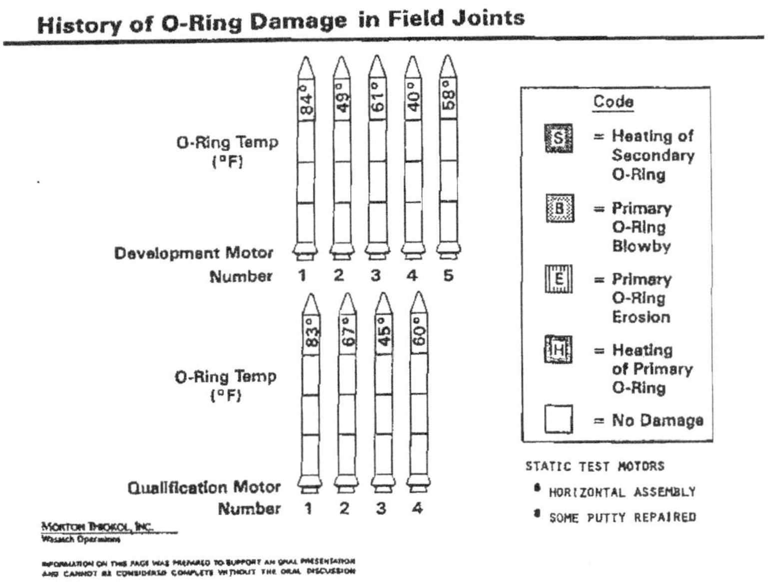

PCSSCA, volume v, p. 895.

39 Most accounts of the Challenger reproduce a scatterplot that apparently demonstrates the analytical failure of the pre-launch debate. This graph depicts only launches with O-ring damage and their temperatures, omitting all damage-free launches (an absence of data points on the line of zero incidents of damage):

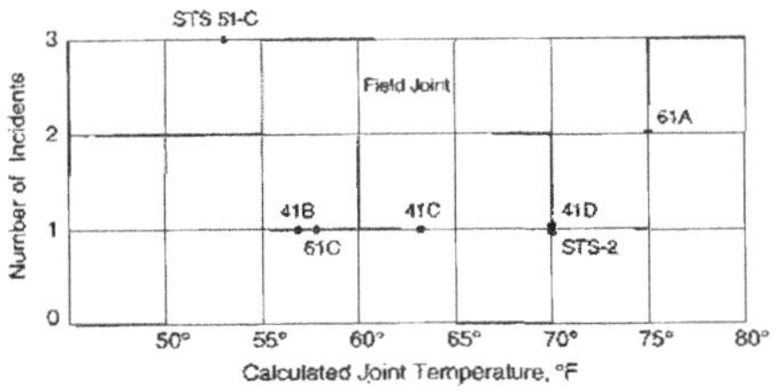

First published in the shuttle commission report (*PCSSCA*, volume I, p. 146), the chart is a favorite of statistics teachers. It appears in textbooks on engineering, graphics, and statistics—relying on Dalal, Fowlkes, Hoadley, "Risk Analysis of the Space Shuttle: Pre-*Challenger* Prediction of Failure," who describe the scatterplot as having a central role in the launch decision. (The commission report does not say when the plot was made.) The graph of the missing data-points is a vivid and poignant object lesson in how not to look at data when making an important decision. But it is too good to be true! First, the graph was *not* part of the pre-launch debate; it was *not* among the 13 charts used by Thiokol and NASA in deciding to launch. Rather, it was drawn *after* the accident by two staff members (the executive director and a lawyer) at the commission *as their simulation* of the poor reasoning in the pre-launch debate. Second, the graph implies that the pre-launch analysis examined 7 launches at 7 temperatures with 7 damage measurements. That is not true; only 2 cases of blow-by and 2 temperatures were linked up. The actual pre-launch analysis was much thinner than indicated by the commission scatterplot. Third, the damage scale is dequantified, only counting the number of incidents rather than measuring their severity. In short, whether for teaching statistics or for seeking to understand the practice of data graphics, why use an inaccurately simulated post-launch chart when we have the genuine 13 pre-launch decision charts right in hand? (On this scatterplot, see Lighthall, "Launching the Space Shuttle Challenger;" and Vaughan, *Challenger Launch Decision*, pp. 382–384.)

SOON after the Challenger accident, a presidential commission began an investigation. In evidence presented to the commission, some more charts attempted to describe the history of O-ring damage in relation to temperature. Several of these displays still didn't get it right.[39]

Prepared for testimony to the commission, the chart above shows nine little rockets annotated with temperature readings turned sideways. A legend shows a damage scale. Apparently measured in orderly steps, this scale starts with the most serious problem ("Heating of Secondary O-ring," which means a primary ring burned through and leaked) and then continues in several ordered steps to "No Damage." Regrettably, the scale's visual representation is disordered: the cross-hatching varies erratically from dark, to light, to medium dark, to darker, to lightest—a visual pattern unrelated to the substantive order of the measured scale. A letter-code accompanies the cross-hatching. Such codes can hinder visual understanding.

At any rate, these nine rockets suffered no damage, even at quite cool temperatures. But the graph is not on point, for it is based on test data from "Development and Qualification Motors"—all fixed rockets ignited on horizontal test stands at Thiokol, never undergoing the stress of a real flight. Thus this evidence, although perhaps better than nothing (that's all it is better than), is not directly relevant to evaluating the dangers of a cold-weather launch. Some of these same temperature numbers for test rockets are found in a pre-launch chart that we saw earlier.

Beneath the company logotype down in the lower left of this chart lurks a legalistic disclaimer (technically known as a CYA notice) that says this particular display should not be taken quite at face value—you had to be there:

INFORMATION ON THIS PAGE WAS PREPARED TO SUPPORT AN ORAL PRESENTATION AND CANNOT BE CONSIDERED COMPLETE WITHOUT THE ORAL DISCUSSION

Such defensive formalisms should provoke rambunctious skepticism: they suggest a corporate distrust both of the chartmaker and of any viewers of the chart.[40] In this case, the graph is documented in reports, hearing transcripts, and archives of the shuttle commission.

The second chart in the sequence is most significant. Shown below are the O-ring experiences of all 24 previous shuttle launches, with 48 little rockets representing the 24 flight-pairs:

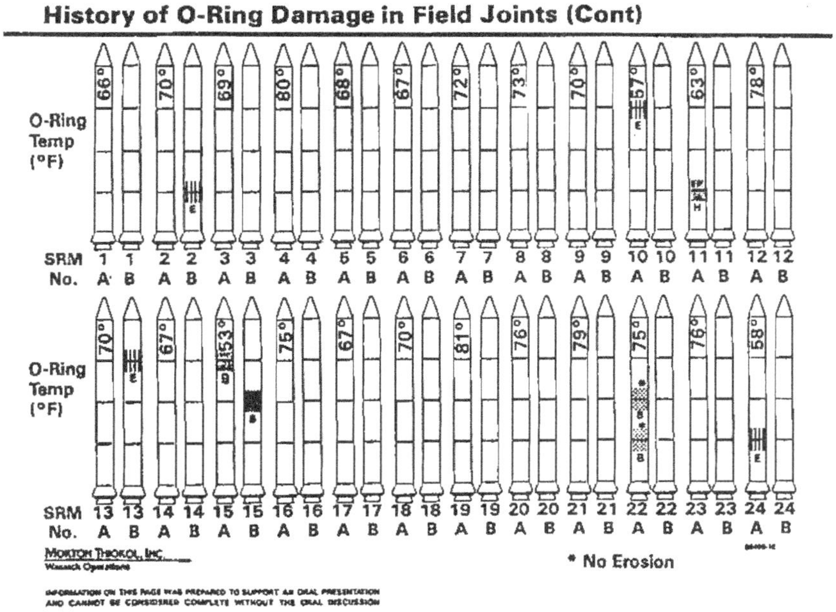

PCSSCA, volume v, p. 896.

Rockets marked with the damage code show the seven flights with O-ring problems. Launch temperature is given for each pair of rockets. Like the data matrix we saw earlier, this display contains *all* the information necessary to diagnose the relationship between temperature and damage, if we could only see it.[41] The poor design makes it impossible to learn what was going on. In particular:

The Disappearing Legend At the hearings, these charts were presented by means of the dreaded overhead projector, which shows one image after another like a slide projector, making it difficult to compare and link images. When the first chart (the nine little rockets) goes away, the visual code calibrating O-ring damage also vanishes. Thus viewers need to memorize the code in order to assess the severity and type of damage sustained by each rocket in the 48-rocket chart.

[40] This caveat, which also appeared on Thiokol's final approval of the Challenger launch (reproduced here with the epigraphs on page 26), was discussed in hearings on Challenger by the House Committee on Science and Technology: "U. Edwin Garrison, President of the Aerospace Group at Thiokol, testified that the caveat at the bottom of the paper in no way 'insinuates . . . that the document doesn't mean what it says.'" *Investigation of the Challenger Accident*, pp. 228–229, note 80.

[41] This chart shows the rocket pair SRM 4A, SRM 4B at 80°F, as having *undamaged* O-rings. In fact, those rocket casings were lost at sea and their O-ring history is unknown.

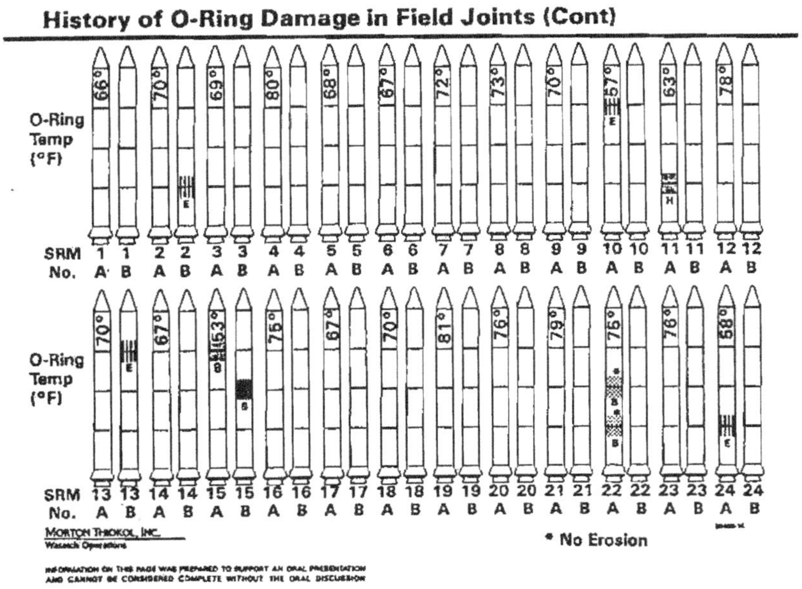

PCSSCA, volume v, p. 896. This image is repeated from our page 47.

Chartjunk Good design brings *absolute attention* to data. Yet instead of focusing on a possible link between damage and temperature—the vital issue here—the strongest visual presence in this graph is the clutter generated by the outlines of the 48 little rockets. The visual elements bounce and glow, as heavy lines activate the white space, producing visual noise. Such misplaced priorities in the design of graphs and charts should make us suspicious about the competence and integrity of the analysis. Chartjunk indicates statistical stupidity, just as weak writing often reflects weak thought: "Neither can his mind be thought to be in tune, whose words do jarre," wrote Ben Jonson in the early 1600s, "nor his reason in frame, whose sentence is preposterous."[42]

Lack of Clarity in Depicting Cause and Effect Turning the temperature numbers sideways obscures the causal variable. Sloppy typography also impedes inspection of these data, as numbers brush up against line-art. Likewise garbled is the measure of effect: O-ring anomalies are depicted by little marks—scattered and opaquely encoded—rather than being totaled up into a summary score of damage for each flight. Once again Jonson's Principle: these problems are more than just poor design, for a lack of visual clarity in arranging evidence is a sign of a lack of intellectual clarity in reasoning about evidence.

Wrong Order The fatal flaw is the *ordering* of the data. Shown as a time-series, the rockets are sequenced by date of launching—from the first pair at upper left SRM No. 1 1 A B to the last pair at lower right 24 24 A B (the launch immediately prior to Challenger). The sequential order conceals the possible link between temperature and O-ring damage, thereby throwing statistical thinking into disarray. The time-series

[42] Ben Jonson, *Timber: or, Discoveries* (London, 1641), first printed in the Folio of 1640, *The Workes . . .*, p. 122 of the section beginning with *Horace his Art of Poetry*. On chartjunk, see Edward R. Tufte, *The Visual Display of Quantitative Information* (Cheshire, Connecticut, 1983), pp. 106–121.

chart at left bears on the issue: Is there a time trend in O-ring damage? This is a perfectly reasonable question, but not the one on which the survival of Challenger depended. That issue was: Is there a temperature trend in O-ring damage?

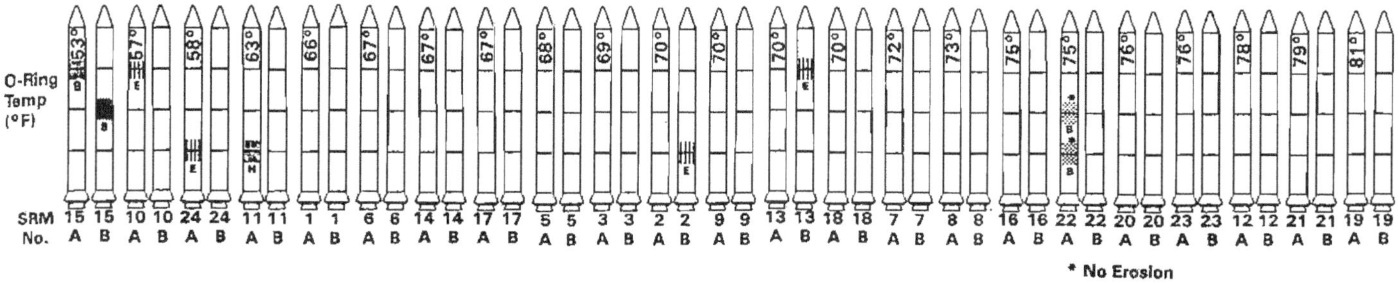

Information displays should serve the analytic purpose at hand; if the substantive matter is a possible cause-effect relationship, then graphs should organize data so as to illuminate such a link. Not a complicated idea, but a profound one. Thus the little rockets must be *placed in order by temperature, the possible cause*. Above, the rockets are so ordered by temperature. This clearly shows the serious risks of a cold launch, for most O-ring damage occurs at cooler temperatures. Given this evidence, how could the Challenger be launched at 29°?

In the haplessly dequantified style typical of iconographic displays, temperature is merely ordered rather than measured; all the rockets are adjacent to one another rather than being spaced apart in proportion to their temperature. Along with proportional scaling—routinely done in conventional statistical graphs—it is particularly revealing to include a symbolic pair of rockets way over at 29°, the predicted temperature for the Challenger launch. Another redrawing:

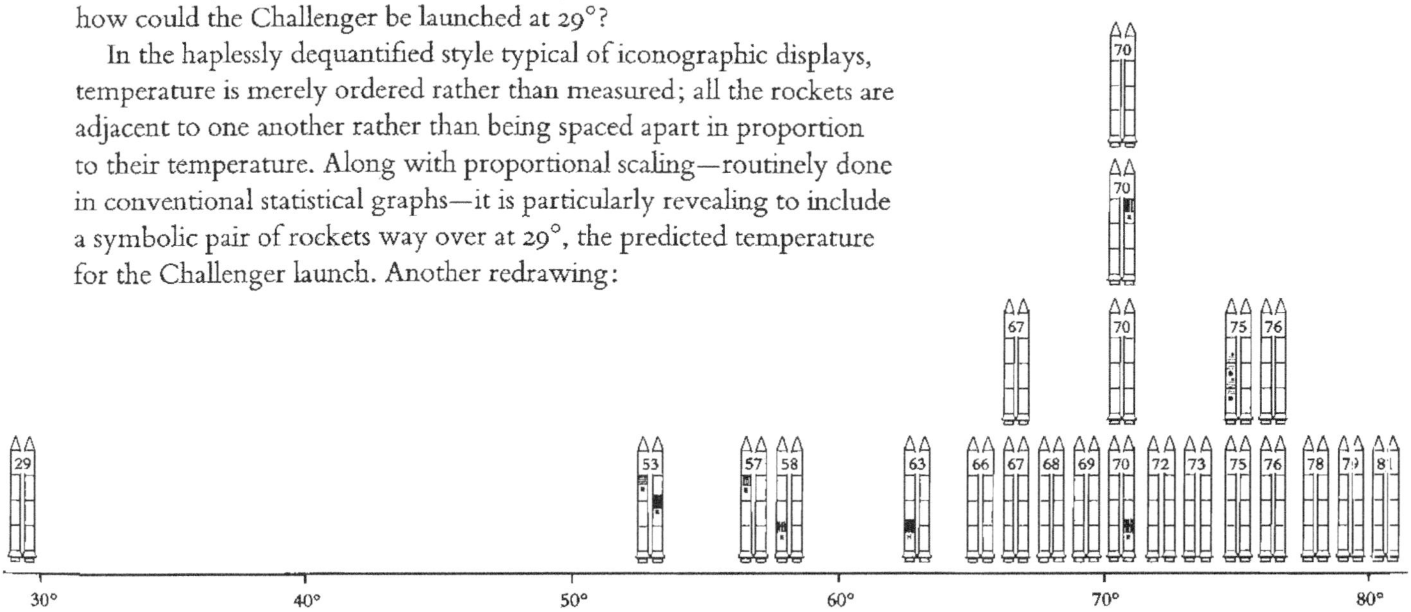

Even after repairs, the pictorial approach with cute little rockets remains ludicrous and corrupt. The excessively original artwork just plays around with the information. It is best to forget about designs involving such icons and symbols—in this case and, for that matter, in nearly all other cases. These data require only a simple scatterplot or an ordered table to reveal the deadly relationship.

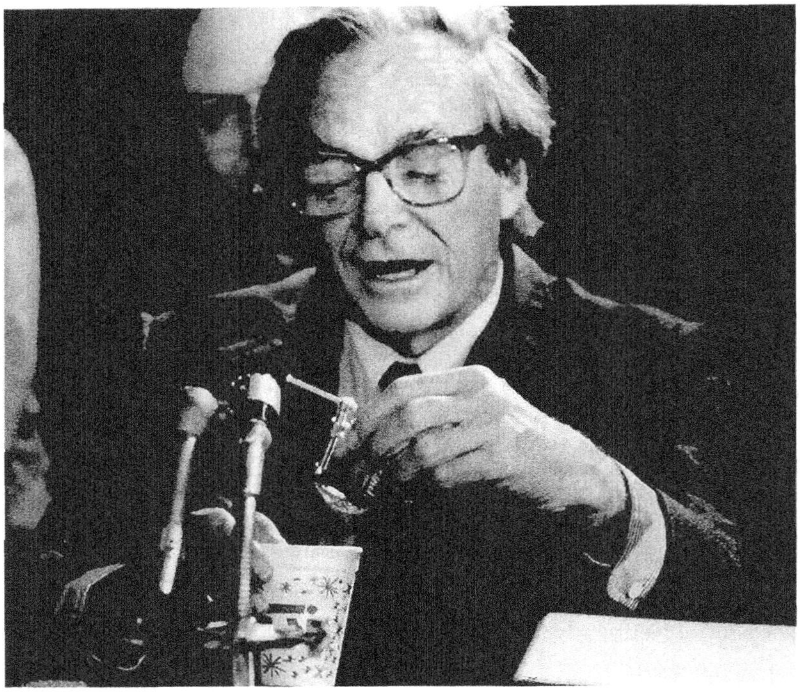

Photograph by Marilynn K. Yee, NYT Pictures, *The New York Times*.

AT a meeting of the commission investigating the shuttle accident, the physicist Richard Feynman conducted a celebrated demonstration that clarified the link between cold temperature and loss of resiliency in the rubber O-rings. Although this link was obvious for weeks to engineers and those investigating the accident, various officials had camouflaged the issue by testifying to the commission in an obscurantist language of evasive technical jargon.[43] Preparing for the moment during the public hearing when a piece of an O-ring (from a model of the field joint) would be passed around, Feynman had earlier that morning purchased a small clamp at a hardware store in Washington. A colorful theater of physics resulted. Feynman later described his famous experiment:

> The model comes around to General Kutyna, and then to me. The clamp and pliers come out of my pocket, I take the model apart, I've got the O-ring pieces in my hand, but I still haven't got any ice water! I turn around again and signal the guy I've been bothering about it, and he signals back, "Don't worry, you'll get it!". . . .
>
> So finally, when I get my ice water, I don't drink it! I squeeze the rubber in the C-clamp, and put them in the glass of ice water. . . .
>
> I press the button for my microphone, and I say, "I took this rubber from the model and put it in a clamp in ice water for a while."
>
> I take the clamp out, hold it in the air, and loosen it as I talk: "I discovered that when you undo the clamp, the rubber doesn't spring back. In other words, for more than a few seconds, there is no resilience in this particular material when it is at a temperature of 32 degrees. I believe that has some significance for our problem."[44]

[43] One official "gave a vivid flavor of the engineering jargon—the tang end up and the clevis end down, the grit blast, the splashdown loads and cavity collapse loads, the Randolph type two zinc chromate asbestos-filled putty laid up in strips—all forbidding to the listening reporters if not to the commissioners themselves." James Gleick, *Genius: The Life and Science of Richard Feynman* (New York, 1992), p. 422.

[44] Richard P. Feynman, "*What Do You Care What Other People Think?" Further Adventures of a Curious Character* (New York, 1988), pp. 151–153. Feynman's words were edited somewhat in this posthumously published book; for the actual hearings, see *PCSSCA*, volume IV, p. 679, transcript.

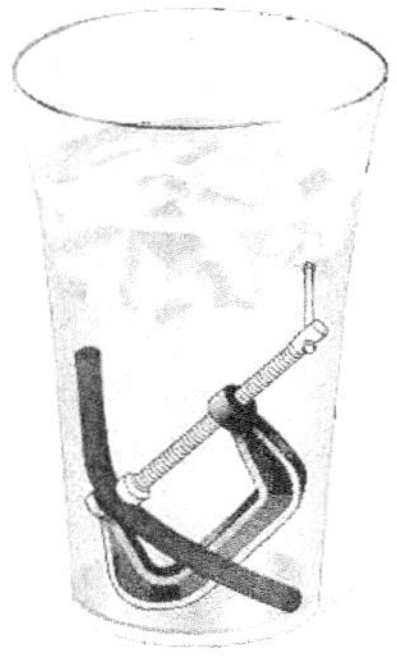

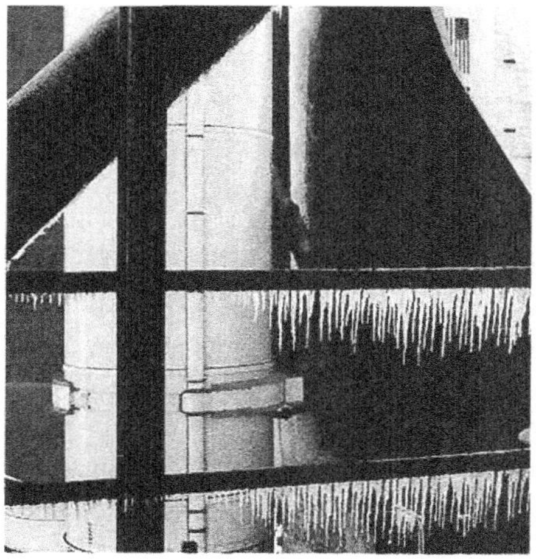

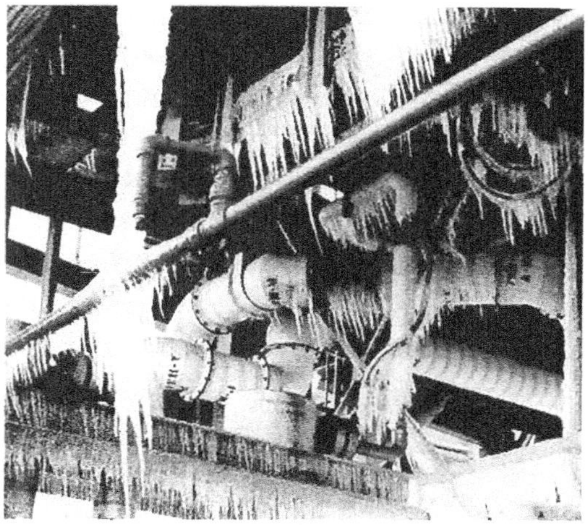

To create a more effective exhibit, the clamped O-ring might well have been placed in a transparent glass of ice water rather than in the opaque cup provided to Feynman. Such a display would then make a visual reference to the extraordinary pre-flight photographs of an ice-covered launch pad, thereby tightening up the link between the ice-water experiment and the Challenger.[45]

With a strong visual presence and understated conclusion ("I believe that has some significance for our problem"), this science experiment, improvised by a Nobel laureate, became a media sensation, appearing on many news broadcasts and on the front page of *The New York Times*. Alert to these possibilities, Feynman had intentionally provided a vivid "news hook" for an apparently inscrutable technical issue in rocket engineering:

> During the lunch break, reporters came up to me and asked questions like, "Were you talking about the O-ring or the putty?" and "Would you explain to us what an O-ring is, exactly?" So I was rather depressed that I wasn't able to make my point. But that night, all the news shows caught on to the significance of the experiment, and the next day, the newspaper articles explained everything perfectly.[46]

Never have so many viewed a single physics experiment. As Freeman Dyson rhapsodized: "The public saw with their own eyes how science is done, how a great scientist thinks with his hands, how nature gives a clear answer when a scientist asks her a clear question."[47]

AND yet the presentation is deeply flawed, committing the same type of error of omission that was made in the 13 pre-launch charts. Another anecdote, without variation in cause or effect, the ice-water experiment is *uncontrolled and dequantified*. It does not address the questions *Compared with what? At what rate?* Consequently the evidence of a one-glass exhibit is equivocal: Did the O-ring lose resilience because it was clamped hard, because it was cold, or because it was wet? A credible experimental

[45] Above, icicles hang from the service structure for the Challenger. At left, the photograph shows icicles near the solid-fuel booster rocket; for a sense of scale, note that the white booster rocket is 12 ft (3.7 m) in diameter. From *PCSSCA*, volume I, p. 113. One observer described the launch service tower as looking like "... something out of Dr. Zhivago. There's sheets of icicles hanging everywhere." House Committee on Science and Technology, *Investigation of the Challenger Accident*, p. 238. Illustration of O-ring experiment by Weilin Wu and Edward Tufte.

[46] Feynman, "*What Do You Care What Other People Think?*", p. 153.

[47] Freeman Dyson, *From Eros to Gaia* (New York, 1992), p. 312.

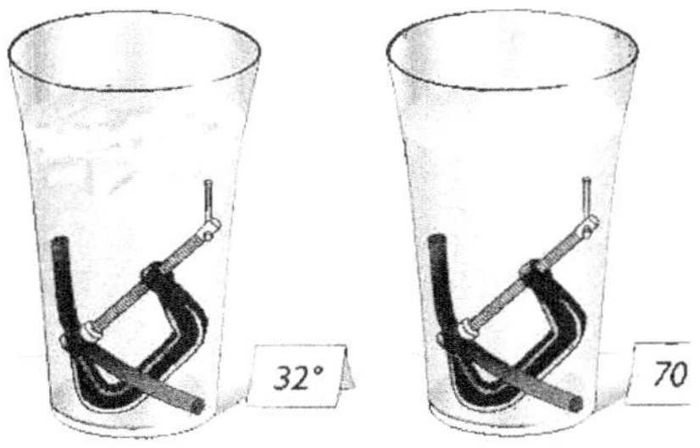

design requires at least two clamps, two pieces of O-ring, and two glasses of water (one cold, one not). The idea is that the two O-ring pieces are alike in all respects save their exposure to differing temperatures. Upon releasing the clamps from the O-rings, presumably only the cold ring will show reduced resiliency. In contrast, the one-glass method is not an experiment; it is merely an experience.

For a one-glass display, neither the cause (ice water in an opaque cup) nor the effect (the clamp's imprint on the O-ring) is explicitly shown. Neither variable is quantified. In fact, neither variable varies.

A controlled experiment would not merely evoke the well-known empirical connection between temperature and resiliency, but would also reveal the overriding *intellectual* failure of the pre-launch analysis of the evidence. That failure was a lack of control, a lack of comparison.[48] The 13 pre-launch charts, like the one-glass experiment, examine only a few instances of O-ring problems and not the causes of O-ring success. A sound demonstration would exemplify the idea that in reasoning about causality, *variations in the cause* must be explicitly and measurably linked to *variations in the effect*. These principles were violated in the 13 pre-launch charts as well as in the post-launch display that arranged the 48 little rockets in temporal rather than causal order. Few lessons about the use of evidence for making decisions are more important: story-telling, weak analogies, selective reporting, warped displays, and anecdotes are not enough.[49] Reliable knowledge grows from evidence that is collected, analyzed, and displayed with some good comparisons in view. And why should we fail to be rigorous about evidence and its presentation just because the evidence is a part of a public dialogue, or is meant for the news media, or is about an important problem, or is part of making a critical decision in a hurry and under pressure?

Failure to think clearly about the analysis and the presentation of evidence opens the door for all sorts of political and other mischief to operate in making decisions. For the Challenger, there were substantial pressures to get it off the ground as quickly as possible: an unrealistic and over-optimistic flight schedule based on the premise that launches were a matter of routine (this massive, complex, and costly vehicle was named the "shuttle," as if it made hourly flights from Boston to New York); the difficulty for the rocket-maker (Morton Thiokol) to deny the demands of its major client (NASA); and a preoccupation with public relations and media events (there was a possibility of a televised conversation between the orbiting astronaut-teacher Christa McAuliffe and President Reagan during his State of the Union address that night, 10 hours after the launch). But these pressures would not have prevailed over credible evidence against the launch, for many other flights had been delayed in the past for good reasons. Had the correct scatterplot or data table been constructed, no one would have dared to risk the Challenger in such cold weather.

[48] Feynman was aware of the problematic experimental design. During hearings in the afternoon following the ice-water demonstration, he began his questioning of NASA management with this comment: "We spoke this morning about the resiliency of the seal, and if the material weren't resilient, it wouldn't work in the appropriate mode, or it would be less satisfactory, in fact, it might not work well. I did a little experiment here, and *this is not the way to do such experiments*, indicating that the stuff looked as if it was less resilient at lower temperatures, in ice." (*PCSSCA*, volume IV, pp. 739–740, transcript, emphasis added.) Drawing of two-glass experiment by Weilin Wu and Edward Tufte.

[49] David C. Hoaglin, Richard J. Light, Bucknam McPeek, Frederick Mosteller, and Michael Stoto, *Data for Decisions: Information Strategies for Policymakers* (Cambridge, Massachusetts, 1982).

Conclusion: Thinking and Design

RICHARD Feynman concludes his report on the explosion of the space shuttle with this blunt assessment: "For a successful technology, reality must take precedence over public relations, for Nature cannot be fooled."[50] Feynman echoes the similarly forthright words of Galileo in 1615: "It is not within the power of practitioners of demonstrative sciences to change opinion at will, choosing now this and now that one; there is a great difference between giving orders to a mathematician or a philosopher and giving them to a merchant or a lawyer; and demonstrated conclusions about natural and celestial phenomena cannot be changed with the same ease as opinions about what is or is not legitimate in a contract, in a rental, or in commerce."[51]

[50] Richard P. Feynman, "Appendix F: Personal Observations on the Reliability of the Shuttle," *PCSSCA* volume II, p. F5; also, Feynman, "*What Do You Care What Other People Think?" Further Adventures of a Curious Character* (New York, 1988), p. 237.

[51] Galileo Galilei, letter to the Grand Duchess Christina of Tuscany, 1615, in *The Galileo Affair: A Documentary History*, edited and translated by Maurice A. Finocchiaro (Berkeley, 1989), p. 101.

In our cases here, the inferences made from the data faced exacting reality tests: the cholera epidemic ends or persists, the shuttle flies or fails. Those inferences and the resulting decisions and actions were based on various visual representations (maps, graphs, tables) of the evidence. The quality of these representations differed enormously, and in ways that governed the ultimate consequences.

For our case studies, and surely for the many other instances where evidence makes a difference, the conclusion is unmistakable: if displays of data are to be truthful and revealing, then the design logic of the display must reflect the intellectual logic of the analysis:

> *Visual representations of evidence should be governed by principles of reasoning about quantitative evidence. For information displays, design reasoning must correspond to scientific reasoning. Clear and precise seeing becomes as one with clear and precise thinking.*

For example, the scientific principle, *make controlled comparisons*, also guides the construction of data displays, prescribing that the ink or pixels of graphics should be arranged so as to depict comparisons and contexts. Display architecture recapitulates quantitative thinking; design quality grows from intellectual quality. Such dual principles—both for reasoning about statistical evidence *and* for the design of statistical graphics—include (1) *documenting* the sources and characteristics of the data, (2) insistently enforcing appropriate *comparisons*, (3) demonstrating mechanisms of *cause and effect*, (4) expressing those mechanisms *quantitatively*, (5) recognizing the inherently *multivariate* nature of analytic problems, and (6) inspecting and evaluating *alternative explanations*. When consistent with the substance and in harmony with the content, information displays should be documentary, comparative, causal and explanatory, quantified, multivariate, exploratory, skeptical.

And, as illustrated by the divergent graphical practices in our cases of the epidemic and the space shuttle, it also helps to have an endless commitment to finding, telling, and showing the truth.

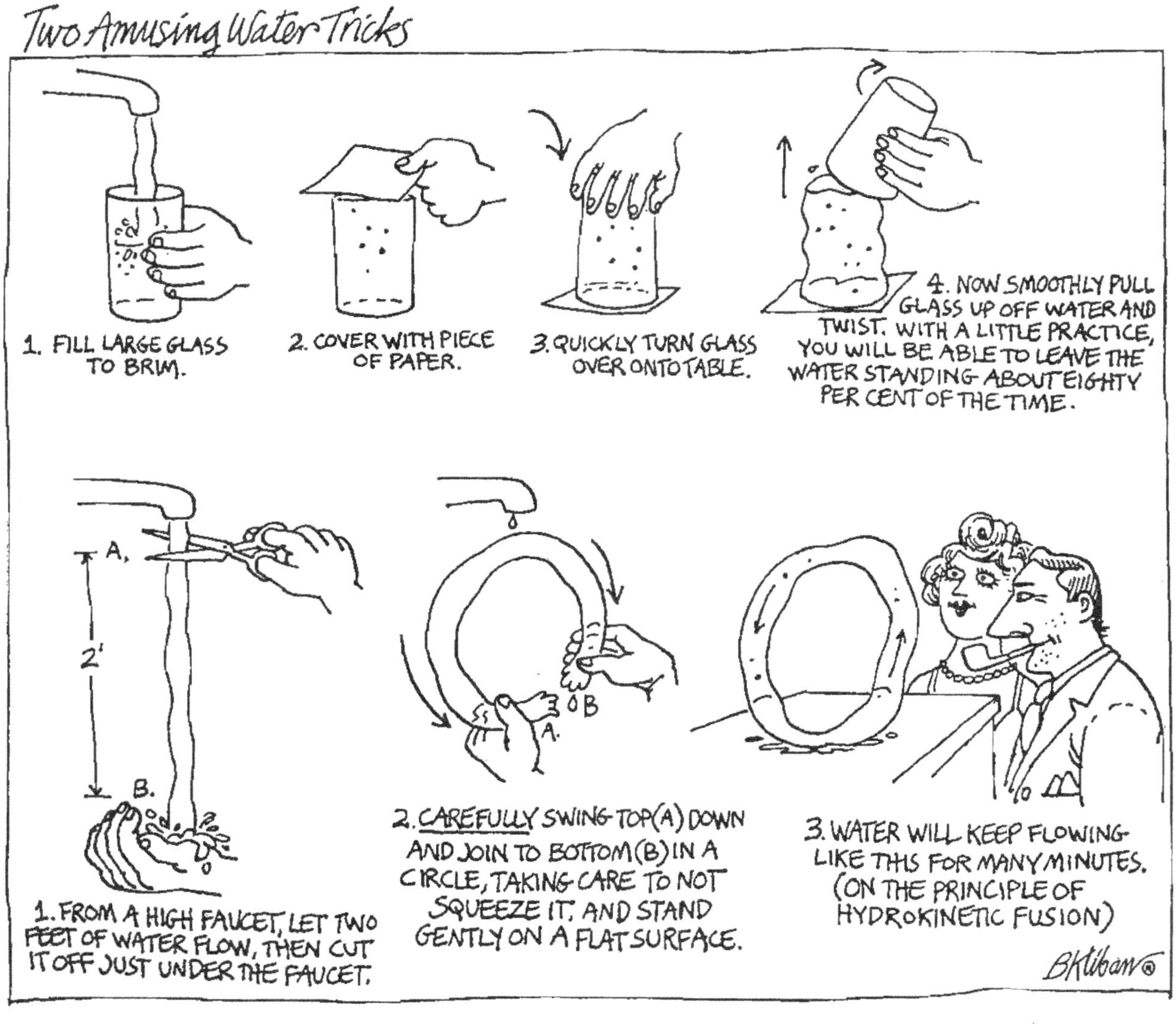

B. Kliban, *Advanced Cartooning and Other Drawings* (New York, 1993), p. 25.

3 Explaining Magic: Pictorial Instructions and Disinformation Design*

MAGIC, the production of entertaining illusions, has an appeal quite independent of the local specifics of language or culture. In seemingly causing an object to vanish or an assistant to levitate, conjurers amaze, delight, and even shock their audiences by the apparent violation of the universal laws of nature and our daily experience of those laws.[1] Since these principles of physics hold *everywhere*, magic is conceivably a cosmological entertainment, with the wonder induced by theatrical illusions appreciated by all, regardless of planetary system.

Explanations of magic involve pictorial instructions demonstrating a sequence of performance, a step-by-step description of conjuring activities.[2] To document and explain a process, *to make verbs visible*, is at the heart of information design.

Also, as is the case for all sorts of narratives, explanations of magic tell a four-dimensional story, using words and images to navigate through time and three-space where conjuring activities take place. It is hard to imagine how the motionless, two-dimensional flatland of paper can fully disclose the swift fluidity of sleight of hand.

In magical performances, knowledge about the revealed frontview (what appears to be done) fails to yield reliable knowledge about the concealed backview (what is actually done)—and it is the audience's misdirected assumption about such symmetric reliability that makes the magic. Comprehensive visual accounts of illusions must simultaneously depict the revealed and the concealed. As a result, such explanations are intriguing exercises in design.

Magicians, like other theatrical performers, are professionals in communicating and presenting information. Thus writings on the *stagecraft* of magical performances may well contribute to our understanding of information design.

Finally, the techniques of conjuring are especially relevant to theories of information display. To create illusions is to engage in *disinformation design*, to corrupt optical information, to deceive the audience. Thus the strategies of magic suggest *what not to do* if our goal is truth-telling rather than illusion-making.

*Jamy Ian Swiss, a professional magician, is co-author of this chapter.

[1] See Earle Coleman, *Magic: A Reference Guide* (Westport, Connecticut, 1987), p. xii. In anthropology and histories of 12th to 17th century ideas, "magic" refers to pre-scientific belief systems—astrology, divination, prophecy, numerology, magic healing, witchcraft, demons—usually as competitors to religious beliefs; see Keith Thomas, *Religion and the Decline of Magic* (New York, 1971). Our interest here is only in *conjuring*, the creation of entertaining illusions.

[2] Ernst Gombrich, "Pictorial Instructions," in Horace Barlow, Colin Blakemore, and Miranda Weston-Smith, eds., *Images and Understanding* (Cambridge, 1990), pp. 26–45.

In explaining magic, diagrams on paper illuminate spatial depth and detail, simultaneously exhibiting the revealed illusion and unveiling the concealed gimmick, the different views of audience and performer. From a superbly illustrated book, *The Royal Road to Card Magic*, this drawing at right describes a parlor trick in which some cards are placed inside an envelope while, by stealth, the target card remains outside. Remarkably, *ten* layers are depicted: (1) left thumb, (2) three of hearts, (3) envelope, (4–7) stack of four cards within the envelope, (8) right thumb, (9) other side of the envelope, and (10) ghosted fingers behind the whole thing. Another layer of content comes from the annotation, which accents the visual separations by pointing to various levels. Both diagonals of the envelope read accidentally in perspective and suggest an added (although representationally incorrect) depth. Perspective is also enforced by the thicker lines around the left thumb compared to the outline of the wrist.

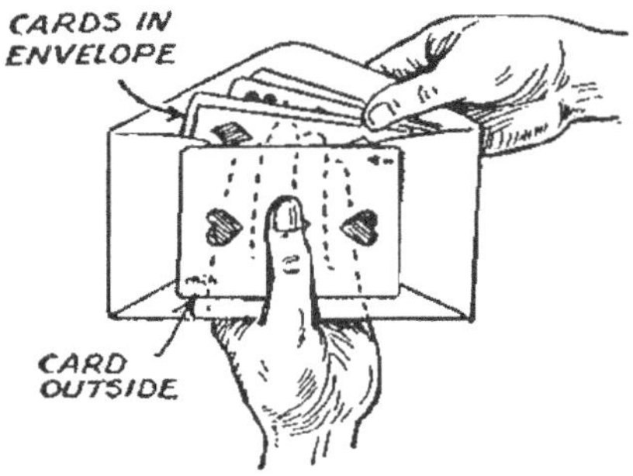

Jean Hugard and Frederick Braué, *The Royal Road to Card Magic* (New York, 1948), p. 114.

Below we see the front and back views, the revealed and concealed hands executing a *Downs Eureka Pass*. First a coin displayed in the right hand vanishes via the *backpalm*, a deft one-handed maneuver whereby an exposed coin is quickly concealed behind the fingers, disappearing under the cover of a tossing motion of the right hand. Such a covering gesture is based on a fundamental principle of Gestalt psychology and of magical misdirection: larger motions hide or blur smaller motions. The sequence continues as another coin is brought to the right fingertips by the left hand, which also secretly steals away the original coin from the back of the right hand. Repeating the cycle, the right hand waves and again causes the visible coin to disappear via a backpalm, the left brings another coin forward and steals the vanished coin, and so on through as many cycles as audience and magician can stand. Since the left hand must hide an increasing accumulation of potentially clinking coins, the repeated cycles grow more difficult. At left, the audience's view; at right, behind the scenes.

T. Nelson Downs, *Modern Coin Manipulation* (London, 1900), pp. 90–92.

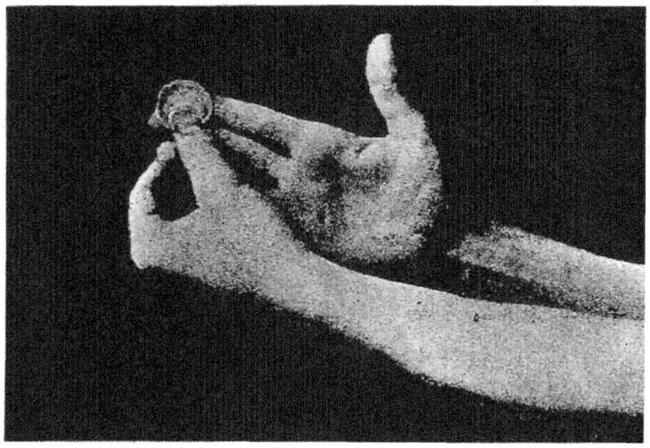

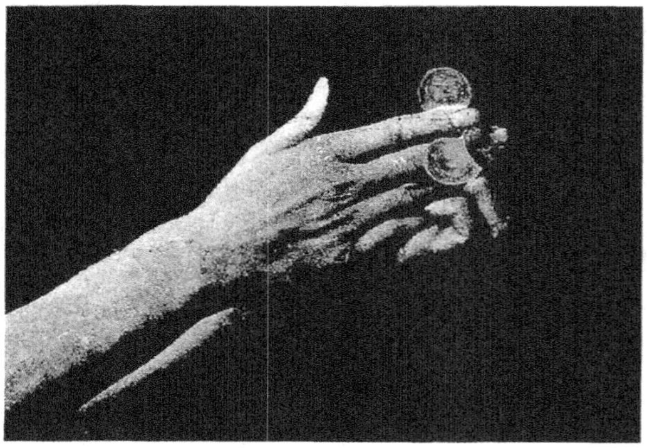

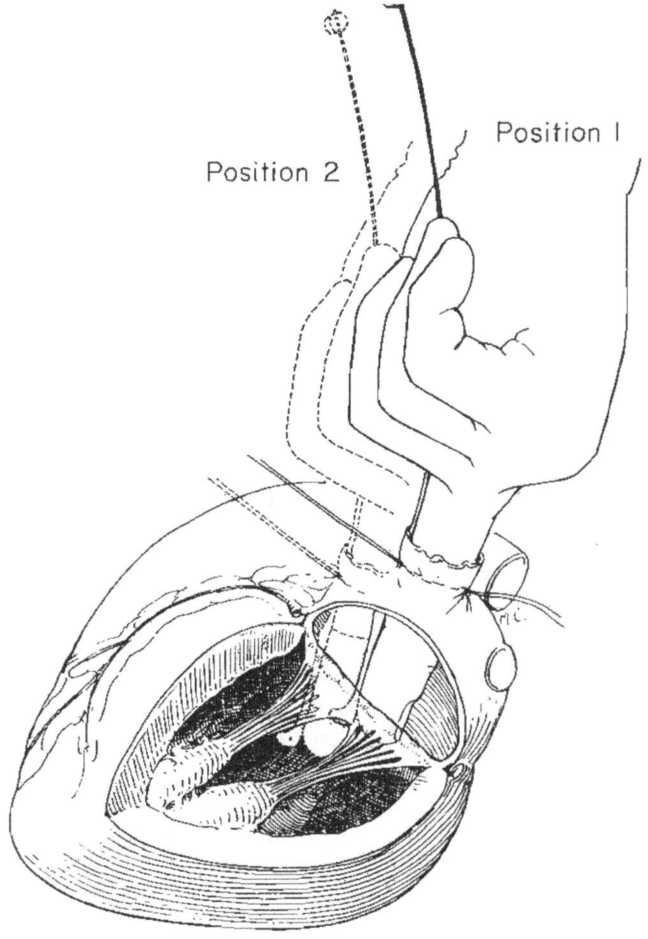

Dwight E. Harken, "Surgery of the Mitral Valve," in Dwight E. Harken, ed., *Cardiac Surgery 1* (Philadelphia, 1971), p. 226.

[3] "Surgery of the Mitral Valve," p. 226.

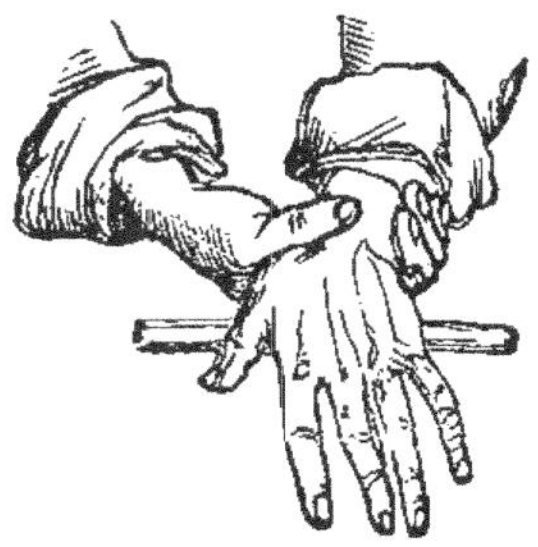

Multiple, layered views exemplify the special power of diagrams, a capacity to show places or activities that we are unable to see directly from one fixed viewpoint in the real world. This drawing from an instruction manual for heart surgery unveils positions of the surgeon's finger and knife (a valvulotome) cutting the hidden fibers and opening up the mitral valve: "A number 13 valvulotome is used as a sharpened edge of the finger, not as a saw. Maneuvers 1 and 2 are whole hand and valvulotome movements to initiate the opening in the anterolateral fusion bridge."[3] By illustrating sequences of action and hidden views, the diagram outperforms eye or camera in exhibiting the procedure. Also, drawings sometimes have a useful abstracting, idealizing quality; a generic heart is depicted, not a particular or idiosyncratic heart.

In the world of the diagram, showing a sequence of changes over time is identical to showing adjacent layers of information; on paper, time and space are as one. Multiple positions signal either temporal or spatial adjacency, movement or arrest. Although potentially ambiguous, the reading is usually clear; this surgeon does not have two right hands.

Of course an effective way to show two views is to show two views. At right, our flap arrangement discloses a trick dating back at least to 1581: on top, a view of a conjurer's hands as seen by the audience and then, beneath the flap, what goes on backstage.[4]

[4] "Lay the piece of wood across the palm of your left hand . . . with the thumb and all the fingers far apart, lest you be suspected of supporting the wood with them. Next, take your left wrist in your right hand, and grasp it tightly, for the purpose, as you state, of giving the hand more steadiness. Now, suddenly turn the back of your left hand uppermost, and as your wrist moves in your right hand, stretch out the forefinger of your right hand, and as soon as the wood comes undermost, support it with such forefinger. You may now shake the hand, and, after a moment or two, suffer the wood to drop. . . . This will, doubtless, create much amusement." [John Wyman?], *The Magician's Own Book, or the Whole Art of Conjuring* (New York, 1857), p. 25. Also in Henri Decremps, *Testament de Jerome Sharp, Professeur de Physique amusante* (Paris, 1789); and Thomas Hill, *A brief and pleasant treatise, entitled, Natural and Artificial Conclusions* (London, 1581). Redrawn, with a flap added.

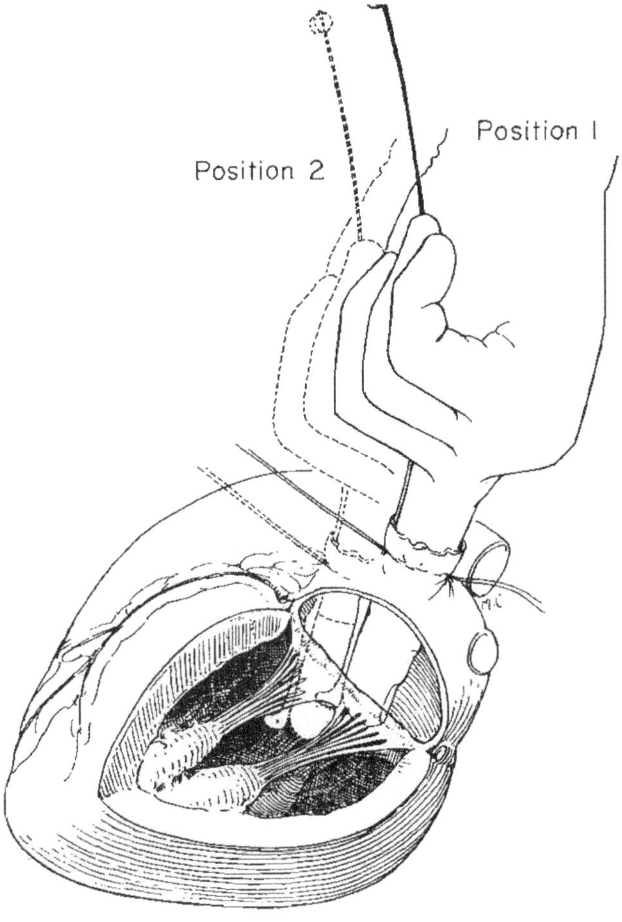

Dwight E. Harken, "Surgery of the Mitral Valve," in Dwight E. Harken, ed., *Cardiac Surgery 1* (Philadelphia, 1971), p. 226.

[3] "Surgery of the Mitral Valve," p. 226.

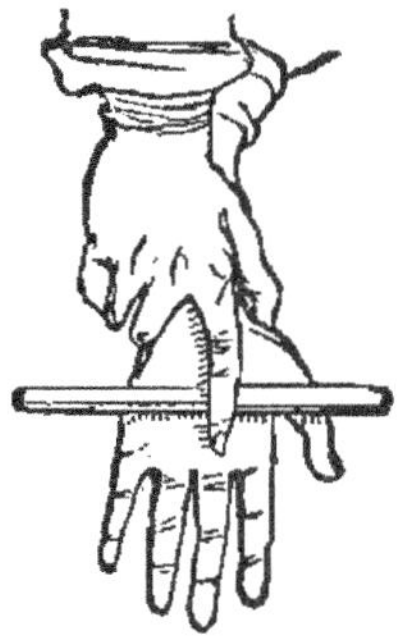

Multiple, layered views exemplify the special power of diagrams, a capacity to show places or activities that we are unable to see directly from one fixed viewpoint in the real world. This drawing from an instruction manual for heart surgery unveils positions of the surgeon's finger and knife (a valvulotome) cutting the hidden fibers and opening up the mitral valve: "A number 13 valvulotome is used as a sharpened edge of the finger, not as a saw. Maneuvers 1 and 2 are whole hand and valvulotome movements to initiate the opening in the anterolateral fusion bridge."[3] By illustrating sequences of action and hidden views, the diagram outperforms eye or camera in exhibiting the procedure. Also, drawings sometimes have a useful abstracting, idealizing quality; a generic heart is depicted, not a particular or idiosyncratic heart.

In the world of the diagram, showing a sequence of changes over time is identical to showing adjacent layers of information; on paper, time and space are as one. Multiple positions signal either temporal or spatial adjacency, movement or arrest. Although potentially ambiguous, the reading is usually clear; this surgeon does not have two right hands.

Of course an effective way to show two views is to show two views. At right, our flap arrangement discloses a trick dating back at least to 1581: on top, a view of a conjurer's hands as seen by the audience and then, beneath the flap, what goes on backstage.[4]

[4] "Lay the piece of wood across the palm of your left hand . . . with the thumb and all the fingers far apart, lest you be suspected of supporting the wood with them. Next, take your left wrist in your right hand, and grasp it tightly, for the purpose, as you state, of giving the hand more steadiness. Now, suddenly turn the back of your left hand uppermost, and as your wrist moves in your right hand, stretch out the forefinger of your right hand, and as soon as the wood comes undermost, support it with such forefinger. You may now shake the hand, and, after a moment or two, suffer the wood to drop. . . . This will, doubtless, create much amusement." [John Wyman?], *The Magician's Own Book, or the Whole Art of Conjuring* (New York, 1857), p. 25. Also in Henri Decremps, *Testament de Jerome Sharp, Professeur de Physique amusante* (Paris, 1789); and Thomas Hill, *A brief and pleasant treatise, entitled, Natural and Artificial Conclusions* (London, 1581). Redrawn, with a flap added.

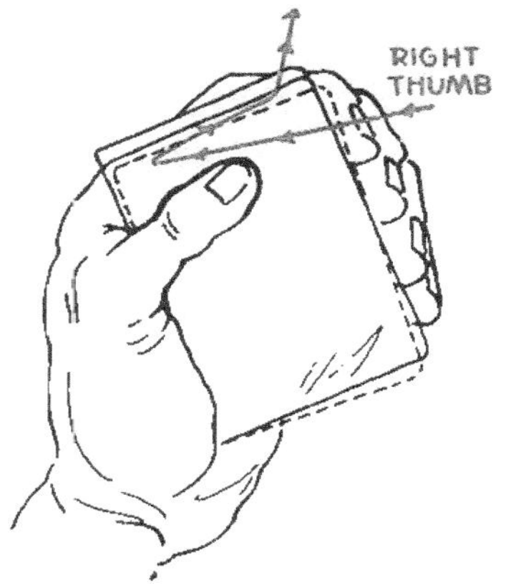

Jean Hugard and Frederick Braué, *Expert Card Technique* (Minneapolis, 1940), p. 18. Redrawn.

In the *strike second deal* (at right), the dealer appears to deliver the top card from the deck but in fact secretly substitutes the card immediately below. For magicians, this technique helps turn one card into another; for card hustlers, it serves to deliver a particular card to an ally or victim. To begin this maneuver, the left thumb pushes the top card slightly aside, thereby exposing a small part of the card beneath. Simultaneously the *right* thumb moves down to the exposed surface of the lower card, sweeps it rightward, and deals it off. Following the path shown in red, the right thumb "strikes" the lower or second card, hence the technique's name. As the lower card leaves the deck, the left thumb squares up the top card, in order to neutralize its potentially incriminating offset. To achieve the desired effect requires a "dead certainty of execution, for perfect timing and for perfect gripping of the cards."[5] Books on magic describe such dynamics and mechanics in great detail, but these paper accounts do not capture any of the sparkle of live action. As Hugard and Braué rightly note: "In the hands of an expert it is absolutely unbelievable that the second card can be drawn off the deck when no movement of the top card is perceptible."[6]

Although apparently nothing special, this diagram above is effective and clever, using subtle techniques to show a moderately complex sequence. An arrow-line neatly traces out the three-space path of the otherwise absent right thumb. For the cards, a change in outline from solid to dotted indicates a change in position of the top card as it is moved aside to give access to the second card. The solid outline of the deck double-functions: when the top card is viewed as being in its shifted (dotted) position, the solid line (which previously located the top card) now represents the position of the *lower* card—a verbally complicated but visually transparent concept. To improve the design, the diagram was rotated 180° from the original, now showing the sleight from the viewpoint of the operator rather than the audience. After all, the audience for this illustration is the student of magic.

Turning now to sequences with three or more states, here is a fine explanation of the *Charlier cut*, with words and images together in tight sequence, just as in a lesson with a teacher-magician, who speaks while slowly demonstrating the moves. Again, an illustration reveals no sense of the deftness of this crisp maneuver when performed live.

[5] *Expert Card Technique*, p. 17.

[6] *Expert Card Technique*, p. 19. The strike second deal happens in a fraction of a second; Hugard and Braué describe the technique in 2.6 pages of text and illustrations. The current record for the longest description of a single sleight is the book of 29 pages, 14 photographs, *and* 14 drawings explaining "the invisible pass," a move completed in less than two seconds. See Jean Hugard and Frederick Braué, *The Invisible Pass* (Brooklyn, New York and Alameda, California, 1946).

Jean Hugard and Frederick Braué, *The Royal Road to Card Magic* (New York, 1948), p. 172.

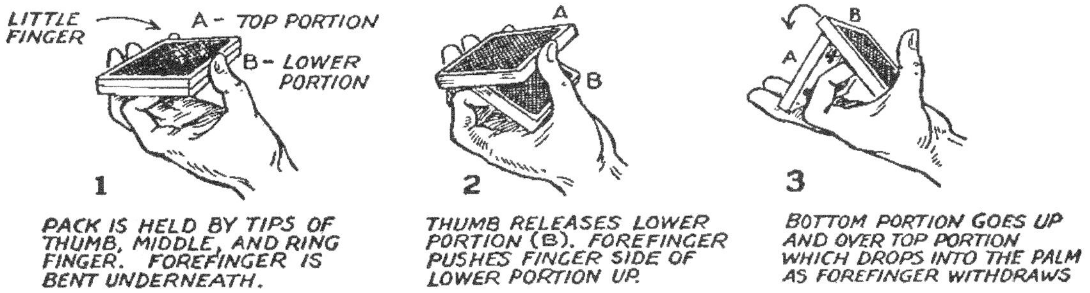

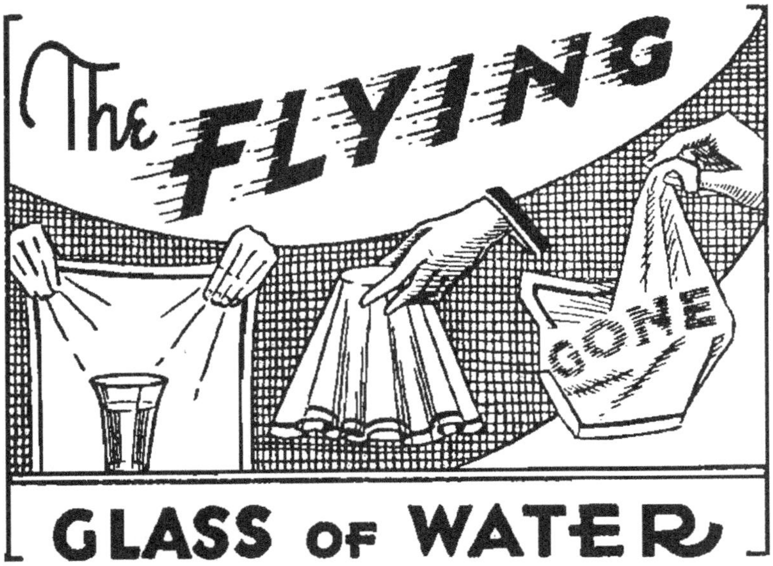

Lyle Douglas, *Complete Five-in-One Catalog* (Dallas, 1932), p. 101. Redrawn.

The Flying Glass of Water, from a 1932 magic catalog, illustrates a three-step sequence, reading left to right. This narration shows what the audience sees, rather than revealing the gimmick (send in $1.00 for that). To begin, a glass and cloth are displayed, and then the cloth apparently covers the glass

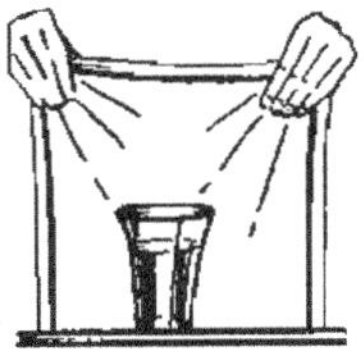

and, then, a flourish and a magical moment

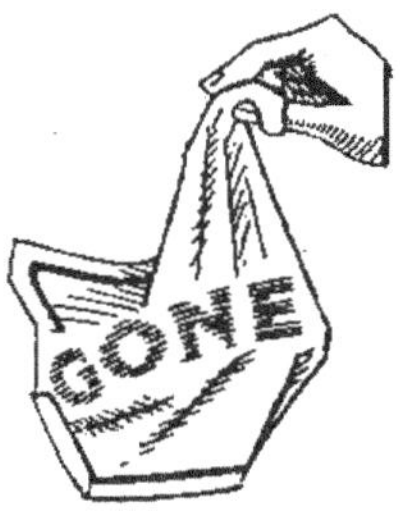

as the glass of water vanishes. On the silent and motionless flatland of paper, how smoothly **GONE** depicts voice, movement, the lightness of vanishing, the absence of weight—at least in this particular context. Vibrating stripes animate and lighten the word, making it airy and more active than a plain GONE.[7] With text also serving as image, the idea, word, and drawing add up to a coherent and vivid whole.

[7] Paul Rand, designer of the striped IBM logotype, writes: "Stripes are dazzling, sometimes hypnotic, usually happy. . . . Stripes attract attention. . . . The stripes of the IBM logo serve primarily as an attention-getting device. They take commonplace letters out of the realm of the ordinary. They are memorable. They suggest efficiency and speed." Paul Rand, *A Designer's Art* (New Haven, 1985), pp. 39–42. Usually the substantive meaning of visual devices is intensely contextual. Stripes suggest dazzle or deft speed when allied with a magic trick or computers but something else when marking the uniforms of military officers or prisoners.

In *The Flying Glass of Water*, changes in position of the disembodied hands, the rising background grid, and the FLYING letters altogether loosely signal left-to-right flow, reinforcing the already understood direction of reading at least in left-right conventions of the occidental world. On paper flatland, unlike video, viewers are able to control the pace, sequence, direction, and focus of viewing. When this illustration is read quickly, the magician's illusion is performed smoothly; under the dissecting microscope of a slow reading, however, the trick falls apart, now diagnosed as the substitution of a thin circular ring or plastic disk for the glass in the second step, while the absent right hand disposes of the glass under the table. *The Flying Glass of Water* is shown as observed from the audience, although those hands do in fact belong to would-be magicians, the fantasizing readers of the catalog.

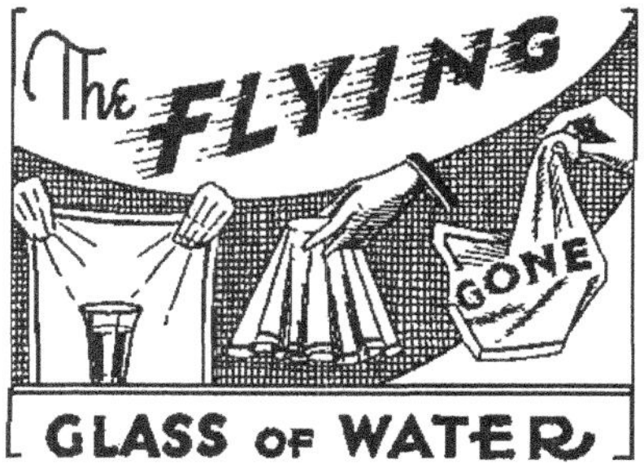

Lyle Douglas, *Complete Five-in-One Catalog* (Dallas, 1932), p. 101. Redrawn.

Richard Kaufman, *Coinmagic* (New York, 1981), p. 105, "One-Hand Triple Spellbound No. 2," by Sol Stone. Redrawn.

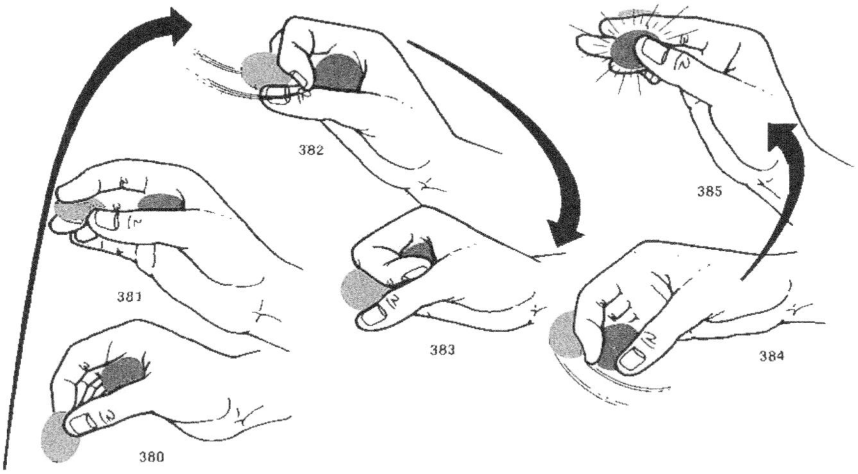

Above, in a difficult manipulation, the magician's hands quickly exchange a silver coin for a copper one. Timing is crucial in magic, and the complex and rapid performance required for deft conjuring is not easy to illustrate. For this sleight, the author notes that the swift moves "must be done in a one-two-three up and down wave of your hand."[8] Depicting the action at a rate of two frames per beat, the multiple images flow over time and through space, just as a statistical graphic records a time-series. (In fact, the magician's hands trace out a two-dimensional time-series; a similar statistical design is this account at right of Japanese economic history, as years track the points on a two-space grid of inflation and unemployment—the "Phillips curve," or non-curve.[9]) Heavy arrows conduct the rhythm of images, while streamers in frames 382 and 384 indicate finer movements of fingers and coins. In this trick, like many others, small maneuvers of fingers are masked by larger hand movements. To expose the method, these drawings depict the hand tipped at varying angles toward the reader. Yet a slightly different angle of adjustment will assure that the audience sees

[8] Richard Kaufman, *Coinmagic*, p. 104.

[9] Data sources: OECD, *Quarterly Labour Force Statistics, 1992* and continuing; OECD, *Labour Force Statistics, 1967–1987* (Paris, 1989); IMF, *International Financial Statistics Yearbook, 1992* (Washington, 1992), and continuing.

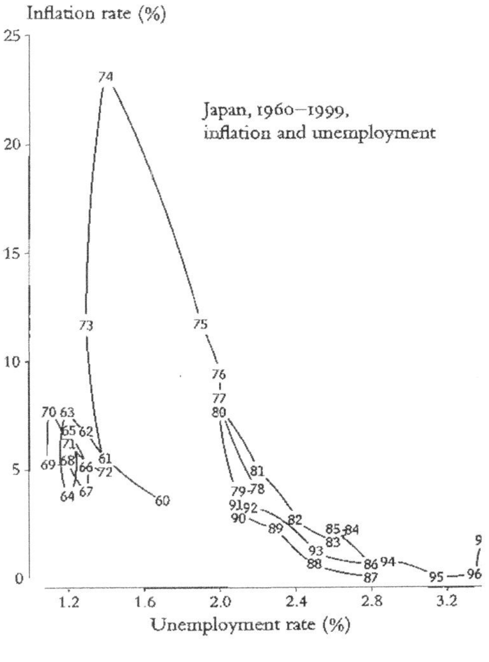

only a silver coin magically transformed into a copper coin. Magicians are preoccupied with such viewing angles, which make the difference between a successful deception and a disastrous exposure. And so for illustrators: Are readers to see the produced effect or *how* to produce the effect, or both, and by means of what angles?

Many traditional illustrations of magic do not convey such a finely detailed sense of sequence and rhythm as that shown at far left. Nonetheless the artwork is unpolished: the hands are silhouetted by a heavy outline (its uniform line-weight contradicts perspective); the strong dark arrows unintentionally cause the hands to read as if they are continually moving forward. In a later work, above right, the same artist-author-magician effectively portrayed motion by combining multiple, blurred, overlapping images and lines tracking movements, a device often used in comics.

Ghosting of multiple images, like blurring, can signal motion in pictorial descriptions. At right, a delightful illustration from Descartes' *Principles of Philosophy* shows a bug crawling outward along a rotating ruler. Both the bug's changing location and the sequence of alphabetic labels indicate direction of rotation (counter-clockwise) of the ruler, although an arrow pointing in the direction of rotation would clarify the reading. Particularly engaging are the ghosted letters X Y Y.

Illustrations of magic tricks are simply workaday instructions for practitioners. Because of efforts to restrict secrets to professionals, the literature is somewhat fugitive and often privately published, cheaply printed with homemade diagrams traced over photographs of tricks. Rarely will such work be equal to that of those scientific masters of motion, such as Etienne-Jules Marey[10] and the Webers, who constructed this exquisite sequence of multiple overlapping images:

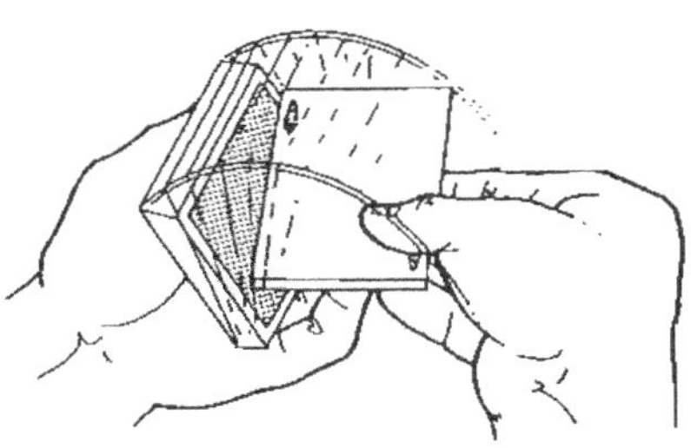

Richard Kaufman, *The Complete Works of Derek Dingle* (Boulder, Colorado, 1982), p. 83.

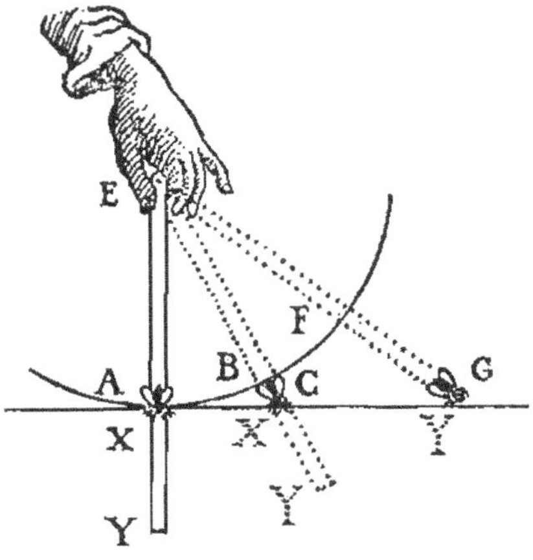

René Descartes, *The Principles of Philosophy* (Amsterdam, 1644), translated by Valentine Rodger Miller and Reese P. Miller (Dordrecht, 1983), pp. 113–114.

[10]See Marta Braun, *Picturing Time: The Work of Etienne-Jules Marey (1830–1904)* (Chicago, 1992).

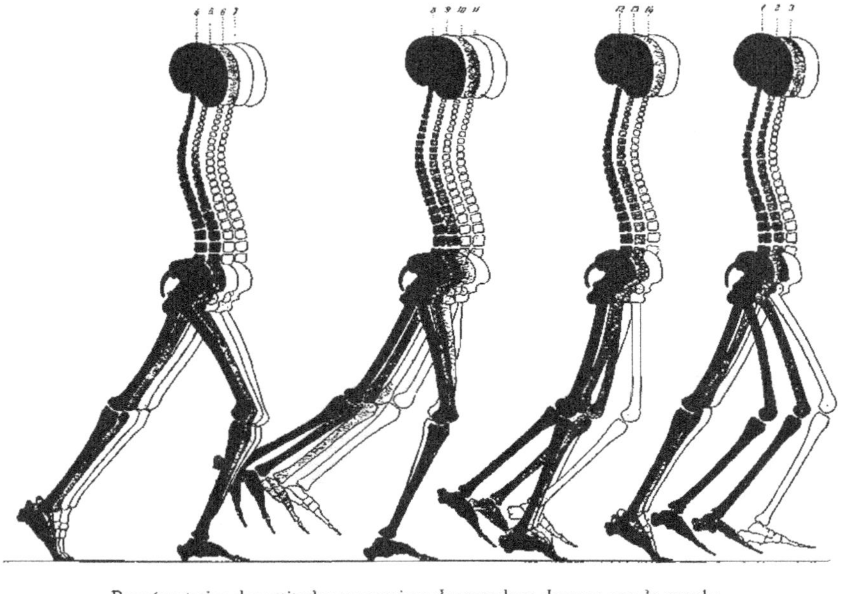

Représentation des attitudes successives des membres dans un pas de marche.

E. J. Marey, *Développement de la méthode graphique par l'emploi de la photographie: supplément à la méthode graphique dans les sciences expérimentales* (Paris, 1885), p. 37. Marey's drawing is based directly on the work of Wilhelm and Eduard Weber.

These three panels below show some fish magic, the "distraction display" of the colorful male stickleback, as it seeks to lure a group of egg-eating predators away from its nest. Several methods depicting movement combine to create a lively narrative of threat and decoy: (1) separate diagrams show paragraphs of activity, (2) dotted lines track motion within images, and (3) just as a sequence of varying positions of a single object indicates motion, here varying postures of the many fish together signal motion. The three panels are separated by a gentle and effective visual move, simply the absence of background; heavy-handed compartments made from thick lines are never necessary in order to tell one image from another. This is a superb arrangement, a design so good as to be unnoticeable, transparent to the interesting content at hand.

Drawn by Patricia J. Wynne, in Gerard J. FitzGerald, "The Reproductive Behavior of the Stickleback," *Scientific American*, 268 (April 1993), pp. 80–85. FitzGerald describes the activities of the diagram: "... when females attack in larger groups, the male must resort to more subtle means to save his eggs. Like some species of birds that pretend to have broken wings to lure predators away from their nests, male three-spine sticklebacks use a decoy display. The male tricks the raiders away from his nest by 'promises' of food elsewhere. He rolls on his side, swims up into the water column and out of his territory. He then pokes his snout into the substrate well away from his nest. This erratic swimming and snout poking closely resembles a feeding movement and is often sufficient to lure the raiders away from the nest." (p. 85). See also Karl von Frisch, *Animal Architecture* (New York, 1974, translated by Lisbeth Gombrich), pp. 153, 161–164, for more on stickleback nesting behavior.

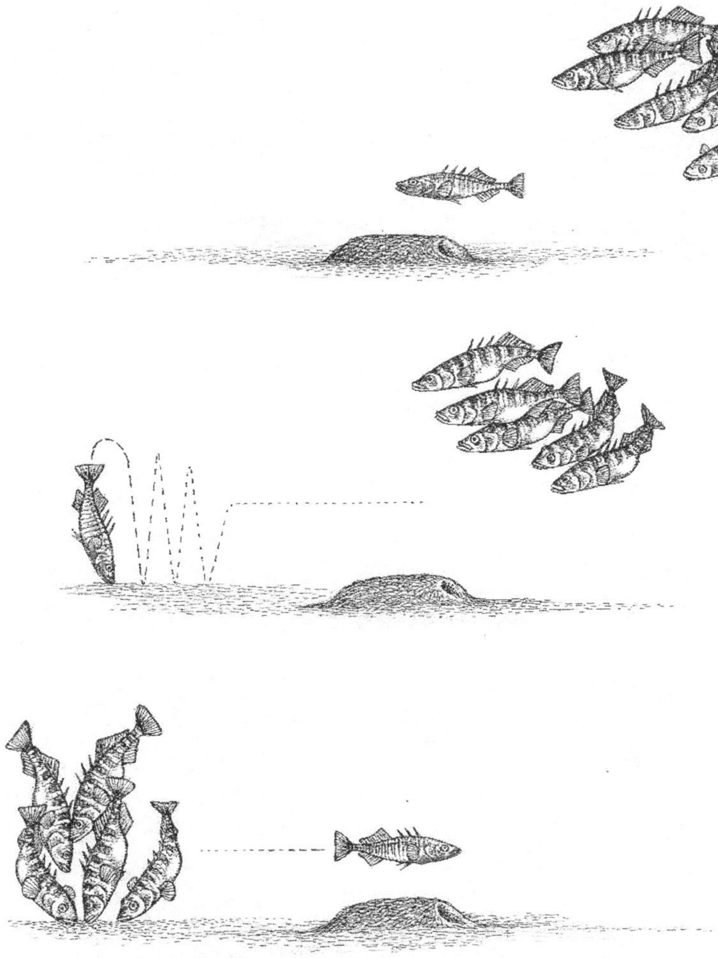

DISTRACTION DISPLAY is a tactic a male may use to protect his nest from raiding females (*top*). The guardian male swims away from the nest, poking his snout into the ground several times (*middle*). This action resembles a feeding movement that lures the attacking females away from the nest (*bottom*).

SOME 400 years of writings on magic make a very clear point about the design of information: *there is no magic in still-land.* Although the still flatland of two-dimensional paper works reasonably well for explaining the step-by-step mechanics of a trick, paper is hopeless for revealing the swift dexterity of motion that makes for convincing illusions presented to an audience. In still-land, there is no spark of conjuring, no sense that a magician may have temporarily repealed the laws of everyday physics. Furthermore, a fundamental technique of illusion-making—*retention of vision*, the mind's brief holding of an image after the image has departed the scene—requires precise timing of swift movements. The fixity of images on paper, despite clever techniques for showing motion, greatly limits representations of the quick rhythms of magic:

> It is difficult to explain "Sleights" on paper, even with the aid of illustrations, because it is almost impossible to show by words or pictures exactly what one means. A demonstration would be the best way of explaining a good "sleight" to a learner who wished to get the utmost value out of the effect and to master the part which misdirects the attention of the audience at the critical moment.[11]

[11] Okito [the stage name of Theodore Bamberg], *Quality Magic* (London, no date, probably 1922), p. 3.

Is there, then, magic in video-land? Moving images surely capture the fluidity of motion that produces the astonished surprise resulting from a good trick. A polished and witty video is David Williamson's 1990 tape, *Sleight of Dave*, which first shows a magical effect and then unveils the method, along with explaining techniques of stagecraft. Some video recordings of magic performances, however, have serious problems of credibility, and not just because they look like television. How are we to assess an illusion seen on video? Did the assistant vanish from the box because the camera was turned off or because of a real trick? Magic is at its best alive, seen by our own eyes, rather than through the eyes of an illustrator or the lens of a camera.

The literature of magic is haunted by another issue of information design: how to combine text with images. In perhaps 80 percent of the work, two nearly separate stories march along apart, as a trick is described in words and then again in pictures, or in clumps of words with scattered pictorial interruptions. Sometimes it is helpful to see the entire sequence together. But when we teach step-by-step sequences in live-land, usually a few words describe a visual element (with words and object linked by pointing gestures), then some more words describe another view, and so on. In contrast, readers of pictorial instructions often have to spend too much of their time coordinating small steps buried in large blocks of text with small steps buried in a long sequence of illustrations. It is all as heavy-handed as Euclid, with endless back-and-forths between triangle ABC mentioned in the text and triangle ABC shown in the diagram. In contrast at right, *The Royal Road to Card Magic*, an exemplar of pictorial instruction, tightly links its shared verbs of text and of image—"pivots up to cross over and drop on."

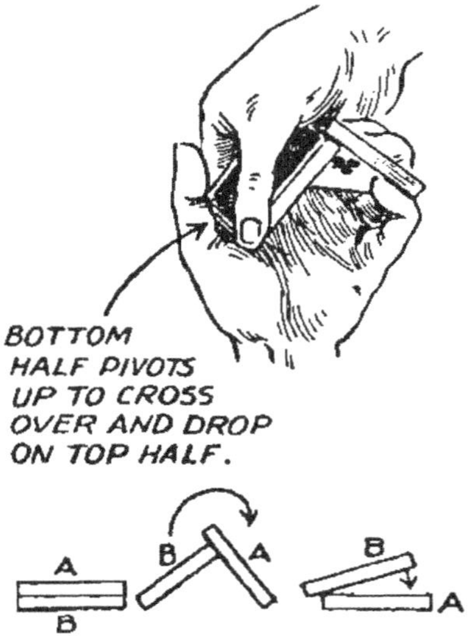

Jean Hugard and Frederick Braué, *The Royal Road to Card Magic* (New York, 1948), p. 156.

Magic and Disinformation Design

MAGICAL illusions are based on techniques that deny, conceal, obscure, and manipulate optical information. In viewing magic performances, the spectator's astonishment

> . . . is a species of perplexity *caused by concealing important facts or factors or by obscuring the issues*. . . . Since bafflement and its various shades of meaning, including mystification, mean frustration by confusion—by concealment of important factors and by making intricate—successful deception is exactly the act of doing these things plus blocking the spectator from penetrating through them to solution of the problem.[12]

To create illusions is to engage in *disinformation design*. An inventory of conjuring methods consequently provides evidence about *what not to do* in the proper arrangement of information—where the point is not at all to baffle the audience but rather to unveil and explain complex data clearly, accurately, unmistakably.

In conjuring, strategies of *disguise* and *attention control* work to regulate the optical information available to the spectator.[13] As we have seen for the backpalm and the copper-silver coin exchange, a common technique is to disguise smaller motions by means of larger motions; the fingers craftily manipulate while the hand grandly waves. The attention-attracting but resolution-reducing character of motion is described by Henning Nelms:

> Although movement attracts attention, it also diminishes visibility. When a thread is used to support a light object, it can be seen from a surprising distance even when its color matches the background. However, the slightest movement makes it disappear. A large movement can be used to conceal a small one. For example, the weak spot in *The Strong Man's Secret* [a trick based on a cut-and-restored string] is the action of cutting the loop. The technique . . . can be made more deceptive if you keep the knife still and force the string against it by a sudden movement of the left hand. . . . The large movement of the left hand and the string draws every eye away from the knife so that no one can observe the unnatural way in which the string is cut.[14]

And in detective stories, the small clue that solves the mystery may be similarly disguised: "It is Agatha Christie, too, who regularly contrives that just as the clue is dropped a distracting incident occurs. Here we are close to the art of the stage conjurer."[15] As well as close to the arts of propaganda, strategic intelligence, and politics[16]—although for magic, at least, the targets of the deception are aware and pleased that they are being deceived. Related issues have engaged researchers in visual perception for more than a century, in work on *visual masking*, "the reduction of the visibility of one stimulus, called the target, by a spatiotemporally overlapping or contiguous second stimulus, called the mask."[17] In conjuring, The Mask makes the magic; elsewhere, The Mask makes a lie.

[12] Dariel Fitzkee, *Magic by Misdirection* (San Rafael, California, 1945), p. 124. In his essay on perception, magic, and ecological physics (the tacit regularities of the everyday physical world), James J. Gibson writes: "An event that would violate the laws of ecological physics if it occurred would be impossible. Nevertheless, someone who knows how to manipulate and control the information available to an observer for *perceiving* events can make [an observer] perceive such an impossibility. (Note that the observer can *perceive* a happening without necessarily *believing* that it happened: [the observer] may assume that it was a 'trick'. Seeing does *not* always entail believing.) The magician does so by suppressing the optical information for what really happened or by preventing the observer from picking it up and, more rarely, by producing information for the impossible happening." James J. Gibson, "Ecological Physics, Magic, and Reality," in Edward Reed and Rebecca Jones, eds., *Reasons for Realism* (Hillsdale, New Jersey, 1982), p. 219.

[13] Dariel Fitzkee, *Magic by Misdirection* (San Rafael, California, 1945), p. 114.

[14] Henning Nelms, *Magic and Showmanship: A Handbook for Conjurers* (New York, 1969), p. 206.

[15] J. I. M. Stewart, *Myself and Michael Innes* (London, 1987), p. 177.

[16] Jeremy Bentham, *Handbook of Political Fallacies* (Baltimore, 1952: London, 1824); Allen Dulles, *The Craft of Intelligence* (New York, 1963); Paul Ekman, *Telling Lies: Clues to Deceit in the Marketplace, Politics, and Marriage* (New York, 1985, 1992); and Ray Hyman, "The Psychology of Deception," *Annual Review of Psychology*, 40 (1989), pp. 133–154.

[17] Bruno G. Breitmeyer, *Visual Masking: An Integrative Approach* (Oxford, 1984), p. 2.

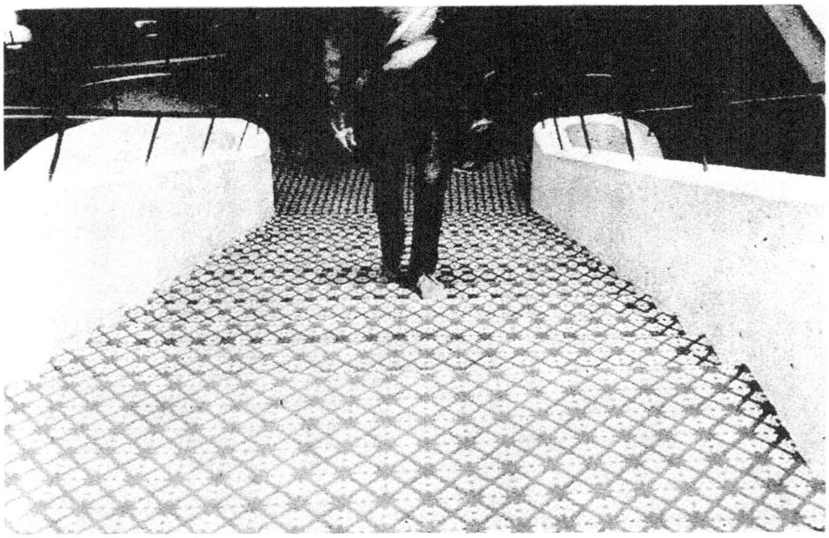

John Archea, Belinda Collins, and Fred Stahl, *Guidelines for Stair Safety* (Washington, D.C., National Bureau of Standards, 1979), p. 47.

Here we see some distinctly unmagical disinformation design, as a noisy and repetitive carpet pattern masks the edge of each step in this treacherous staircase.[18] Shrill and strident visual activities will tend to dominate the information space, scrambling finely detailed but relevant content. Below, in a sinister piece of disinformation from a billboard advertising cigarettes, a thick frame clutters the words of warning (by activating the negative white space between word and box) just as a waving hand masks small moves of the fingers in switching coins.

[18] John Templer, *The Staircase: Studies of Hazards, Falls, and Safer Design* (Cambridge, Massachusetts, 1992), p. 142, describes another distracting design: "At one New York City railroad station, the stair treads had been treated with a material consisting of lines parallel to the tread edge. Over a six-week period (until the problem was corrected), more than 1400 people fell on this stair."

SURGEON GENERAL'S WARNING: SMOKING CAUSES LUNG CANCER, HEART DISEASE, EMPHYSEMA, AND MAY COMPLICATE PREGNANCY

The sans serif, capital letters minimize distinctions among letters and words, contributing to the difficulty of reading. "Where scrutiny is damaging, scrutiny is diverted," explains *Magic by Misdirection*.[19]

Such masking of content resembles the obscurantist foolings around of too much of contemporary graphic design. Paul Rand describes the triumph of decoration over information, similar to the mishmash of chartjunk for statistical graphics:

> . . . a collage of chaos and confusion, swaying between high tech and low art, and wrapped in a cloak of arrogance: squiggles, pixels, doodles, dingbats, ziggurats, and aimlessly sprinkled Lilliputian squares; turquoise, peach, pea green, and lavender; corny woodcuts on moody browns and russets; art deco rip-offs, high-gloss finishes, sleazy textures; halos and airbrush effects; tiny color photos surrounded by acres of white space; indecipherable, zany typography; tiny type with miles of leading. . . .[20]

[19] Dariel Fitzkee, *Magic by Misdirection* (Oakland, California, 1945), p. 114.

[20] Paul Rand, *Design, Form, and Chaos* (New Haven, 1993), p. 207. Concerning chartjunk, see Edward R. Tufte, *The Visual Display of Quantitative Information* (Cheshire, Connecticut, 1983), 100–121.

Sometimes, of course, the disinformation is in the data rather than the method of display. Thoughtful designs may skillfully present false information, as in this famous example in the history of magic. →

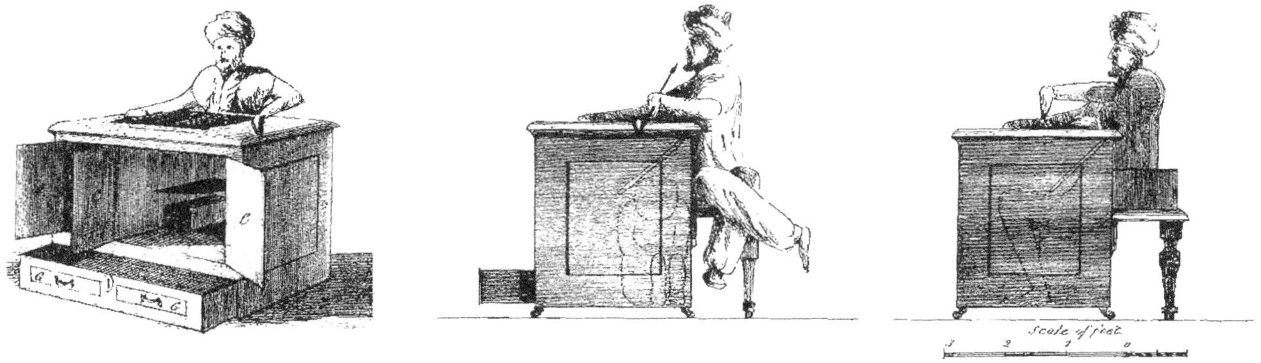

Robert Willis, *An Attempt to Analyse the Automaton Chess Player* . . . (London, 1821), pp. 2, 37, 41.

These drawings document a theory of concealed workings of the Automaton Chess Player, a sensation in Europe during the late 1700s. The apparatus seemingly played chess by mechanical means, defeating many human opponents (including perhaps Napoleon, who allegedly tested the machine by making illegal moves, only to be corrected each time).[21] Developed by Wolfgang von Kempelen in 1769, the contraption went on tour for 50 years in various guises. While in France, Benjamin Franklin played and lost, and then wrote a letter of introduction for the keepers of the machine to another ambassador![22]

Decked out in Turkish dress, the magical automaton stiffly moved chess pieces with its left hand, rolled its eyes, and, when checking its human opponent, shook its head thrice. To begin each performance, von Kempelen briefly opened the cabinet and moved a candle around various compartments, revealing what appeared to be either empty space or intricate gears and levers.

A thorough analysis of the automaton was published in 1821 by Robert Willis in a book of 36 pages and 11 diagrams. These drawings (three are shown above) were widely copied, redrawn, and republished. Using a sometimes murky visual language of dotted outline, Willis depicts a human chess-player hidden behind a false wall in the cabinet, who secretly climbs up inside the Turk in order to move the pieces. Printed separately, these diagrams are inconveniently isolated from the explanatory text. This arrangement requires dozens of cross-references, filtered through an elaborate 19-letter code of call-outs (below), linking text to legend to 11 different diagrams bound in the front and back of the book:

[21] Sources: Charles Michael Carroll, *The Great Chess Automaton* (New York, 1975); Milbourne Christopher, *The Illustrated History of Magic* (New York, 1973), pp. 30–47; Robert Willis, *An Attempt to Analyse the Automaton Chess Player* . . . (London, 1821); and David Brewster, *Letters on Natural Magic* (London, 1834), pp. 270–282.

[22] Detecting clever frauds requires a professional illusionist, such as a magician. Intelligences even as bright as Franklin's are easily fooled by skilled conjurers. See Martin Gardner, "Magicians in the Psi Lab: Many Misconceptions," *Skeptical Inquirer*, 8 (Winter, 1983–1984), pp. 111–116; Ray Hyman, "Scientists and Psychics," and James Randi, "Science and the Chimera," in George O. Abell and Barry Singer, eds., *Science and The Paranormal* (New York, 1981), pp. 119–141, 209–222.

THE FOLLOWING LETTERS OF REFERENCE ARE EMPLOYED IN ALL THE PLATES.

A Front door of the small cupboard.
B Back door of ditto.
CC Front doors of the large cupboard.
D Back door of ditto.
E Door in the trunk.
F Door in the thigh.
GG The drawer.
H Machinery in front of the small cupboard.
I Screen behind the machinery.
K Opening caused by the removal of part of the floor of the small cupboard.
L A box which serves to conceal an opening in the floor of the large cupboard, made to facilitate the first position; and which also serves as a seat for the player in the third position.
M A similar box to receive the toes of the player in the first position.
N The inner chest, filling up part of the trunk.
O The space behind the drawer.
PQ The false back, turning on a joint at Q.
R Part of the partition formed of cloth stretched tight, which is carried up by the false back, to form the opening between the chambers.
S The opening between the chambers.
T The opening connecting the trunk and chest, which is partly concealed by the false back.
U Panel which is slipped aside to admit the player.

Robert Willis, *An Attempt to Analyse the Automaton Chess Player* . . . (London, 1821), p. 36.

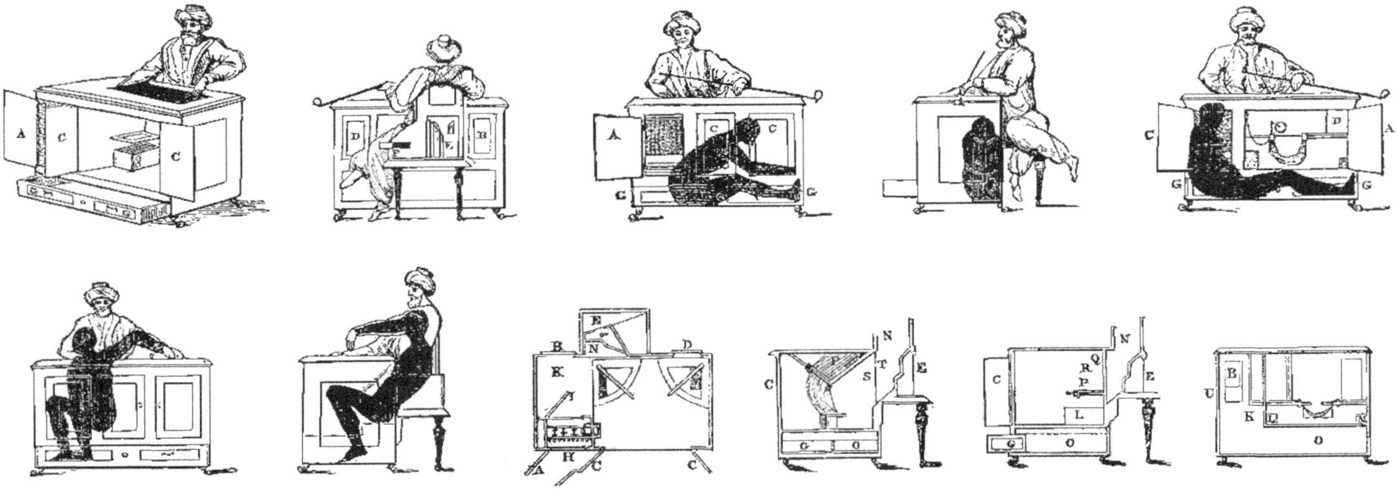

David Brewster, *Letters on Natural Magic* (London, 1834), pp. 270–282.

Among those who shared Willis' opinion and admired the "logical reasoning" of his solution were Edgar Allan Poe and Scottish physicist Sir David Brewster.[23] In 1834 Brewster completely appropriated Willis' explanation of the chess machine, including all 11 diagrams. Brewster's redrawings above make crisp and consistent visual distinctions: line for the revealed, darkened silhouette for the concealed. Effectively layering the information, the line-drawing remains visible against the finer vertical lines of the silhouette, a technique also used in maps for carrying multiple layers of data. These redrawings fail to reproduce the scale of measurement shown in the original, as incomplete plagiarism leads to dequantification. Although Brewster integrates the small diagrams into his text, he still retains the clumsy call-outs of Willis, and, for no good reason, places the captions several pages away from the diagrams themselves. Nevertheless, the illustrations developed a vigorous life of their own. They were reproduced in 12 editions of *Letters on Natural Magic* and often borrowed by other explainers of magic.[24] Because of their clarity, plausibility, and vividness, Brewster's drawings became the definitive account of the mechanical chess-player.

Yet the most important fact about these technically well-executed diagrams is that they are *false*, detailed wrong guesses about how the automaton worked. The main thing that Willis (and thus Brewster) got right was that a human chess-master was hidden inside. But the person residing in the box never climbed up into the Turk; and the other proposals concerning the automaton's inner mechanisms were incorrect.[25] These much-copied drawings resemble "urban legends," picturesque stories told and retold about bizarre happenings that can never be traced to actual events or particular eye-witnesses. A student of folklore described the principle that governs the exuberant proliferation of such fictional narratives: "Rule 1: The truth never stands in the way of a good story."[26] Or, for that matter, a good illustration.

[23] Charles Michael Carroll, *The Great Chess Automaton* (New York, 1975), describes a long history of guessing and plagiarism in writings about the automaton.

[24] Such borrowing is common. Raymond Toole Stott [*A Bibliography of English Conjuring 1581–1876* (Derby, 1976), p. 76] writes: "Reginald Scot, in his *Discovery of Witchcraft*, denied the existence of witchcraft and . . . explained in detail how tricks popularly regarded in the nature of witchcraft were performed. Thus was born the first work to expound the technique of conjuring, and with it began a long course of literary theft which, as Sidney S. Clarke pointed out in his *Annals of Conjuring*, had been the bane and disgrace of the conjuring profession for more than 300 years. *The Art of Iugling*, the first work to be devoted exclusively to legerdemain, *Hocus Pocus Junior*, the first illustrated work on the subject, and Henry Dean's *The Whole Art of Legerdemain or Hocus Pocus in Perfection*, were all founded upon Scot's famous work. . . . [T]he tricks in Samuel Rid's *The Art of Iugling* were mostly copied word for word from Scot's pages."

[25] The machine was more intricate than anyone imagined. The automaton was a puppet, animated with long sticks from below by the director concealed inside.

[26] Jan Harold Brunvand, *The Mexican Pet* (New York, 1986), p. 205.

SEVERAL of the classic texts of magic advocate two primary principles for successful illusion-making, *suppressing context* and *preventing reflective analysis*. Here, for example, is Professor Hoffmann in 1876:

> The first rule to be borne in mind by the aspirant [magician] is this: "*Never tell your audience beforehand what you are going to do.*" If you do so, you at once give their vigilance the direction which it is most necessary to avoid, and increase ten-fold the chances of detection. . . . It follows, as a practical consequence of this first rule, that *you should never perform the same trick twice on the same evening*. The best trick loses half its effect on repetition, but besides this, the audience knows precisely what is coming, and have all their faculties directed to find out at what point you cheated their eyes on the first occasion.[27]

[27] Professor Hoffmann [Angelo John Lewis], *Modern Magic: A Practical Treatise on the Art of Conjuring* (New York, c. 1876), p. 3 (italics in original). Henning Nelms, *Magic and Showmanship: A Handbook for Conjurers* (New York, 1969), p. 175: "The oldest rule in conjuring is: *Never explain beforehand.*" Nelms also points out the limits of this rule.

These techniques of disinformation design, *when reversed*, reinforce strategies of presentation used by good teachers. Your audience *should* know beforehand what you are going to do; then they can evaluate how your verbal and visual evidence supports your argument. And so we have some practical advice for giving a talk or paper.

1. Near the beginning of your presentation, tell the audience:

What the problem is
Why the problem is important
What the solution to the problem is.

If a clear statement of the problem cannot be formulated, then that is a sure sign that the content of the presentation is deficient.

Magicians rarely perform the same trick twice in front of the same audience because they are aware that repetition helps people learn, remember, understand.[28] Unlike magicians, you should give your audience a second chance to get the point. And a third. Repeated variations on the same theme will often clarify and develop an idea.

2. To explain complex ideas or data, use the method of PGP:

Particular *General* *Particular*

For example, to help your audience understand a multivariate table of data, briefly introduce the table and point to a *particular* number and say what it means; then step back and describe the *general* architecture of the table; finally reinforce it all with a second *particular*, explaining what another number means.[29] These two particulars can be selected to make a substantive point as well as to explain the data arrangement. With PGP, your argument is more credible, for you have more than a single anecdote (you have two) to accompany the general theory.

To mask the optical information that would reveal their methods, magicians systematically reduce our ability to resolve their movement. In contrast, you should give *high-resolution* talks that are clear and also rich in content. Seek *to maximize the rate of information transfer* to your audience. Yet many presentations rely on *low-resolution* devices to communicate information—reading aloud from images projected

[28] Harlan Tarbell, *The Tarbell Course in Magic* (Brooklyn, 1927, 1971), 1, p. 51: "Never repeat a trick at the same performance. . . . What your audience has missed the first time, they will watch for the second time, and so may discover your secret." Daniel Fitzkee, *Magic by Misdirection* (Oakland, California, 1945), p. 219: "The same misdirection expedient must never be used twice in the same program. This is even worse craftsmanship than doing the same trick twice." In the current-day practice of magic, however, the same effect may indeed be repeated, produced by a different method each time, a chaining of magical effects that makes for a striking performance.

[29] The idea of PGP (as described by Robert E. K. Rourke) is discussed in Frederick Mosteller, "Classroom and Platform Performance," *The American Statistician*, 34 (February 1980), p. 13.

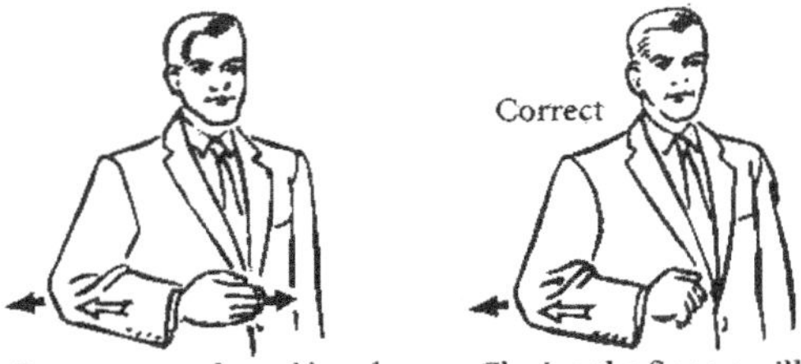

Open, arrow-shaped hand counteracts the pointing effect of the movement.

Closing the fingers will eliminate the effect of pointing two ways at once.

POINTING WITH ELBOW

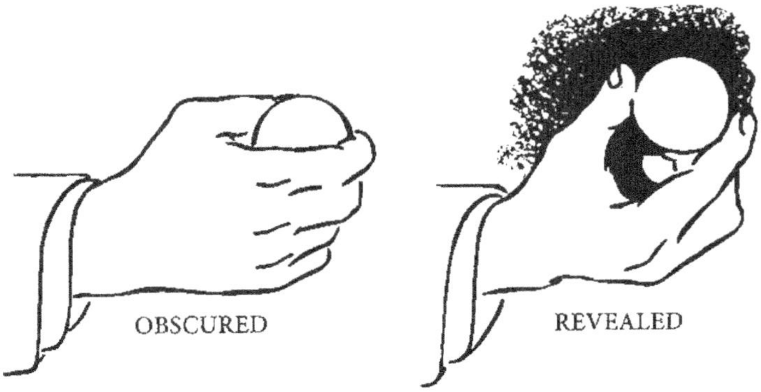

When handling a small prop, show as much of it as possible and display it against a contrasting background.

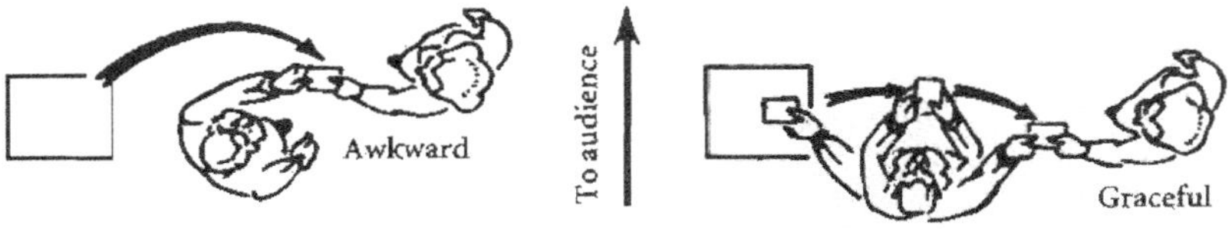

CHANGE HANDS WHEN PASSING PROP ACROSS YOUR BODY

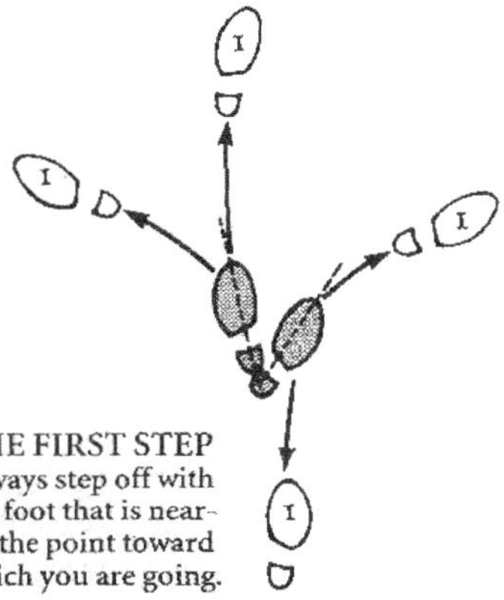

THE FIRST STEP
Always step off with the foot that is nearest the point toward which you are going.

Henning Nelms, *Magic and Showmanship: A Handbook for Conjurers* (New York, 1969), pp. 188, 280, 286, 304.

up on the wall from computer screens or from the dreaded overhead projector, or talk talk talk. Instead, try a high-resolution method:

3. *No matter what, give everybody in the audience one or more pieces of paper, packed with material related to your presentation.*

Handouts can show pictures, diagrams, data tables, research methods, references, names of people at the meeting, or the complete text of the paper outlined in your talk. Unlike evanescent projected images, permanent and portable paper has credibility. Paper serves as a testimonial record documenting your talk, letting your audience know that you take responsibility for what you say. People can file your handouts away and then come back in a month and ask, "Didn't you say this?"

ALONG with the perils of disinformation design, the practice of magic also exemplifies the *stagecraft* of theatrical performance, the professional techniques that can help us improve our presentations.[30] The literature on the staging of magic reveals that there is a lot going on in a good performance, and that mastery of this detail requires constant attention and enthusiastic practice (sometimes several years are needed to perfect a few minutes of material for a magic act). These diagrams above from Nelms' book on stagecraft give a sense of the intense detail involved in a magic performance. The message for our own work is clear:

4. *Analyze the details of your presentation; then master those details by practice, practice, practice.*

Good teachers know all about the value of preparation and practice. Frederick Mosteller, a superb statistics teacher and one-time magician, writes "rehearsals are extremely helpful, and rehearsals with timing very instructive. Rehearsals are, I think, the single best way of improving

[30] See Bruce Tognazzini, "Principles, Techniques, and Ethics of Stage Magic and Their Application to Human Interface Design," in *Interchi '93 Conference on Human Factors in Computing Systems* (Amsterdam, 1993), pp. 355–362.

one's lecture work."[31] Magicians practice in front of a mirror, friend, or video camera; when you practice, work on what your audience *sees* and also *hears*. To detect mannerisms of speech, turn off the video and listen to the audio only.

Finally, plan your arrival and departure so as to make a difference:

5. Show up early. Something good is bound to happen.

6. Finish early.

By arriving early, you can look the place over, have time enough to recover from a problem (for example, the room is already occupied; or the projector is missing), check the lights, and greet people as they gradually arrive to await your performance.[32] Give the talk and finish early: "People will be pleased with a nice short speech. I believe that Paul Halmos, a very great lecturer, noted that in a lifetime of giving and attending mathematics lectures he had never heard complaints about a seminar ending early."[33] Even magicians are urged to get on with their entertaining performances: "Always leave them wanting more. Get to the point. Be brief. Keep interesting them. Quit before they've had enough."[34]

Conclusion

THE techniques of disinformation and the pseudo-explanation of the automaton chess-player illustrate once again the supreme and enduring test of all information design, the integrity of the content displayed:

Is the display revealing the truth?
Is the representation accurate?
Are the data carefully documented?
Do the methods of display avoid spurious readings of the data?
Are appropriate comparisons and contexts shown?

Sometimes we have a clear empirical test of visual truth-telling: Was a wise decision made and prudent action taken on the basis of the displayed information? Thus, in our examples, the epidemic ends or persists, the space shuttle survives or explodes, the stairs escort us safely or trip us up, the map efficiently guides us to our destination or it confuses and misleads us.

Also professional standards of quantitative and graphical integrity point the way. For example, economists agree that graphs depicting money over a period of time should show inflation-adjusted (constant) monetary units.[35] To use undeflated monetary units is to distort the evidence, mixing up changes in the value of money with real changes in the data, just as rainbow color-coding of quantitative data confounds what happens in a color scheme with what happens in the data.

[31] Frederick Mosteller, "Classroom and Platform Performance," *The American Statistician*, 34 (February 1980), p. 14. See Judith M. Tanur, "Fred as Educator," in *A Statistical Model: Frederick Mosteller's Contributions to Statistics, Science, and Public Policy* (New York, 1990), ed. S. E. Fienberg, D. C. Hoaglin, W. H. Kruskal, and J. M. Tanur, pp. 111–129.

[32] Joseph Lowman, *Mastering the Techniques of Teaching* (San Francisco, 1984), p. 49.

[33] Mosteller, "Classroom and Platform Performance," p. 16.

[34] Dariel Fitzkee, *Showmanship for Magicians* (San Rafael, California, 1943), pp. 78, 91. Similarly, Henning Nelms, *Magic and Showmanship: A Handbook for Conjurers* (New York, 1969), p. 229: "Stop before the audience has had enough; a wise showman always sends them away wanting still more." Recall Samuel Johnson's famous comment on Milton's *Paradise Lost*: "None ever wished it longer. . . . " *The Lives of the Most Eminent English Poets* (London, 1783), volume 1, p. 249.

[35] Paul A. Samuelson and William D. Nordhaus, *Economics* (New York, 1983), pp. 104–105, 226–228; Edward R. Tufte, *The Visual Display of Quantitative Information* (Cheshire, Connecticut, 1983), pp. 64–68.

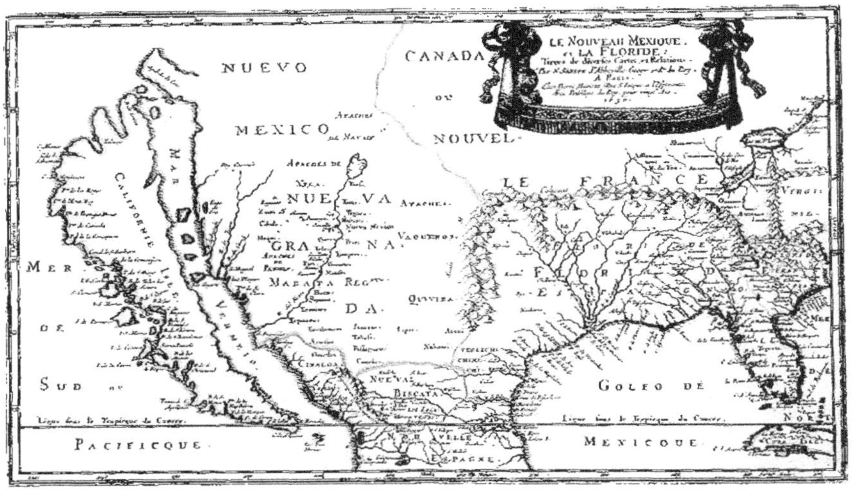

[36] R. V. Tooley, *California as an Island* (London, 1964); John Leighly, *California as an Island* (San Francisco, 1972); Glen McLaughlin with Nancy Mayo, *The Mapping of California as an Island* (Saratoga, California, 1995). The map shown here is from Nicolas Sanson, *Cartes générales de toutes les parties du monde* (Paris, 1658).

The accuracy of visual representations can be checked against the real thing, if someone is willing to do the work. Errors do persist, however. A 1622 map depicting California as an island was reproduced in 182 variants, as the distinctive mistake traces out a disturbingly long history of rampant plagiary. The last copyist published in 1745, after which California cartographically rejoined the mainland.[36] Then there is Albrecht Dürer's gloriously wrong engraving of 1513 that portrays a fanciful two-horned, armor-plated rhinoceros. Copied repeatedly in guides and textbooks and even made into a monument, the bogus rhinoceros, along with a fable about its battles with the elephant, was taken as real for some 200 years until finally confronted with too many sightings of actual rhinoceros.[37]

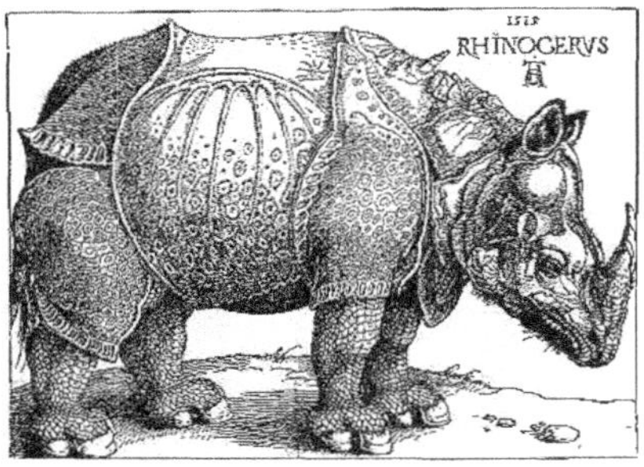

[37] F. J. Cole, "The History of Albrecht Dürer's Rhinoceros in Zoological Literature," *Science, Medicine, and History: Essays on the Evolution of Scientific Thought and Medical Practice* (London, 1953), ed. E. Ashworth Underwood, pp. 337–356.

AND for the world of magical illusions, standards of truth-telling in illustration should at least rule out six-fingered conjurers, two of whom apparently perform below:[38]

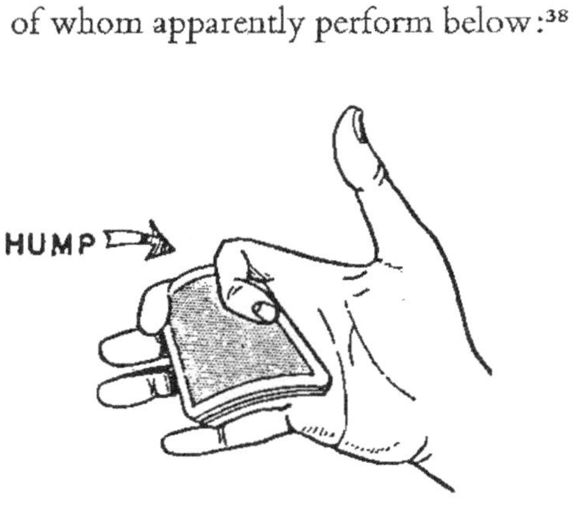

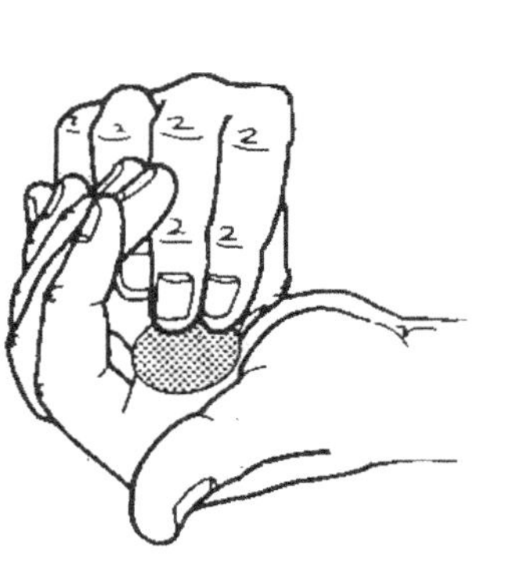

[38] At far left, Cliff Green, *Professional Card Magic* (New York, 1961), p. 128, showing an error by the well-known illustrator, Edward Mishell. The extra finger is not needed in performing the depicted manipulation. Unnoticed for years, the slip was spotted by Richard Kaufman, who then drew a homage to Mishell's sixth finger—at near left, Richard Kaufman, *Coinmagic* (New York, 1981), p. 260.

Based on Ad Reinhardt, *Abstract Painting 6, Blue, 1952*, oil on canvas, 76 by 64 cm, or 30 by 25 in.

Painting is special, separate, a matter of meditation and contemplation, for me, no physical action or social sport. As much consciousness as possible. Clarity, completeness, quintessence, quiet. No noise, no schmutz, no schmerz, no fauve schwärmerei. Perfection, passiveness, consonance, consummateness. No palpitations, no gesticulation, no grotesquerie. Spirituality, serenity, absoluteness, coherence. No automatism, no accident, no anxiety, no catharsis, no chance. Detachment, disinterestedness, thoughtfulness, transcendence. No humbugging, no button-holing, no exploitation, no mixing things up.

Ad Reinhardt, statement for the catalog of the exhibition, "The New Decade: 35 American Painters and Sculptors," Whitney Museum of American Art, New York, 1955.

4 *The Smallest Effective Difference*

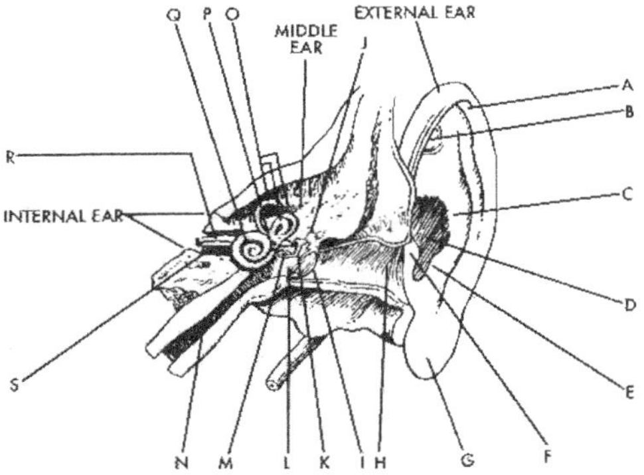

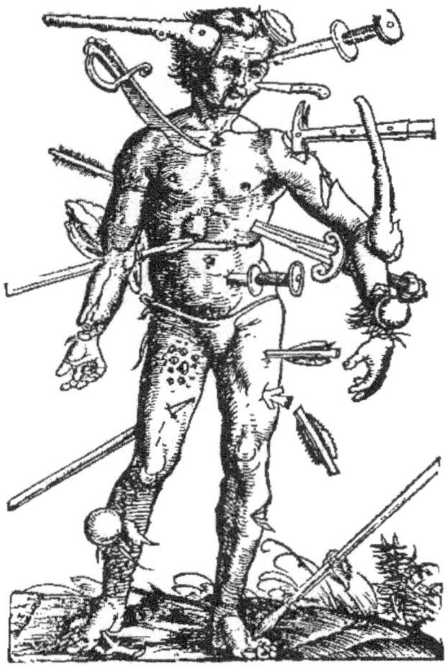

The ear is from *The Random House Dictionary of the English Language* (New York, 1971), p. 447. The Wound Man is from Hans van Gersdorff, *Feldtbüch der Wundartzney* (Augsburg, 1517, 1542).

RESEMBLING the needles of acupuncture, some 25 thick pointer-lines penetrate this human ear. Heavier than the linework for the ear itself, the pointers merely link elements in the drawing to letter-codes in a parts list—a minor task generating much noise and clutter. This poor ear evokes a woodcut published in 1517, "The Wound Man," an image that serves as a walking table of unfortunate contents for combat injuries whose treatment is explained later in Gersdorff's *Fieldbook of Wound Surgery*. At least these injuries represent the real thing, inflicted in battle rather than by the thick pencils of inept graphic design.

The fat pointer-lines are altogether disproportionate to their trivial errand. Such incongruities and irrelevancies are avoided by following the design strategy of *the smallest effective difference:*

> Make all visual distinctions as subtle as possible,
> but still clear and effective.

Relevant to nearly every display of data, the smallest effective difference is the Occam's razor ("what can be done with fewer is done in vain with more") of information design. And often the happy consequence of an economy of means is a graceful richness of information, for *small* differences allow *more* differences. As Wallace Stevens wrote, "In ghostlier demarcations, keener sounds."

In the study of perception, *just noticeable differences* measure the very limits of human abilities to detect the faintest of differences between, say, two adjacent colors almost exactly alike in a continuous spectrum of 100,000 colors.[1] Ad Reinhardt's paintings (left) rely on such vaporous distinctions, with some gradations revealing themselves only after many minutes of focused viewing. This is fine for art but not for data. Rather than operating at such an exquisite threshold of perceptual acuity, data displays must be clear, assured, reliable, sturdy. In designing information, then, the idea is to use *just notable differences*, visual elements that make a clear difference but no more—contrasts that are definite, effective, *and* minimal. That is, distinctions stronger than Reinhardt's but far less heavy-handed than the ear pointers.

[1] T. E. Cohn and D. J. Lasley, "Visual Sensitivity," *Annual Review of Psychology*, 37 (1986), pp. 495–521.

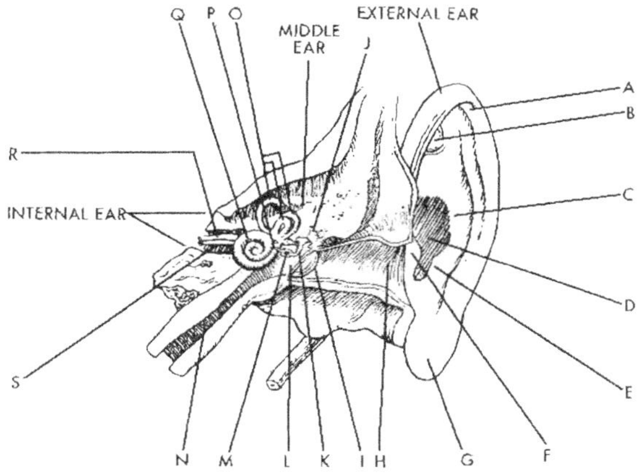

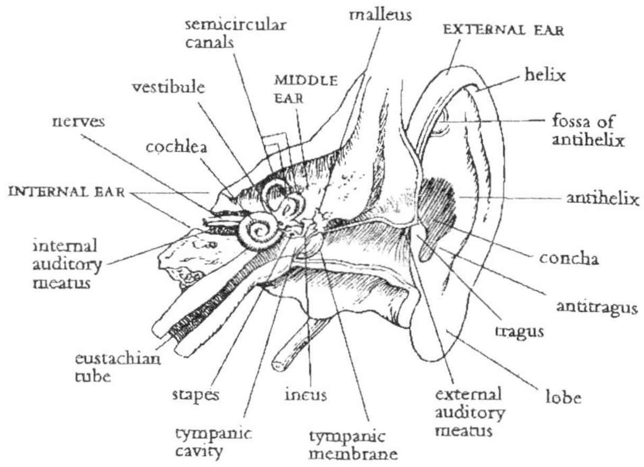

The idea of the smallest effective difference helps in designing the various secondary and structural elements in displays of information—arrows, pointer lines, dimension lines, tic marks, scales, compass roses, broken lines for incomplete elements, grids, meshes, rules, underlines, frames, boxes, compartments, codes, legends, highlights, accents, bevels, shadows, and fills defining areas and surfaces. Muting these secondary elements will often reduce visual clutter—and thus help to clarify the primary information. Minimal contrasts of the secondary elements (figure) relative to the negative space (ground) will tend to produce a visual hierarchy, with layers of inactive background, calm secondary structure, and notable content. And, conversely, when *everything* (background, structure, content) is emphasized, *nothing* is emphasized; the design will often be noisy, cluttered, and informationally flat.[2]

Strong contrasts between secondary elements and the background will also visually activate the background. In the original ear (top left), white stripes show up between the dominant pointer-lines. A redrawing (top right) minimizes the pointers—*thereby clarifying the ear itself*—and also replaces the coded list of parts with direct labels.

Here various secondary elements are redesigned in accord with the idea of minimal contrasts. Based on universal ideas of figure-ground, large-motion-covers-small-motion, hierarchical layering, and content-driven design, the strategy of the smallest effective difference applies to all display technologies; these examples come from paper, video, and computer screen (liveland examples illustrating the strategy are found in Chapter 3, on magic and disinformation design). Calming the grid down clarifies the imprisoned data, as in these cases (right and below) of statistical graphics, spreadsheet entries, and visual timetables.

[2] Variations of these ideas are discussed in terms of data-ink ratios, chartjunk, data density, and layering-separation in *The Visual Display of Quantitative Information,* chapters 5, 6, 8; *Envisioning Information,* chapters 3, 5. At the back of this book are sheets of my graph paper with very light grids (smallest effective difference) of 1 centimeter (page 158) and 0.5 inch (page 159), designs useful for laboratory notebooks.

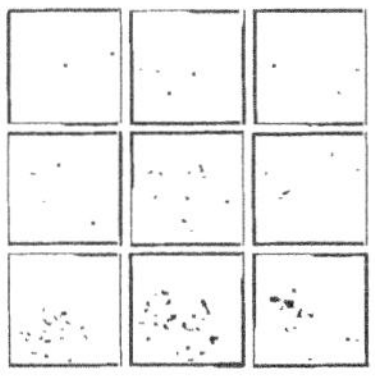

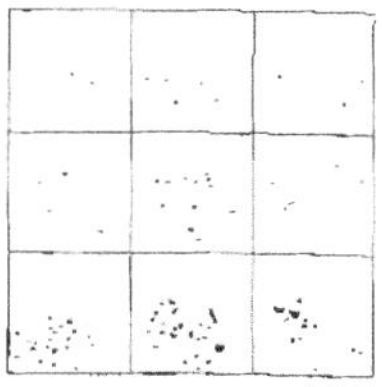

1866	516	9998
758	510	7310
658	150	4465
698	121	3274

1866	516	9998
758	510	7310
658	150	4465
698	121	3274

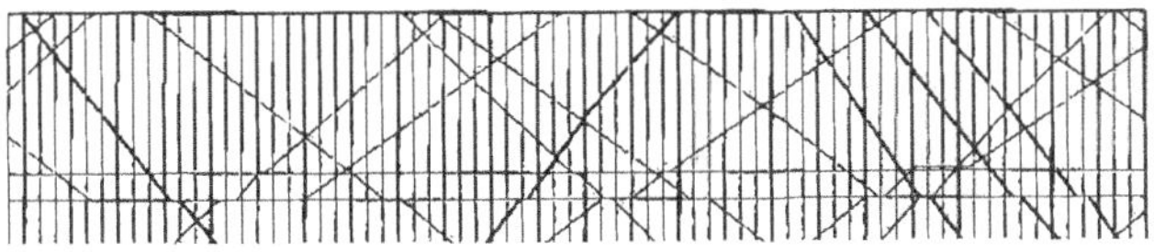

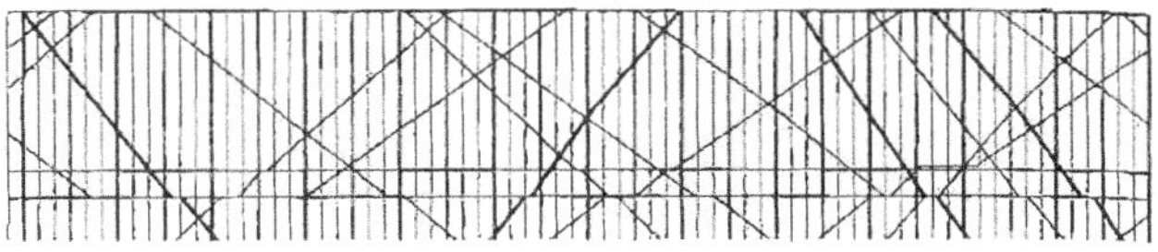

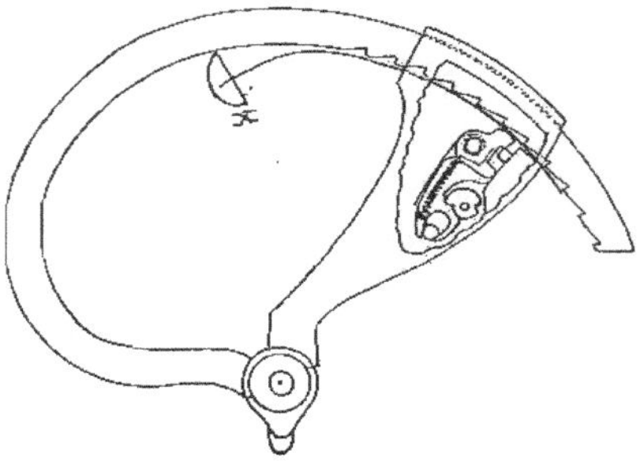

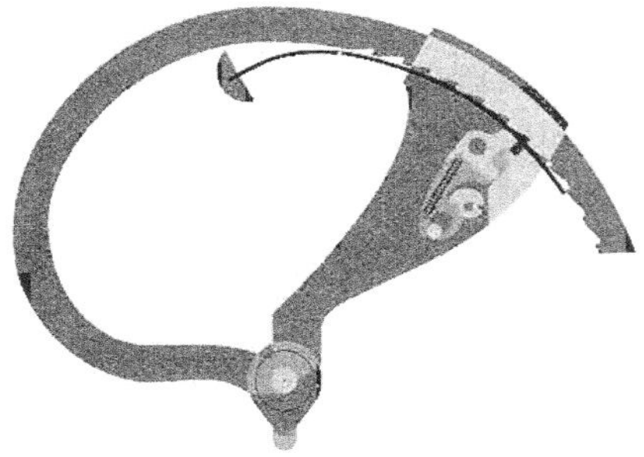

[3] Harry Houdini, *Handcuff Secrets* (London, 1909), p. 35. "The majority of the ratchet cuffs can be opened by a small piece of apparatus as shown in [the] illustration, which consists of a strip of fine steel about 3½ inches long and ¼ inch wide, with a knob on the end. This is inserted through the handcuff where the lock snaps."

Above left, the illustration fails to distinguish between the handcuff and Houdini's thin metal strip for secretly unlocking the handcuff.[3] In the redrawing at right, the strip is separated from the handcuff by means of a small visual move. Small differences can send clear signals. Consider these two color fields indicating selected text on a computer screen. Below left, the ragged edge has a strong but irrelevant presence. Also, as text is selected and deselected, the contrasty field appears and disappears, resulting in a jumpy texture of change. Thus the dark field generates both spatial clutter and temporal lurches. At right, a lighter field simply highlights the selected material:

Minimal (but clear) distinctions reduce the clutter of visual noise. Minimal contrasts enrich the visual signal by increasing the number of distinctions that can be made within a single image, as we saw in comparing the blue and the rainbow oceans. Design by means of the smallest effective difference helps to maximize the resolution of our images. In practice, the size of smallest effective difference will depend on the context, priority of particular visual elements in the overall story, number

Minimal (but clear) distinctions reduce the clutter of visual noise. Minimal contrasts enrich the visual signal by increasing the number of distinctions that can be made within a single image, as we saw in comparing the blue and the rainbow oceans. Design by means of the smallest effective difference helps to maximize the resolution of our images. In practice, the size of smallest effective difference will depend on the context, priority of particular visual elements in the overall story, number

The strategy of small but clear differences applies to moving images as well as to tables, diagrams, and statistical graphics. Revisions of the animated thunderstorm in Chapter 1 (also below, showing before and after) muted the prominent secondary elements, clarified the storm, and added some new information.

Redesigned animation by Edward Tufte and Polly Baker, with the assistance of Matthew Arrott, Colleen B. Bushell, and Michael McNeill; scientific data from Robert B. Wilhelmson, Brian F. Jewett, Crystal Shaw, and Louis J. Wicker (Department of Atmospheric Sciences and the National Center for Supercomputing Applications, University of Illinois at Urbana-Champaign); original visualization by Matthew Arrott, Mark Bajuk, Colleen B. Bushell, Jeffrey Thingvold, Jeffery B. Yost, National Center for Supercomputing Applications, University of Illinois at Urbana-Champaign.

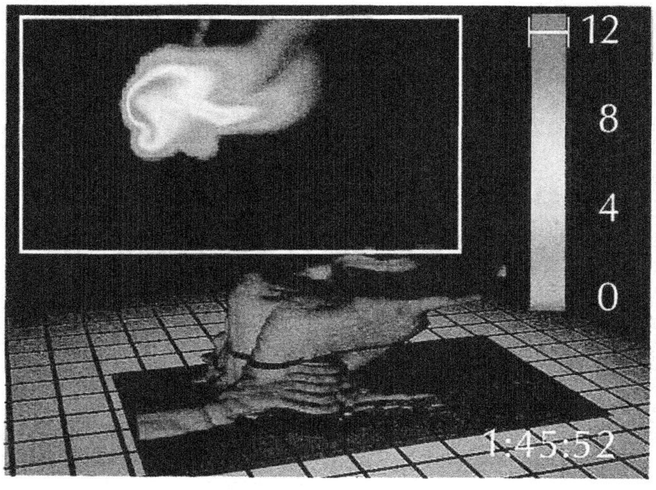

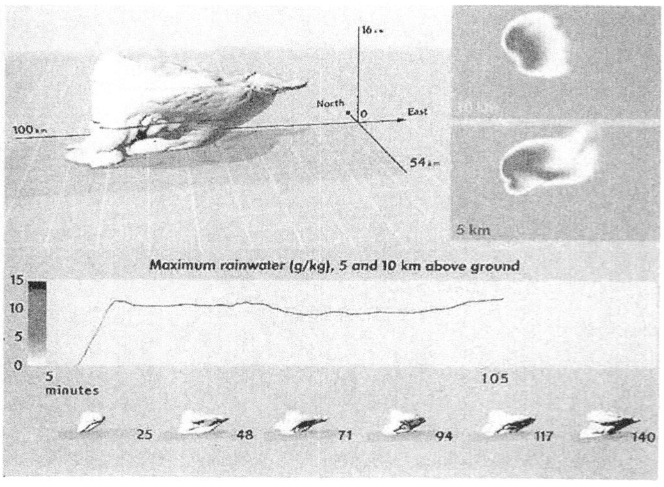

Showing the Japan Sea and the great trenches of the western Pacific, this classic map below makes extraordinary use of small and effective differences. The General Bathymetric Chart of the Oceans depicts depth (the blue, bathymetric tints) and altitude (tan, hypsometric tints) in 21 color gradations—with "the deeper or the higher, the darker the color" serving as the visual metaphor for the color scale. To indicate depth, the contour lines are labeled by numbers, a design that enhances accuracy of reading and nearly eliminates any need to refer back to the legend. Every color tint on the map signals four variables: latitude, longitude, sea or land, and depth or altitude measured in meters. Then, on a visual layer separated from the blue tints, thin gray lines trace out the routes of the oceanographic ships that measured the depth (outside of areas with detailed surveys, such as ports and coastlines).

These gray lines are a small miracle of information design. Floating on top of the ocean and coexisting with the blue tints and contours, the thin lines depict a distinct, second layer of data relevant to the depths below. There is sufficient visual space for the gray lines because the representation of depth does not use up all the informational possibilities of color in the map. And since the contours are directly

General Bathymetric Chart of the Oceans, International Hydrographic Organization (Ottawa, Canada, 5th edition, 1984). 5.06.

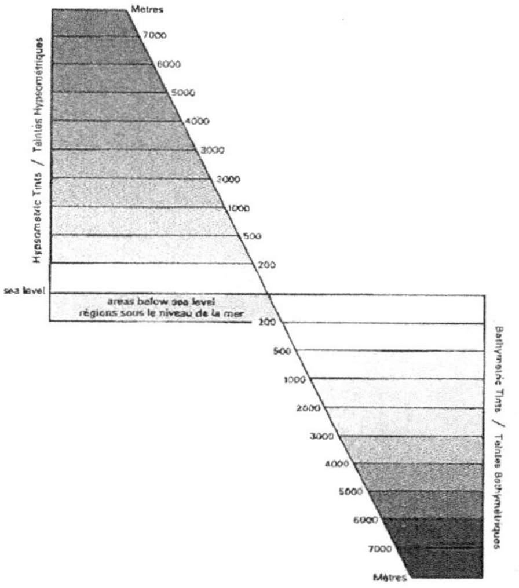

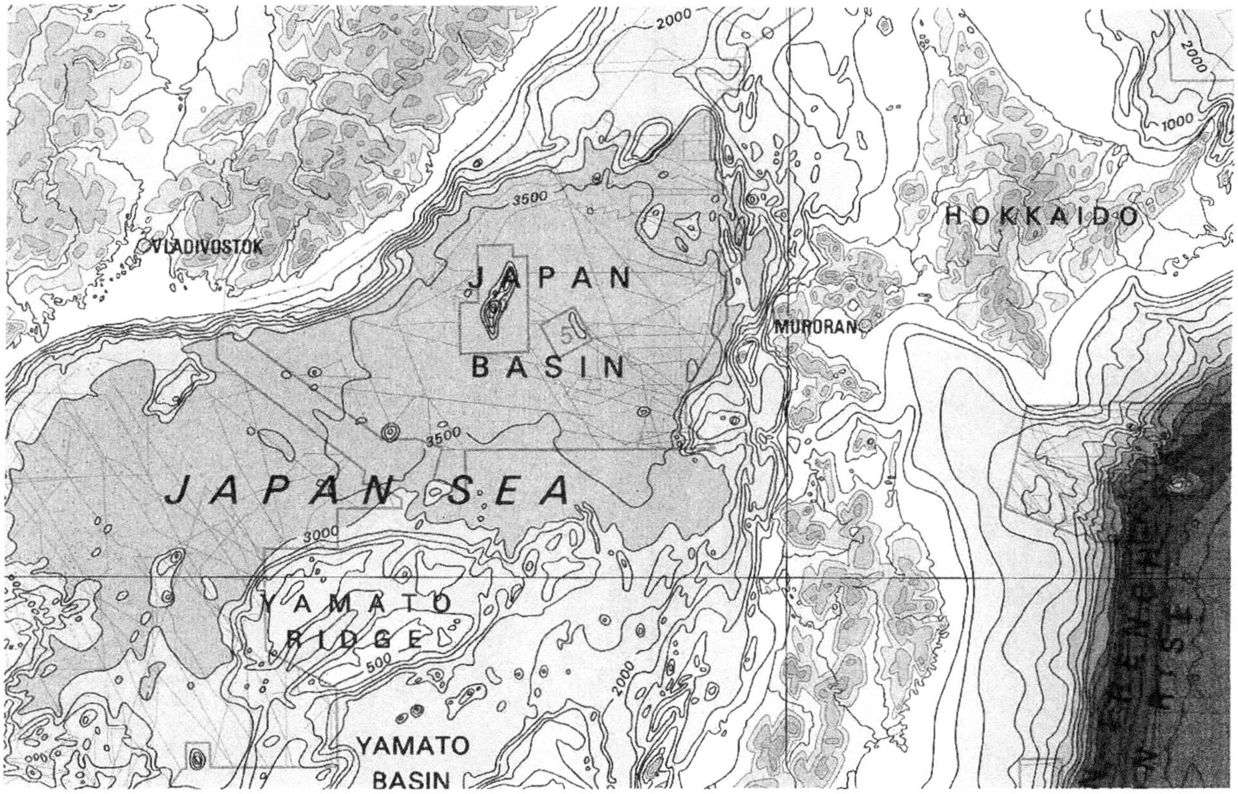

labeled with numbers, the fine distinctions in blue remain clear and readable. By indicating depth with visually minimal gradations in color, the cartographers were able to add an extra two-dimensional layer of gray-line data right on top of the ocean contours. Minimal differences allow more differences.

In ghastly contrast below, a rainbow encodes depth. Although often found in scientific publications, such a visually naive color-scale would be laughed right out of the field (or ocean) of cartography. These aggressive colors, so unnatural and unquantitative, render the map incoherent, with some of the original data now lost in the soup.

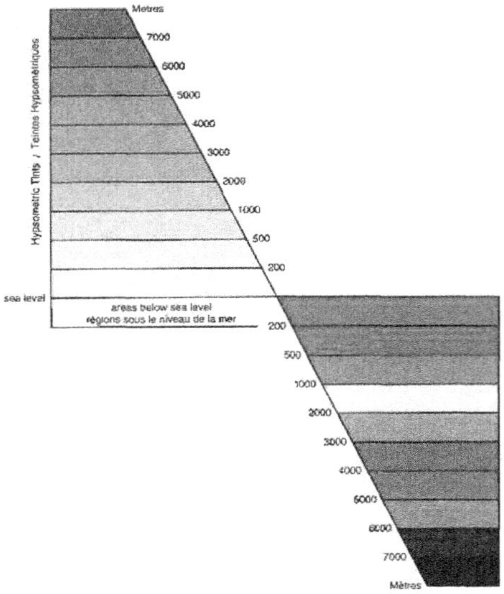

Minimal distinctions reduce visual clutter. Small contrasts work to enrich the overall visual signal by increasing the number of distinctions that can be made within a single image; thus design by means of small effective differences helps to increase the resolution of our images. In practice, the appropriate size of small contrasts will depend on the context, priority of particular elements in the overall visual story, number of differentiations made within an image, and characteristics of those viewing the image. Despite these local complications, the global principle of the smallest effective difference resolves many visual issues—serving perhaps even as an algorithm for automated design.

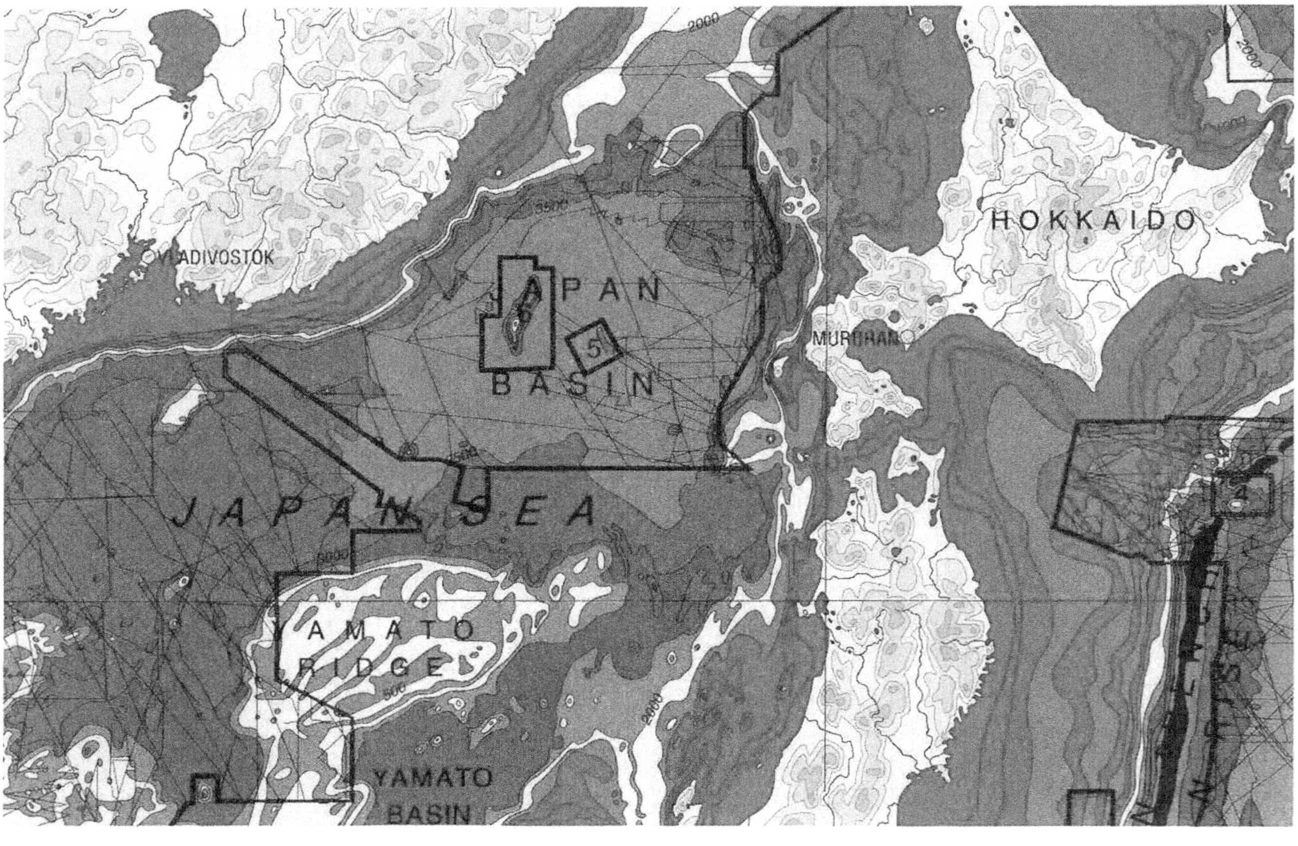

A candid but rational inquiry into the progress and establishment of Christianity may be considered as a very essential part of the history of the Roman empire. While that great body was invaded by open violence, or undermined by slow decay, a pure and humble religion gently insinuated itself into the minds of men, grew up in silence and obscurity, derived new vigour from opposition, and finally erected the triumphant banner of the Cross on the ruins of the Capitol.

But this inquiry, however useful or entertaining, is attended with two peculiar difficulties. The scanty and suspicious materials of ecclesiastical history seldom enable us to dispel the dark cloud that hangs over the first age of the church. The great law of impartiality too often obliges us to reveal the imperfections of the uninspired teachers and believers of the Gospel; and, to a careless observer, *their* faults may seem to cast a shade on the faith which they professed. But the scandal of the pious Christian, and the fallacious triumph of the Infidel, should cease as soon as they recollect not only *by whom*, but likewise *to whom*, the Divine Revelation was given. The theologian may indulge the pleasing task of describing Religion as she descended from Heaven, arrayed in her native purity. A more melancholy duty is imposed on the historian. He must discover the inevitable mixture of error and corruption which she contracted in a long residence upon earth, among a weak and degenerate race of beings.

Edward Gibbon, *The History of the Decline and Fall of the Roman Empire* (London, 1776–1788), chapter XV.

5 Parallelism: Repetition and Change, Comparison and Surprise

For prose, parallelism helps bring about clarity, efficiency, forcefulness, rhythm, balance. "The matching of phrase against phrase, clause against clause, lends an unmistakable eloquence to prose," writes Richard Altick, employing a parallel structure.[1] In *Decline and Fall of the Roman Empire,* Edward Gibbon describes the spread of Christianity in prose filled with intricate parallels. Repetitions, elaborations, and contrasts advance the argument, as Gibbon sardonically justifies writing an impartial, objective history of religion. Especially effective is the second sentence, in which four parallel verbs (*insinuated, grew, derived, erected*) render a terse account of Christianity in the Roman empire. Gibbon also uses parallelism to make his key point, with an italicized *by whom* contrasted with *to whom.* Complexly organized, like a fugue, the sentences roll and rumble—and sting with latent sarcasm. All this in the one-dimensional flow of words.

[1] Richard Altick, *Preface to Critical Reading* (New York, 1963), p. 210.

Now consider information displays in two- and three-space: What are the strategies of *visual* parallelism? Are there visual analogs to syntactical and rhetorical principles? Analogs to the more subtle aspects of parallelism in language, such as ellipsis and deliberately faulty parallelism?

Like *by whom* and *to whom* in Gibbon, paired images enforce a direct visual parallelism. At right, in this *before/after* of a magic trick, parallel verbs and images (*torn/restored*) are connected by means of some exotic arrow-letters. And, below, two divergent views of the sculpture *Cheval à l'arrêt* by Edgar-Hilaire Degas expressly contrast the surface with an x-ray revelation of the wire innards. Comparisons between photograph and x-ray are straightforward because the horse is about the same size and takes a similar stance in the two views.

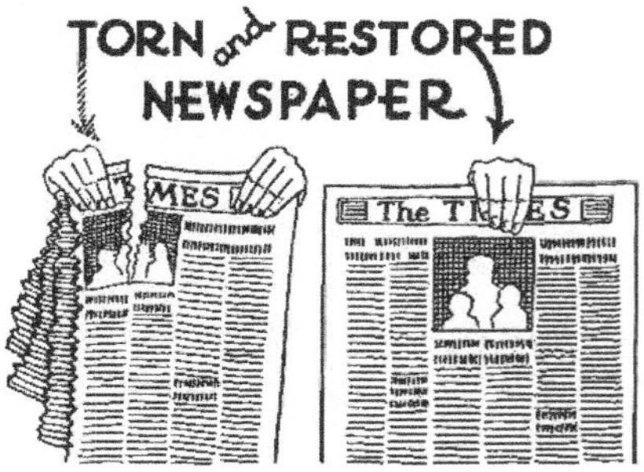

Lyle Douglas, *Complete Five-in-One Catalog* (Dallas, 1932), p. 101. Redrawn.

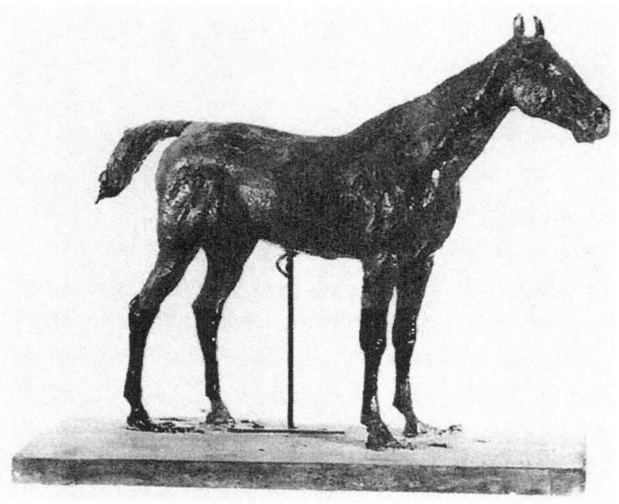

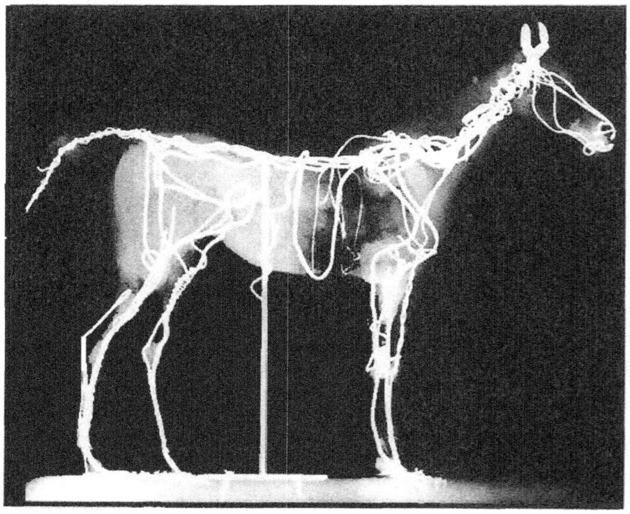

Laboratoire de Recherche des Musées de France, *La science et l'art* (Paris, 1989, second edition), pp. 28–29.

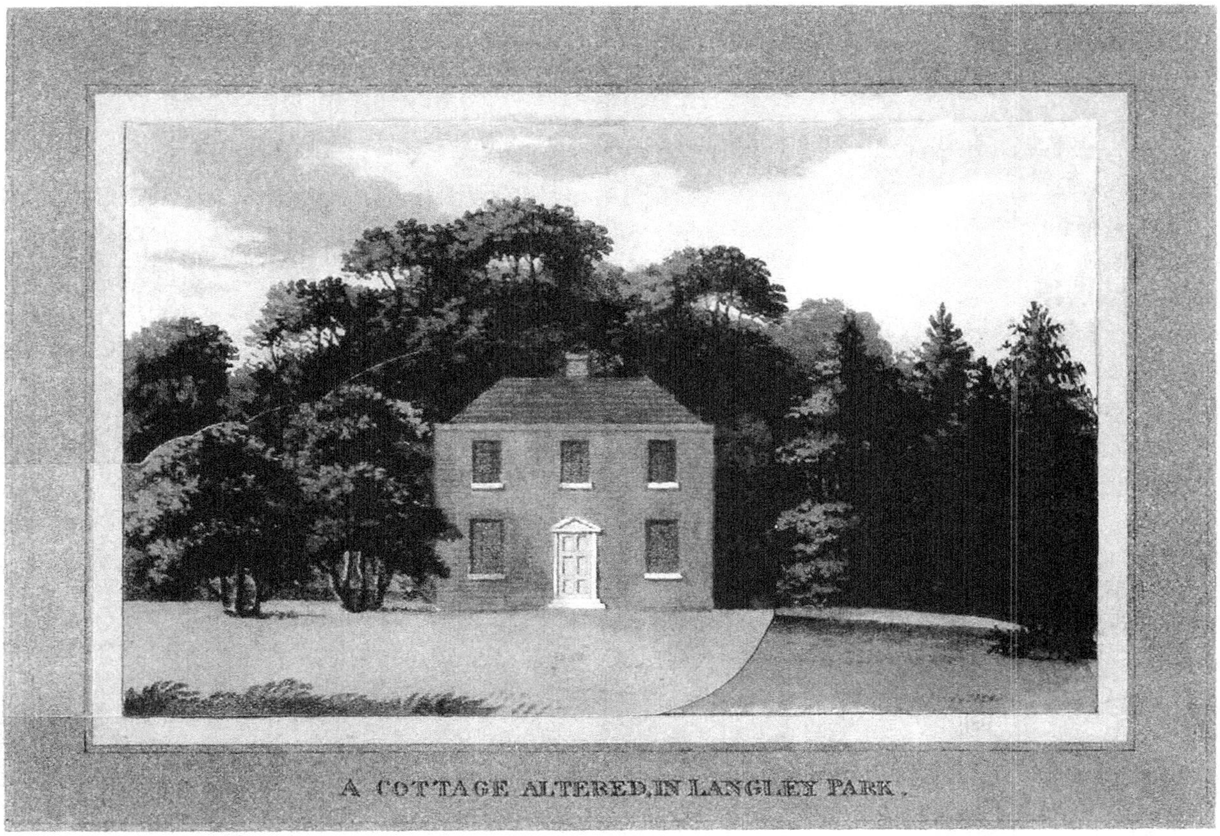

Humphry Repton, *Observations on the Theory and Practice of Landscape Gardening* (London, 1803), at pp. 162–163.

The horses of Degas are *parallel in space*, located close together on the paper. Spatial parallelism takes advantage of our notable capacity to compare and reason about multiple images that appear simultaneously within our eyespan. We are able to canvass, sort, identify, reconnoiter, select, contrast, review—ways of seeing all quickened and sharpened by the direct spatial adjacency of parallel elements.

Parallel images can also be distributed temporally, with one like image following another, *parallel in time*. For time-bound sequences, comparisons must be made by contrasting a remembered image with a currently viewed image, a sometimes difficult task.

Lifting the flap above provides an example of parallelism in time, a *before/after* presentation of an architectural redesign (a Doric portico added to a cosy cottage). At the instant of unveiling, the new image delights the eye. Concealing and then revealing the fanciful construction project, the flap is integrated into the surroundings by means of its contoured shape and small size; its *local* quality concentrates our attention on how *before* differs from *after*, more so than for a large rectangular flap laid over the entire scene.

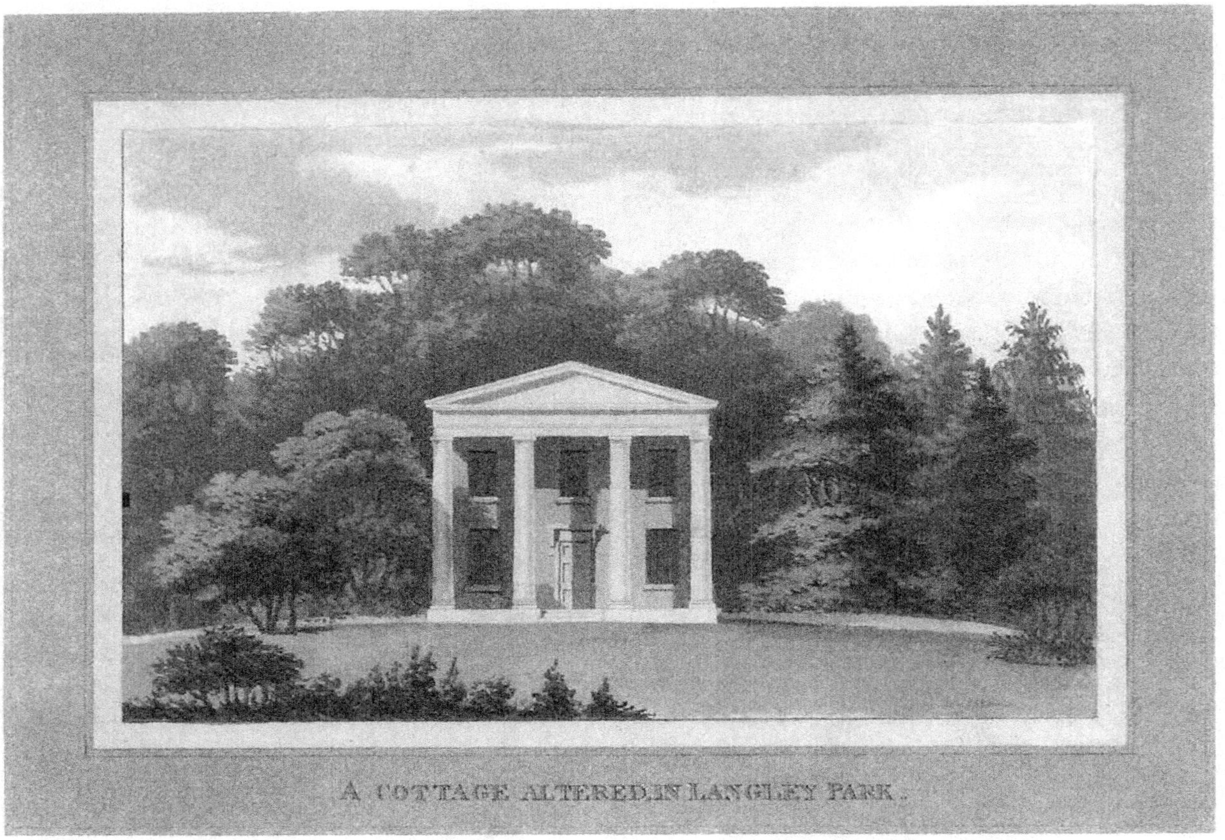

Since the proposed redesign merely applies a façade to the old building, the viewing sequence becomes: first the cottage on the flap, then the grandiose decoration beneath, and finally the parallel ghost of the old cottage peeking through the new façade. This interplay of content with the method of display yields a parallelism of layered depth.

Furthermore, rapidly flipping the flap, veiling and unveiling, brings about a nearly simultaneous visual comparison of the old and new buildings exactly in position.[2] This temporal flip-parallelism enhances the reading of differences, which is the exact purpose of comparisons in parallel. Such flips avoid the disorienting back-and-forth movements of the eye needed to compare adjacent but separate images.

Humphry Repton, the British architect, used *before/after* flaps in some 100 presentations during the early 1800s, both in his books on landscape theory and in pitching proposals to clients.[3] His redesigns could easily be presented without flaps—though without magic—by means of spatial parallelism, by paired images (above, left and right). And, despite the enchantment of flaps, comparisons are usually more effective when the information is adjacent in space rather than stacked in time.

[2] A similar display for statistical data is described in John W. Tukey and Paul A. Tukey, "Computer Graphics and Exploratory Data Analysis: An Introduction," *The Collected Works of John W. Tukey, Volume V, Graphics: 1965–1985*, ed. William S. Cleveland (Pacific Grove, California, 1988), pp. 419–436.

[3] Humphry Repton, *Designs for the Pavilion at Brighton* (London, 1808); Edward Malins, ed., *The Red Books of Humphry Repton* (London, 1976); J. C. Louden, ed., *The Landscape Gardening and Landscape Architecture of the late Humphry Repton* (London, 1840). See Dorothy Stroud, *Humphry Repton* (London, 1961); Nikolaus Pevsner, *Studies in Art, Architecture and Design* (London, 1968), volume 1, pp. 138–155; Stephen Daniels, *Fields of Vision* (Princeton, 1993).

PARALLELISM connects visual elements. Connections are built among images by position, orientation, overlap, synchronization, and similarities in content. Parallelism grows from a common viewpoint that relates like to like. Congruity of structure across multiple images gives the eye a context for assessing data variation. Parallelism is not simply a matter of design arrangements, for the perceiving mind itself actively works to detect and indeed to generate links, clusters, and matches among assorted visual elements.[4]

The linking mechanism of parallel designs can be subtle and elegant, consistent with the guiding principle that *good form is clear but not a spectacle*. For example, images in graceful parallel begin this charming book by Margaret Morris. Employing her abstract notational system for documenting body movement and posture, an encoded chart on the title page records the author's position—head, arms, hands, body, legs—in her picture at left! Connections between photograph and diagram are made by common centering, by short explanatory notes, and, for a few viewers perhaps, by a reading of the notation itself.

[4] E. H. Gombrich, *The Sense of Order* (Ithaca, New York, 1979). What various minds do with various images is a complicated and unsettled matter. On recognition systems, see Ulric Neisser, *Cognition and Reality: Principles and Implications of Cognitive Psychology* (San Francisco, 1976); and Stephen M. Kosslyn, *Image and Mind* (Cambridge, Massachusetts, 1980).

Margaret Morris, *The Notation of Movement* (London, 1928), frontispiece and title page.

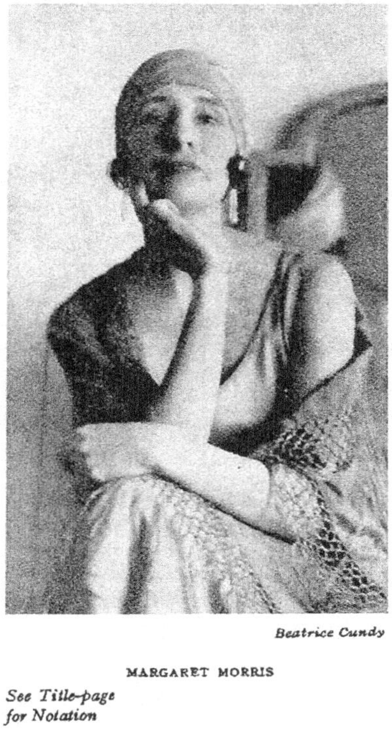

Beatrice Cundy

MARGARET MORRIS

See Title-page for Notation

THE NOTATION OF MOVEMENT

TEXT, DRAWINGS AND DIAGRAMS

BY

MARGARET MORRIS

With an Introduction by

H. LEVY, M.A., D.Sc., F.R.S.E.

Professor of Mathematics, Imperial College of Science & Technology

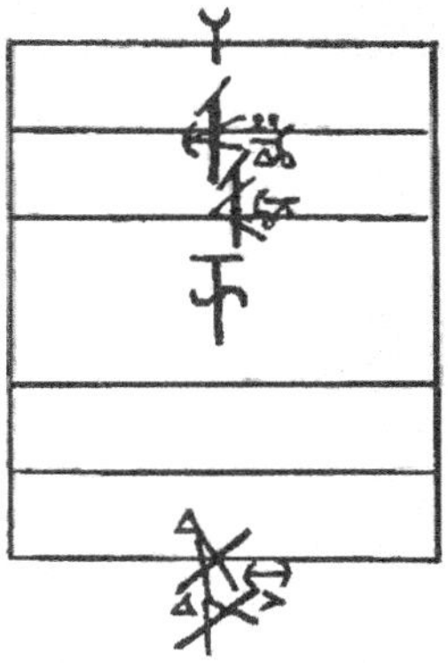

The position in Frontispiece written in notation

LONDON

KEGAN PAUL, TRENCH, TRUBNER & Co., Ltd.

BROADWAY HOUSE, CARTER LANE, E.C.

1928

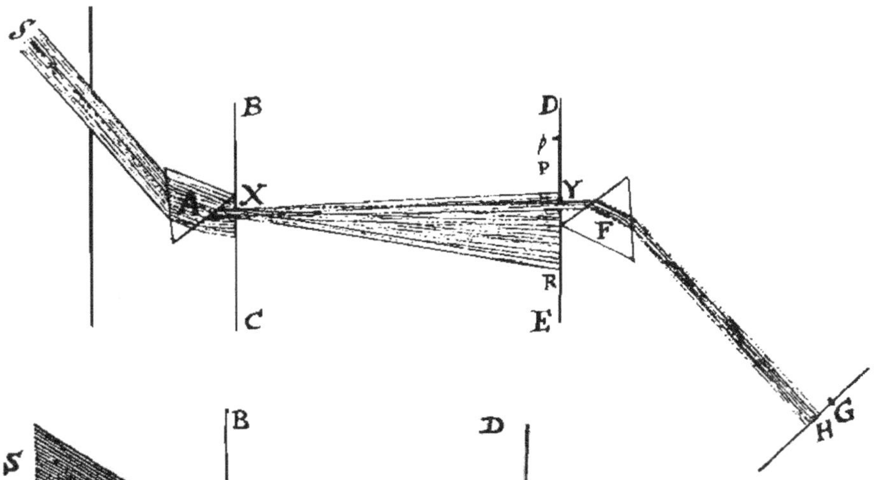

Isaac Newton, optical lectures, manuscript, University Library Cambridge, Add 4002, loose slip.

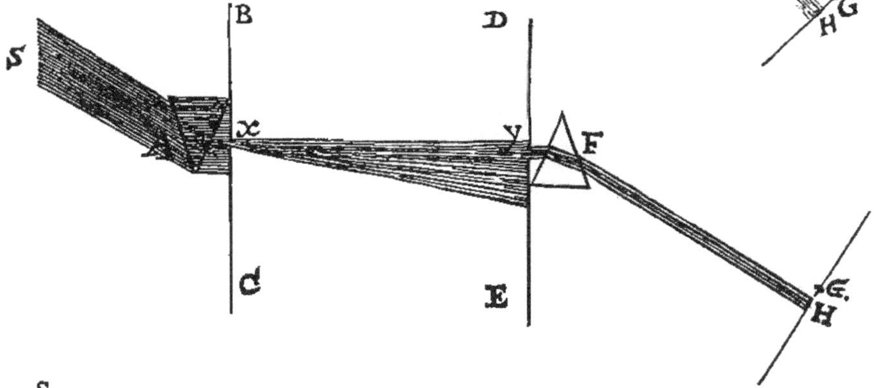

Oldenburg, *Philosophical Transactions*, 85 (July 15, 1672), 5016.

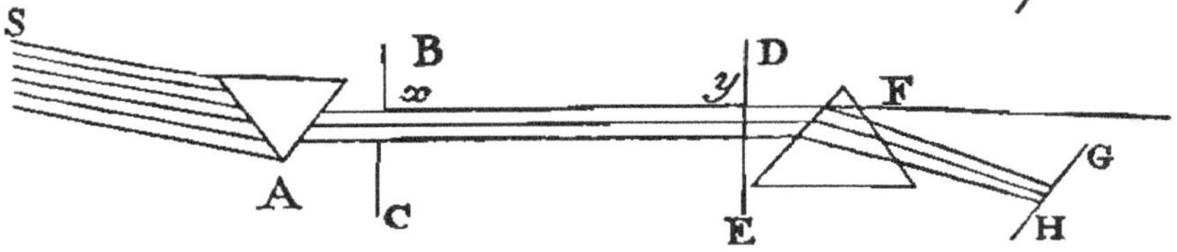

Isaaci Newtoni opera quæ exstant omnia. Commentariis illustrabat Samuel Horsley (London, 1779–1785), volume IV, 317.

Multiple parallel images—a transparent, powerful, and widely used method of enforcing visual comparisons—show here three versions of the same finding. At top is Isaac Newton's own sketch of his famous experiment demonstrating that a second refraction of a colored ray does not alter its color. Sunlight is refracted into a rainbow at the left prism; green light only is allowed to pass through the slit at BXC; and it remains green (not becoming a rainbow) after it passes through a second prism and falls on plane HG. Editors altered Newton's work in later publications, as shown in the two drawings beneath Newton's original. Lohne sternly describes the corruption of the diagrams:

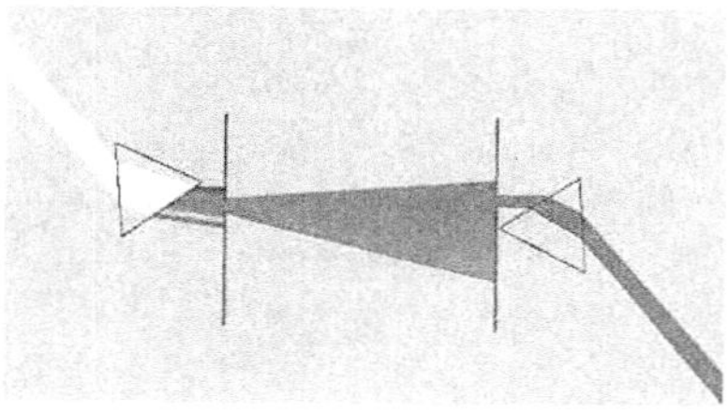

> Newton himself attended to the minutest details of this and other prismatic experiments and was no less accurate in executing their diagrams. In illustrating the crucial experiment . . . he saw to it that the refractions at entrance and emergence from the prism should be exactly equal. This equality ensures minimal deviation of the ray as well as minimal distortion of images. Editors of Newton's optical letters and lectures have been very negligent in such particulars, their diagrams often violating fundamental optical laws. We may be lenient with the first editor, Oldenburg, who in 1672 had no competent draughtsmen, but we cannot excuse Horsley and more recent bowdlerizers of this most celebrated figure.[5]

[5] J. A. Lohne, "The Increasing Corruption of Newton's Diagrams," *History of Science*, 6 (1967), pp. 71–73. Historical diagrams reproduced from Lohne.

Christopher Wilmarth, the sculptor, described an unusual birthday present in his "The True Story of the Gift of the Bridge." The story concludes poignantly with a parallel sequence of fading text.

> I was going to be twenty, or rather I was twenty, and Susan was coming over to my old place on West Broadway and North Moore to give me my birthday present. . . . Susan had been giving me the "just wait till you see what I'm giving you" look for days and I was getting curious. . . . She arrived, animated and bright, and suggested that my gift was "elsewhere". . . .
>
> There were two ways to get to the Brooklyn Bridge on foot: through the I.R.T. subway station past the old bronze plaque that said it was the first subway, and by going up the stairs from William Street. I always preferred the William Street way because the bridge would bounce into view as I climbed the steps, and I could hum things to myself and mostly no one was around to hear.
>
> When we got there (to the William Street stairs) Susan was grinning and chuckling and hurrying me up onto the bridge but I was in the dark. I really didn't think that any substantial gift could be hidden on the bridge and not be found by someone passing by. When we had walked to the middle of the bridge where the expansion joint is, near the police phone, Susan made a gesture of presentation and triumph. I looked thick and stumbly so she said to me "Don't you see it?" and then—I did! Right in the middle of the bridge, under the railing on the uptown tips of the footwalk planks so you would hardly notice them, were painted, one letter to a plank end, the words: FOR CHRISTOPHER ON HIS BIRTHDAY LOVE SHIFRAH. It was great! I loved that bridge so much and here Susan had gone and given it to me. It said so! Right there in the middle.
>
> Every so often after that I'd go down for a walk on the bridge alone, or with Susan, and we would see how my birthday card was doing. If there were other people around we would never let on about the letters, just check them out and not say anything. After a while a board would go bad and be replaced, so a letter or two would disappear or the railing would be painted and the drips would fuzz the words. Slowly over the years the inscription would become more and more cryptic. By the end of September nineteen seventy-one all the letters had gone.[6]

```
1963      FOR CHRISTOPHER ON HIS BIRTHDAY LOVE SHIFRAH
1964      F R CHRI  OPH R  N  IS BIRTH A  LOVE SHIFR
1965      F R CHRI  OP  R  N  IS BIRT  A  L VE SHIFR
1966      F   C RI   P  R  N  IS BIR   A    VE SHIFR
1967      F   C RI   P     N  IS BIR        VE S IFR
1968          C RI   P        I  BIR         E S IF
1969          C R    P            IR         E S IF
1970          C      P            IR         E   IF
1971                 P             R              F
Oct 1971
```

Here, appearing together all at once in deteriorating parallel, are *text* (reading across), *time-series* (reading down), *image* (representing the object itself), and *symbol* (of the fading image, as IF repeats again and again, surviving longer than any other letters). And the typographic array even resembles a bridge.

[6] Christopher Wilmarth, "The True Story of the Gift of the Bridge," in *Christopher Wilmarth: Matrix 29*, brochure, Wadsworth Atheneum (Hartford, Connecticut, 1977).

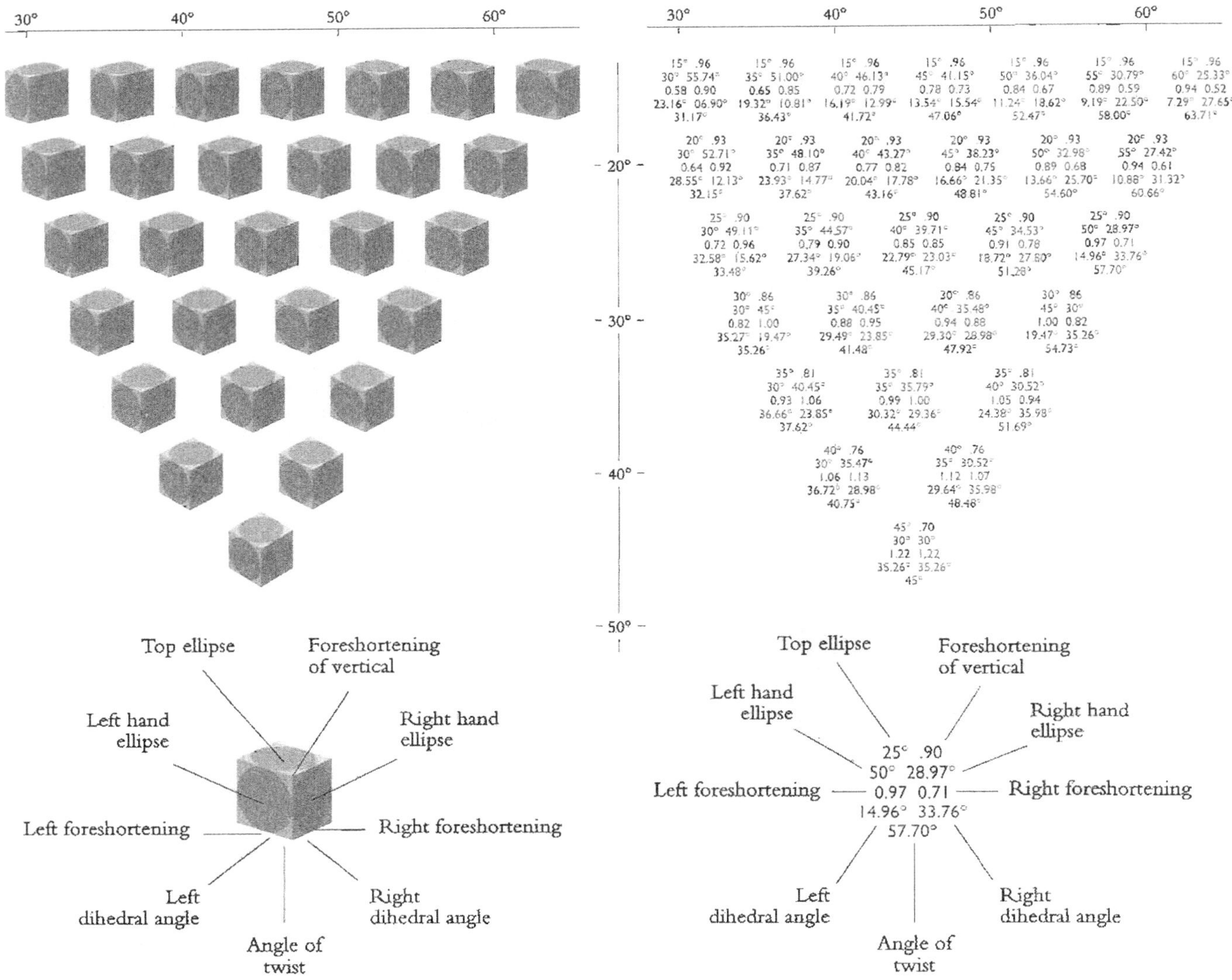

By means of multiple parallels, these drawings show the cube in trimetric projection, a method for translating three-space objects onto paper flatland. At upper left, a matrix of visual elements organizes 28 cubes on a two-dimensional grid of incrementally varying angles of twist (along the rows) and tilt (up and down). At upper right, a corresponding data matrix shows 252 numbers, with 9 numbers describing the particulars of each cube. An interesting visual effect occurs within the right matrix: each cluster of numbers roughly outlines the shape of a cube, and consequently the negative (white) space of the data matrix matches the negative space of the visual matrix of cubes, reinforcing the parallelism of their content. Finally, the legends (presented in rigorous parallel beneath the visual and the data matrices) explain the individual entries. All the pairwise parallelism connects and makes coherent the matrices and legends in this well-designed assembly of information—visual, textual, and numerical.

Based on B. Coe, *An Atlas for Trimetric Drawing* (Royal College of Art, London, 1981), as reproduced in Fred Dubery and John Willats, *Perspective and Other Drawing Systems* (New York, 1983), pp. 42–43.

To show that the earth is spherical (which practically no one had doubted for centuries), in 1533 Peter Apian drew these agreeable diagrams depicting how the earth masks sunlight falling on the moon.[7] Pictures and words in parallel demonstrate that an eclipse of the moon by the earth casts a circular shadow; and if the earth were some other shape, a non-circular shadow would appear. The repetitions are perhaps made less tedious by the changing characters of sun, moon, and earth, and by the interchange of sun and moon halfway through. All told the entire performance consists of eight parallel accounts—four sentences, four drawings—of the same point, along with four translations in parallel. Apian's representation is utterly flat and without dynamics, treating the sun, earth, and moon as fixed cardboard cutouts rather than as three-dimensional objects moving in space. Visual simplifications mask substantive complications; for example, if the earth were a cube, it could cast the shadows shown in the second, third, and fourth scenes above.

Hoc Schema demonſtrat terram eſſe globoſam.

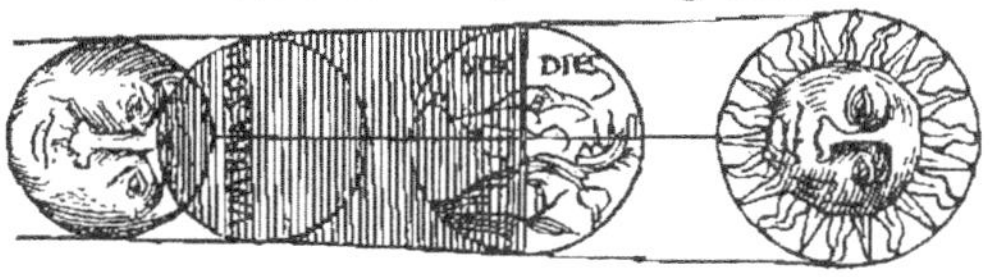

'This diagram shows that the earth is round.'

Si terra eſſet tetragona, vmbra quoq; tetragonæ figuræ in eclipſatione lunari appareret.

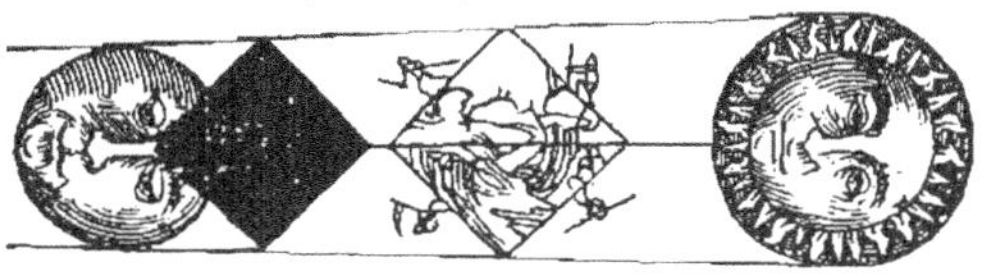

'If the earth were four-cornered, its shadow in a lunar eclipse would also appear to be a four-cornered figure.'

Si terra eſſet trigona, vmbra quoq; triangularem haberet formulam.

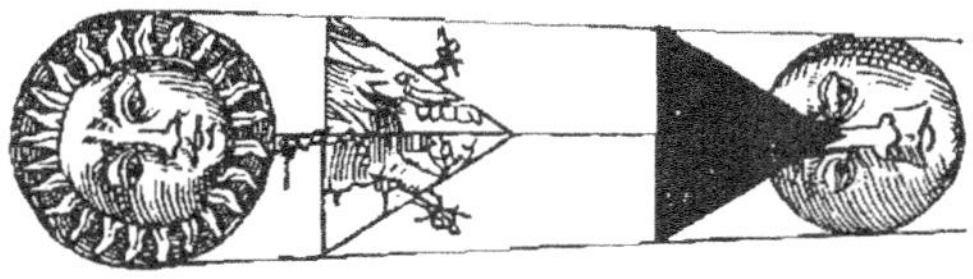

'If the earth were three-cornered, its shadow would also have a triangular shape.'

Si terra hexagonæ eſſet figuræ, eius quoq; vmbra in defectu lunari hexagona appareret, quæ tamen rotunda cernitur.

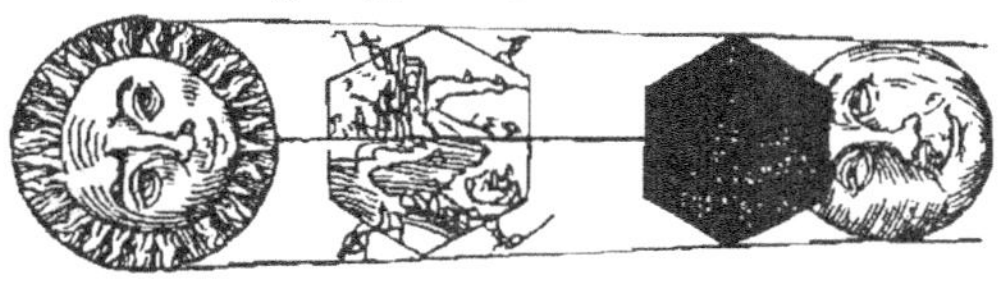

'If the earth were a hexagonal figure, its shadow in a lunar eclipse would also appear to be hexagonal, so it is clearly seen to be round.'

Peter Apian, *Cosmographicus liber* (Antwerp, 1533), fol. 6v.

Below are 20th-century displays of a similar but not identical projection, the two-dimensional shapes made by a cube traversing a plane (that is, the cross-sections created by slices through a cube).[8] Three classes of shapes result, varying with the angle and orientation of the cube (lighter color) relative to the projection plane (darker), as arrayed in parallel columns at left. Shown are cubes entering via the vertex, the edge, and the square face. Note the slice resulting in a regular hexagon. Then at right, a rain of cubes intersect the traversing plane. Observing how a plane articulates three-space objects might help us understand how four-dimensional objects would reveal themselves to the three-space in which we live.

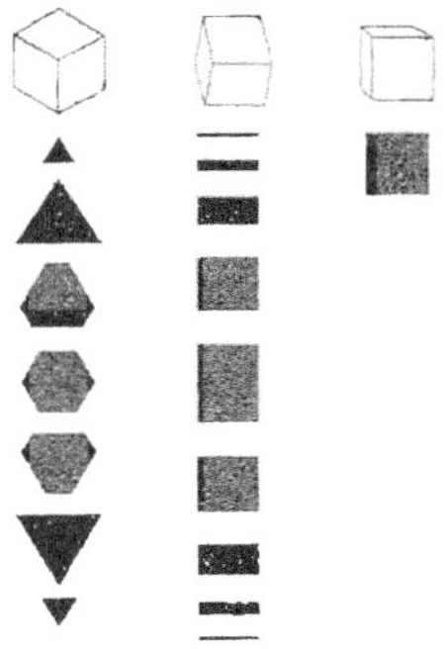

Based on Claude Bragdon, *A Primer of Higher Space: The Fourth Dimension* (Rochester, New York, 1913), plate 30.

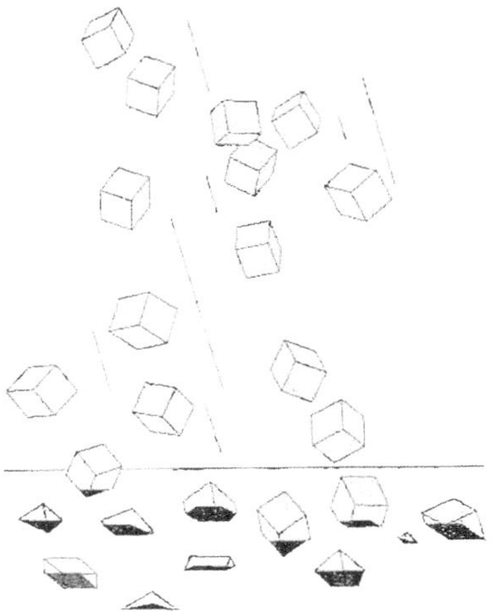

[7] S. K. Heninger, Jr., *The Cosmographical Glass: Renaissance Diagrams of the Universe* (San Marino, California, 1977), pp. 35–36. Translations are from Heninger. The "flat error" is dissected in Jeffrey B. Russell, *Inventing the Flat Earth* (New York, 1991).

[8] On projections by shadows and slices, see Thomas F. Banchoff, *Beyond the Third Dimension: Geometry, Computer Graphics, and Higher Dimensions* (New York, 1990).

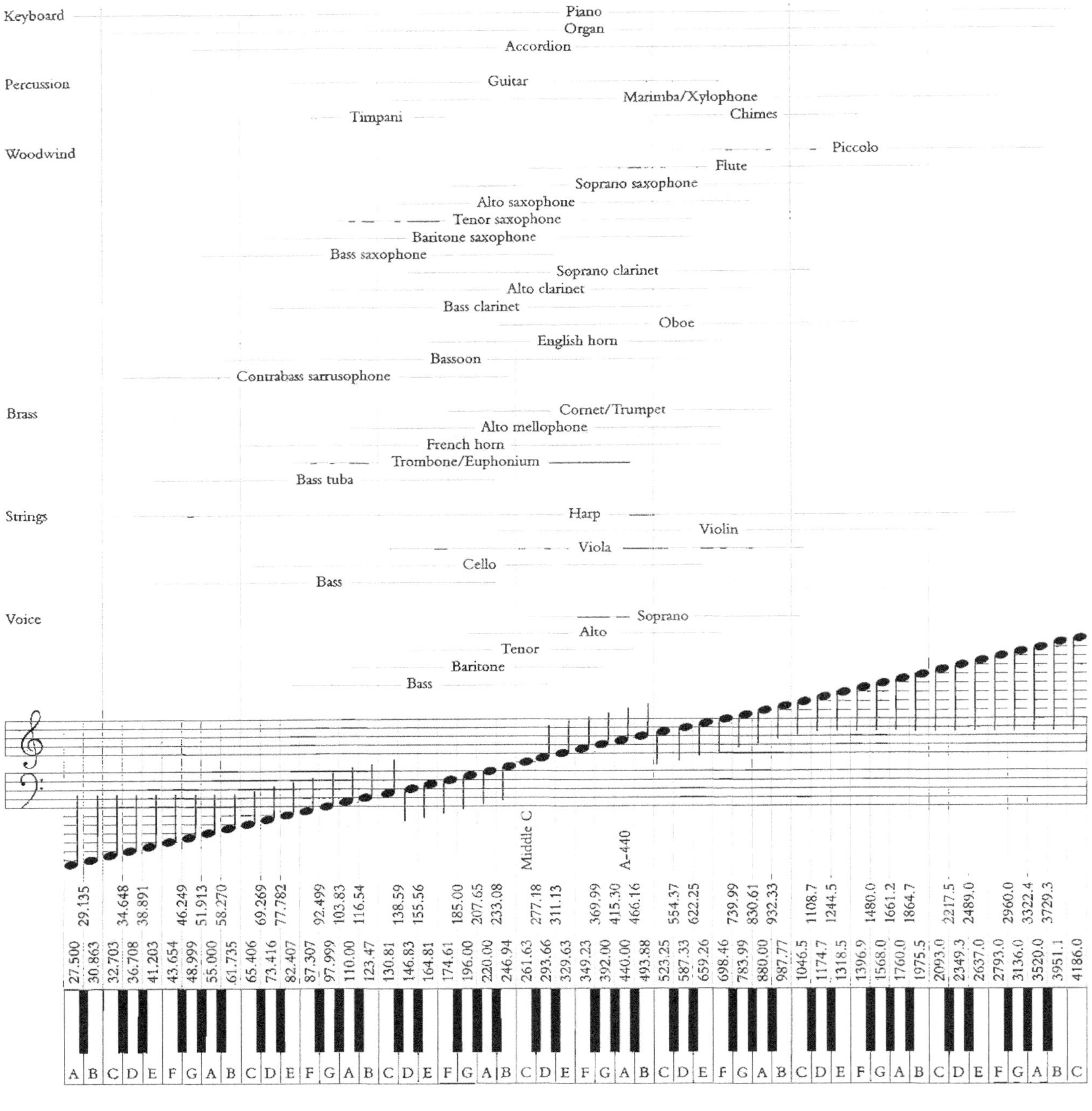

Multiple parallelism is a natural design strategy for explanations of music and sound, as repeated comparisons are made with respect to frequency and time. Above, many overlapping parallel tracks run on the common dimension of the 88 keys of the piano keyboard. Frequencies of sounds, notes of the musical scale, ranges of singing voices, and families of musical instruments are aligned, described, compared, contrasted, remembered.

John R. Pierce, *The Science of Musical Sound* (New York, 1992), pp. 18–19; adapted from a drawing in Donald E. Hall, *Musical Acoustics: An Introduction* (Pacific Grove, California, 1991), inside back cover. Redrawn.

In this superb computer-companion to a recording of Beethoven's Ninth Symphony, visual parallelism describes the musical parallelism of the grand fourth movement. Below, in an image from the computer screen (shown at its original, full size), the left column of little boxes arrays six motifs as played by the orchestra; the right column shows the same motifs as later sung by soloists and chorus. Clicking on one of the 12 boxes on this screen plays the selected musical segment. Then the listener-viewer can hear the *joy theme* (stanza 2) in the 4-part *strings* and then hear the same theme as later performed by the 4-part *voices* of the soloists. This synchronized parallelism between the silent visual explanation on the screen combined with the sound of the music is stunningly effective, as separate channels of information move together. Computer-teachers do not have to talk loudly in the background against the music itself. The effect is similar to following the music by means of a printed score augmented with detailed notes. Listeners can also move through the music as they wish, hearing passages as many times as it takes to understand what is going on.

Robert Winter, *CD Companion: Ludwig van Beethoven, Symphony No. 9*, program design by Robert Winter and Robert Stein, The Voyager Company, Santa Monica, California, 1989, "The Art of Listening," screen 91.

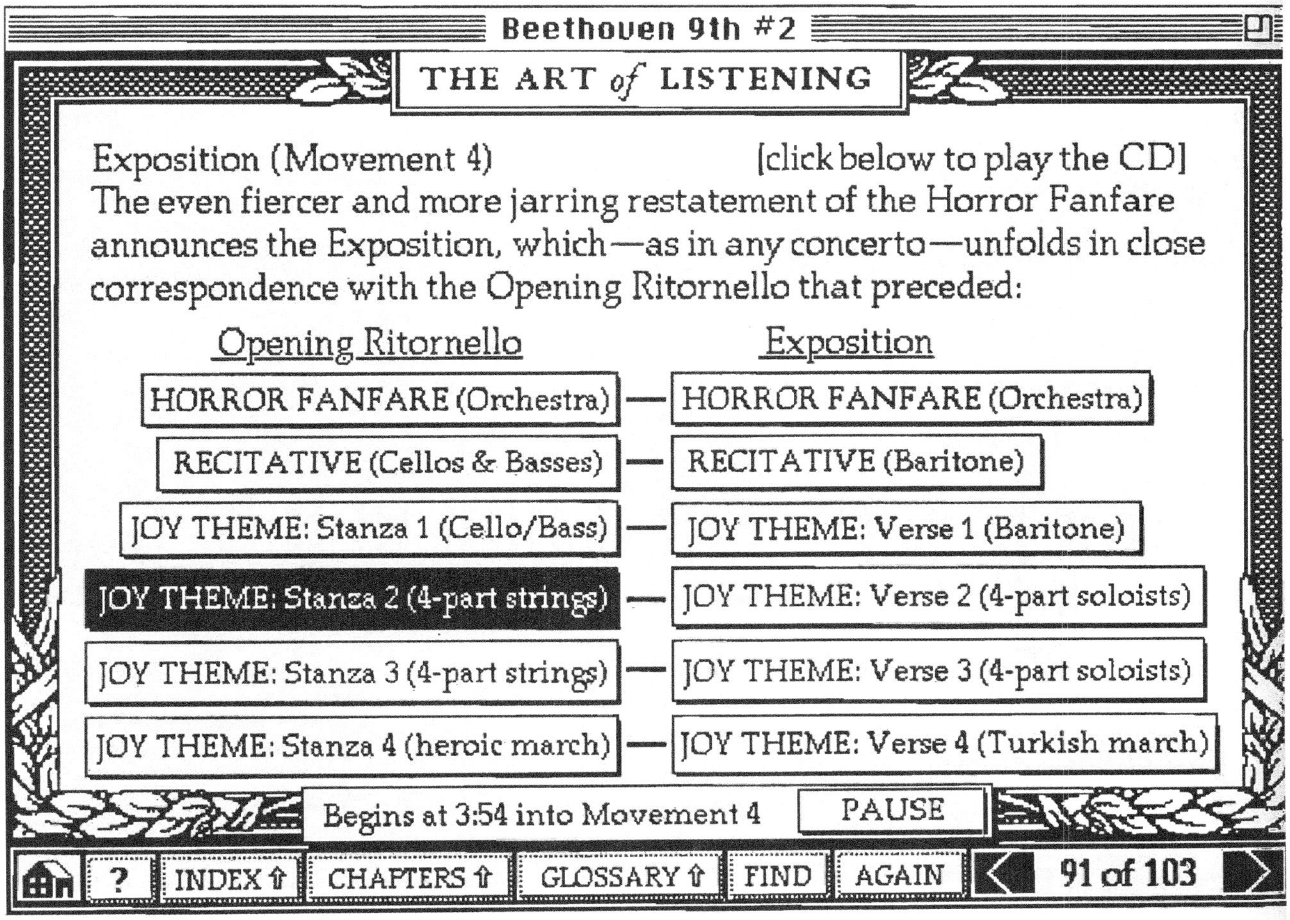

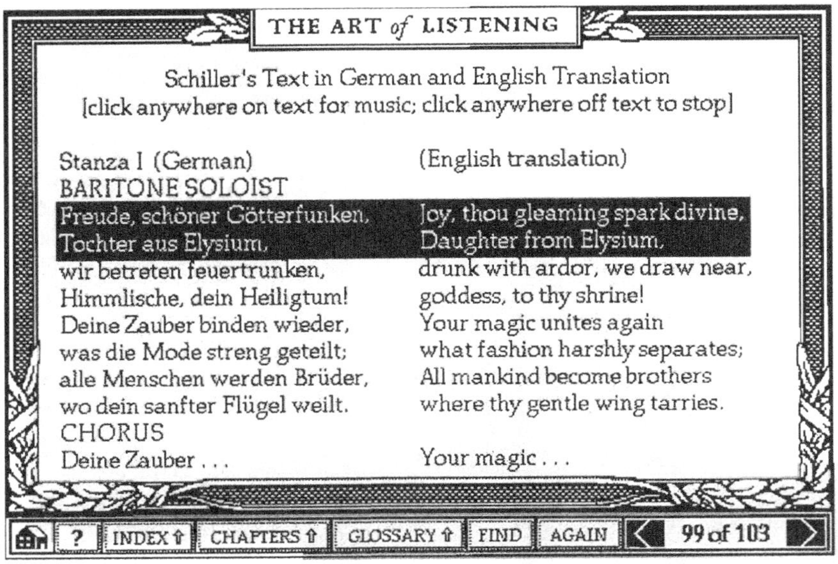

Robert Winter, *CD Companion: Ludwig van Beethoven, Symphony No. 9*, "The Art of Listening," screen 99.

Approximately one thousand images and examples accompany the music, including an explanatory visual account that flows along with the entire symphony (e.g., "the first of two closing themes, soft, legato, and lyrical"). Above, from the fourth movement, we see the German text of the soloists along with an English translation, both in parallel with the music, as reversed text shows the lines currently being sung.

These methods reveal musical complexities. Below, the simultaneous voices of a fugue are dissected, first by sounding out the separate lines one-at-a-time with computer tones and then in full orchestration—as we learn to hear and to distinguish among several parallel voices within the whole. And how pleasant that the ponderous frame (left and above), with its quaint laurel overgrowth, has finally vanished.[9]

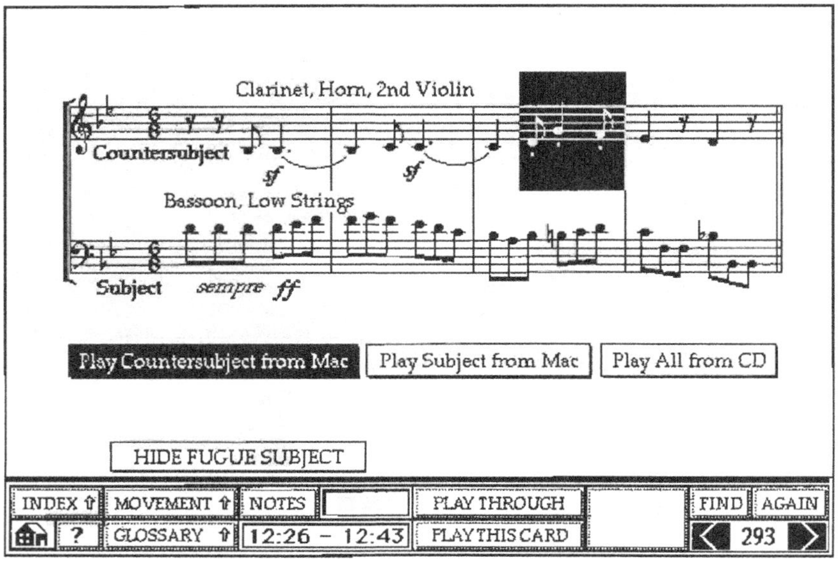

Robert Winter, *CD Companion: Ludwig van Beethoven, Symphony No. 9*, "A Close Reading, screen 293, fugue subject."

[9] The framing apparatus consumes 30% of the scarce area on the low-resolution computer screen. The enlargement below shows 11 different frames (leaving out the laurel growth) surrounding the text like Chinese boxes:

Four-pixel black line
Two-pixel white line
Two-pixel black line

Ten-pixel checkerboard

One-pixel black line
One-pixel white line
Two-pixel black line

Twenty-four pixels of white space

One-pixel black line
One-pixel drop shadow (two sides of box)
Five-pixel white space

After the frame finishes, only enough space remains on the screen to show 642 characters (image at far left), a competent showing for a computer display but terrible compared with real text, such as in books and newspapers, which have typographic densities (characters per unit area) 3 to 50 times greater than computer screens. On most computer displays, information is broken up into low-resolution clumps scrolling or flipping through time. Despite the thin content of some screens, this companion to Beethoven's Ninth Symphony—with its parallelism of text, image, and music—is a useful, natural, and endlessly patient teacher.

Here is a musical streams-of-story, an appealing history of "marketing trends and stylistic patterns in the development of pop/rock music." Topping the chart is a time-series that tracks sales of popular and rock music as a share of total record sales, although the names are not scaled in proportion to their contributions to the grand total. Bold letters indicate some 24 stylistic categories, fountains flowing into musical streams (e.g., **SHOCK ROCK**, lower left). Several fashions, including **BUBBLEGUM** and **SURF**, did not last, to the relief of a grateful world. In these overlapping parallel time-series, a few names of the 470 artists

Steve Chapple and Reebee Garofalo, *Rock 'N' Roll is Here to Pay: The History and Politics of the Music Industry* (Chicago, 1977), inside front and inside back covers. Concept and design by Reebee Garofalo; graphics by Damon Rarey; copyright 1975 by Robert L. Garofalo.

are repeated, as they resurface in fresh currents. The multiple, parallel flows locate music-makers in two dimensions—*linking* musical parents and offspring from 1955 to 1974, and *listing* contemporaries for each year.[10] With an intense richness of detail (measuring in at 20% of the typographic density of a telephone book), this nostalgic and engaging chart fascinates many viewers—at least those of a certain age. Also the illustration presents a somewhat divergent perspective on popular music: songs are not merely singles—unique, one-time, *de novo* happenings—rather, music and music-makers share a pattern, a context, a history.

[10] Among the missing are The Weavers, Pete Seeger, Bonnie Raitt, and Lou Reed and The Velvet Underground.

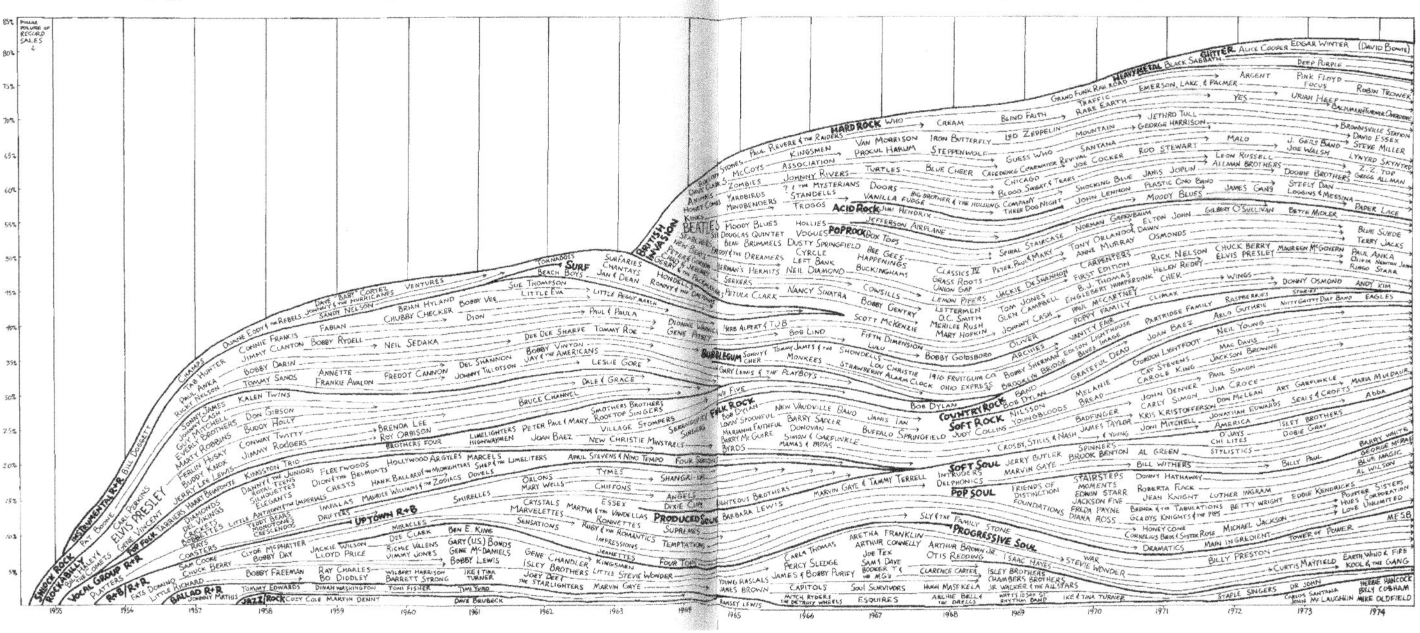

Multiple flows are traced in parallel against a common time-scale in this historic "cyclogram" narrative of the *Salyut 6* space flight, which orbited the Earth for 96 days in the longest space mission of its time (December 10, 1977 to March 16, 1978).[11] Prepared by the two Russian Cosmonauts Georgi Grechko and Yuri Romanenko aboard *Salyut 6*, the meter-long chart was laid out before the journey so that "in a single view it would reveal the entire flight program. We thought it would be handy and convenient to have such a chart aboard the space station." After only two weeks in orbit, however, the overview took on a new interpretation, becoming instead a constant reminder of the lengthy ordeal ahead. And so the orbiting cosmonauts redesigned their chart, first dividing the schedule into freshly marked weeks, counting up (1, 2, 3 . . . weeks completed) and counting down (14, 13, 12 . . . weeks remaining), then breaking up the timetable fractionally, adding marks at one-third of the voyage, one-half, two-thirds, and three-fourths. Their cyclogram eventually measured the demanding passage of time with fully *eight* methods, all plodding along in parallel: phases of the moon, holidays, weeks (red tick marks), fraction of total flight, dates (each newly completed day was colored with a red triangle), elapsed days, total weeks to go and total weeks finished. These tediously redundant counting

[11] This account is based on interviews with Cosmonaut Georgi Grechko (May 1994); his handwritten manuscript describing the cyclogram (Moscow, 1993); the detailed analysis of *Salyut 6* in James E. Oberg, *Red Star in Orbit* (New York, 1981), pp. 162–182; the biography of Grechko in Gordon Hooper, *The Soviet Cosmonaut Team* (Woodbridge, Suffolk, England, 1986), pp. 169–171; and the Sotheby's auction catalog, *Russian Space History: Property of the Industries, Cosmonauts, and Engineers of the Russian Space Program* (New York, December 11, 1993), items 122, 123, 124.

schemes were, however, as Georgi Grechko reports, "witless ploys that did not help much." Persisting in their information redesign, the cosmonauts finally folded the chart like an accordion so that it revealed no more than 15 days into the future: "The rest of the flight we unfolded the accordion, paying close attention so that the uncolored part of the cyclogram was never bigger than the colored. This made us more comfortable in this flight of world-record duration." Although their endurance record was surpassed, these two cosmonauts remain forever the first to redesign an information display while in outer space.

Transitions between day and night are shown by contours outlining gray bands of darkness and yellow bands of daylight, as the vertical axis shows the time of a single orbit (91 minutes, starting at the equator). This grid plots time by time: orbit time in minutes (vertical) by trip time in days (horizontal).[12] For example, on the 84th day reading up, one full orbit around Earth consisted of 20 minutes of daylight, then 40 minutes of night, and then 30 minutes more of daylight. All told, the cosmonauts experienced some 1500 sunrises and 1500 sunsets during their mission. Lines marked ТЕРМИНАТОР (terminator) show the beginning and end of total light; ИКВ (infrared vertical), the viewing method in partial light; and, at night, ПВКО, the method for navigating by the stars in darkness.

[12] Since time in orbit is interchangeable with distance, the cyclogram resembles a graphical timetable. For space-by-time and time-by-time grids, see Edward R. Tufte, *Envisioning Information* (Cheshire, Connecticut, 1990), pp. 32, 45, 97–113.

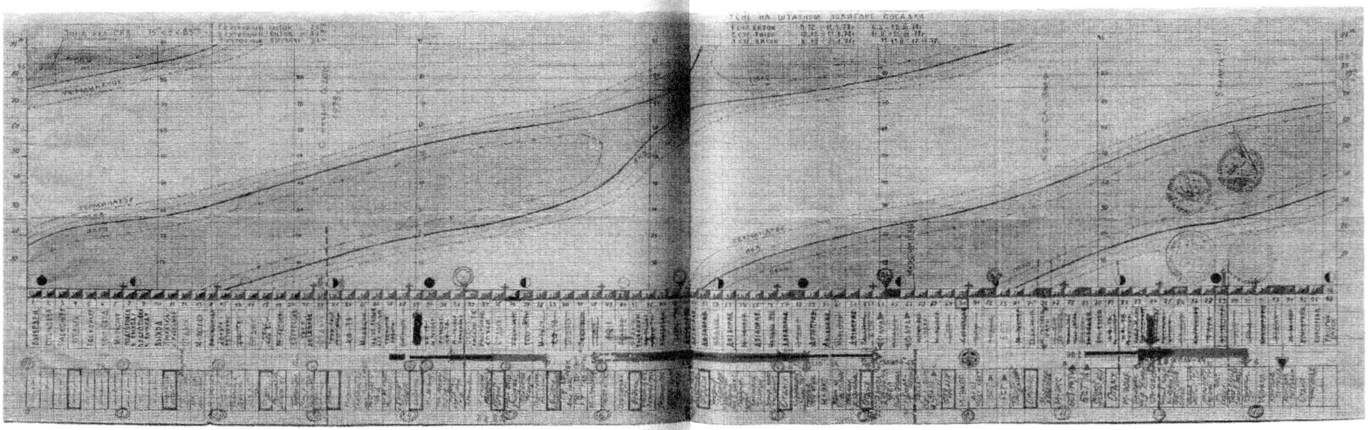

Timing cycle for ignition of engines to make orbit corrections: "Zone of corrective engines."

Happy New Year! С Новым годом! 1978г

Visit by *Soyuz 27*, January 10–16. Grechko caught a cold, probably from one of the guests. Visits are marked by solid red lines between the planned and actual schedules.

Shadow on site of landing.

A cargo ship brought up an electric muscle-stimulator (МИОСТИМУЛЯЦ) to supplement the daily exercise regime, which the cosmonauts were neglecting.

Markings for space-mail delivery.

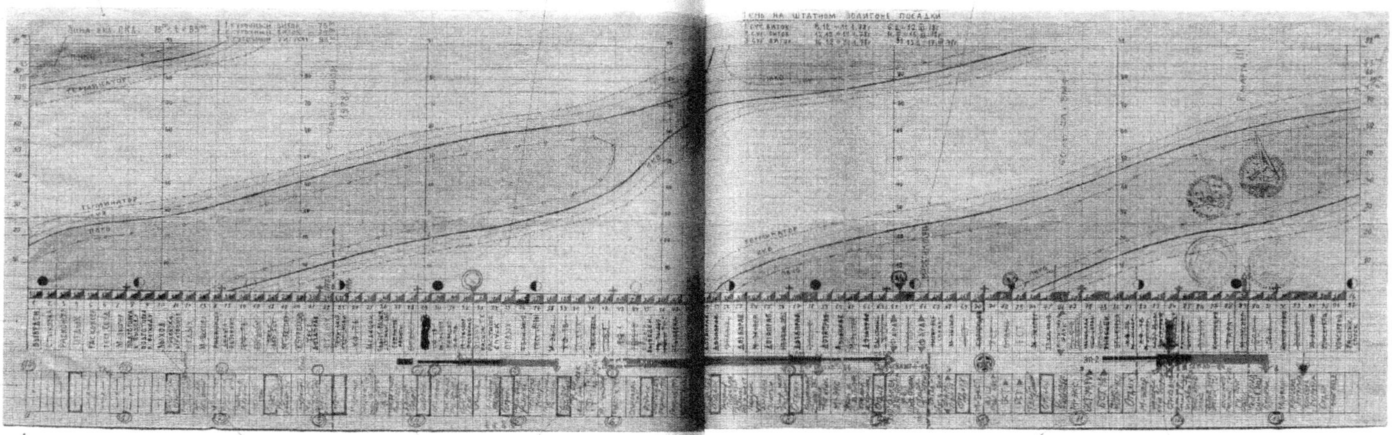

Grechko and Romanenko arrive at space station *Salyut 6*, via *Soyuz 26*.

Actual activity for each day, recorded in red pen, while in orbit. As the flight goes on, the pen tip squashes and broadens.

Planned activity for each day, schedule prepared prior to flight, with variously colored pens. Note the many deletions and changes (e.g., [handwritten sample]).

Red boxes (ОТДЫХ ОТДЫХ, rest) indicate every 6th day of rest (revised schedule).

Spacewalk (ВЫХОД ВЫХОД, exit) by Grechko on December 20. When Grechko returned, Romanenko decided on the spur of the moment to look around outside. While pushing himself through the tight airlock, he lost his grip and began to drift away from the spacecraft! Romanenko's line was not secure; at the last second, Grechko caught hold of the line and pulled his floating colleague to safety. The cosmonauts waited until months after their return to Earth before saying anything to authorities about their near-disaster. Romanenko went on to spend 430 days in space on this and later flights.

Visit by *Progress 1*, January 20 to February 6. This automated cargo ship, without a crew, brought equipment, fresh fruit, mustard, horseradish, bread, music tapes and a cassette recorder, clothes, linen, air filters, an atlas, newspapers, and mail.

"БАНЯ" СПВП (БАНЯ) "Steamroom," a traditional Russian bath. Surrounded by quotation marks, the word is used here sarcastically, mocking the engineering jargon (the acronym СПВП) that calls a space-bath "A System of Taking Water Procedures."

On a television broadcast of February 10, Grechko noted a birthday: "Hello everyone. Today marks the one hundred and fiftieth birthday of Jules Verne, the remarkable French writer. There's hardly a person who hasn't read his books, at any rate not among the cosmonauts, because Jules Verne was a dreamer, a visionary who saw flights in space. I'd say this flight too was predicted by Jules Verne."

A visiting cosmonaut quietly mentioned to Romanenko that Grechko's father had just died. Romanenko decided to tell Grechko only after they were safely back to earth.

This red arrow celebrates the 84th day in orbit when *Salyut 6* equaled the space endurance record set five years earlier by America's *Skylab 4*. A thick red line extends from the 84th to the 91st day, when Grechko and Romanenko exceeded the previous endurance record by the officially necessary ten percent.

February 23, the 60th anniversary of the Soviet Army and Navy. The cosmonauts observed notable dates to mark the progress on their very long stay in space.

8 марта !!! March 8, International Women's Day. Grechko and Romanenko made a television broadcast and prepared mail to send back on *Soyuz 28*.

Visit by *Soyuz 28*, March 2–10. In addition to a Czech cosmonaut (who became the first non-Soviet, non-American in space), the visitors brought a package with fresh onions, garlic, Bulgarian peppers, lemons, apples, milk, gingerbread, and honey.

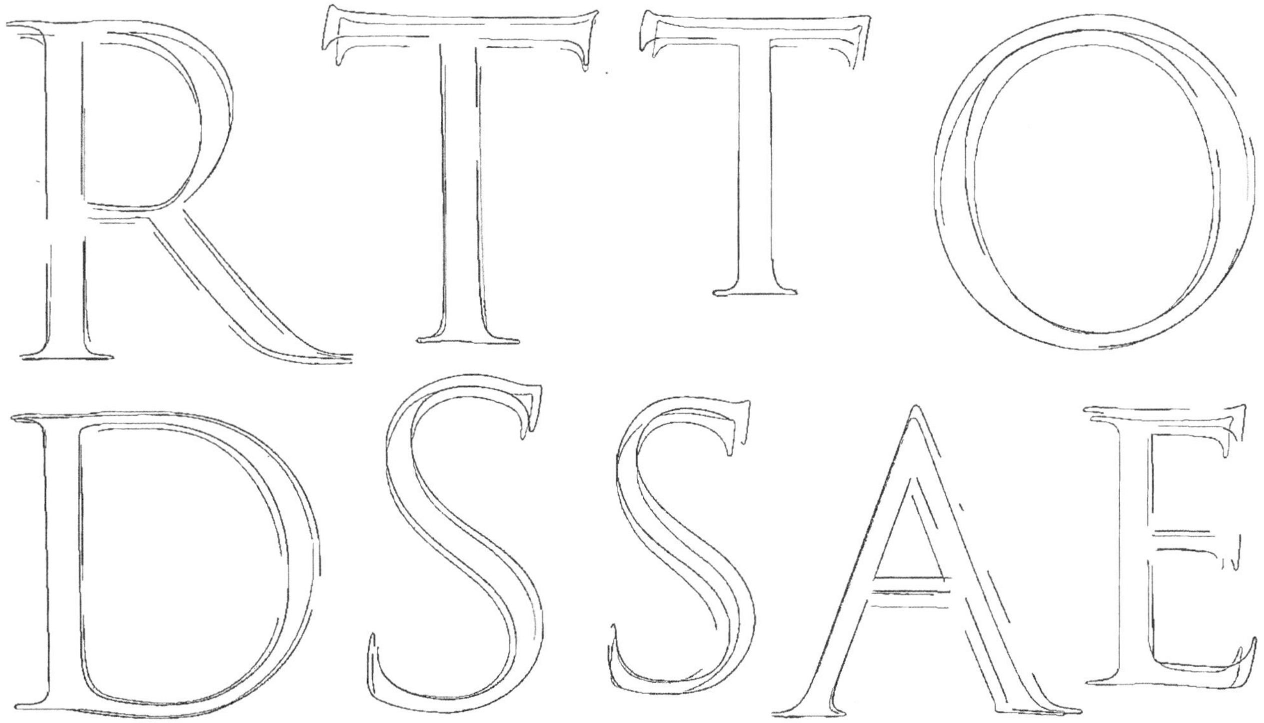

Edward M. Catich, *The Origin of the Serif: Brush Writing and Roman Letters* (Davenport, Iowa, 1968), pp. 53–57.

Parallel designs abound in the study of letterforms, as repeated and subtle comparisons are made across complex shapes. Edward Catich provides evidence (above) that the Roman letters of the Trajan Inscription varied from occurrence to occurrence, indicating that uniform stencils were not used to reproduce the letters but rather that they were painted with a brush as a guide for the stonecutters. To intensify comparisons and to reveal variations in shapes, the letters are shown in *superimposed parallelism*, directly overlapping rather than side by side, a bit like Repton's architectural before/after but without a flap. The black outline shows one instance of the letter, the gray another, similar to the parallelism of tracing paper. Breaks in the lines reflect damage to the original letters in stone.

Below, side-by-side parallelism depicts the brushstrokes for painting the letter H as used by sign writers. Three pairs of letters juxtapose the wrong and correct methods, comparing sequence, direction, and path followed by the brush. "It is clear which stroke sequence in making H is quicker and preferable, and which H represents the possibility of smearing over wet strokes," concludes Catich, master scholar of the serif and one-time Chicago signwriter.[13]

[13] Catich, *The Origin of the Serif*, p. 275.

Catich, *The Origin of the Serif*, pp. 274–275. Redrawn.

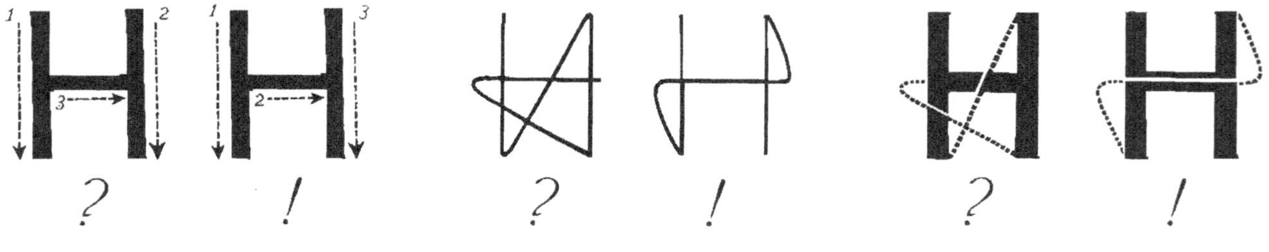

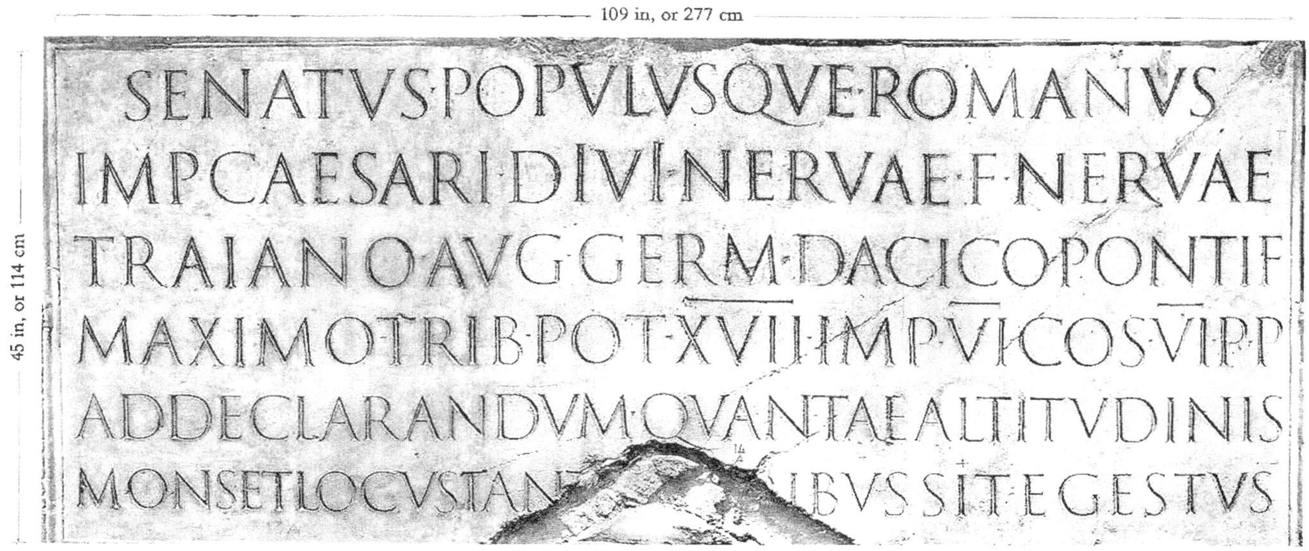

Above, cast of the Trajan Inscription from Catich, *The Origin of the Serif,* p. 82. Below, interpoints from Catich, p. 58 (rearranged); pp. 18, 58, 188–190 are the sources for the discussion here. Dimensions of the inscription are from Edward Johnston, *Writing & Illuminating, & Lettering* (London, 1932), pp. 409–410.

In the Trajan Inscription, words are separated by *interpoints* (the Romans did not space words). Catich pulls out these interpoints and arrays them in a parallel sequence, as spatial adjacency helps to compare the differing shapes of the same element. The idea is to depict variation, which here again testifies to the use of the brush (causing non-uniformities) rather than the stencil in sketching the inscription:

Another parallel sequence of images appears below in this reproduction from the modern classic on the letterforms of Luca Pacioli. Beginning in the seventh line, five small grids are arranged in series to portray geometric grids for constructing Roman letters. Here designer Bruce Rogers and writer Stanley Morison have seamlessly integrated the images into their text. Providing a pleasant contrast with the large ornate initial-letter, the sequence of five small grids is the visual parallel of five words:

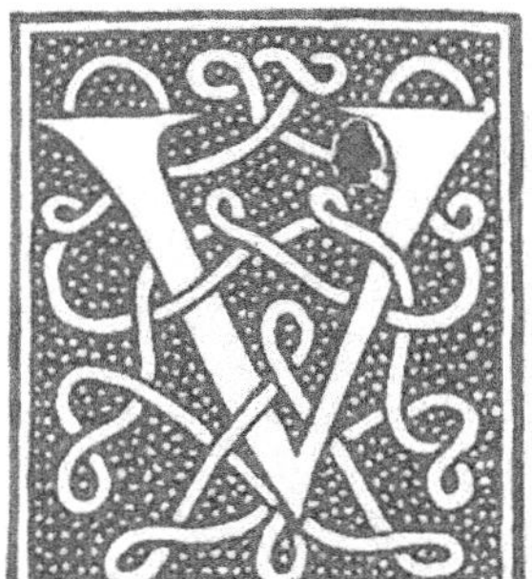
ERY few of us, familiar as we are with the description "Roman Letter"—and the thing itself—understand at first why a thing so simple to look at should be so difficult to make, and above all, why it should be considered necessary to erect a geometrical scaffolding with □ ○ ⊠ ⊞ and ■ in support of an obviously simple construction. Yet simple as the A B C looks we all know it is difficult because we have all tried at one time or another to make a set of capitals, or at least to write our name . . .

Stanley Morison, *Fra Luca de Pacioli* (New York: The Grolier Club, 1933), p. 77. An account of this beautiful book and its printing of 390 copies is found in Joseph Blumenthal, *Bruce Rogers: A Life in Letters* (Austin, 1989), pp. 147–152.

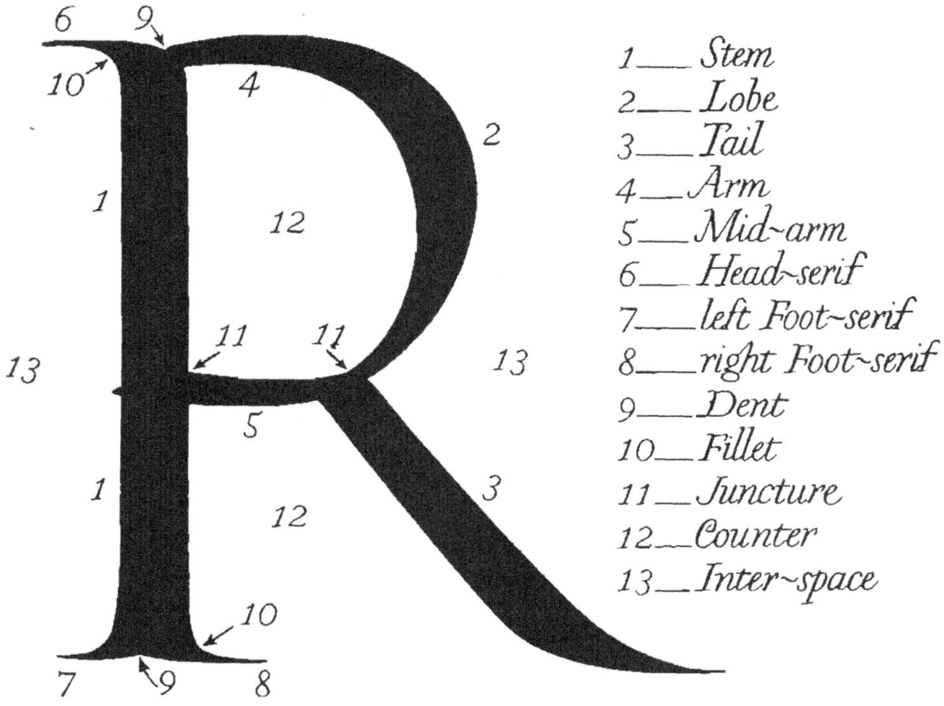

Edward M. Catich, *Letters Redrawn from the Trajan Inscription in Rome* (Davenport, Iowa, 1961), plate 24.

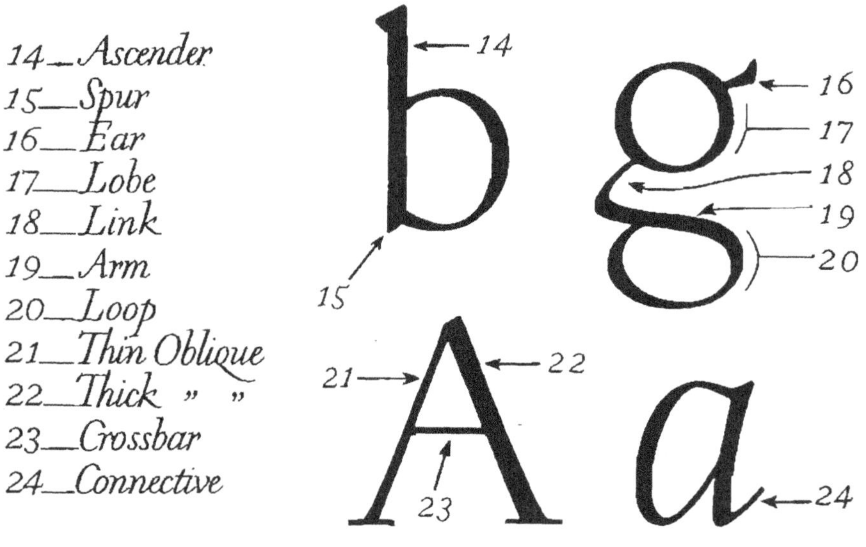

Above, a code connects image and label: *image→number→number→noun* or, reading the other direction, *noun→number→number→image*. Some 48 numbers loiter around the images and words. This one-time code is unique, an exclusive for this illustration. Such codes prevent us from seeing each part and its name right together, an efficient merger which assists our memory. In short, codes obstruct parallelism; replacing codes with direct labels unifies the information. Codes and keys are sometimes necessary for highly complex data (geological field maps, for example),

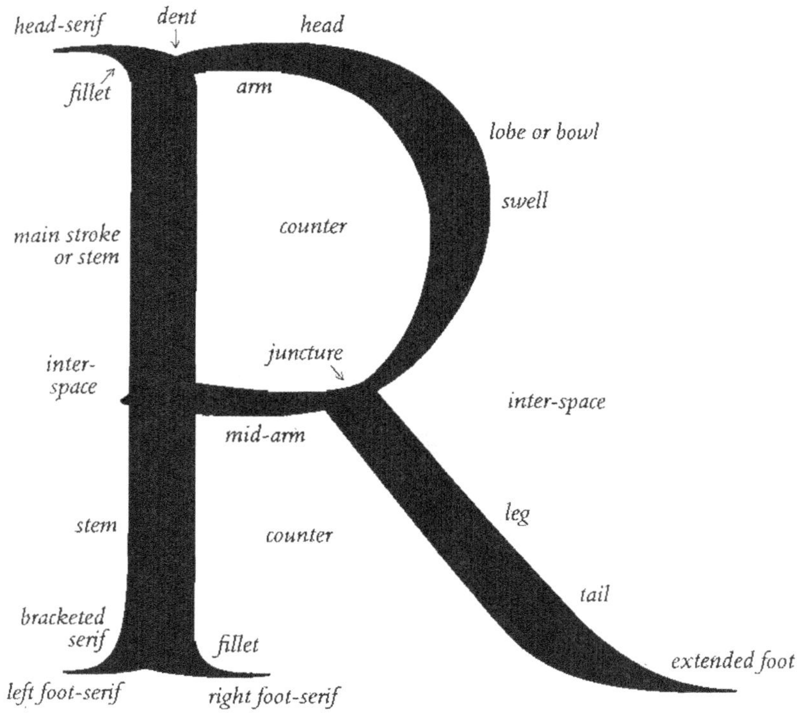

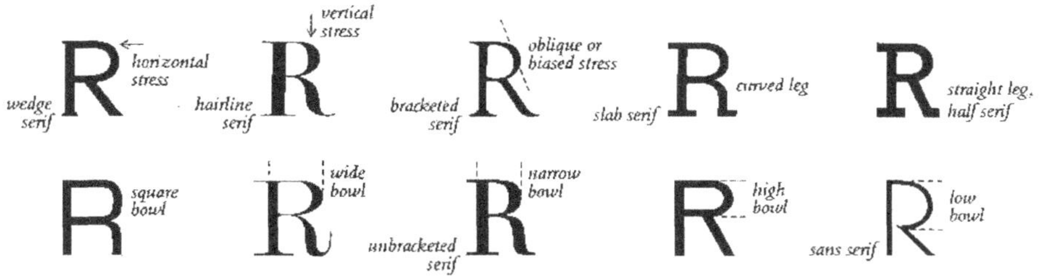

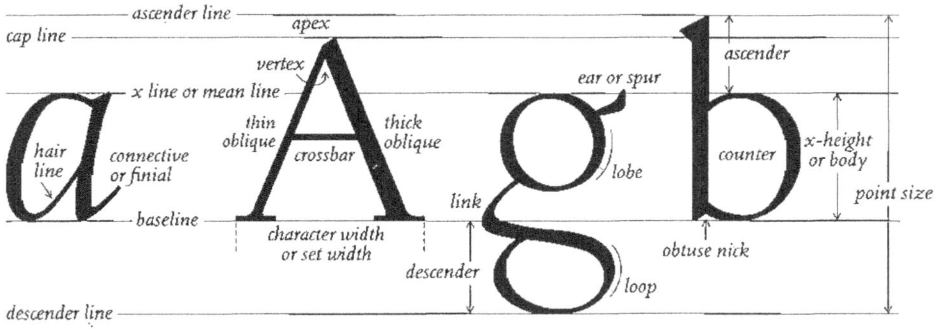

Sources for the terms in the revised illustration are: Matthew Carter, letter, November 9, 1992; Edward M. Catich, *Letters Redrawn from the Trajan Inscription in Rome* (Davenport, Iowa, 1961), plate 24; Stanley C. Hlasta, *Printing Types and How to Use Them* (Pittsburgh, 1950); Alexander Lawson, *Printing Types: An Introduction* (Boston, 1971); Ruari McLean, *Typography* (London, 1980); Christopher Perfect and Gordon Rookledge, *Rookledge's International Typefinder* (London, 1983); Walter Tracy, *Letters of Credit* (Boston, 1986); Hugh Williamson, *Methods of Book Design* (New Haven, 1983); Daniel Berkeley Updike, *Printing Types* (Cambridge, Massachusetts, 1922, 3rd edition, 1966).

or when there are a great many scattered elements (the photograph of 146 astronomers on the next page). As publication-layout programs for computers finally eliminate the arbitrary distinction between word and image, it will be easier to construct the artwork for direct labels, merging elaborate images with detailed text. Above, the redesign uses direct labels. And, instead of the original 24 letter-parts, a total of 66 directly named elements are now indicated—in a tight parallelism of image and noun.

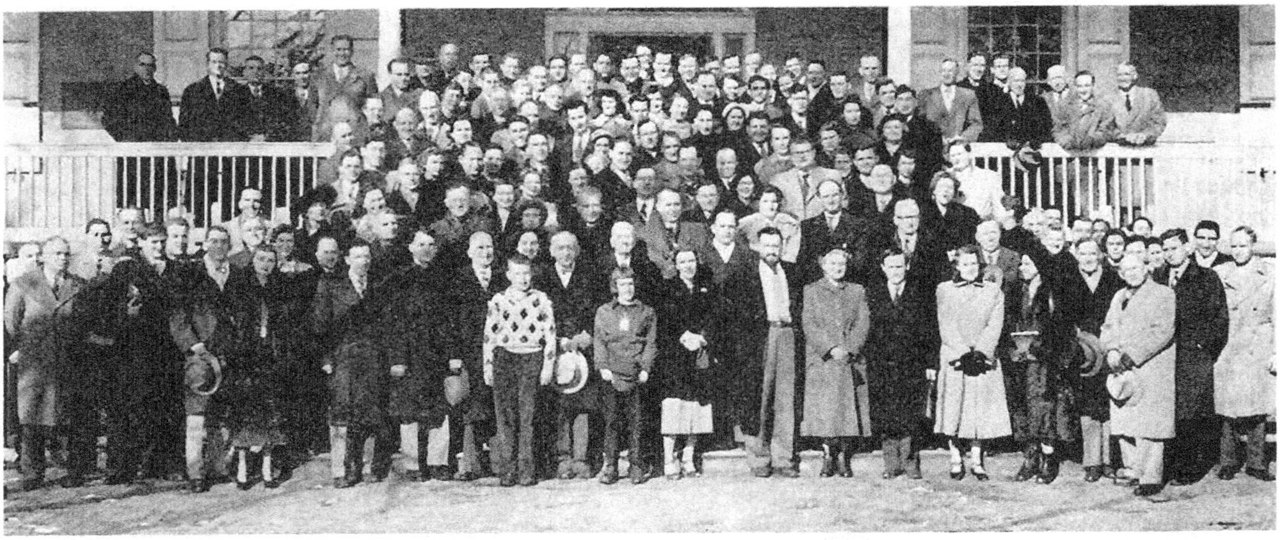

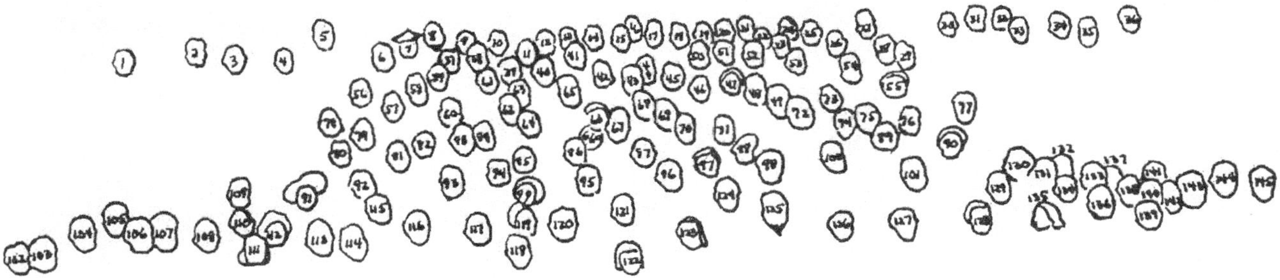

1. Dimitroff
2. Cameron
3. Adams
4. Layzer
5. Irwin
6. Binnendijk
7. Rieber
8. Smiley
9. Dyer
10. Keller
11. Vyssotsky
12. Mitchell
13. Protheroe
14. Deutsch
15. Matthews
16. T. G. Cowling
17. Wildt
18. Sitterly
19. Orral
20. Hoag
21. Wyller
22. Mrs. Merrill
23. Mrs. Henry Smith
24. McKrosky
25. Merrill
26. Henry Smith
27. Bestul
28. Scott
29. Savedoff
30. Yeagley
31. R. H. Wilson
32. Ashbrook
33. Sutton
34. Alden
35. Schopp
36. Heines
37. Weston
38. Harlan Smith
39. Mrs. Harlan Smith
40. Keenan
41. Stearns
42. Sarah Lee Lippincott
43. Munch
44. Mrs. Stearns
45. Miss Roman
46. King
47. Mrs. Gossner
48. Davis
49. Streeter
50. Cuffey
51. Mrs. Sitterly
52. Naqvi
53. Gossner
54. Mrs. Savedoff
55. Mrs. Lewis
56. Leavitt
57. Brouwer
58. Federer
59. Miss Morrow
60. Miss Hutzler
61. Huffer
62. Malitosky
63. Wood
64. Seyfert
65. Blitzstein
66. Miss Reilly
66a. Miss Allen
67. Haddock
68. Hagen
69. Thomas
70. Whipple
71. Harris
72. Eggen
73. Miss Williams
74. Mrs. Mayall
75. Hall
76. Miss Jones
77. Owren
78. Wolff
79. Rabinowitz
80. Hynek
81. Eckert
82. Mrs. Eckert
83. Omer
84. Yoss
85. Miss Weber
86. Miss Underhill
87. Allan Cook
88. Mrs. Whipple
89. Ice
90. Mrs. Menzel
91. Mrs. van de Kamp
92. Mrs. Baker
93. Aller
94. Mrs. Federer
95. Schilt
96. Miller
97. McLaughlin
98. Mrs. Woodward
99. Mrs. Deutsch
100. Goldberg
101. Menzel
102. Barton
103. Whitford
104. Duke
105. Green
106. van de Kamp
107. Baker
108. Chamberlin
109. Spitzer
110. Chester Cook
111. Mrs. Chamberlin
112. Miss Damkoehler
113. Hertz
114. Kameny
115. Kiess
116. Warwick
117. Joy
118. Toni Federer
119. Miss Schwartzman
120. Nassau
121. Robertson
122. Barbara Federer
123. Mrs. Miller
124. Millman
125. Edmondson
126. Miss Barney
127. Schwarzschild
128. Mrs. Schwarzschild
129. Gingrich
130. Miss Swope
131. Stuecklen
132. Kerr
133. Clemence
134. Miss Hill
135. Miss Wright
136. Olivier
137. Bappu
138. Miss Johns
139. Zinszer
140. Yowell
141. Milford
142. Mrs. Owren
143. Epstein
144. Wrubel
145. de Jonge

Captions to pictures, legends on maps, labels, and codes are partial representations of the image itself, running in parallel with the image. Above, we see a mix of photograph, drawing, number, and word that make *five* partial, parallel descriptions. It all began at the 84th meeting of the American Astronomical Society in Haverford, Pennsylvania on December 27, 1950, when a photograph was taken of the 146 attendees. They arranged themselves somewhat haphazardly—certainly not in a few orderly rows—on the steps of Founders Hall. What with this

Popular Astronomy, 59 (February 1951), pp. 58–59.

chaotically two-dimensional and dense clustering of faces in the photograph, a conventional typographic caption would not do. Instead this diagram arrays numbered heads as an intermediary code, linking the picture to names of the 146 attendees.[14] Five descriptions of the astronomers run in parallel: (1) photograph, (2) hand-drawn heads, (3) handwritten numbers, (4) list of numbers sequencing the names, (5) list of names. The disembodied heads were traced with a thick pencil onto paper laid over the photograph, resulting in unarticulated lumps that look pretty much alike. Several landmark heads, nonetheless, enable viewers to find their way: the large hat 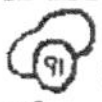, the profile , another hat , and the goatee 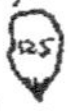 all serve as differentiating signs to give the eye reference points in locating other faces.

[14] That is, 145 as counted to the end of the list, plus 66a, Miss Allen.

Encodings can easily complicate matters. These drawings of sunspots from Christopher Scheiner's *Rosa ursina sive sol* make a complexifying use of letters as codes. Sunspots are lettered A, B, C . . . recording the

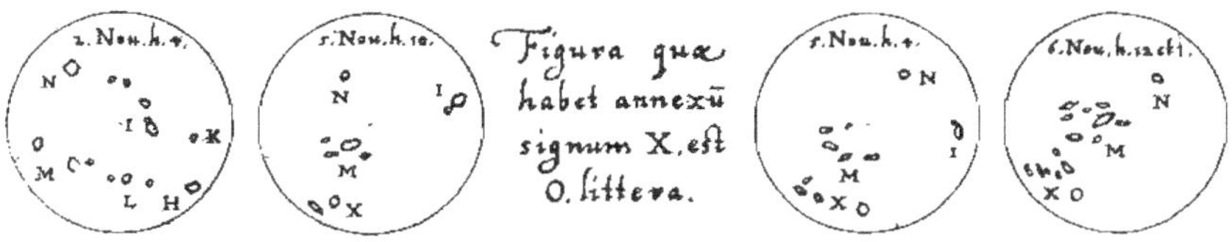

Christopher Scheiner, *Rosa ursina sive sol* . . . (Bracciani, 1626–1630), p. 63.

order that each spot was observed. Spot and letter are parallel. Codes sometimes cause confusion; here, the sunspot marked with the letter O is accompanied by another mark indicating that the letter itself is not a sunspot! Thus X means "This O does not represent a sunspot, rather this O labels another O-like mark which does represent a sunspot." Description of this apparatus in the Latin original (above) breaks up the sequence, and may induce viewers to meditate upon quirky labeling schemes and theories of meaning rather than upon sunspots. In practice, probably about two-thirds of such codes can be avoided, by means of thoughtful design, direct labels (rather than intermediate codes), and close integration of explanatory text with images.

In this curious diagram at right, the images and letter-labels run in tight parallel. Rather than serving as a code linking text and figure, the letters represent themselves as vowels. Thus this singular account—you heard it here first—of the vowel pipe:

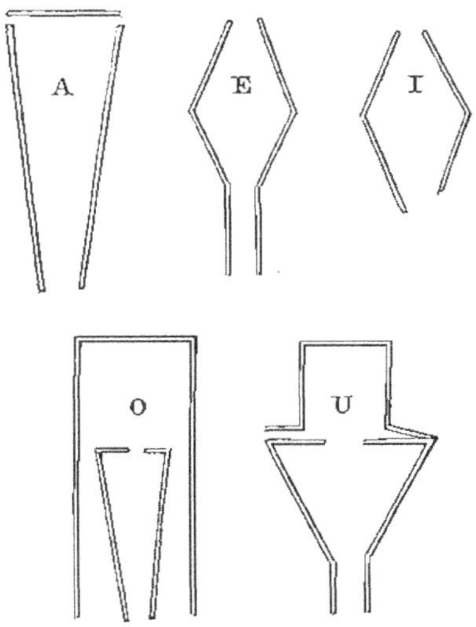

> Toward the end of the nineteenth century a bold and almost successful attempt was made to construct a talking automaton. In the year 1779, the Imperial Academy of Science at St. Petersburgh proposed as the subject of one of their annual prizes an inquiry into the nature of vowel sounds, A, E, I, O, and U, and the construction of an instrument for artificially imitating the sounds. This prize was gained by M. Kratzenstein, who showed that all the vowels could be distinctly pronounced by blowing through a reed into the lower ends of the pipes of the annexed figures, where the corresponding vowels are marked on the different pipes.[15]

[15] David Brewster, *Letters on Natural Magic* (London, 1833), p. 207.

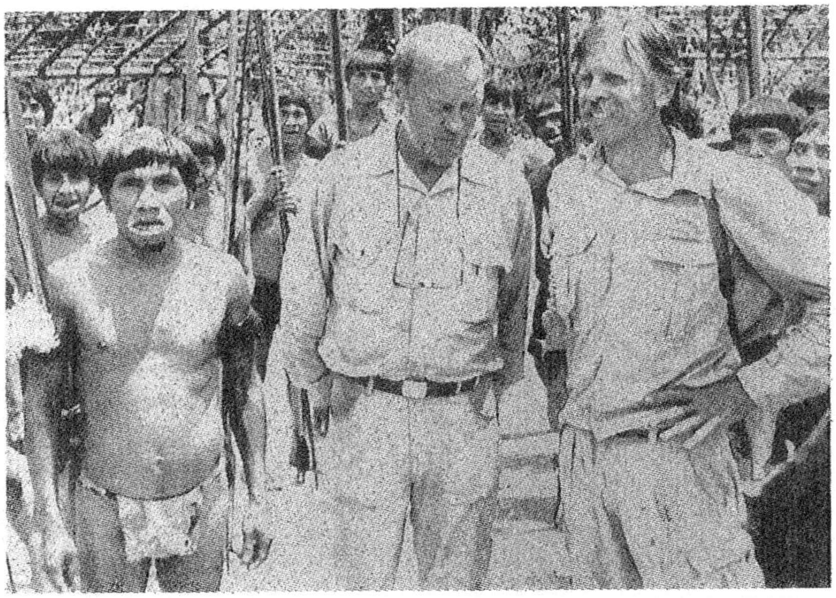

James Brooke for The New York Times

Napoleon A. Chagnon, left, American anthropologist, and Charles Brewer-Cariás, Venzuelan naturalist at Konabuma-teri, one of 10 Yanomami villages that remained isolated from outside world.

The New York Times (September 18, 1990), p. c8, as reported in *Lies of Our Times*, 1 (October 1990), p. 2.

INSTANCES of faulty parallelism occur in design as well as in language. Above, the orderly parallelism that connects caption with photograph unfortunately comes all undone. The man at left in the loin cloth is *not* Napoleon Chagnon, American anthropologist, no matter what the caption says. The man in the loin cloth was evidently invisible to the writer of the caption.

Faulty parallelisms are found in Repton's before-and-after displays, as many of his redesigns show substantial embellishments quite beyond the scope of architectural work. In the paradise of *after*, stylishly dressed visitors watch as new deer graze in new meadows—elements all missing from the grim *before*.[16] Below left, only a few tiny boats appear in the seascape of a *before* flap; at right, in *after*, the proposed renovations are enhanced with a fine view of a grand total of nine boats sailing about, presumably attracted by the improved landscape.

[16] Another Repton before/after: "Where in the unimproved view servants swept up horse droppings in front of the house, in the improved view Sir Windsor Hunloke and his wife promenade on the terrace." Stephen Daniels, *Fields of Vision* (Princeton, 1993), p. 85.

Humphry Repton, *Designs for the Pavillon at Brighton* (London, 1808), p. 41.

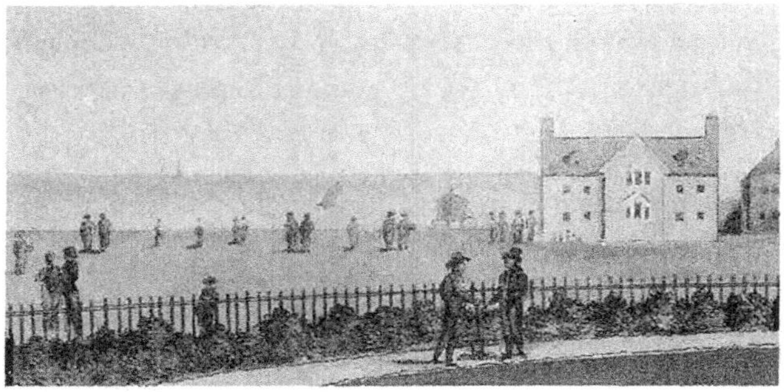

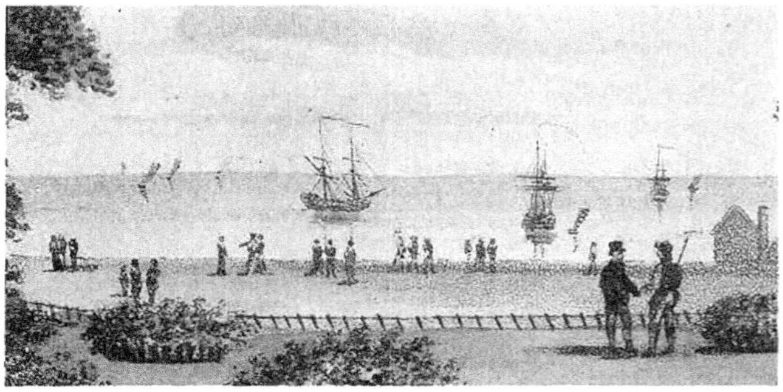

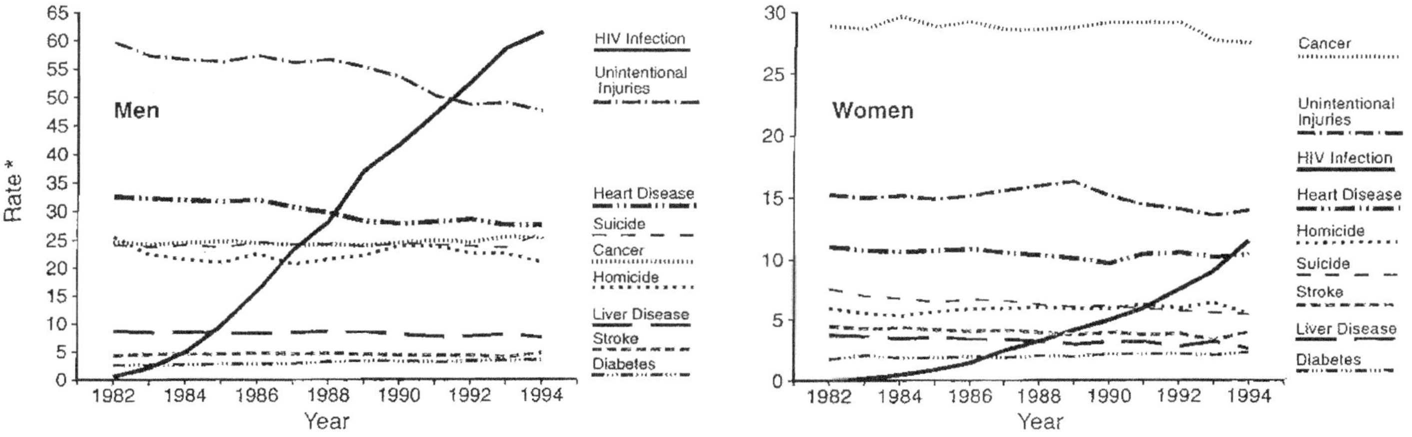

*Per 100,000 population

Two unparallelisms—one effective, one inaccurate—appear in these graphs on the major causes of death from 1982 to 1994 among men (left) and women (right) aged 25 to 44. First, the epidemic of HIV-AIDS infection is shown to surge upward against the steady background levels of other causes of death, as the dark solidity of the HIV line contrasts to the dot-dash lines. Compared with the seven other leading causes of death, the distinctive and unparallel slopes of the HIV-AIDS lines are properly accented. There is, however, a regrettable lack of parallelism in the vertical scales of death-rates for men and for women. Equal vertical distances represent different quantities, which makes visual comparisons of slopes (rates of change) between the two graphs most difficult and also obscures the fact that men in this age group have an overall risk of death more than double that of women. And placing the denominator of the rate in a footnote undermines the substantive reading of the measurement scales. In any case, why put the numerator in one place and the denominator in another?

"Update: Mortality Attributable to HIV Infection Among Persons Aged 25–44 Years—United States, 1994," *Morbidity and Mortality Weekly Report*, 45 (February 16, 1996), pp. 122–123.

EMBODYING inherent links and connections, parallelism synchronizes multiple channels of information, draws analogies, enforces contrasts and comparisons. Our examples have inventoried all sorts of design strategies that collate like with like: pairing, orientation, simultaneity, overlap, superimposition, flowing together on a common track, codes, pointer lines, sequence, adjacency, analogy, similar content. Parallelism provides a coherent architecture for organizing and learning from images—as well as from words and numbers, the allies of images. And by establishing a structure of rhythms and relationships, parallelism becomes the poetry of visual information.

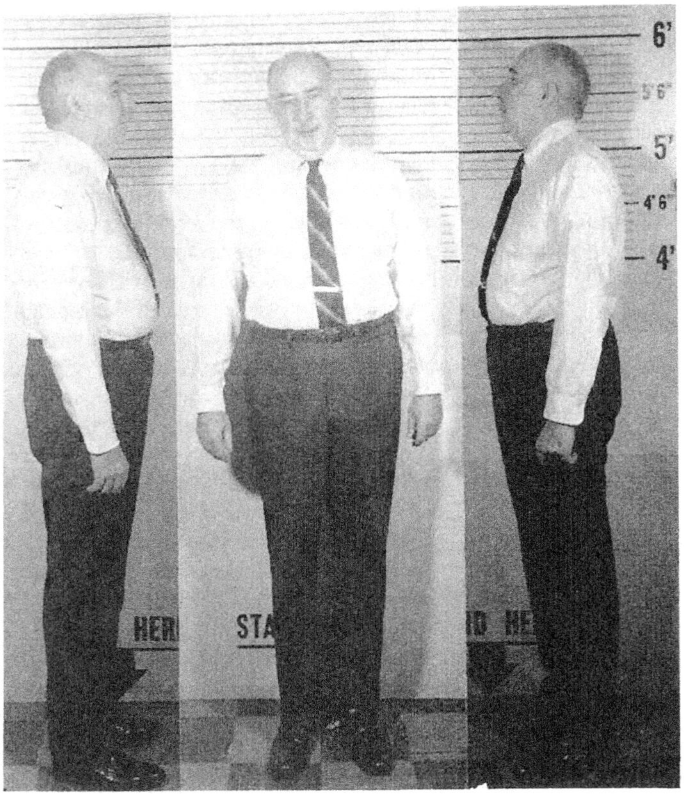
6'
5'6"
5'
4'6"
4'

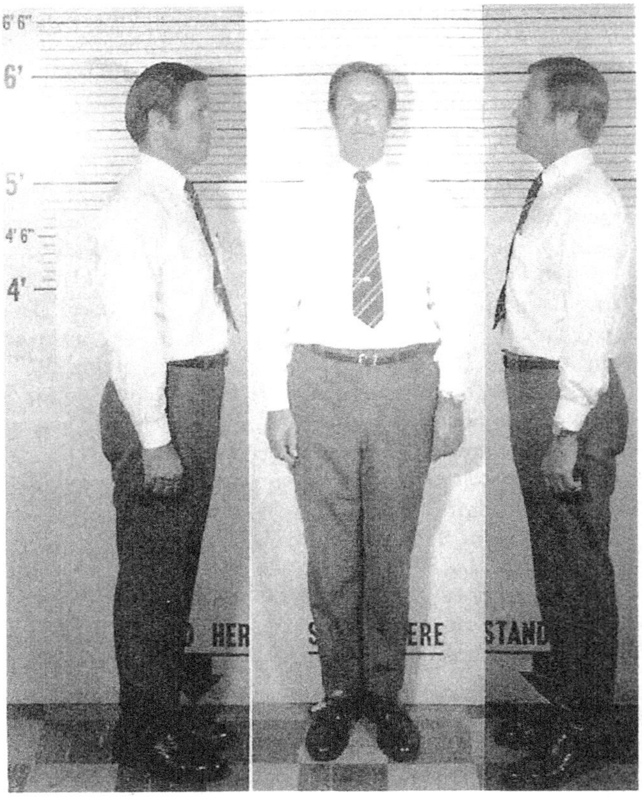
6'6"
6'
5'
4'6"
4'

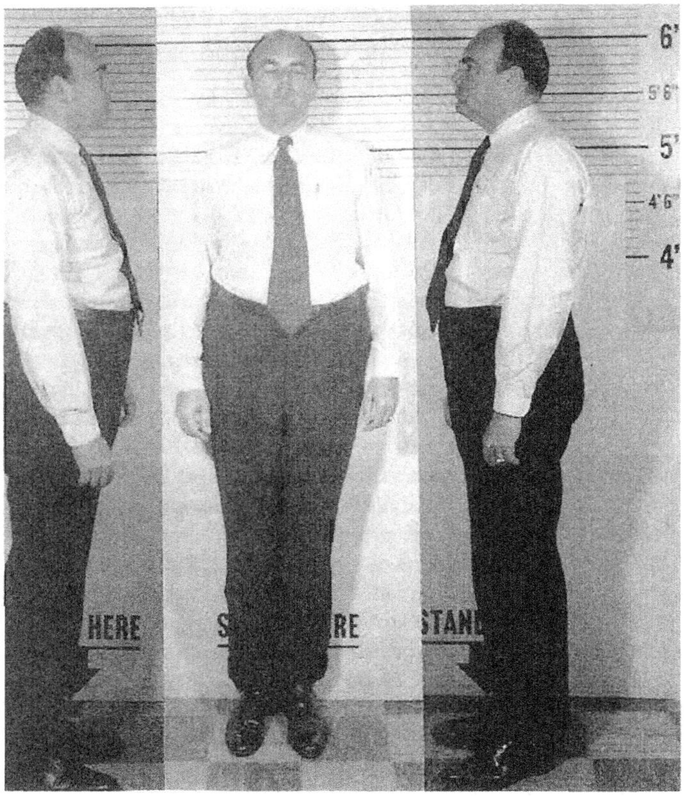
6'
5'6"
5'
4'6"
4'

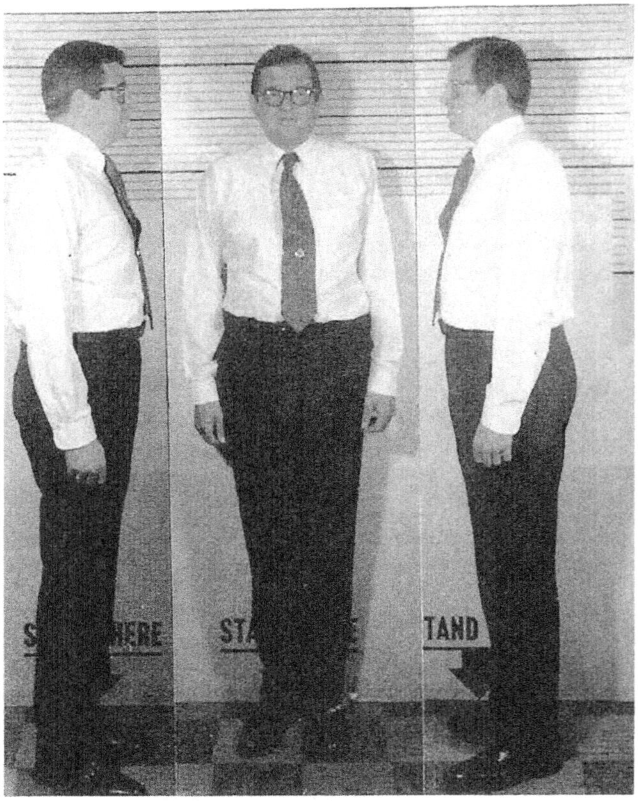

6 *Multiples in Space and Time*

MULTIPLE images reveal repetition and change, pattern and surprise—the defining elements in the idea of *information.*

Multiples directly depict comparisons, the essence of statistical thinking.

Multiples enhance the dimensionality of the flatlands of paper and computer screen, giving depth to vision by arraying panels and slices of information.

Multiples create visual lists of objects and activities, nouns and verbs, helping viewers to analyze, compare, differentiate, decide—as we see below with 12 hands in 12 positions for making 12 sounds.

Multiples represent and narrate sequences of motion.

Multiples amplify, intensify, and reinforce the meaning of images.

Clockwise, from top left: four of President Richard Nixon's closest associates: John Mitchell, H. R. Haldeman, Charles Colson, and John Ehrlichman, photographs taken when they were arraigned on March 9, 1974, after their indictments in the Watergate cover-up.

Manoel da Paixão Ribeiro, *Nova Arte de Viola* (Lisbon, 1789), appended figure v.

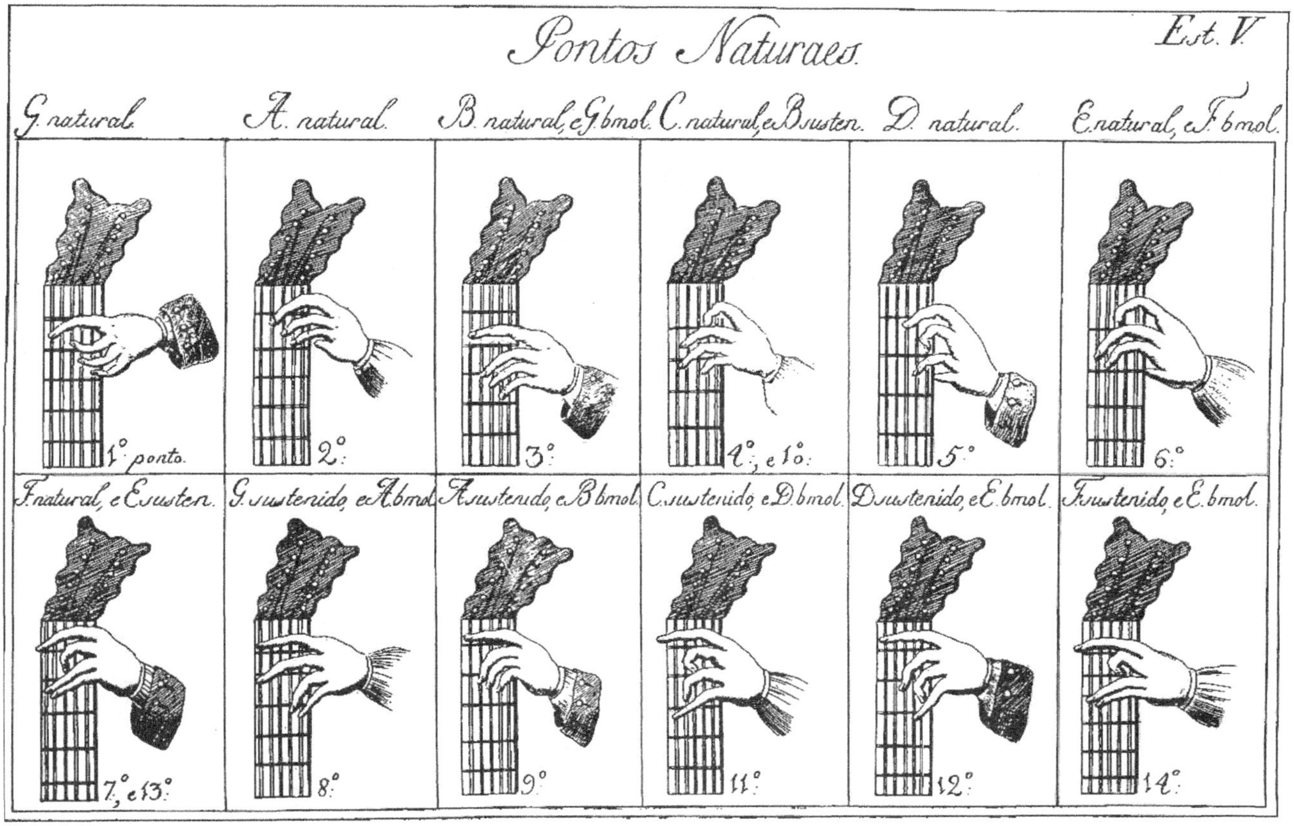

CHRISTIAAN HUYGENS reported his discoveries about Saturn in *Systema Saturnium*, published in 1659. Multiple images are used throughout to reveal new findings, narrate movements of the planet and its satellites, and catalog previous research. Below, a double-page spread shows a sharp, clear view of the rings of Saturn—the first such view, ending years of misconception that had started with Galileo's fragmentary glimpse and incorrect interpretation of the rings in 1610. Also below, a text-image sequence describes a series of nightly observations of the motion of Titan, Saturn's largest satellite. Galileo had used the same design, many years earlier, in his description (at right) of the four inner satellites of Jupiter.[1] A tight collation of explanatory text and small drawings, much like a scientific notebook, the Galileo-Huygens design narrates a sequence of observational slices in a time-series, as changes in the multiple images represent the verbs of motion.

In an another superb display of data, Huygens used multiple images to record and compare previous views of Saturn along with the names

Die vigeſimaquinta hora 1. min: 40. ita ſe habebat

Ori. * * ○ Occ.

conſtitutio, aderant enim duæ tantum Stellæ ex orientali plaga, eæque ſatis magnæ. Orientalior à media diſtabat min: 5. media verò à Ioue min: 6.

Die vigeſima ſexta hora 0. min: 40. Stellarum coordinatio eiuſmodi fuit. Spectabantur enim Stellæ

Ori. * * ○ * Occ.

tres, quarum duæ orientales, tertia occidentalis à Ioue: hæc ab eo min: 5. aberat, media verò orientalis ab eodem diſtabat min: 5. ſec: 20. Orientalior verò à media min: 6. in eadem recta conſtitutæ, & eiuſdem magnitudinis erant. Hora deinde quinta conſtitutio ferè eadem fuit, in hoc tantum diſcrepans, quod

Ori. * * •○ * Occ.

[1] Galileo Galilei, *Sidereus Nuncius* (Venice, 1610), pp. 19–30; above, p. 24.

Christiaan Huygens, *Systema Saturnium* (The Hague, 1659), pp. 24–25.

24 CHRISTIANI HVGENII

Forma verò anſarum diſtincte hac vice percipi potuit, quam figura hæc exhibet;

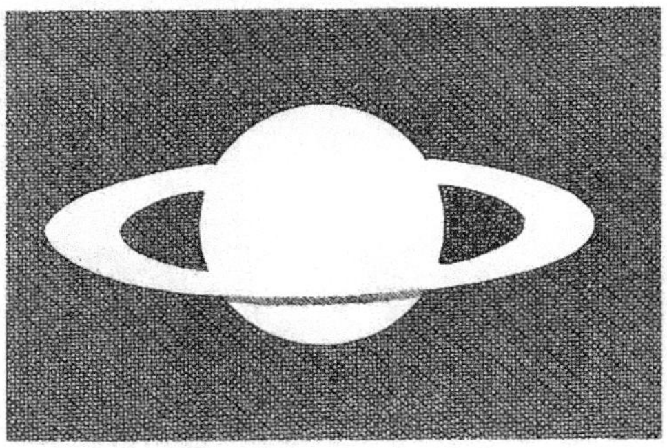

atque ea ad ultimam uſque harum obſervationum talis extitit.

24 Febr. hora dimidia poſt mediam noctem, comes erat in mediocri diſtantia, orientem verſus, rectâ anſarum paulo inferior.

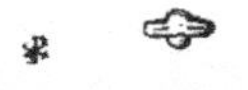

25 Febr. horâ eadem orientalis denuo comes cernebatur, una Saturni diameter ab ipſo remotus.

14 Martij

SYSTEMA SATVRNIVM. 25

14 Martij, hora 12, comes recta fere infra Saturnum obſervatus, unius circiter diametri longitudine diſtans; paulum tamen verſus occidentem declinabat. *Comes infra Saturnii tranſire viſus.*

16 Martij, hora 11, ad latus occiduum poſitus erat, fere in maxima diſtantia, inferiorque paulo eâ quæ per anſas ducitur.

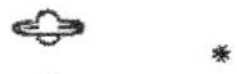

21 Martij, hora 11, rurſus ad eandem partem conſiſtebat comes, motu latitudinis integra Saturni diametro ſupra anſarum lineam elatus, longitudinis motu tantum dimidia diametro diſtans. *Idê ſupra Saturnii tranſiens.*

22 Martij, horæ quadrante ante undecimam; rurſus integra diametro ſuperior erat rectâ anſarum, ac fere ſupra orientalis anſæ extremam cuſpidem collocatus.

26 Martij, hora 10½ comes in maxima diſtantia videbatur; quam accuratè hac vice dimenſus, inveni inter comitem centrumque Saturni intervallum trium ſcrupulorum primorum, 16 ſecundorum.

Hucuſque obſervationes, & plures quidem quam neceſſe fuerat, recenſui; rem gratam tamen iis me facturum ratus, qui triennio iſto ſimul forſitan mecum novo

D Planetæ

of the astronomers who published these views. Depicted below are 13 interpretations of Saturn—all of them wrong—based on observations made before Huygens solved the puzzle of the rings. A foldout from *Systema Saturnium*, this multiple visually reviews the scientific literature from 1610 to 1645. All these squashed images appear to be stuck flat on the projection plane, as the rings were read two-dimensionally rather than as three-dimensional objects encircling the planet:

> Astronomers offered all manner of geometrical contrivances to explain the planet's behavior—two crescents attached to a tumbling planet; two large, dark satellites (the dark triangles) and two bright ones outside of those; or, perhaps an egg-shaped planet with four black spots. The most popular idea was some sort of vaporous exhalation of the planet condensed into an ever changing cloud or a thin elliptical corona that rotated with the planet.[2]

People can see more clearly if they have the right idea, as our cases of the cholera epidemic and Challenger accident suggest. Reasoning about planets in general and then developing a geometric model based on his discovery of Titan, Huygens became the first to see the rings as rings.

[2] James Elliot and Richard Kerr, *Rings: Discoveries from Galileo to Voyager* (Cambridge, 1984), p. 23. My other guides are A. F. O'D. Alexander, *The Planet Saturn* (London, 1962); and H. J. M. Bos, "Huygens, Christiaan," in Charles C. Gillispie, ed., *Dictionary of Scientific Biography* (New York, 1981), vol. 6, pp. 597–613.

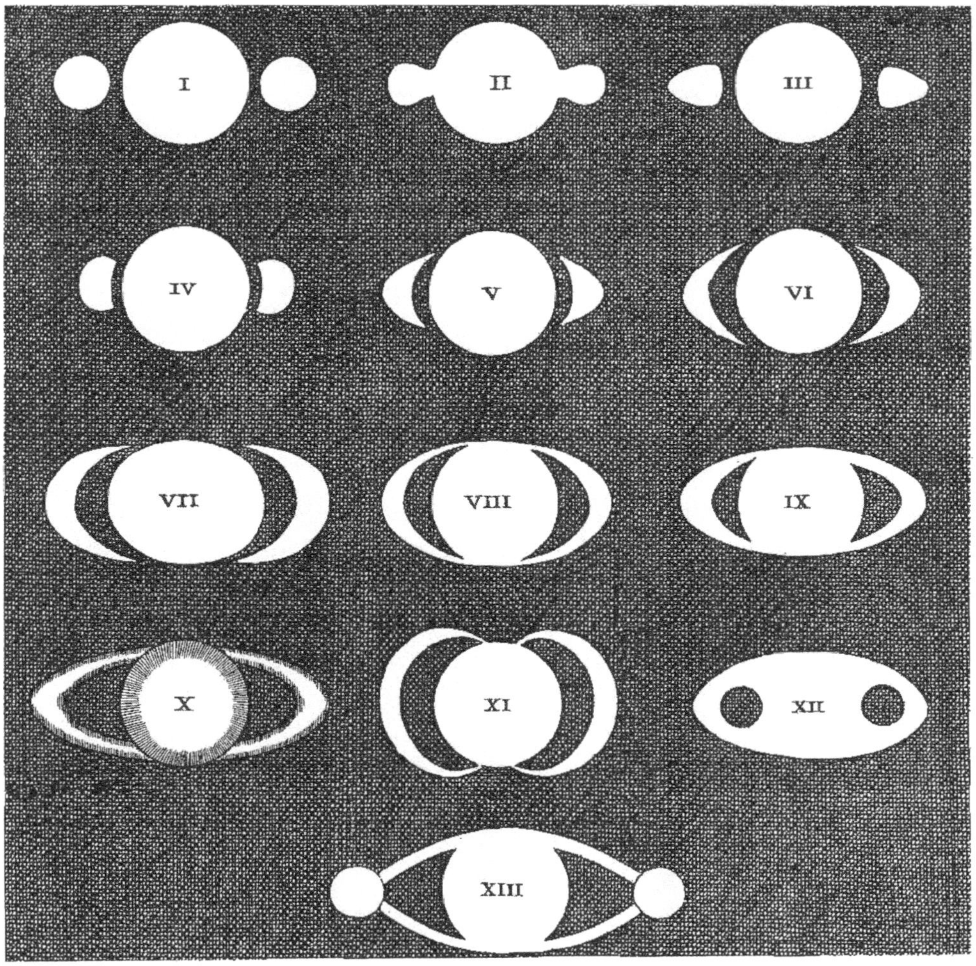

Christiaan Huygens, *Systema Saturnium* (The Hague, 1659), foldout plate at pp. 34–35. The observations shown are:

I. Galileo, 1610
II. Scheiner, 1614
III. Riccioli, 1641 or 1643
IV–VII. Hevel, theoretical forms
VIII–IX. Riccioli, 1648–1650
X. Divini, 1646–1648
XI. Fontana, 1636
XII. Biancani, 1616; Gassendi, 1638, 1639
XIII. Fontana and others, 1644, 1645.

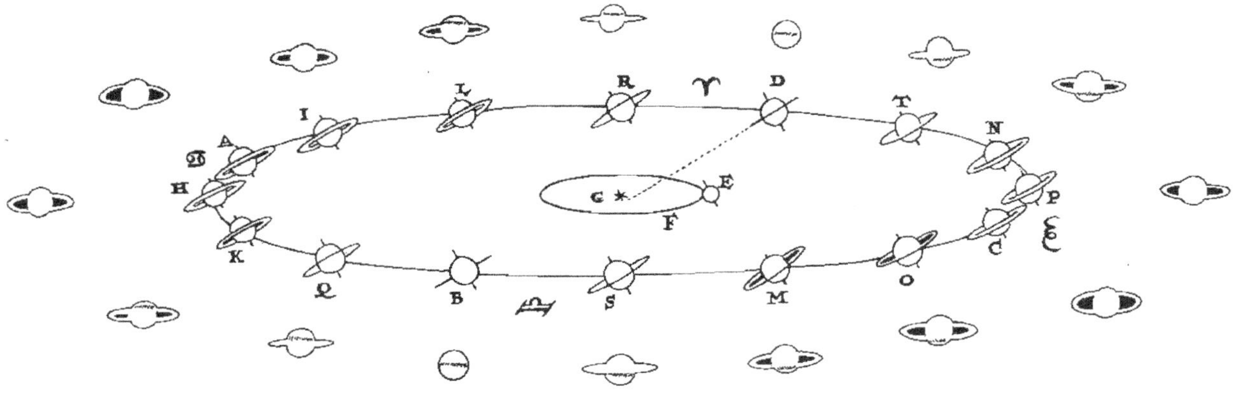

In this exquisite multiple from *Systema Saturnium*, the small inner ellipse traces Earth's annual journey around the Sun; the larger ellipse shows Saturn in orbit (some 29.5 Earth-years long) as viewed from the heavens. The outermost floating images depict Saturn as viewed through telescopes located on Earth—so that each matched pair of Saturns compares Earth-view with heaven-view. All told, we have 32 Saturns, at different locations in three-space and from the perspective of two different observers.[3] Huygens' substantive idea is to explain the periodic changes in Saturn's rings, when viewed from Earthbound telescopes. As the diagram indicates, twice each Saturn-year, the thin ring becomes oriented edgewise relative to Earth and thus disappears to our eyes—an explanation resolving a 50-year mystery, as astronomers (including Galileo) were baffled by long-run changes in the apparent shape of Saturn. Imaginative and original, this display is a classic, an exemplar of information design.

Huygens presents a series of still images in order to depict motion. To resolve such discontinuous spatial representations of continuous temporal activity, viewers must interpolate between images, closing up the gaps.[4] In the diagram above, about 1.8 Earth-years elapse between Saturns, an insignificant interruption because the depicted motion is smooth, deliberate, incremental. Representation of more abrupt and irregular motion, in contrast, demands a quicker tempo and greater density of time-sampling to build up a sequence of still images. For example, Muybridge shows 18 separate photographs to capture a few seconds of leapfrog. On the other hand, to demonstrate the theory of

Christiaan Huygens, *Systema Saturnium* (The Hague, 1659), p. 55.

[3] On visual narratives, see Kurt Weitzmann, *Illustrations in Roll and Codex: A Study of the Origin and Method of Text Illustration* (Princeton, 1947); H. A. Groenewegen-Frankfort, *Arrest and Movement: An Essay on Space and Time in the Representational Art of the Ancient Near East* (Chicago, 1951); and Scott McCloud, *Understanding Comics* (Northampton, 1993), pp. 60–117.

[4] Below, viewers *extrapolate* to an implicit prior image, as the poor diver is poked by a rescue float. Different time-states are also suggested by the verbs (*grabbed, will flip, counterbalanced*) of the caption.

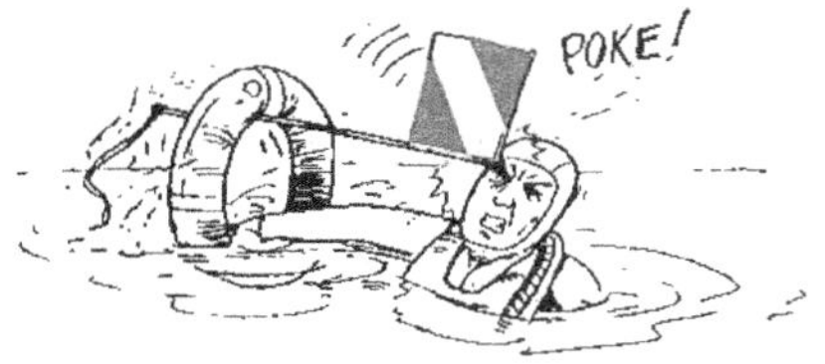

An inner tube grabbed suddenly will flip upright unless counterbalanced.

It would be better to express the moral of the diagram positively: *Grab an inner tube with both hands to keep it balanced.* From Albert Pierce, *Scuba Life Saving* (Champaign, Illinois, 1985), p. 149.

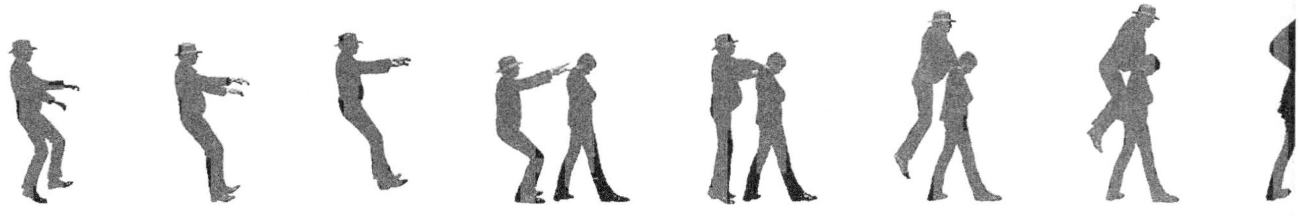

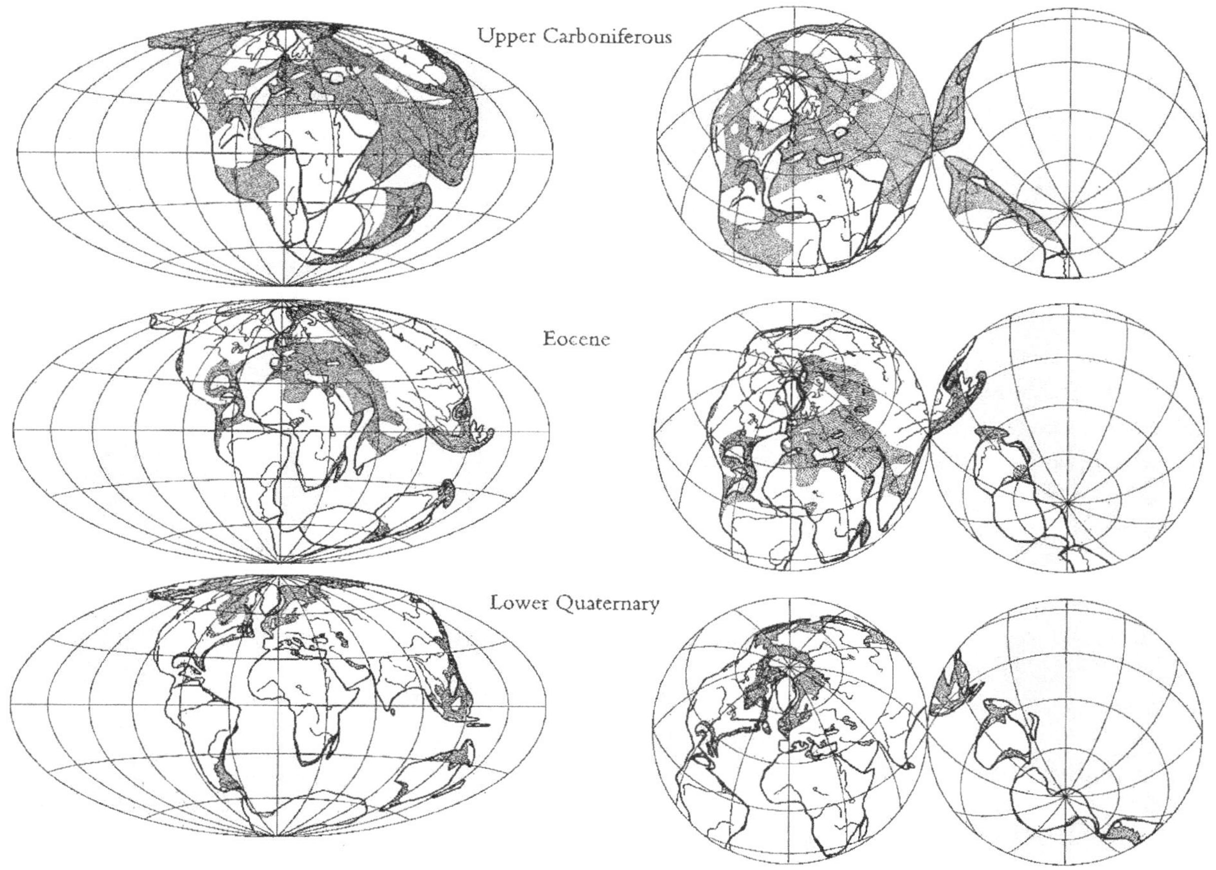

Alfred Wegener, *Die Entstehung der Kontinente und Ozeane* (Braunschweig, 1915; 4th edition, 1929), pp. 18–19. The dark, stippled areas are shallow seas. Redrawn.

continental drift, Alfred Wegener placed projections of the Earth on a time-scale about 300 million years long, showing the original unified land mass ("Pangea") breaking up into today's continents.

For still-land images that depict movement, space replaces time as the sequencing dimension. The adjacency of images helps us to assess change and possibly rates of change within each image and between images in sequence—and we can do so at our own pace. Sequences of still images suffer the obvious (though no less important for being so) loss of the experience of the passage of time, the loss of the rates and rhythms of actual motion. In addition, that loss is sometimes magnified by a design error: many still-land multiples depicting motion omit any explicit time-scale. Dequantification all over again.

Eadweard Muybridge, *Animal Locomotion* (Philadelphia, 1887), plate 169, "Jumping over boy's back (Leapfrog)." Redrawn.

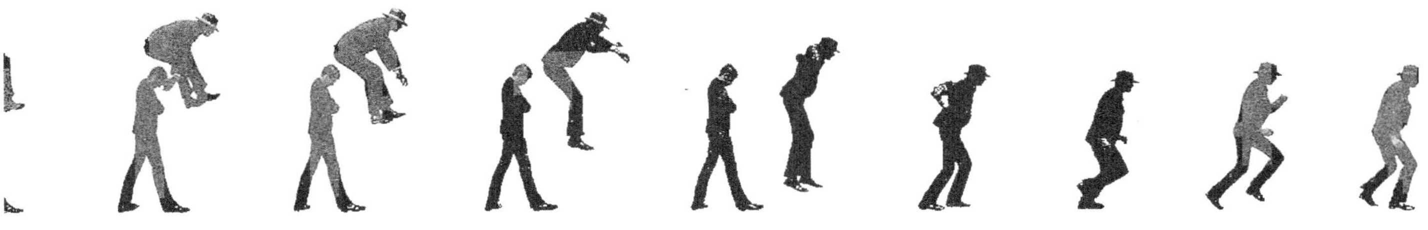

Multiples help to monitor and analyze multi-variable processes—ordinary occurrences in medicine, finance, quality control, and large-scale industrial and engineering operations. By providing a quick, simultaneous look at a continuing flow of different measurements, multiples help sort out the relevant substance from a flood of numbers.

Consider the conventional medical record, the patient's chart. For decades, medical treatment has been documented in folders stuffed with handwritten notes, laboratory reports, orders, print-outs, forms, referral letters, and an occasional identification tag from a transfused unit of blood or implanted prosthesis. For some hospitalized patients, a flow-sheet (similar to a spreadsheet) tabulates measurements; every time a reading is taken, however, another row is opened, a clumsy way to organize a data grid. Charts and flowsheets are bulky, difficult to file and retrieve, and sometimes even illegible. Medical records are gradually being computerized, making them more legible but hardly more comprehensible—since data are as easily lost in pages of print-out as in tangles of handwriting. These data dumps accumulate bits and pieces of information for administrative, regulatory, financial, legal, and clinical purposes. Largely a device for storage (a write-only memory!), the chart was not designed with the medical treatment of the patient in mind.

The page at right shows a *graphical* view of patient status, an overlay summary of the traditional medical record designed primarily to assist in the clinical care of the patient. Illustrated is a long and complex history, involving two medical and two psychiatric problems. Some 24 small images depict laboratory readings, medicines, and x-rays (showing an improvement in a cloudy lung). The legend at near right describes the basic graphical element in the multiple. A common horizontal time-scale, strongly emphasizing recent events, orders the flow of data. On the vertical scale, all measurements are referenced to normal limits (within the whiskered band); the most recent reading is shown both numerically and graphically (in red). Each column of multiples generally represents each medical or psychiatric problem; the lefthand column deals with pneumonia, for example. Thus data are seen in short-run and long-run contexts, and in relation to other measures (allowing, say, comparisons up and down a column between dosages and responses).

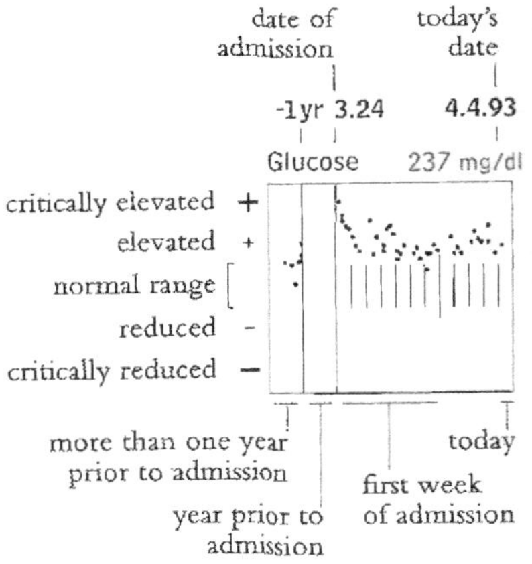

Combining overview with detail, this one-page, high-resolution set of multiples makes sense of thousands of items (the spreadsheet for this display contains 11,616 cells and 1,786 values) now scattered throughout standard medical records. Such graphical summaries will be especially helpful during case conferences or teaching exercises; all the participants, each with a copy, can quickly assess the history and treatment—with an improvement in the rate of information transfer of perhaps 10 to 20-fold compared with the standard talk talk talk presentation.[5]

This architecture—blending quantitative multiples, narrative text, and images—may prove useful for monitoring other data-rich processes.

[5] These two pages are based on Seth M. Powsner and Edward R. Tufte, "Graphical Summary of Patient Status," *The Lancet*, 344 (August 6, 1994), pp. 386–389; also Seth M. Powsner and Edward R. Tufte, "Summarizing Clinical Psychiatric Data," *Psychiatric Services*, 48 (November 1997), pp. 1458–1461. This architecture and the associated computer program received U.S. patent number 5,640,549 on June 17, 1997.

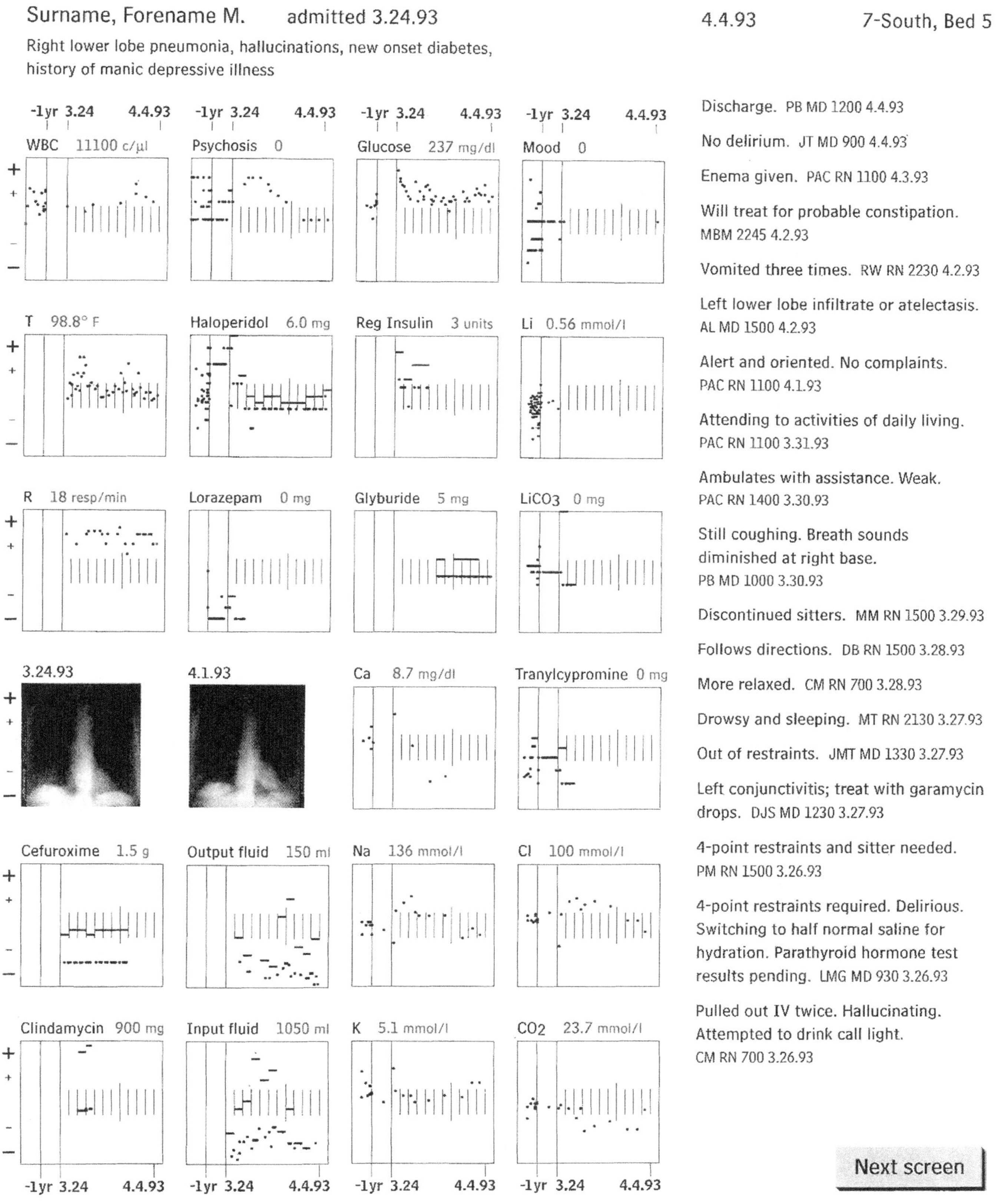
Surname, Forename M. admitted 3.24.93
4.4.93
7-South, Bed 5
Right lower lobe pneumonia, hallucinations, new onset diabetes, history of manic depressive illness
-1yr 3.24 4.4.93
WBC 11100 c/μl
Psychosis 0
Glucose 237 mg/dl
Mood 0
T 98.8° F
Haloperidol 6.0 mg
Reg Insulin 3 units
Li 0.56 mmol/l
R 18 resp/min
Lorazepam 0 mg
Glyburide 5 mg
LiCO3 0 mg
3.24.93
4.1.93
Ca 8.7 mg/dl
Tranylcypromine 0 mg
Cefuroxime 1.5 g
Output fluid 150 ml
Na 136 mmol/l
Cl 100 mmol/l
Clindamycin 900 mg
Input fluid 1050 ml
K 5.1 mmol/l
CO2 23.7 mmol/l
Discharge. PB MD 1200 4.4.93
No delirium. JT MD 900 4.4.93
Enema given. PAC RN 1100 4.3.93
Will treat for probable constipation. MBM 2245 4.2.93
Vomited three times. RW RN 2230 4.2.93
Left lower lobe infiltrate or atelectasis. AL MD 1500 4.2.93
Alert and oriented. No complaints. PAC RN 1100 4.1.93
Attending to activities of daily living. PAC RN 1100 3.31.93
Ambulates with assistance. Weak. PAC RN 1400 3.30.93
Still coughing. Breath sounds diminished at right base. PB MD 1000 3.30.93
Discontinued sitters. MM RN 1500 3.29.93
Follows directions. DB RN 1500 3.28.93
More relaxed. CM RN 700 3.28.93
Drowsy and sleeping. MT RN 2130 3.27.93
Out of restraints. JMT MD 1330 3.27.93
Left conjunctivitis; treat with garamycin drops. DJS MD 1230 3.27.93
4-point restraints and sitter needed. PM RN 1500 3.26.93
4-point restraints required. Delirious. Switching to half normal saline for hydration. Parathyroid hormone test results pending. LMG MD 930 3.26.93
Pulled out IV twice. Hallucinating. Attempted to drink call light. CM RN 700 3.26.93
Next screen

Relying on the links of parallelism, well-crafted multiples provide high-resolution views of complex material. Illustrations of postage-stamp size are indexed by a category or a label, sequenced in time like the frames of a movie, or gathered along a fresh dimension not contained in each small element. For a broad range of problems in presenting numbers and images, small multiples will serve quite well. Since many slices of information are displayed within the eyespan, alert viewers may be able to detect contrasts and correspondences at a glance—uninterrupted visual reasoning. And some multiples, like good graphics of all kinds, are worth more than a glance; careful viewing may reveal subtle differences among the elements.

Fine distinctions in letterforms, for example, appear in the panel at near right: ten geometric constructions of the letter A, published from 1460 to 1529. These compass-and-rule constructions, developed in the Italian Renaissance, attempt to rationalize and make uniform the early inscriptional Roman letters (the Trajan Inscription was hand-painted and then cut into stone in 112 A.D.). The lines lay out a geometry for the systematic production of an entire alphabet. This methodical geometry is sometimes broken, however, in order to draw elegant brushlike curves of variable stroke-width; for these A's, perhaps a few of the serifs are fudged.

At far right, a redrawn panel of ten letters repairs several flaws in the original panel at near right. In the original, three A's are filled and seven are not, thereby creating two distinct—and meaningless—visual clusters (which vanish in the redrawing). Accidental communalities in design can easily induce false groupings in the eyes of viewers, who are often busy searching for visual hints that help to boil down, organize, group, and otherwise make sense of multiple images. False clusterings can result from inexpert use of color; for example, the icons of the upper computer screen here form two spatial clusters, the reds and the blues. Yet the only thing the members of each cluster have in common is the accident of their color, as viewers mistake the decorative tints for real information. Also, since multiples are distributed over time as well as space, false *temporal* clusters (the green sequence between screen 1 and screen 2) can arise as we move from image to image.[6]

The original panel of A's contains another flaw: the grids and the outlines of the letters are at the same visual level, with nearly equal line-weights throughout. In the revised panel, the construction lines are calmed down and differentiated (again, the smallest effective difference). We now see more clearly locations of the cross-bar, curls of the serifs, and thick-thin relationships among the strokes. Supplementing the redrawn letters are quantitative measures of stroke-thickness relative to the side of the square (ratios of 1:12 to 1:8 and corresponding proportions of .083 to .125), a matter of aesthetic controversy among 15th and 16th-century architects of letterforms.

Sources for original set of ten letter-forms in the near-right panel: *The Alphabet of Francesco Torniello da Novara (1517)*, introduction by Giovanni Mardersteig (Verona: Officina Bodoni, 1971), shows the six Italian alphabets (three filled-in and three not, as in their first publication) with bibliography at pp. XXVII–XXVIII; Stanley Morison, *Fra Luca de Pacioli* (New York, 1933), p. 23, shows Schedel, Dürer (at 1 to 10) and Tory. Dürer (at 1 to 9) is reproduced from p. 134 of Albrecht Dürer, *Institutiones geometricae* (Paris, 1532), the first Latin edition of *Unterweysung der Messung* (Nuremberg, 1525). Mardersteig's and Morison's sources are (with variants in spelling of names): Damiano da Moyle, *Alphabetum* (Parma, 1480); Sigismondo Fanti, *Theorica et practica de modo scribendi* (Venice, 1514); Felice Feliciano, *Felice Feliciano Veronese: Alphabetum Romanum*, ed. Giovanni Mardersteig (Verona, 1960); Luca Paciolo, *Divina Proportione . . .* (Rome, 1540); Francesco Torniello, *Opera del Modo de Fare le Littere Maiuscole Antique* (Milan, 1517); Jeofroy Tory, *L'art et science de la proportion des letterres* (Paris, 1529); and Giovam Baptista Verini, *Luminario* (Tusculano, 1526).

[6] Aaron Marcus, *Graphic Design for Electronic Documents and User Interfaces* (New York, 1992), p. 86.

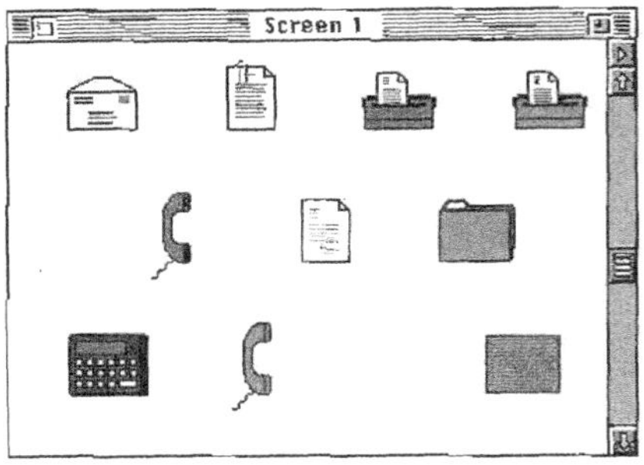

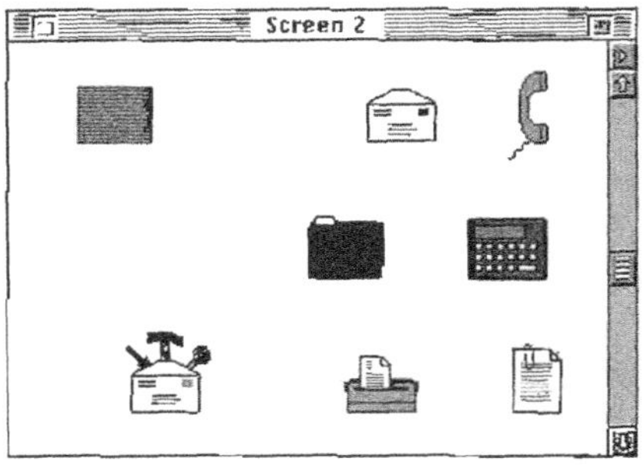

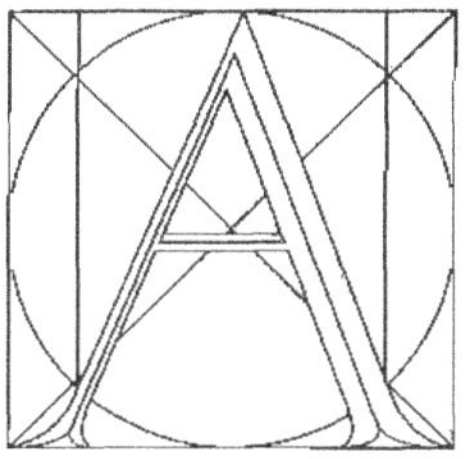

Felice Feliciano,
Città del Vaticano 1460

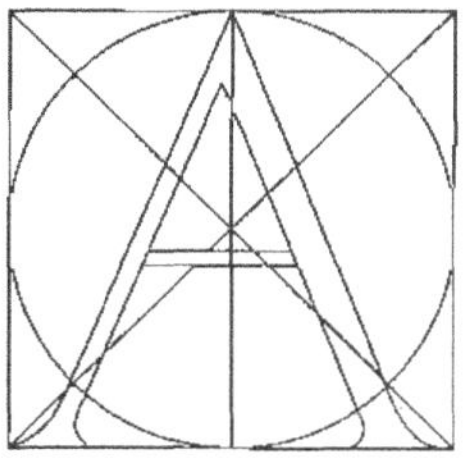

Damiano Moille, Parma 1480

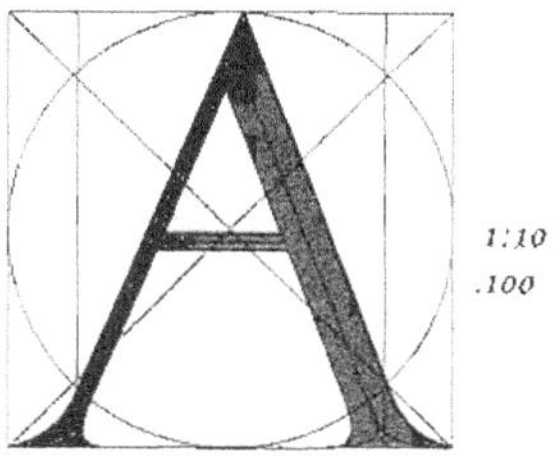

Felice Feliciano,
Città del Vaticano 1460

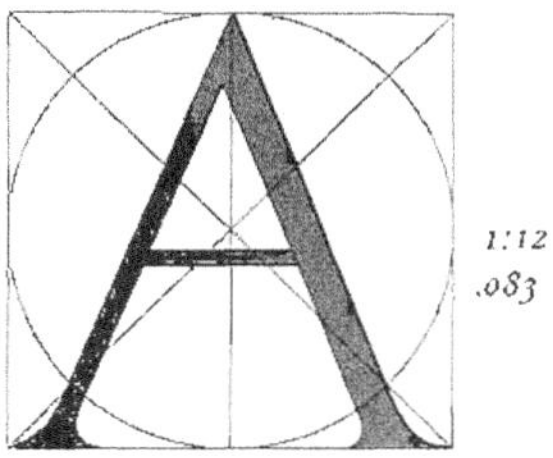

Damiano Moille, Parma 1480

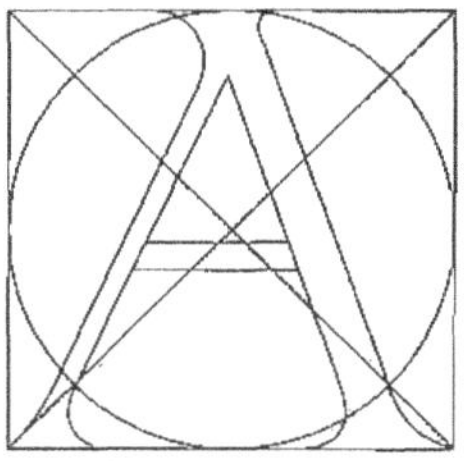

Hartmann Schedel, Munich 1482

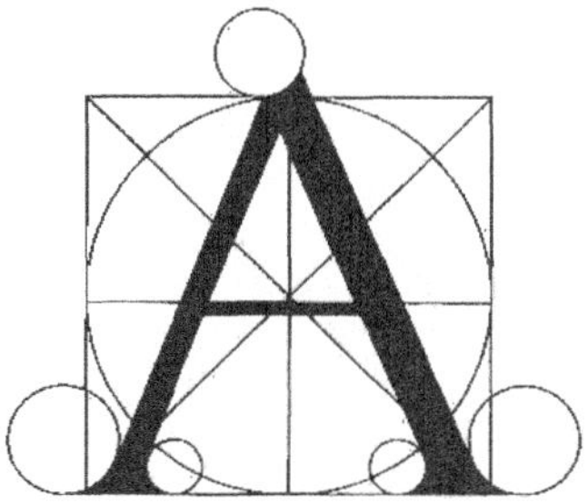

Luca Pacioli, Venezia 1509

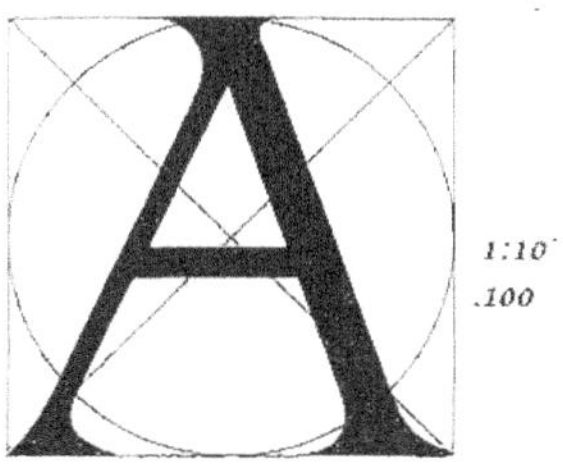

Hartmann Schedel, Munich 1482

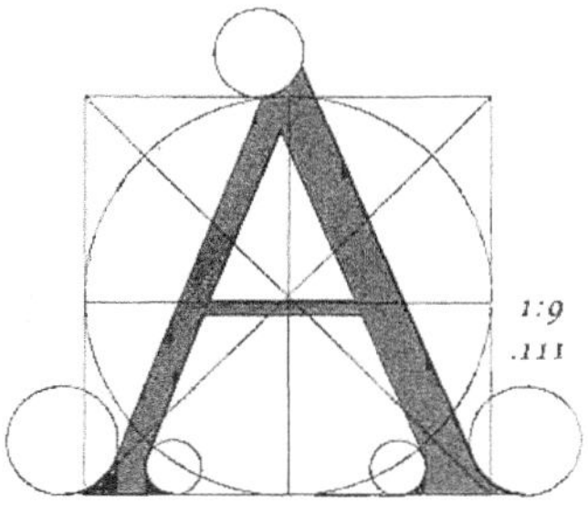

Luca Pacioli, Venezia 1509

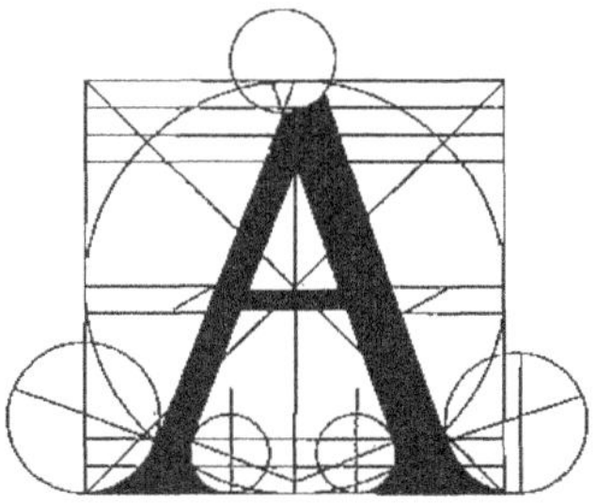

Sigismondo Fanti, Venezia 1514

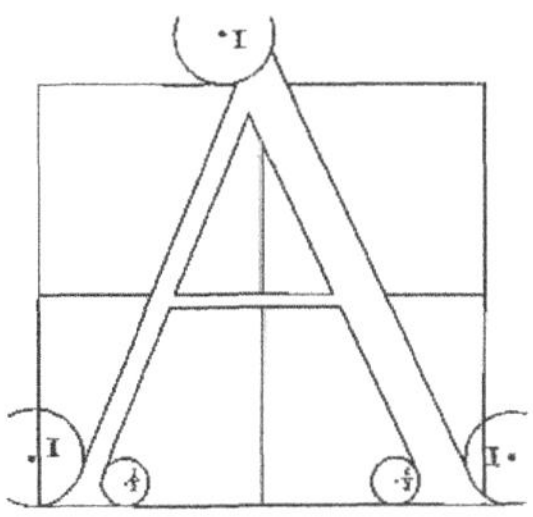

Francesco Torniello, Milano 1517

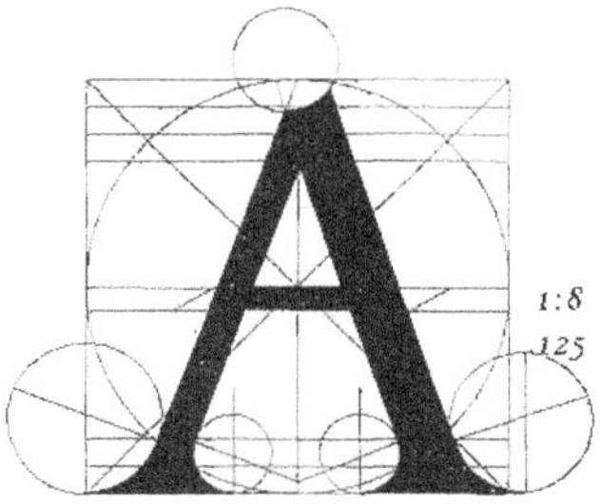

Sigismondo Fanti, Venezia 1514

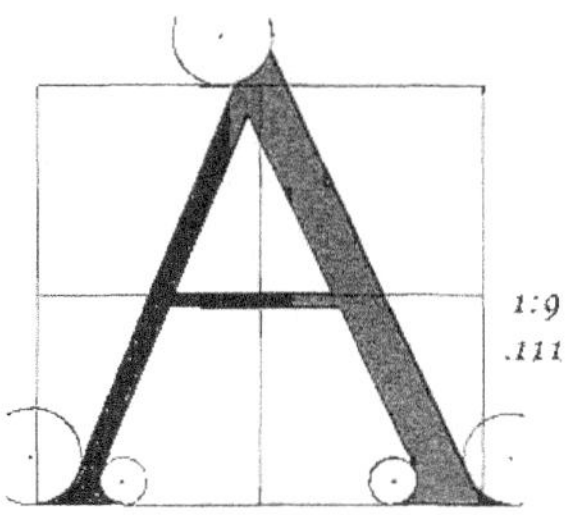

Francesco Torniello, Milano 1517

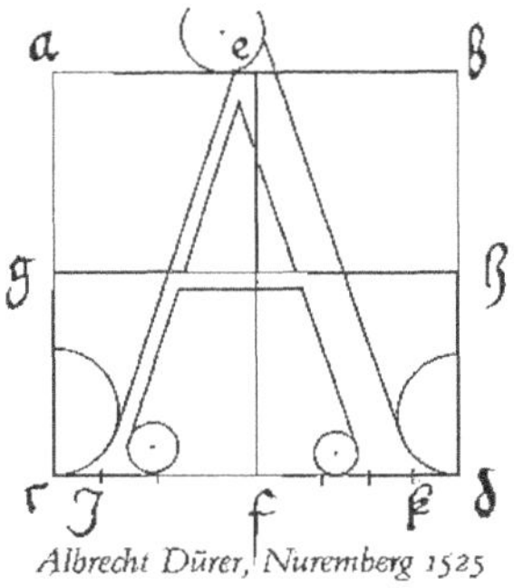

Albrecht Dürer, Nuremberg 1525

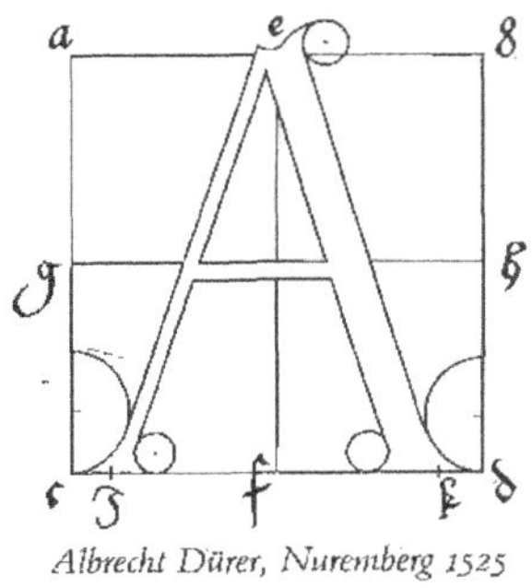

Albrecht Dürer, Nuremberg 1525

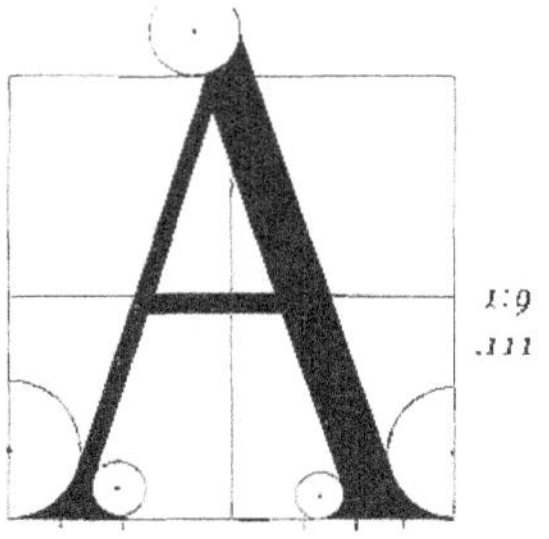

Albrecht Dürer, Nuremberg 1525

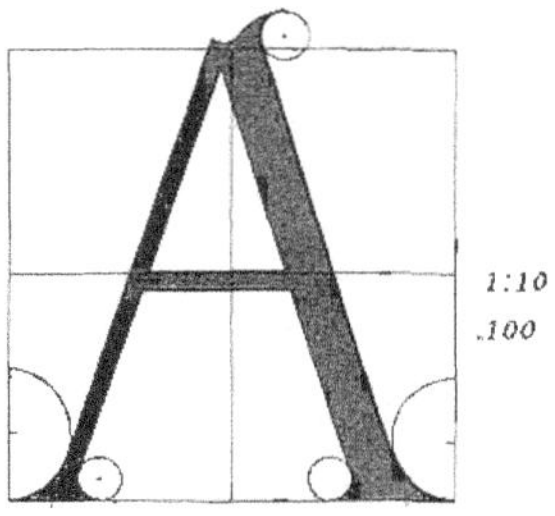

Albrecht Dürer, Nuremberg 1525

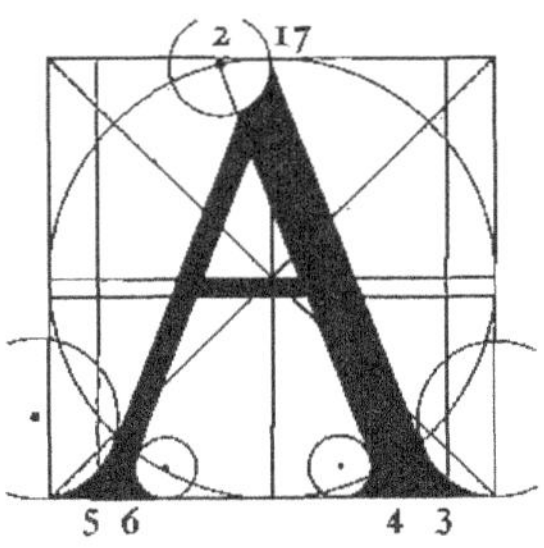

Giovam Baptista Verini, Toscolano 1526

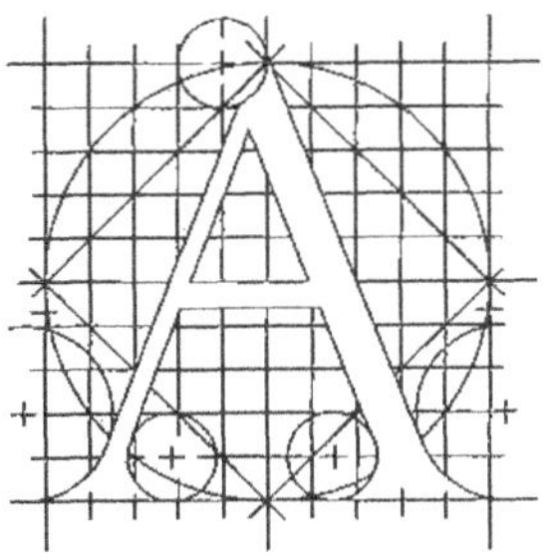

Geofroy Tory, Paris 1529

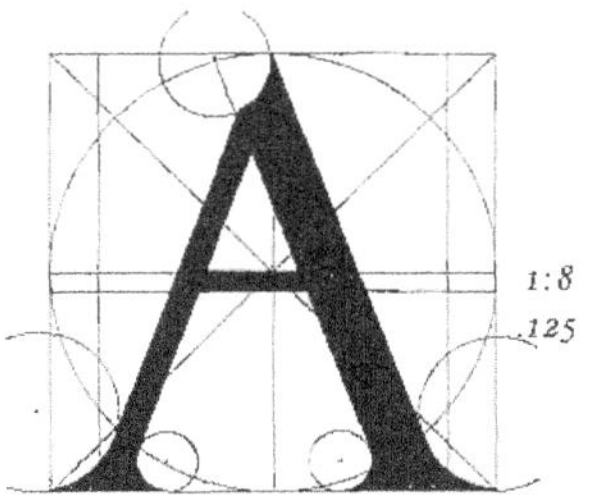

Giovam Baptista Verini, Toscolano 1526

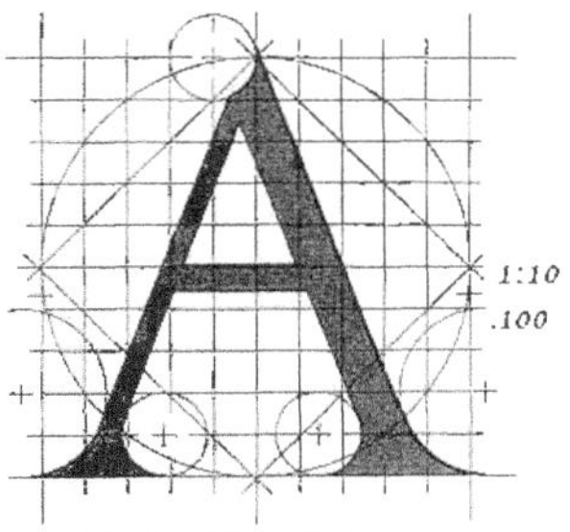

Geofroy Tory, Paris 1529

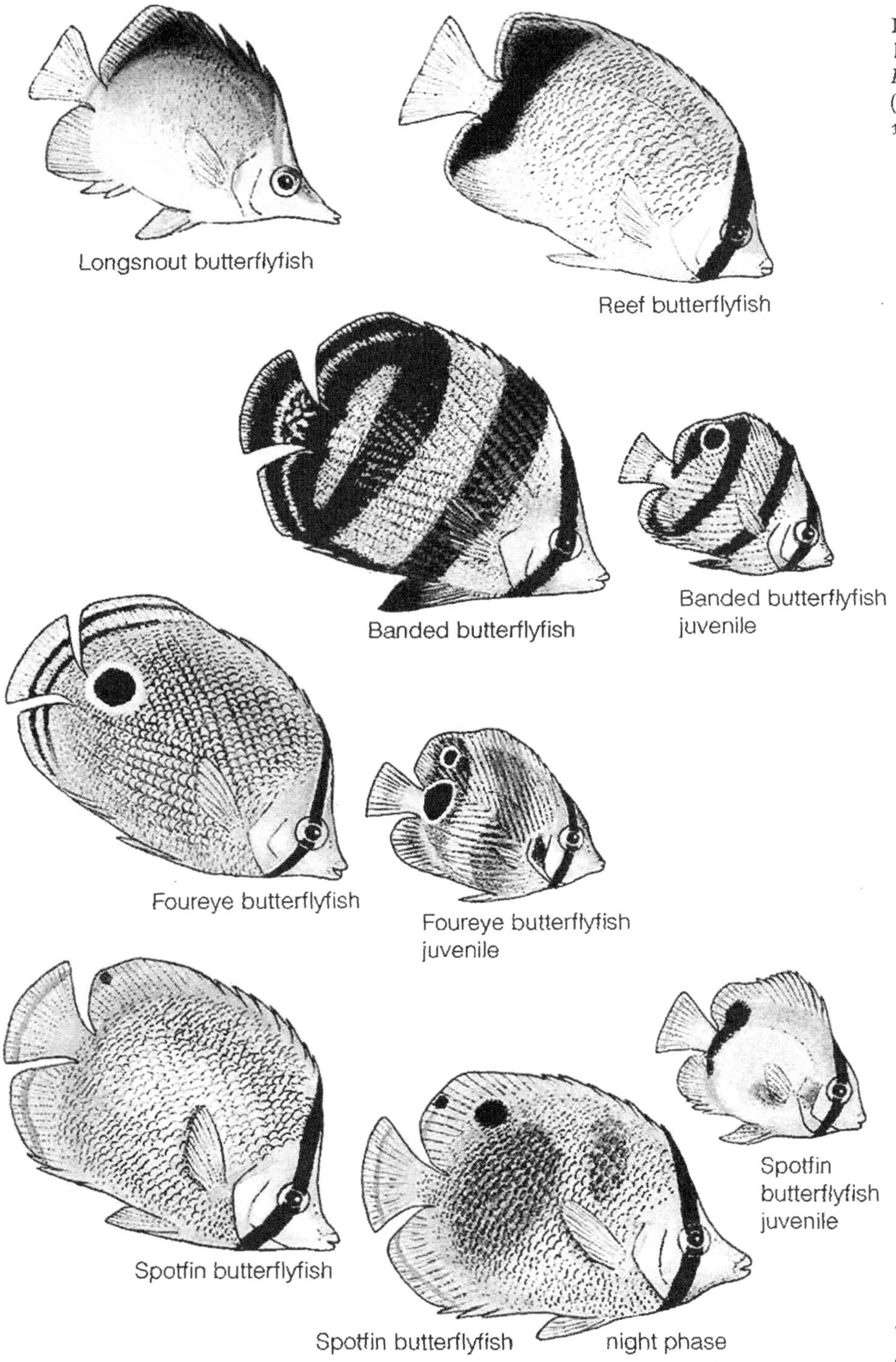

Idaz Greenberg and Jerry Greenberg, *Waterproof Guide to Corals and Fishes of Florida, the Bahamas, and the Caribbean* (Miami, 1986), p. 30. Copyright © 1977, 1986 Idaz and Jerry Greenberg.

Multiples help make fine distinctions and close comparisons among similar nouns, as in the page above from a guide showing various butterflyfishes all nicely lined up in parallel for identification.[7] This handbook is a *submersible* field guide, so that snorkelers and divers can identify fishes by name, sorting among the multiple images while in the water. Since divers will usually see many kinds of fishes, the 64-page

[7] To aid recognition by highlighting elements that make for otherness, some guides use keys or call-outs to indicate differences, as in this example from the fine guide by Paul Humann, *Reef Fish Identification: Florida, Caribbean, Bahamas* (Jacksonville, Florida, 2nd edition, 1994), p. 21.

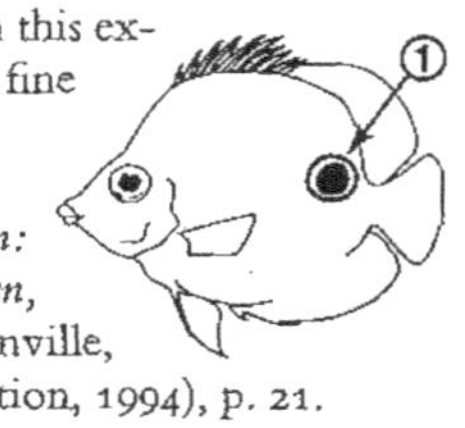

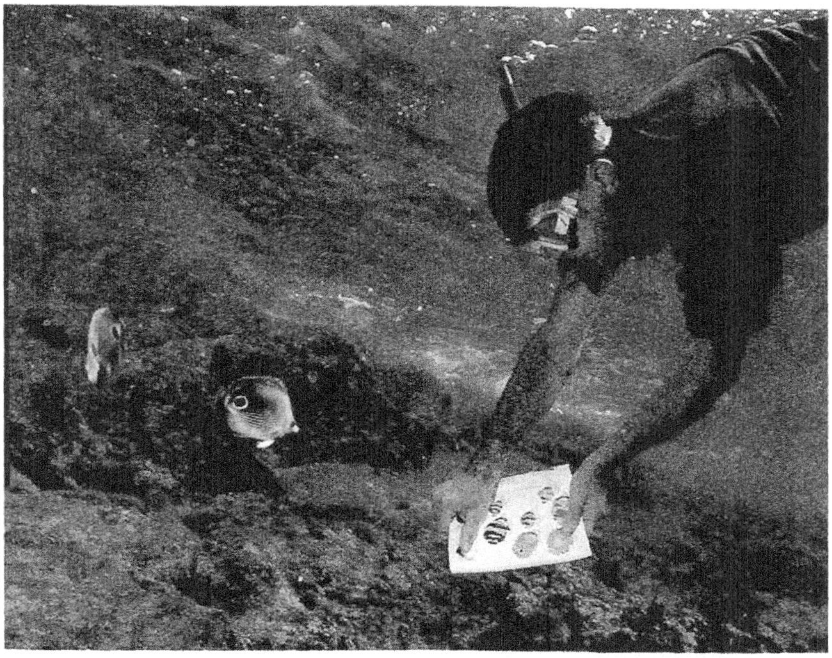

At left, photograph by Roger Kelso, at Long Bay, Virgin Gorda, British Virgin Islands; below, photograph by Edward Tufte, at North Wall, Grand Cayman.

book (above, in action, helping to identify the foureye butterflyfish) demands turning all those wet, sticky pages underwater. To increase the number of images within the viewer's eyespan—and thus reduce the number of pages—such guides can take advantage of the fact that the pages are viewed underwater. There, the refraction of light passing from water to air within the fishwatcher's mask magnifies objects, causing them to appear only three-quarters of their actual distance away.[8] This substantial magnification-in-use suggests that water-books can depict a greater density of material than air-books.

Good design should take into account how, when, and where the information is used. Just as underwater books should minimize page-turning, cookbooks should lie flat on the counter, directional guides should enable glancing back and forth between the road and the instructions (short lines of type, with content-based linebreaks, will help), maps for piloting aircraft at night should allow for reading by dim light, and charts for recording space-flight data (such as the cyclogram) should fold compactly.

The page at left uses multiple images to show small variations within a single category in a large classification system. Another approach is to organize multiple images by the *empirical* frequency of occurrence of the objects represented by the images. Typically, such frequency distributions are highly skewed, as a few items dominate the total count (for example, perhaps 90% or more of all fish sightings consist of only a handful of the thousands of varieties found at least once in a while).[9] Thus for inexperienced divers, a submersible card showing the most commonly-seen fishes might prove more useful in practice than the

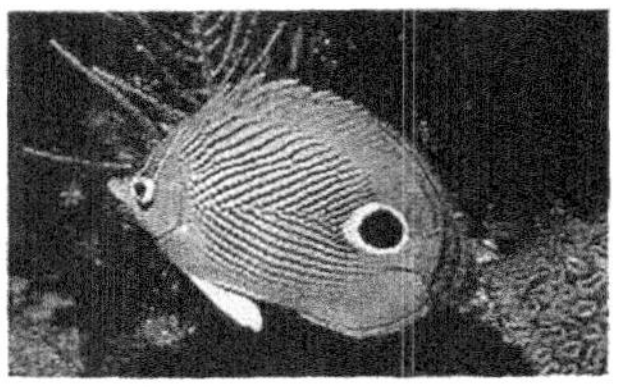

Above, if this is the actual size,

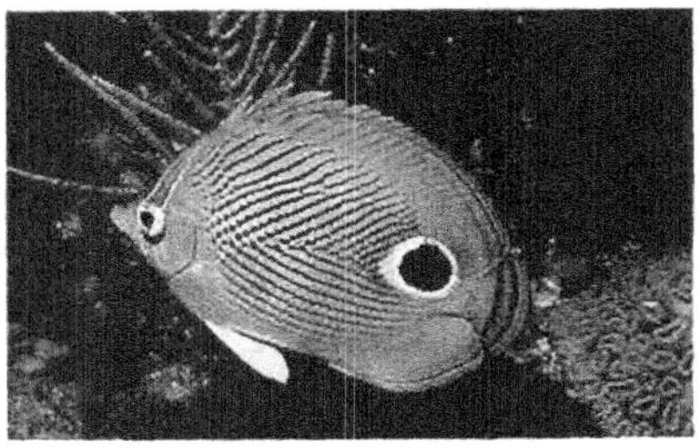

then this is the size seen underwater.

[8] Stanley Miles, *Underwater Medicine* (Philadelphia, 2nd edition, 1966), p. 151; Jeppesen Sanderson, Inc., *Open Water Sport Diver Manual* (Englewood, Colorado, 4th edition, 1984), pp. 2–6 to 2–8.

[9] Herbert Simon, "On a Class of Skew Distribution Functions," *Biometrika* 42 (1955), pp. 425–440.

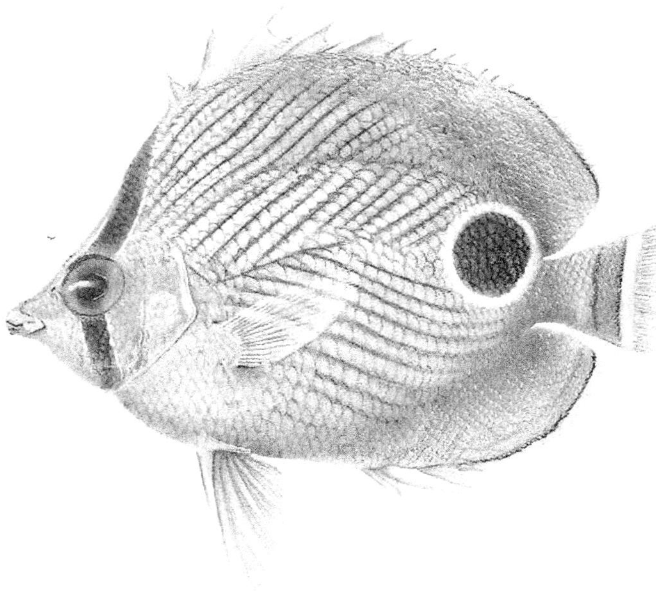

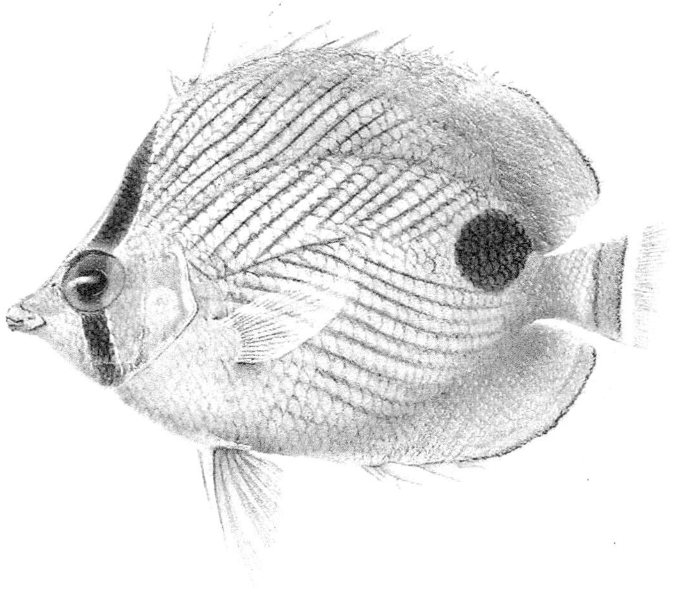

overwhelmingly elaborate taxonomies of encyclopedic guides. Several of these waterproof summary-cards, now published, manage to squeeze in depictions of 60 to 80 commonly found fishes on a two-sided plastic sheet (15 by 23 cm, or 6 by 9 in).[10] Arranging multiples by frequency of occurrence or along some other illuminating dimension (rather than alphabetically, randomly, or taxonomically) may lead to quite efficient learning, whether in water or in air. When the computer is used to collate and display these types of ordered images, however, its great capacity to organize multiple images over multiple dimensions is compromised by the low resolution of the computer screen compared with paper or film. In such relentlessly low-resolution scenes, contrasts among multiple images often must be made temporally from screen to screen—one damn thing after another—rather than spatially within the eyespan. Improved resolution means more effective comparisons.[11]

Our fish presentations here have featured the foureye butterflyfish (*Chaetodon capistratus*), recognized by large false eyes near the tail and by concealed real eyes masked by a dark line passing around the head. This is another example of disinformation design by fishes; recall the stickleback in Chapter 3 on magic. Above left, the dark circle of the false eye is "surrounded by a brilliant white ring."[12] The false eyes are quite showy, more attention-attracting and whimsical than deceptive. Above right, the white ring is redrawn and muted, so that the paired images demonstrate the effect of highlighting.

Antic highlighting for human eyes is catalogued at right. By means of pattern, repetition, and redundancy, multiples evoke the character of various and divergent worlds, sometimes in wonderfully expressive ways. Multiple versions of these prankish glasses reinforce the perception that what we have here is not merely a one-time lapse but rather a chronic silliness—just as the multiple views of the multiple Watergate defendants intensify the atmosphere of feloniousness.

James E. Böhlke and Charles C. G. Chaplin (additions by Eugenia B. Böhlke and William F. Smith-Vaniz), *Fishes of the Bahamas and Adjacent Tropical Waters* (Austin, Texas, 2nd edition, 1993), p. 422.

[10] Submersible plastic cards and booklets showing the more common fish are published by Seahawk Press, Miami, Florida; Natural World Press, Vida, Oregon; Gulf Publishing, Houston, Texas; and, for Paul Humann's fine series, New World Publications, Jacksonville, Florida.

[11] Some evidence about information density for spatial and temporal displays is reported in Nancy Staggers and Mary Etta Mills, "Nurse-Computer Interaction: Staff Performance Outcomes," *Nursing Research*, 43 (1994), pp. 144–150.

[12] *Fishes of the Bahamas and Adjacent Tropical Waters*, p. 422. On the foureye butterflyfish, see Carl Linnaeus, *Systema Naturae* (Leiden, 1758, 10th edition), *Regnum animale*, volume 2, p. 275; and Warren E. Burgess, *Butterflyfishes of the World* (Neptune City, New Jersey, 1978).

Johnson Smith & Company, *Catalogue of Surprising Novelties, Puzzles, Tricks, Joke Goods, and Useful Articles* (Detroit, 1938), p. 284.

Unusual Luminous Glasses - *Surprise Your Friends*

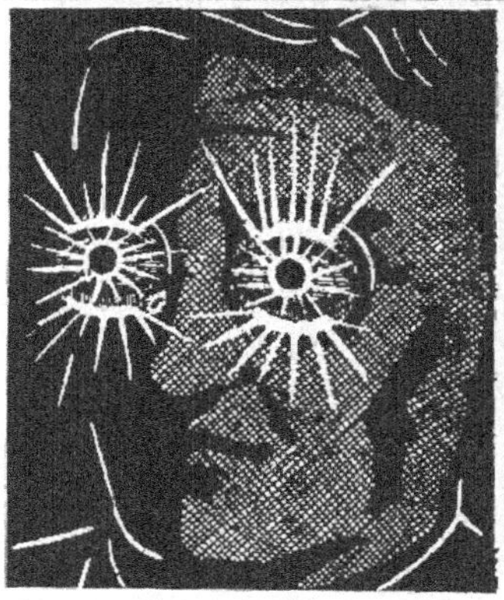

Eyelashes & Pupils

These glasses have luminous eyelashes and pupils in them so that at night they shine radiantly. One glance should scare anybody.
No. 4665. Price Postpaid 19c

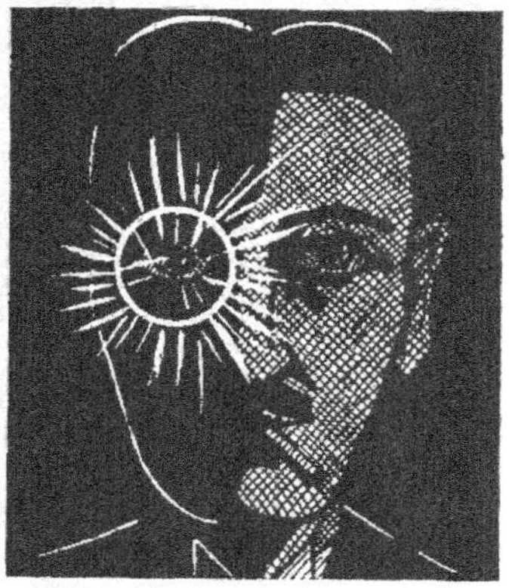

Luminous Monocle

This attractive monocle is just the thing for wearing at night. Take it with you in the theater. The effect will be most novel and surprising.
No. 4666. Price Postpaid 9c

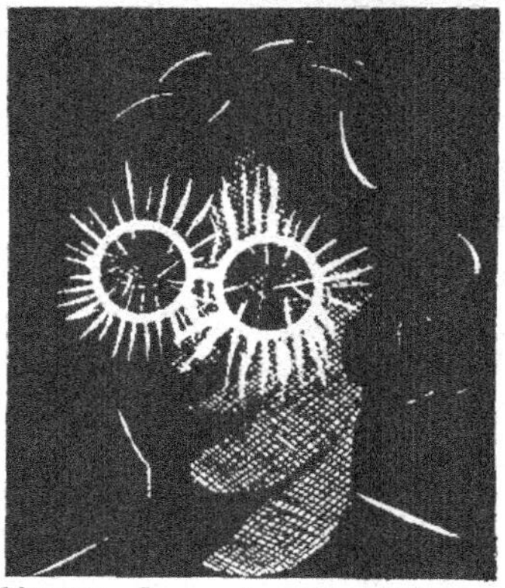

Glasses With Luminous Rims

Glasses with luminous rims. Appear to be ordinary glasses but at night the rims are clearly visible and give a weird effect.
No. 4667. Price Postpaid 19c

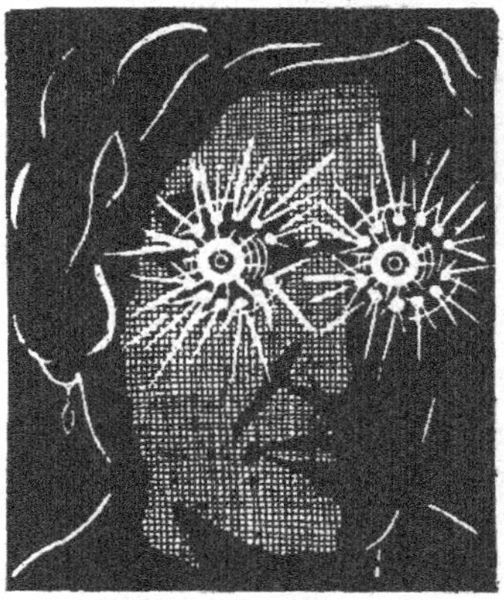

Wobbly Eyes

Wobbly, luminous eyes and spectacles with eyelashes. Roll your eyes in the dark. Usually makes 'em scream with fright when they see it.
No. 4673. Price Postpaid 33c

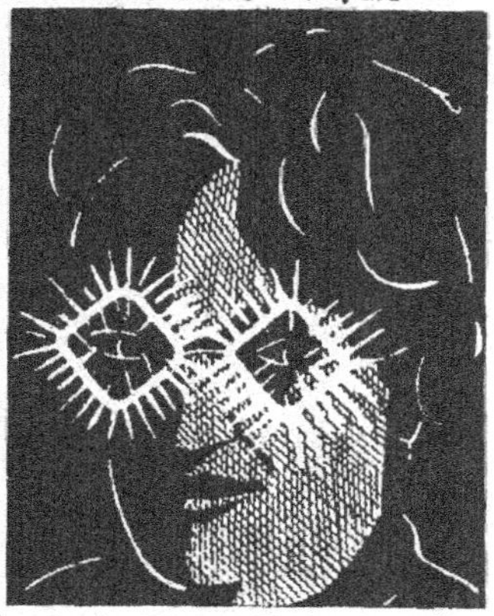

Luminous Spectacles

Celluloid, square spectacles with luminous rims. **The darker the night the brighter they shine.** Leave them lying around in the dark.
No. 4669. Price Postpaid 29c

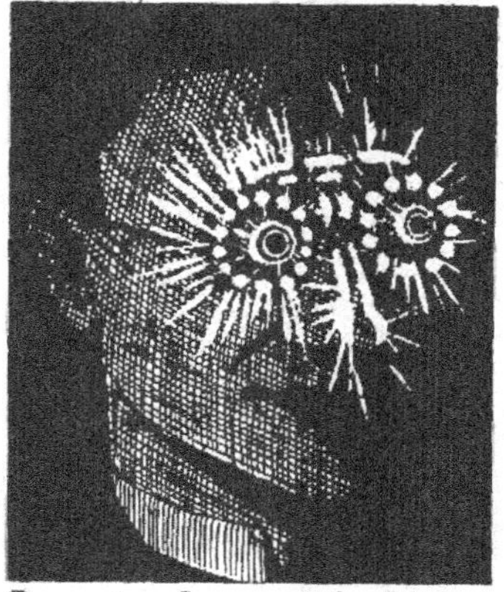

Spectacles with Nose

Giant spectacles with nose, eyes and forehead. Painted with luminous paint. Look weird in the dark. Eyes stand out. Nose shines. Ghastly view.
No. 4670. Price Postpaid 19c

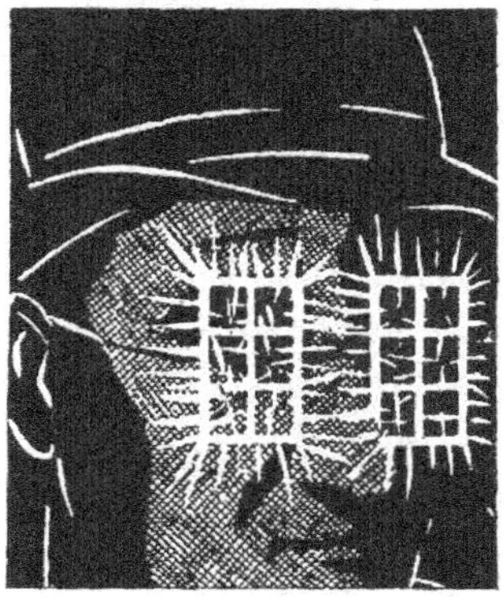

Window Spectacles

Divided into six sections and look like a window pane. The rims are coated with luminous paint and stand out. Something really new.
No. 4671. Price Postpaid 35c

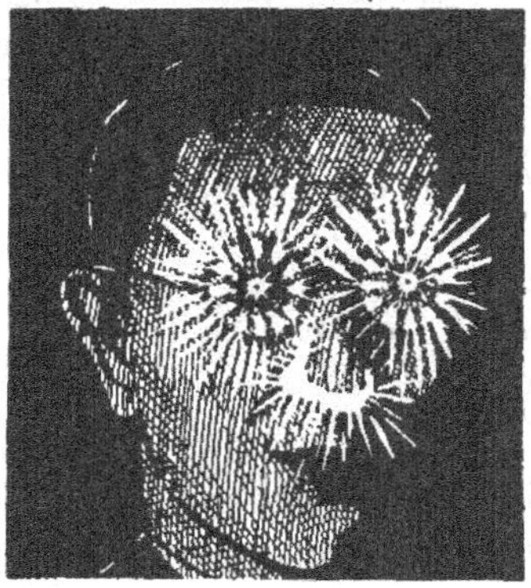

Spectacles & Nose

Spectacles with nose, eyes and forehead painted with luminous paint. Eyes stand out vividly. Nose has distinctive luminous smear.
No. 4672. Price Postpaid 25c

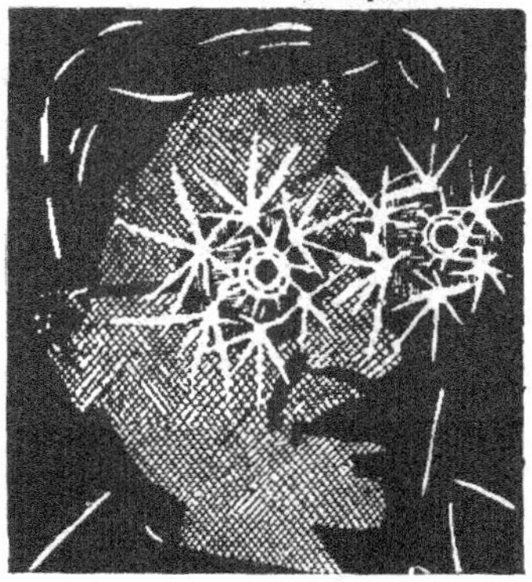

Flashing Glasses

Have wicked eyes and a number of luminous points which shine in the dark. Extremely comical. A good pair to wear when "a'courting."
No. 4668. Price Postpaid 29c

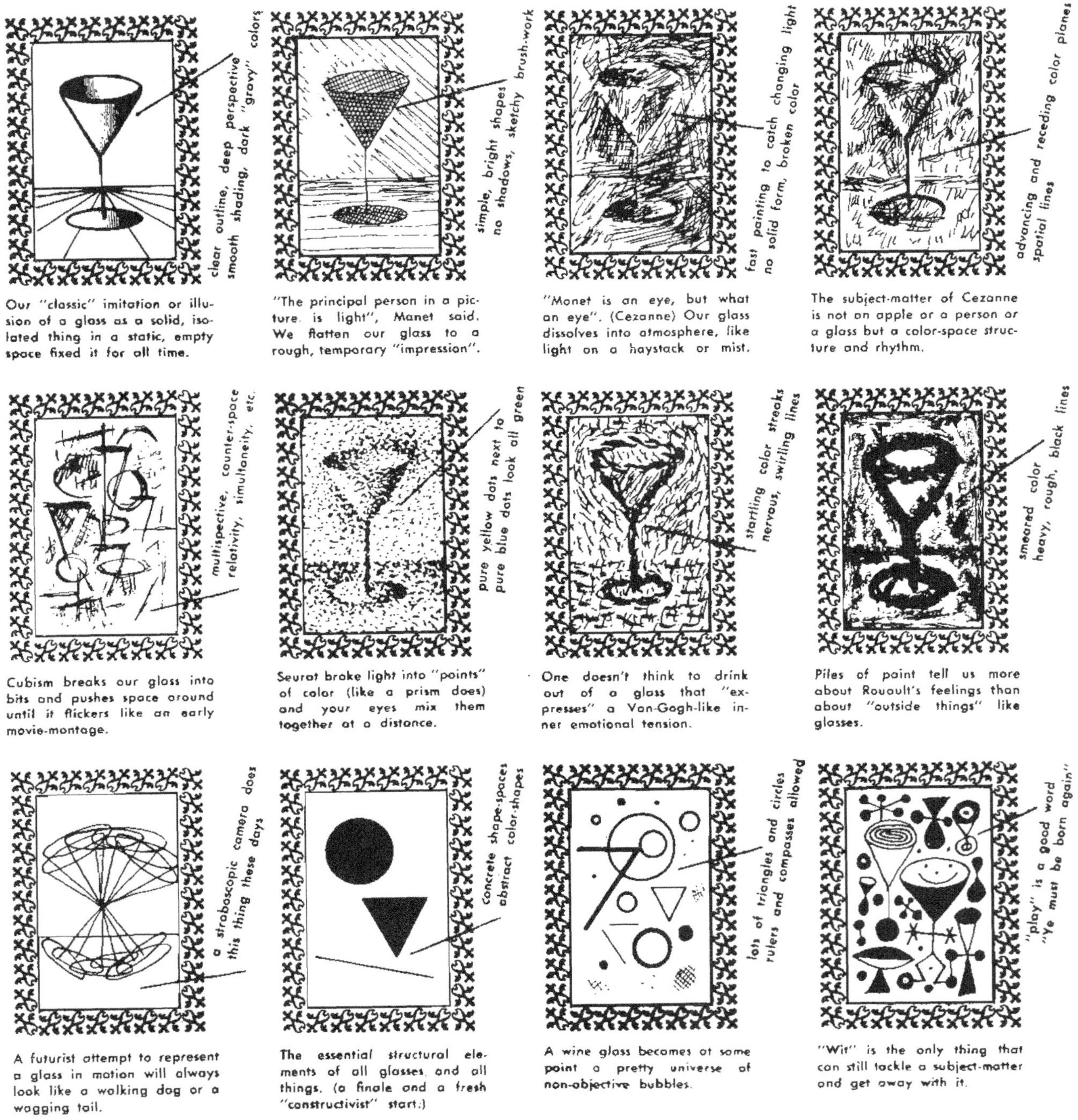

Ad Reinhardt, "How to Look at Things Through a Wine-Glass," *PM*, July 7, 1946. Rearranged, with collateral material omitted.

Multiples organize their images by means of a variety of devices: grids, compartments, call-outs, narrative sequence, overlap (opaque or transparent), and integration of multiple elements into a common field. Such organizational apparatus should be visually minimal; better to use the space for information. Ad Reinhardt's multiple above, a witty introductory tour of modern artists, compares 12 versions of a wine glass. Each intriguing and smartly annotated image is surrounded by a noisy border, administrative bloat that consumes an astonishing 42% of space in each framed rectangle. It resembles all too many computer

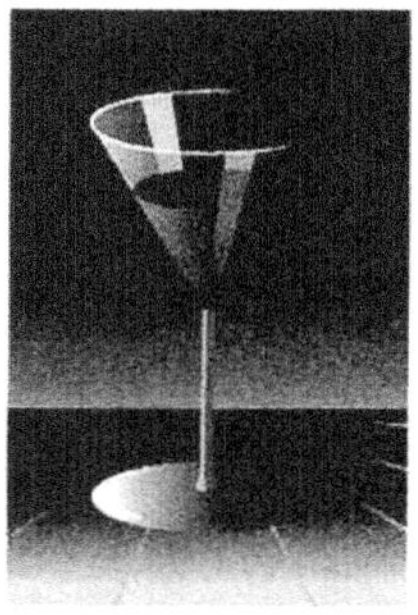

Our "classic" imitation or illusion of a glass as a solid, isolated thing in a static, empty space fixed it for all time.

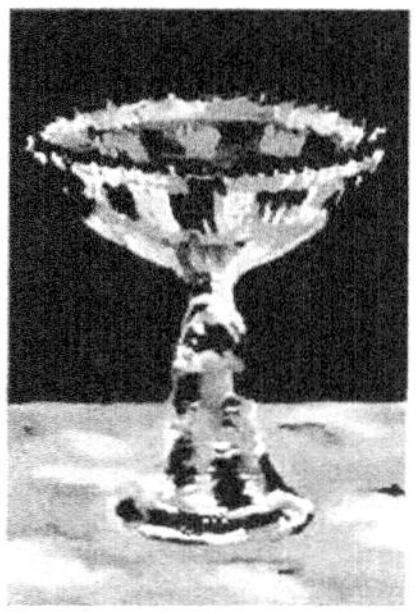

"The principal person in a picture is light", Manet said. We flatten our glass to a rough, temporary "impression".

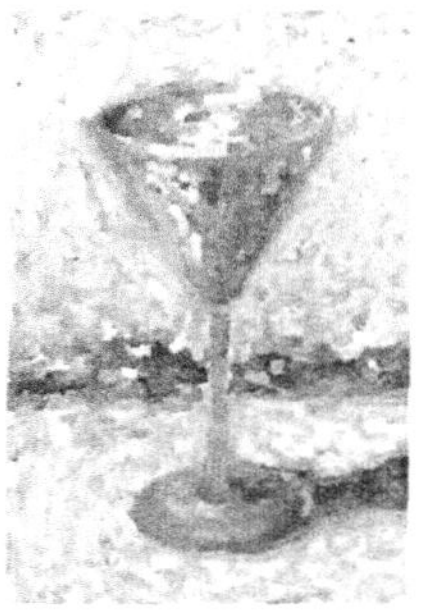

"Monet is an eye, but what an eye". (Cézanne) Our glass dissolves into atmosphere, like light on a haystack or mist.

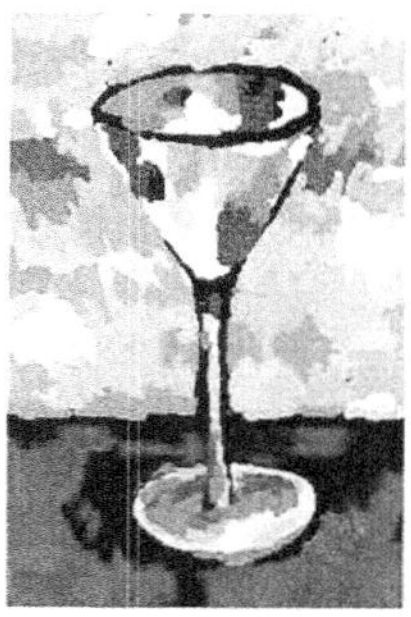

The subject-matter of Cézanne is not an apple or a person or a glass but a color-space structure and rhythm.

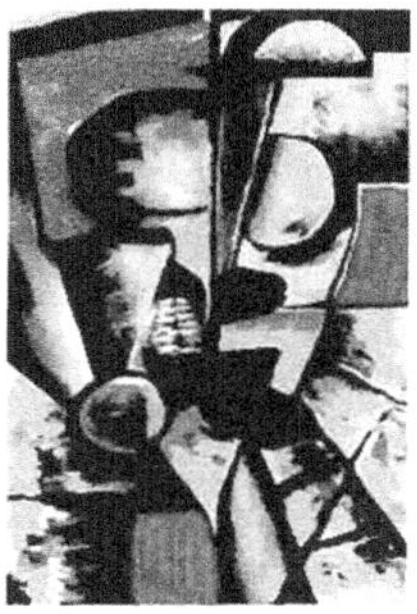

Cubism breaks our glass into bits and pushes space around until it flickers like an early movie-montage.

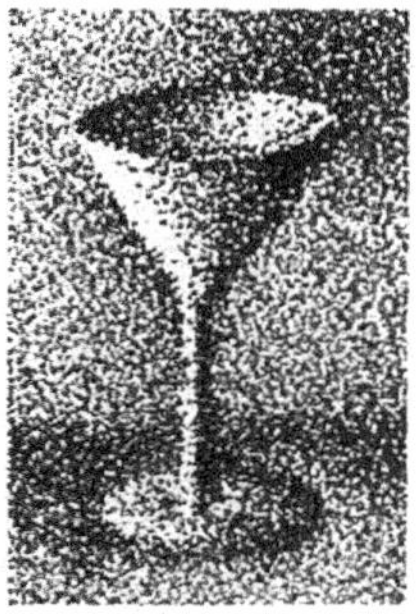

Seurat broke light into "points" of color (like a prism does) and your eyes mix them together at a distance.

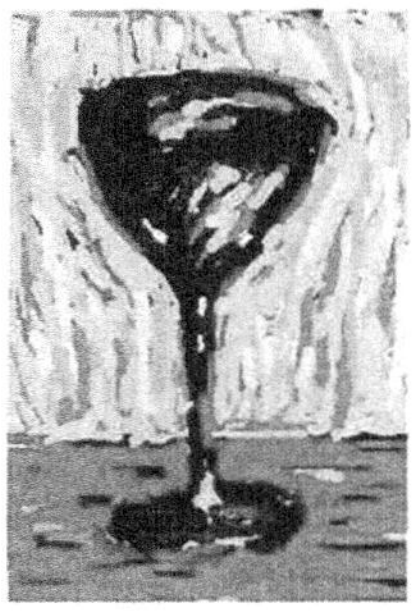

One doesn't think to drink out of a glass that "expresses" a Van-Gogh-like inner emotional tension.

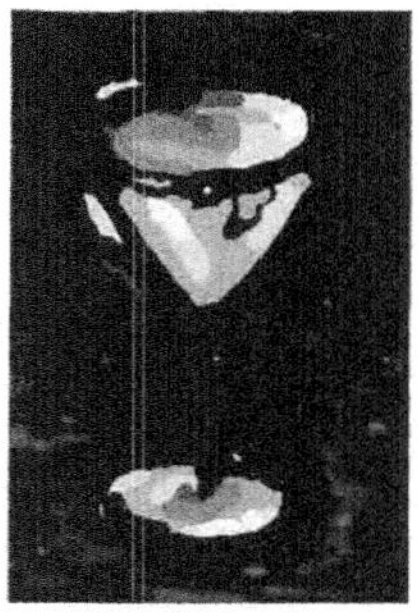

Piles of paint tell us more about Rouault's feelings than about "outside things" like glasses.

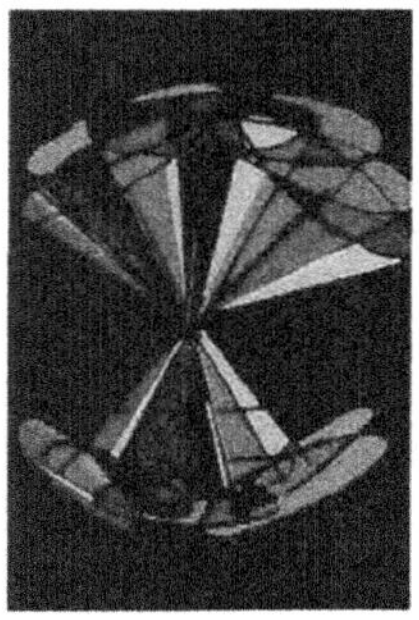

A futurist attempt to represent a glass in motion will always look like a walking dog or a wagging tail.

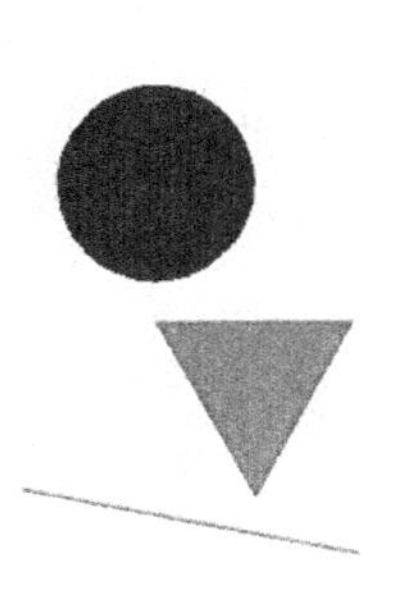

The essential structural elements of all glasses and all things. (A finale and a fresh "constructivist" start.)

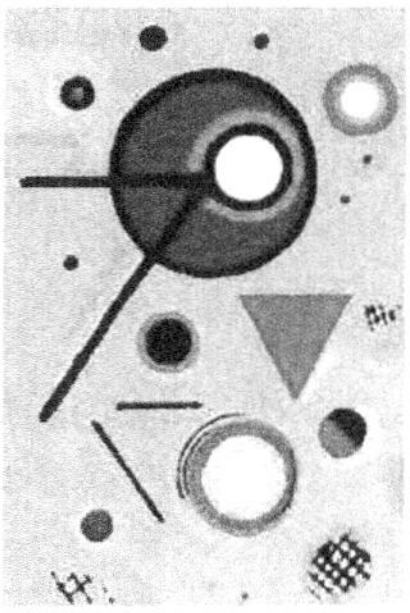

A wine glass becomes at some point a pretty universe of non-objective bubbles.

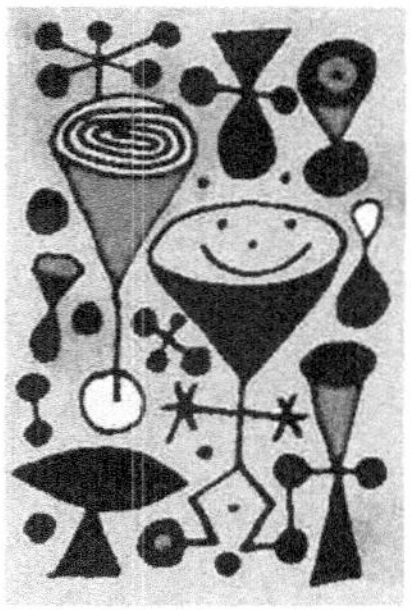

"Wit" is the only thing that can still tackle a subject-matter and get away with it.

displays, where a cramped window showing the user's work is framed by a bureaucratic debris of scroll bars, buttons, titles, icons, and over-produced drawings. Above, my redesign strips away all the frames (for the edge of each picture defines itself well enough) and also adds each artist's typical palette of colors to the original stylized sketches.

In a paragraph accompanying his illustrated history of 20th-century art, Ad Reinhardt wrote what is probably the single best sentence ever written about the point of images for information design: "As for a picture, if it isn't worth a thousand words, the hell with it."

Design and production by Bonnie Scranton and Edward Tufte.

. . . the Water Genie told Haroun about the Ocean of the Streams of Story, and even though he was full of a sense of hopelessness and failure the magic of the Ocean began to have an effect on Haroun. He looked into the water and saw that it was made up of a thousand thousand thousand and one different currents, each one a different color, weaving in and out of one another like a liquid tapestry of breathtaking complexity; and [the Water Genie] explained that these were the Streams of Story, that each colored strand represented and contained a single tale. Different parts of the Ocean contained different sorts of stories, and as all the stories that had ever been told and many that were still in the process of being invented could be found here, the Ocean of the Streams of Story was in fact the biggest library in the universe. And because the stories were held here in fluid form, they retained the ability to change, to become new versions of themselves, to join up with other stories and so become yet other stories . . .

Salman Rushdie, *Haroun and the Sea of Stories* (London, 1990), pp. 71–72.

7 *Visual Confections: Juxtapositions from the Ocean of the Streams of Story*

HERE, as time flows across the page from left to right, is a tiny part of the Ocean of the Streams of Story, a handful of the thousand thousand thousand and one tales. As I have drawn it, an event is the intersection of noun and verb, of subject and action—*something happens*. A plane of events, a slice at a particular time, consists of all possible combinations of nouns and verbs at that time, with as many planes as there are times. A story is a progression of noun-verb incidents; each long strand in the diagram represents one story.

A short story or image sequence (like Marey or Muybridge) is a brief period in a single time-strand, shown by the red line.

And a *confection* is an assembly of many visual events, selected (at the red dots, for example) from various Streams of Story, then brought together and juxtaposed on the still flatland of paper. By means of a multiplicity of image-events, confections illustrate an argument, present and enforce visual comparisons, combine the real and the imagined, and tell us yet another story.

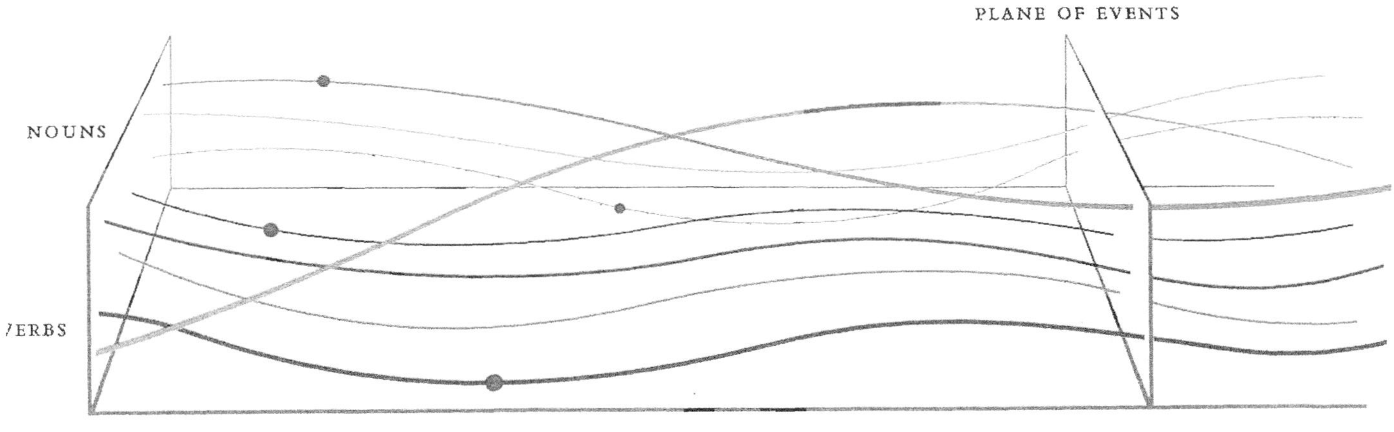

DELIGHTFUL confections, uniquely concocted mixtures of images, fill the illustrated books of the 17th century.[1] An extravagant book about sunspots completed in 1630 by Christopher Scheiner, a Jesuit rival of Galileo, has a curious title, *Rosa ursina sive sol*, mixing together roses, bears, and the sun. This verbal melange is depicted on the title page, which engagingly envisions a rose garden and cave house with five bears occupied with child-rearing, playing, resting, and, of course, observing sunspots. Roses and bears appear so conspicuously here because they were symbols of Scheiner's patron, the Orsini (Ursinus = bear) family.[2] Thus a confectionary image portrays a confectionary title.

On the page at right, another confection serves as a *visual list*. Here Scheiner illustrates seven different techniques for viewing sunspots—through darkened glass or clouds, by various projections and reflections (sometimes involving obelisks)—arranged on a terrace of industrious astronomers observing five suns scattered conveniently about the sky. Down in the basement, details are provided for a particular instrument, a drawing platform attached to a telescope so that the two move together in tracking the sun's motion.[3] The deep and narrow windows, quite impractical for astronomy, suggest an imagined observatory.

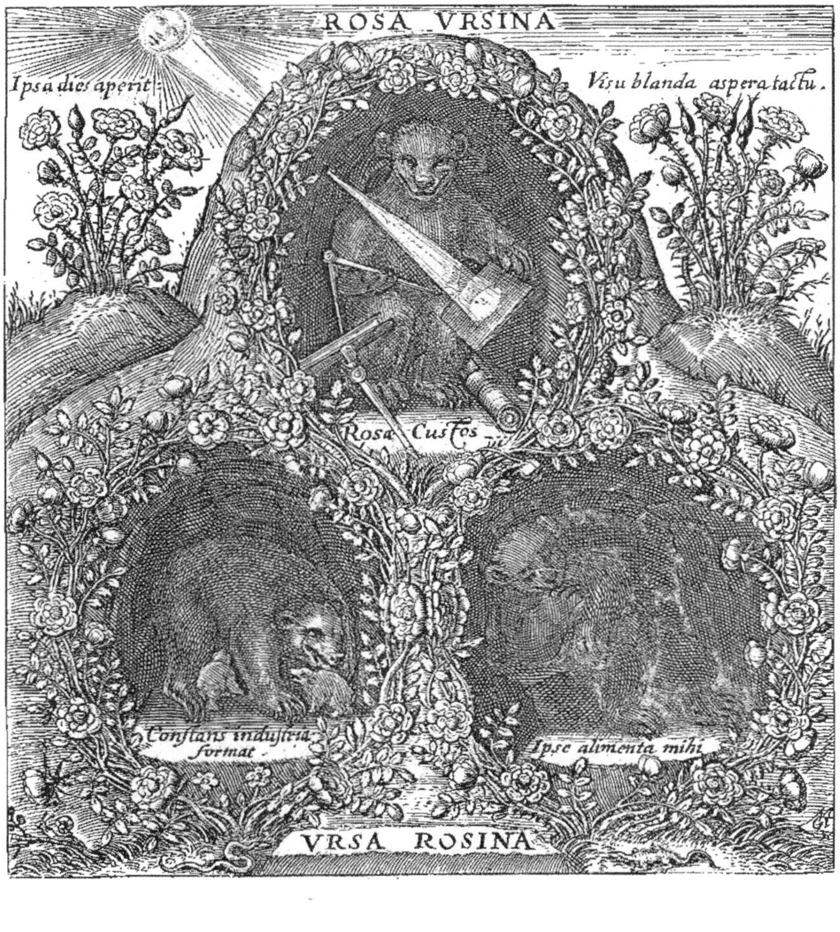

[1] Margery Corbett and Ronald Lightbown, *The Comely Frontispiece: The Emblematic Title-page in England 1550–1660* (London, 1979), report that decorated (and typically richly confectionary) title pages "became general in the early 16th century and spread quickly . . . and were used throughout Renaissance Europe." (p. 3)

[2] The visual logic of Scheiner's title page is described by Craig Williams (Department of Classics, Yale University): "In his preface to the reader, Scheiner compares himself and his research to bears and their activities. Like a bear licking her offspring into shape, he gives form to his work; and like a bear in hibernation, living off its own sustenance, Scheiner insists that he has used only his own original data. By means of elaborate verbal and visual puns that Scheiner develops in several prefaces, the image and its accompanying text also allude to the name, fame, and splendor of his patron's family, the Orsini. The Latin version of their name, *Ursinus*, is identical to the adjective meaning 'bearish,' and the family emblems include the bear and the rose. Scheiner uses the phrase *rosa Ursina*, 'the Orsini rose,' of the family itself, comparable to the most splendid of flowers; and some Orsini mottoes are printed with the image (for example, *ipse alimenta mihi*, 'I am sustenance for myself'). Scheiner's visual creation also metaphorically alludes to sunspots as *rosa Ursina in sole*, the Orsini rose on the sun."

[3] Scheiner's *Oculus, hoc est: fundamentum opticum* . . . (Innsbruck, 1619; Freiburg im Breisgau, 1621, 2nd edition) also has an elaborately allegorical confection for the frontispiece, as seen in Martin Kemp, *The Science of Art* (New Haven, 1990), p. 192.

At left, Christopher Scheiner, *Rosa ursina sive sol* . . . (Bracciani, 1626–1630), extract from title page. At right, *Rosa ursina sive sol* . . . , p. 150.

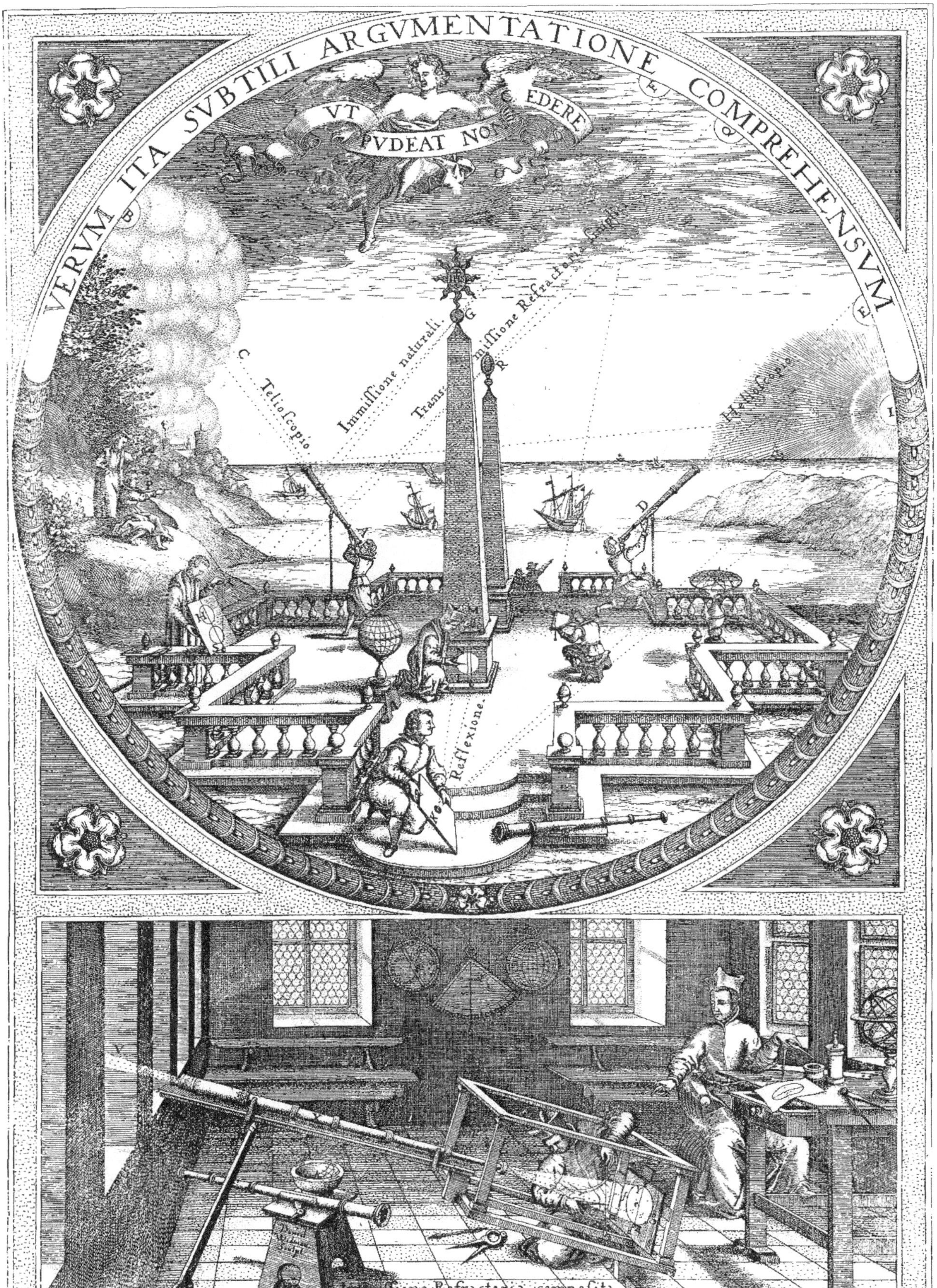
VERVM ITA SVBTILI ARGVMENTATIONE COMPREHENSVM
VT PVDEAT NON CEDERE
Immissione naturali.
Teliofcopio
Transmissione Refractoria Simplici
Heliofcopio
Reflexione.
Immissione Refractoria composita.

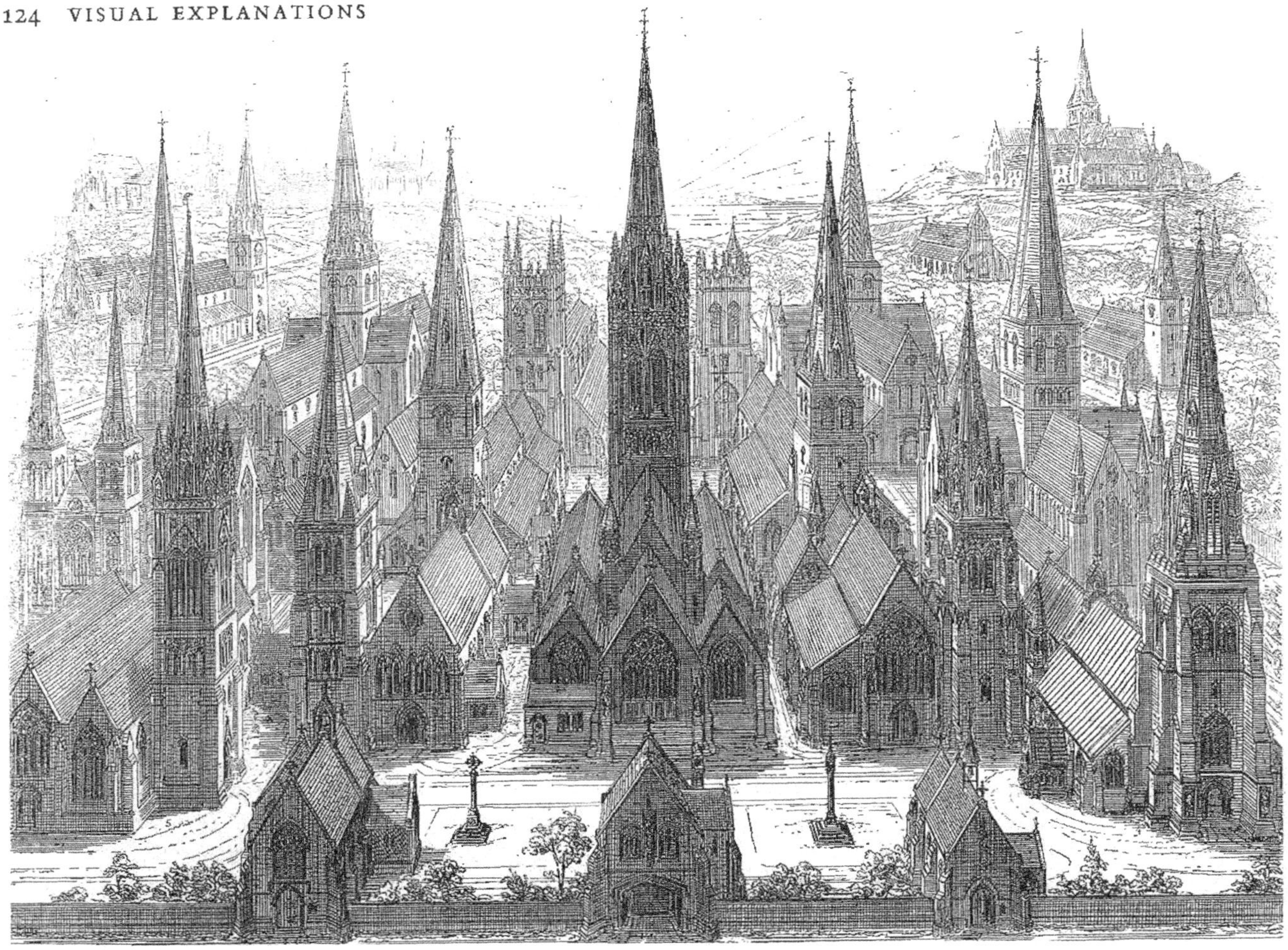

A. Welby Pugin, *An Apology for The Revival of Christian Architecture in England* (London, 1843), frontispiece.

A scenic inventory, this oft-reproduced frontispiece to A. W. Pugin's polemic on the Gothic revival in English architecture gathers together 25 of his churches, chapels, and schools into one grand confection. Kenneth Clark writes that this visual list is

> . . . ranged like a Gothic New Jerusalem before the setting sun. The dramatic effect (largely obtained by the expedient of suppressing cast shadows) is tremendous. Our spirit is exalted by the aspiring pinnacles and soars high above architectural details to the promised land beyond. Were we on earth walking about among these buildings the effect would be less agreeable.[4]

Tiny numbers, usually caught up in the engraving lines, identify each building.[5] These numbers are then keyed to the names of buildings listed in a legend six pages away, where the names read vertically while the frontispiece runs horizontally. To identify a building, the reader must detect and enlarge a number in the drawing, turn some pages, and rotate the book—a clumsy process indeed.

It is fitting that Pugin, who drew this comparative confection, wrote a book two years earlier with the explicitly comparative title *Contrasts: A Parallel Between the Noble Edifices of the Middle Ages, and Corresponding Buildings of the Present Day, Showing the Present Decay of Taste.*

[4] Kenneth Clark, *The Gothic Revival: An Essay in the History of Taste* (London, 1928), pp. 170–171.

[5] This is the actual size of identification numbers in the original frontispiece:

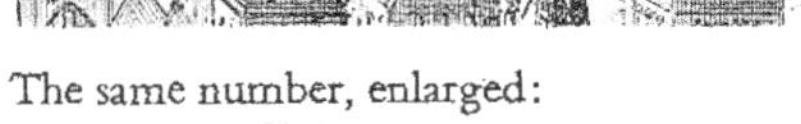

The same number, enlarged:

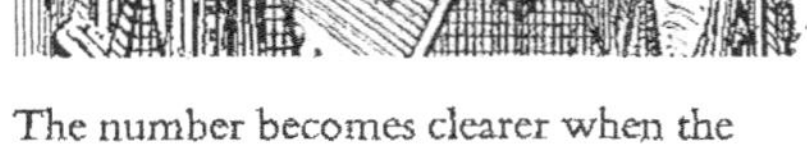

The number becomes clearer when the interference caused by the engraving lines is removed:

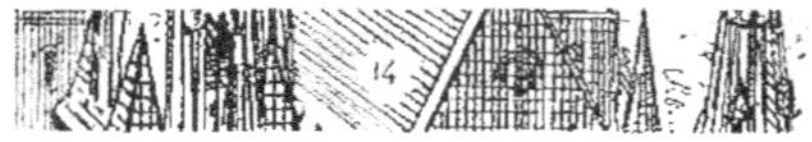

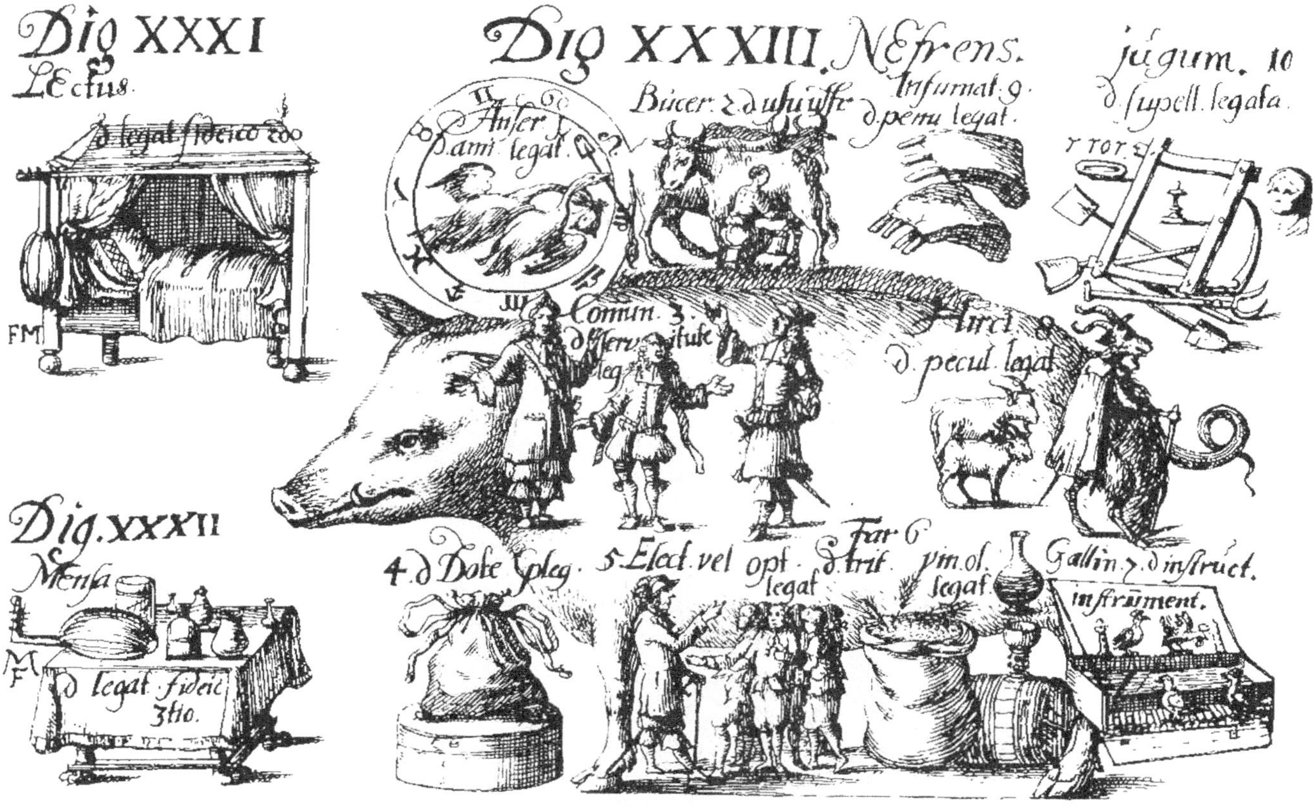

This engraving was designed to assist 17th-century law students in memorizing the *Digest*, 50 books compiling the work of ancient legal authorities. The perfectly sensible theory of design here is that recall is enhanced by allegory, bizarre associations, punning. These "mnemonic-emblematic reductions" compress masses of detailed material into prodigiously elaborate confections. Shown above are three panels, out of hundreds. The larger image (a pig, in this case) represents a book in the *Digest*; smaller superimposed images represent chapters. To remember Book 33, you imagine a young pig, a young animal, *nefrens* in Latin, the letters *ne*, which correspond to the number 33 by means of a complex alphanumeric code (you don't want to know). Near the pig's back foot, we see some chickens on a virginal, a sort of portable harpsichord. That unforgettable image of course means that Chapter 7 of Book 33 deals with bequests of musical instruments (because hens = *galliae* = *g* = 7th letter = Chapter 7). Other complications are happily omitted here. In order to navigate through the sequences of small images, a guide is required (bottom right). Too often in such guides, keys, and codes, the apparatus itself becomes an impediment to understanding—administrative bloat again. And this guide shows a one-time scheme, a labyrinth unique to Buno's book. Ideally, structures that organize information should be transparent, straightforward, obvious, natural, ordinary, conventional—with no need for hesitation or questioning on the part of the reader.

Johannes Buno, *Memoriale Iuris Civilis Romani* . . . (Hamburg, 1673), Books 31–33 (above) and "Præfatio, Schema exhibens ordinem . . . " (bottom).

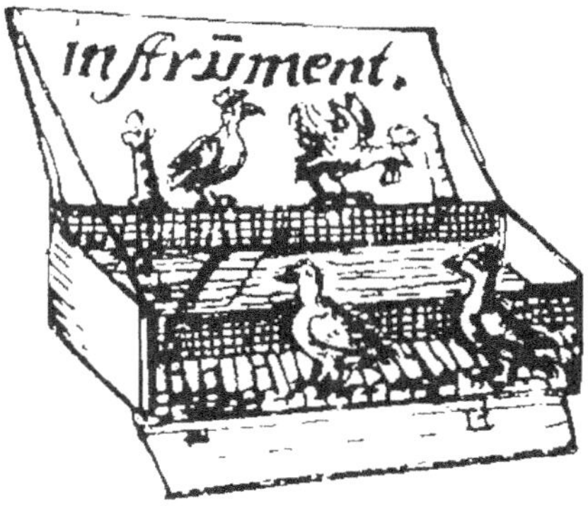

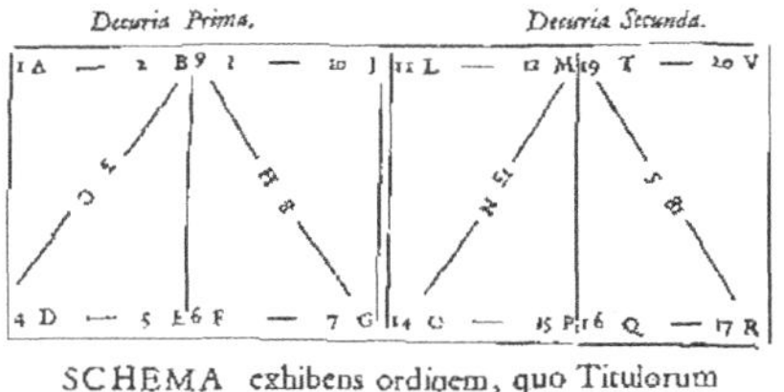

SCHEMA exhibens ordinem, quo Titulorum imagines sunt dispositæ.

Rather than simply being an inventory or parts list, the confection below portrays verbs as well as nouns. Multiple windows describe the Ultimate Weed and its lively interplay with the surroundings. Circled callouts annotate the central image, drawings commenting on a drawing. This superb design also blends words and images into a memorable and distinctive account, reinforced by the text of the caption and the accompanying article. All the particular, real details combine to form a coherent picture of an imagined plant. Describing what the Ultimate Weed *does*, the drawing is about acts, verbs, consequences.

Redrawn by Patricia Wynne, based on her drawing in Gary A. Stobel, "Biological Control of Weeds," *Scientific American*, 265 (July 1991), p. 74.

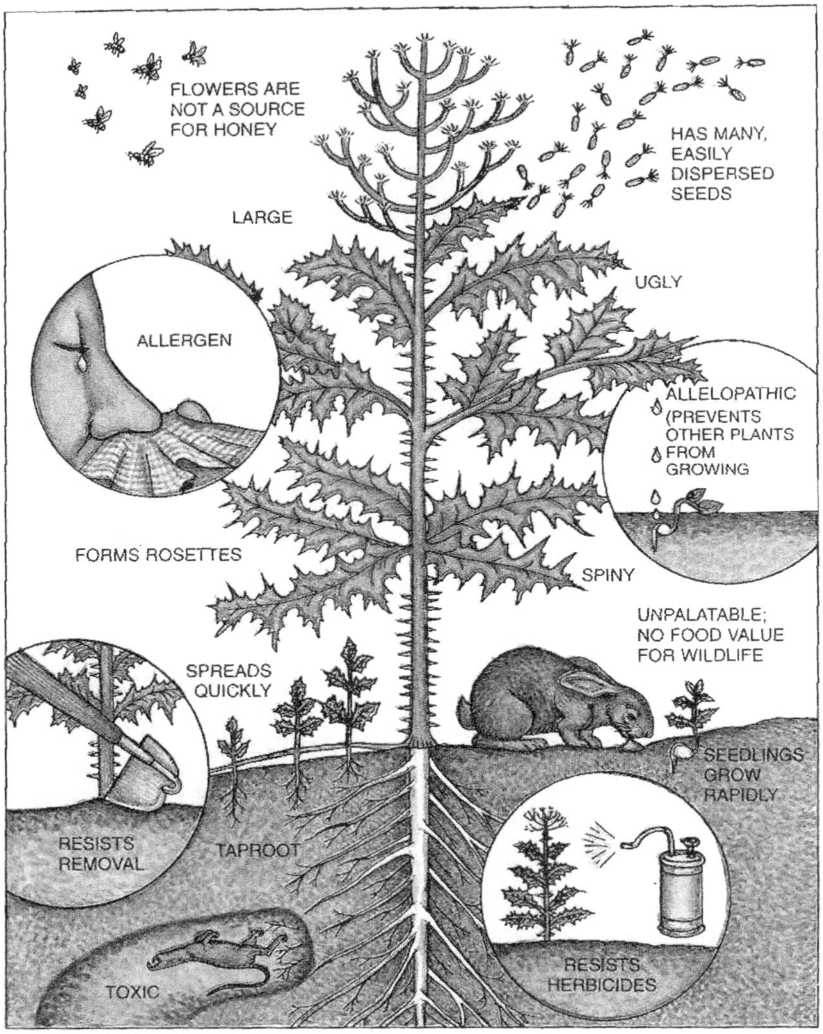

ULTIMATE WEED has no redeeming features. Unsightly and useless, it is unpalatable or toxic to animals and devoid of sugar for honey. It grows tall, proliferates rapidly and actively inhibits the development of other plants (allelopathy). It also triggers allergic reactions in humans. And it won't go away: with its long taproot and rosettes, it resists mechanical removal, and it defies elimination by herbicides.

Drawings combine assorted images of real objects into concocted universes, showing all at once what never has been together. Unlike maps or photographs, confections are not direct representations of pre-existing scenes, nor are they the result of placing data into conventional formats such as statistical charts, tables, or maps. Instead, two general strategies are used to arrange and organize the various images gathered together in confections: *compartments* (for example, the call-out circles for the Ultimate Weed) and *imagined scenes* (the 25 churches and chapels accumulated by Pugin; or, at right, all the symbolic objects collected by Albrecht Dürer in his engraving of 1514, *Melencolia I*). A good many confections use both methods simultaneously (for example, Scheiner's *Rosa ursina* compartmentalizes its imagined scenes).

On the next pages (and in translation below) we see the imagined universe of *Babar's Dream* by Jean de Brunhoff.[6] In an archetypal battle between good and evil, the graceful winged elephants—the angels of kindness, intelligence, courage, patience, perseverance, knowledge, work, hope, love, health, joy, and happiness—drive out the demons of misfortune, anger, stupidity, discouragement, sickness, spinelessness, despair, fear, ignorance, cowardice, laziness. The qualities championed here are *personal* virtues, involving the life of the mind and the life of the individual. Although the orderly angel-elephants resemble an army, with little differentiation among them compared to the dramatically articulated figures of evil, the angels do not proclaim a nationalistic, corporate, or moralistic cause but instead affirm a gracious and serene intelligence. Several of the flying elephants carry symbols characteristic of the virtues: the flowers of hope, the candle of knowledge, the saw of perseverance, the hammer of work, the shield and sword of courage, the clock of patience. And so angelic harmonies banish discordant evils from Celesteville, the home of Babar and Celeste.

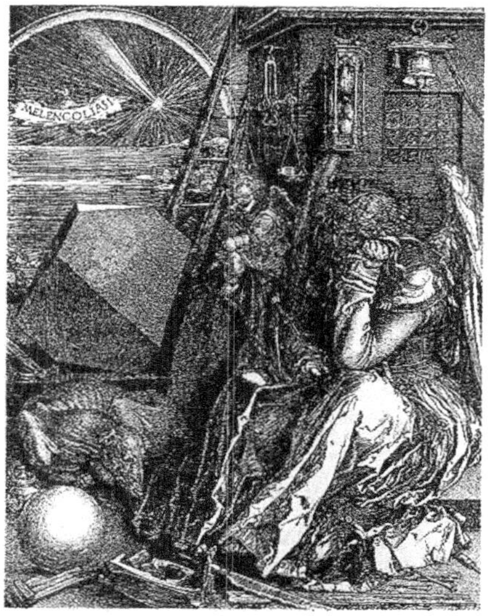

Albrecht Dürer, *Melencolia I*, engraving, 1514, 24 by 19 cm, or 9½ by 7⅜ in.

[6] See Nicholas Fox Weber, *The Art of Babar: The Work of Jean and Laurent de Brunhoff* (New York, 1989), p. 67. *Babar's Dream* contains several notable parallels to Andrea Mantegna's *Pallas Expelling the Vices from the Garden of Virtue* (1499–1502, Musée du Louvre), as Graham Larkin has pointed out to me. See Ronald Lightbown, *Mantegna* (Berkeley, 1986), p. 443; and Suzanne Boorsch, et al., *Andrea Mantegna* (London, 1992), pp. 427–430, for Keith Christiansen's essay on *Pallas*.

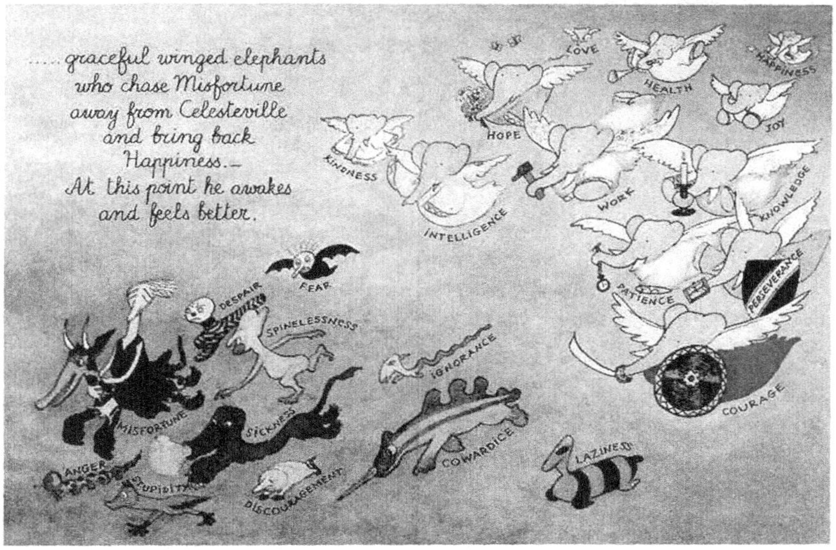

Jean de Brunhoff, *Babar's Dream*, 1933, watercolor and black-line proof, 36 by 53 cm, or 14 by 21 in. Redrawn. Translated by Laurent de Brunhoff and Phyllis Rose. First published in Jean de Brunhoff, *Le Roi Babar* (Paris, 1933), pp. 44–45.

......de gracieux éléphants ailés
qui chassent le Malheur
loin de Célesteville,
et ramènent avec eux
le Bonheur _
A ce moment, il se réveille,
et se sent mieux.

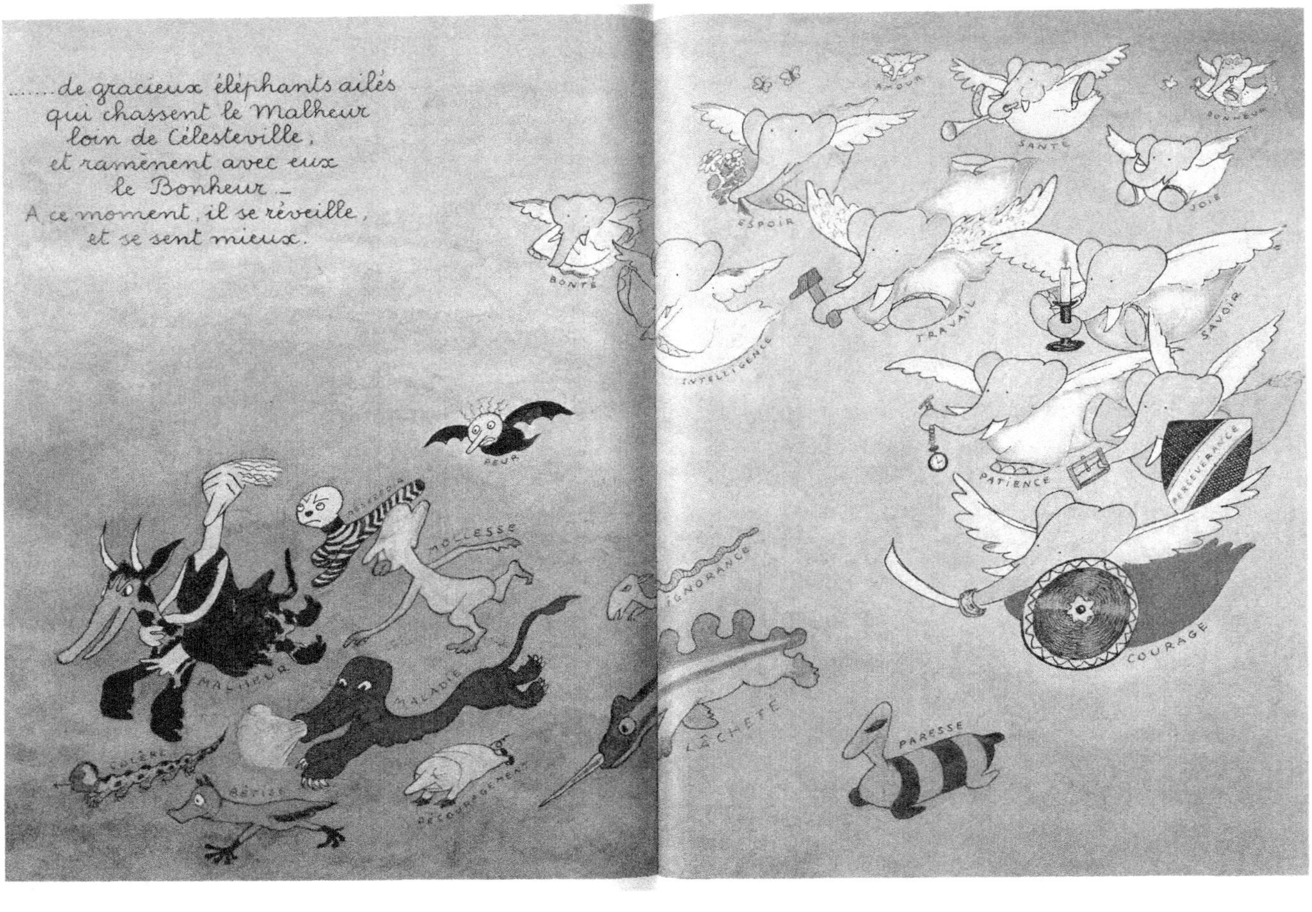

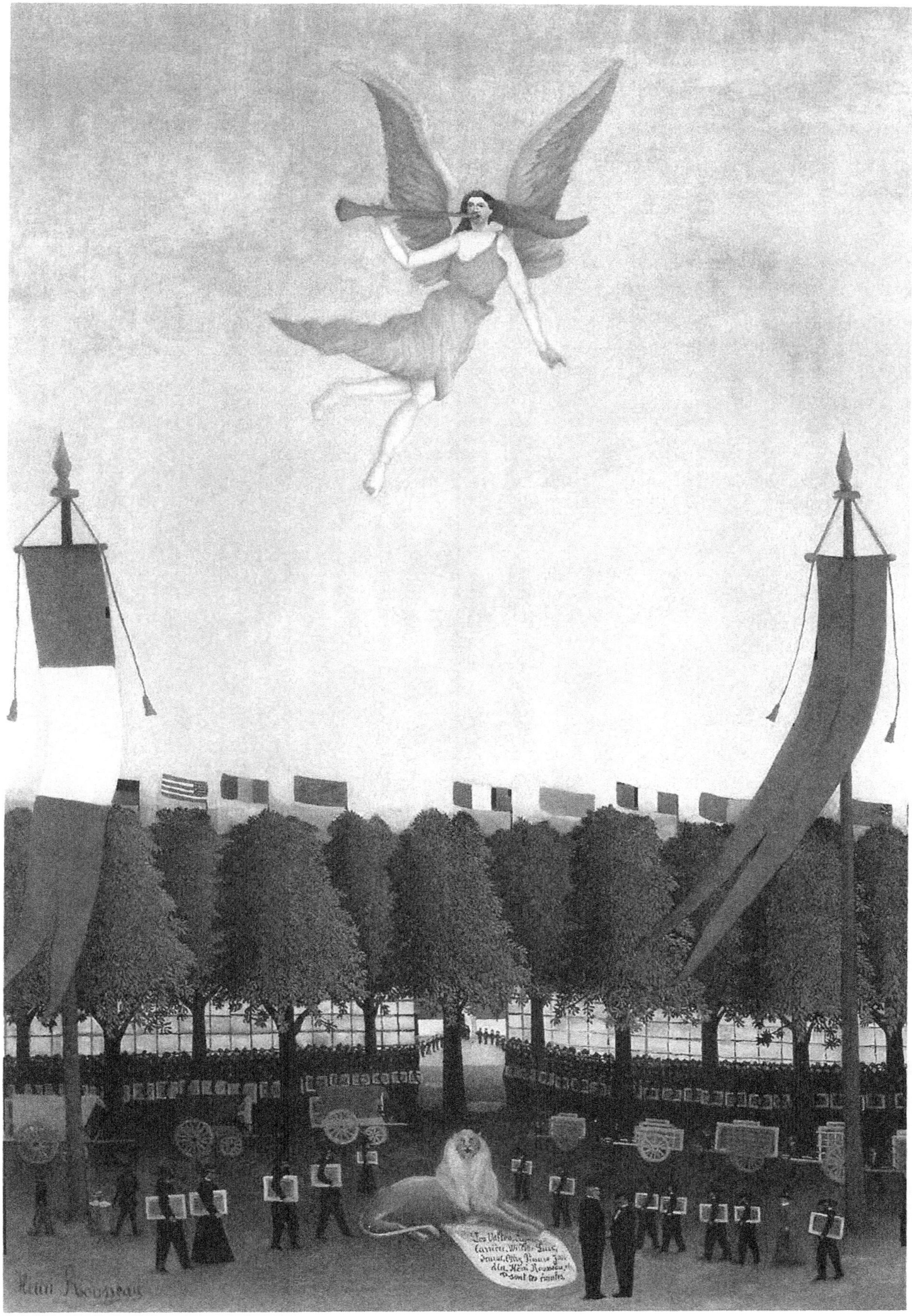

Let us continue in the French winged confection division. The premier artistic work, 27 years earlier than *Babar's Dream*, is Henri Rousseau's 1906 painting with the confectionary title *Liberty Inviting Artists to Take Part in the Twenty-second Exhibition of the Société des Artistes Indépendants*. Interweaving a diversity of real and imaginary images, Rousseau creates a poignant narrative-fantasy that makes an overall general point (celebrating the Salon des Indépendants) and also reveals specific details about the Parisian art world. Some 200 painters, converging on the transparent entrance, bring their work to the exhibition by hand and cart. The rows of multiplied, nearly identical painters express an order in space (a long queue waiting for admission to the Salon) as well as an order in time (a moving flow of artists), similar to the repeated images of motion by Marey and Muybridge.

Integrating words into the complex of images, the scroll held by the lion cites individual artists, a detail that provides a verbal account of the cumulative contribution of the Salon:

> At the bottom center is a lion, obviously drawn from Bartholdi's Lion of Belfort, or, more precisely, from the reproduction located at the Place Denfert-Rochereau in Paris. . . . The lion, here a symbol of courage and the spirit of independence . . . is holding between his paws a rather eclectic list of Salon contributors: "Men such as Les Valton, Signac, Carrière, Willette, Luce, Seurat, Ortiz, Pissarro, Jaudin, Henri Rousseau, etc., etc., are thy [the lion's] emulators."[7]

To complete the confection, Liberty soars over the intricately arranged scene beneath. This angel, clasping a trumpet of Fame, is distinctly cheerier and more active than Dürer's winged figure, melancholy and grounded.

At left, Henri Rousseau, *La liberté invitant les artistes à prendre part à la 22e exposition des Indépendants*, 1906, oil on canvas, 175 by 118 cm, or 69 by 46½ in. Detail below.

[7] Michel Hoog, "Rousseau in His Time," *Henri Rousseau*, essays by Roger Shattuck, Henri Béhar, Michel Hoog, Carolyn Lanchner, and William Rubin (New York, 1985), pp. 170–172.

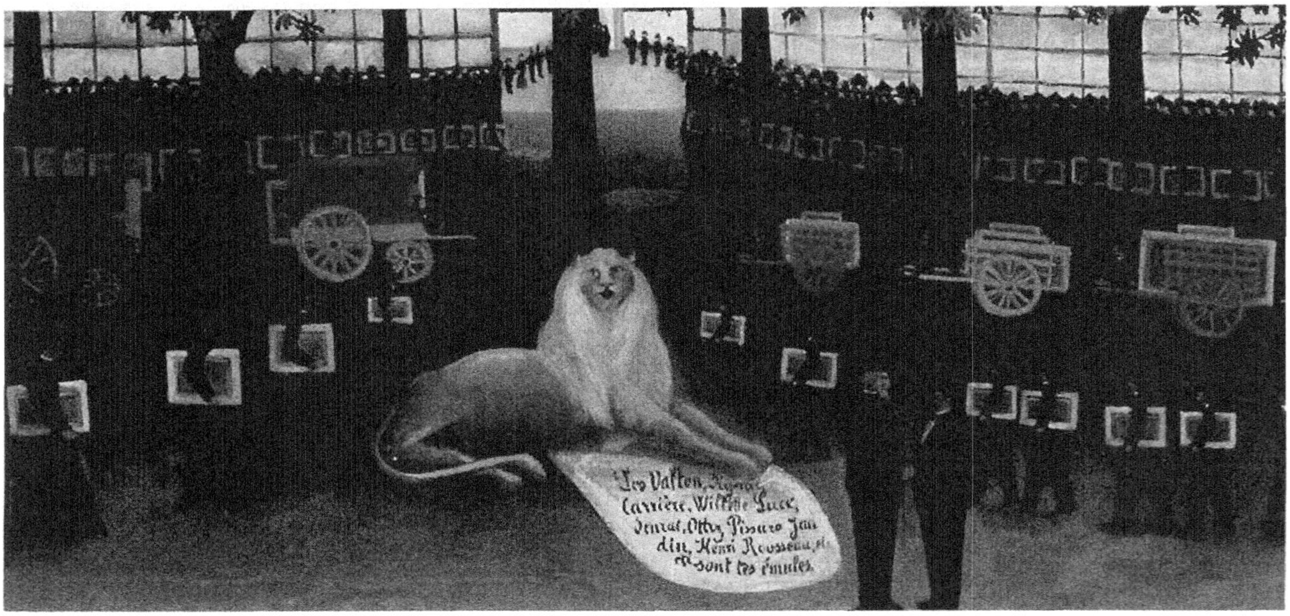

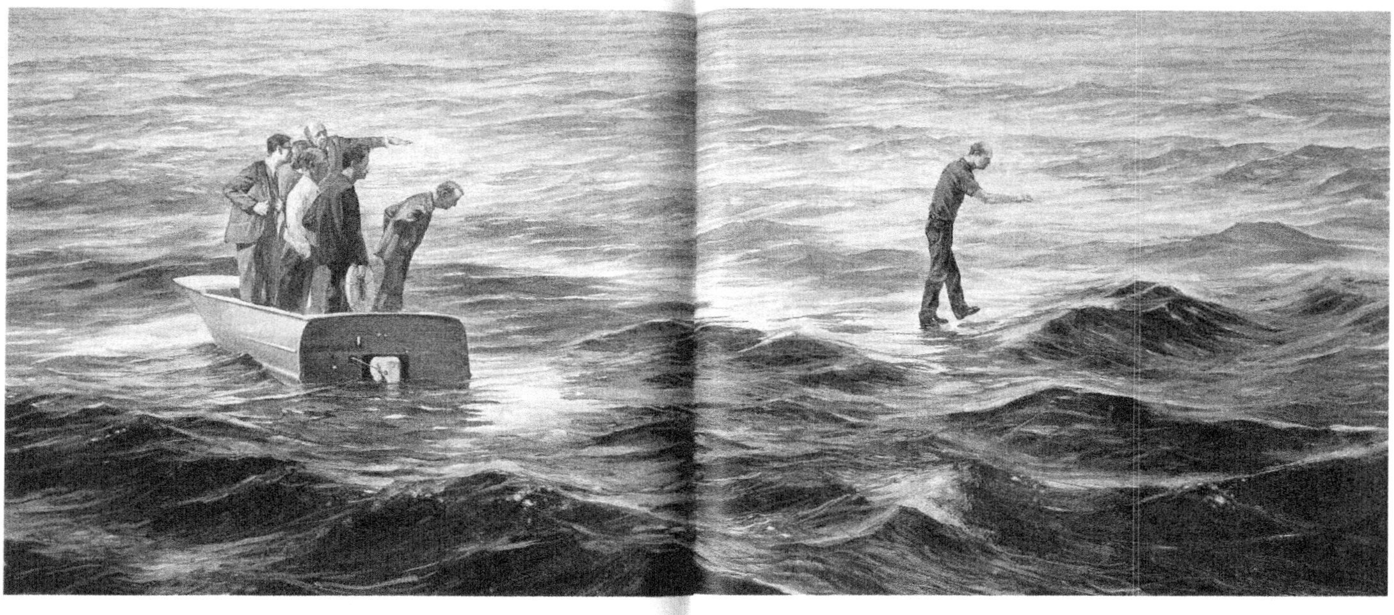

Mark Tansey, *Myth of Depth*, 1984, oil on canvas, 99 by 226 cm, or 39 by 89 in.

LIKE *Babar's Dream*, Mark Tansey's 1984 painting, *The Myth of Depth*, creates an impossibly wonderful scene. Arthur C. Danto writes about this play on flatland and representation in painting:

> . . . the device of showing in a picture what would be a miracle were it to occur in reality is used to great effect. Jackson Pollock is shown walking on the water, like Jesus. Depth (in painting, at least), after all, under the revelation of Greenberg, was an illusion, so what looks like a miracle is merely a matter of necessity; there is only surface here! In the boat, Motherwell studies the water uncertainly, while Greenberg lectures on the nature of flatness. Gorky, doubtful, holds a life preserver. In fact, the painting is Tansey's own lecture on flatness and depth, illusion and reality, and the painting manages to have it both ways: if Pollock has miraculously proven that depth is a myth, the painting in which this miracle is recorded is—like all of Tansey's work—faithful to the idea that pictorial space has depth.[8]

Descriptions of confections seem to provoke the language of miracles, as familiar elements find renewed meaning in astonishing arrangements. A sketched key parallels Tansey's painting:

1. Kenneth Noland
2. Mark Rothko
3. Arshile Gorky
4. Robert Motherwell
5. Clement Greenberg
6. Helen Frankenthaler
7. Jackson Pollock

[8] Arthur C. Danto, *Mark Tansey: Visions and Revisions* (New York, 1992), p. 23; key at p. 136. Most of Tansey's works are confections.

ROBERT BURTON'S *The Anatomy of Melancholy* (1638) begins with a magnificent confection, a title page of ten compartments each corresponding to a numbered stanza in the prefatory poem "The Argument of the Frontispiece." The diagram shows how image and stanza are linked. The poem, which repays study, is at right.

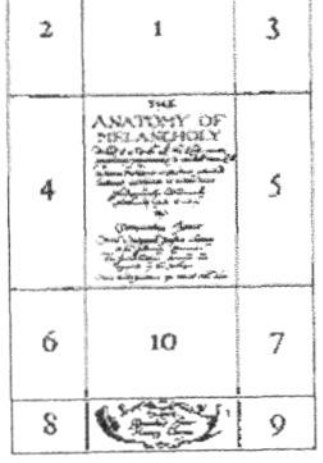

TEN distinct Squares here seene apart,
Are joyn'd in one by Cutters art.

1 *Old* Democritus *under a tree,*
Sits on a stone with book on knee;
About him hang there many features,
Of Cats, Dogs and such like creatures,
Of which he makes Anatomy,
The seat of black choler to see.
Over his head appears the sky
And Saturn *Lord of melancholy.*

2 *To th' left a landscape of* Jealousy,
Presents it self unto thine eye.
A Kingfisher, a Swan, an Hern,
Two fighting Cocks you may discern,
Two roaring Bulls each other hie,
To assault concerning Venery.
Symbols are these; I say no more,
Conceive the rest by that's afore.

3 *The next of* Solitariness,
A portraiture doth well express,
By sleeping dog, cat: Buck and Doe,
Hares, Conies in the desert go:
Bats, Owls the shady bowers over,
In melancholy darkness hover.
Marke well: If't be not as't should be,
Blame the bad Cutter and not me.

4 *I' th' under Columne there doth stand*
Inamorato *with folded hand;*
Down hangs his head, terse and polite,
Some dittie sure he doth indite.
His lute and books about him lie,
As symptomes of his vanity.
If this do not enough disclose,
To paint him, take thy self by th' nose.

5 Hypocondriacus *leans on his arm,*
Winde in his side doth him much harm,
And troubles him full sore God knows,
Much pain he hath and many woes.
About him pots and glasses lie,
Newly brought from's Apothecary.
This Saturn's *aspects signify,*
You see them portray'd in the sky.

6 *Beneath them kneeling on his knee,*
A Superstitious *man you see:*
He fasts, prays, on his Idol fixt,
Tormented hope and fear betwixt:
For hell perhaps he takes more pain,
Then thou dost Heaven it self to gain.
Alas poor Soul, I pity thee,
What stars incline thee so to be?

7 *But see the* Madman *rage down right*
With furious looks, a gastly sight.
Naked in chains bound doth he lie,
And roars amain he knows not why?
Observe him; for as in a glass,
Thine angry portraiture it was.
His picture keep still in thy presence;
Twixt him and thee, ther's no difference.

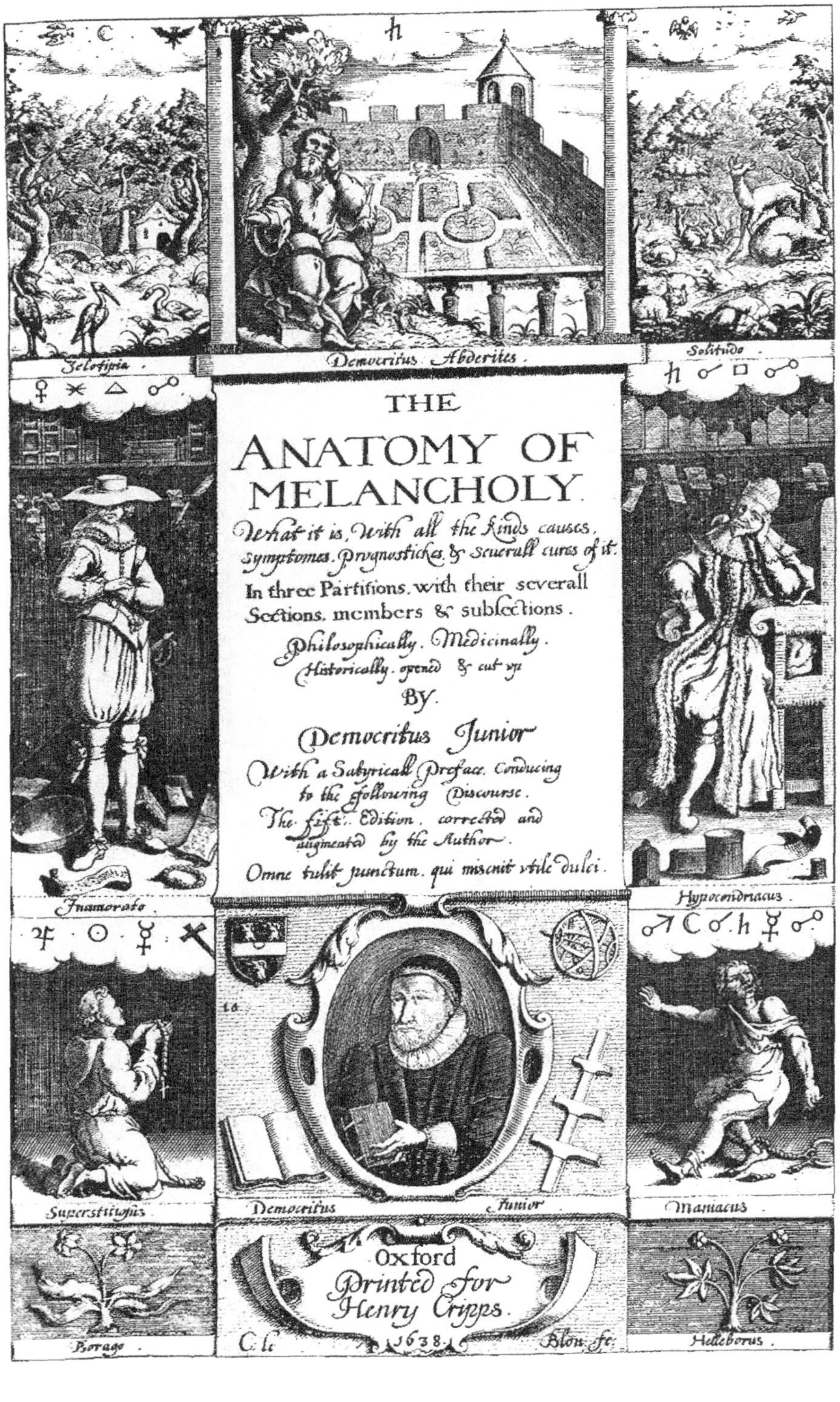

Compartment 10, for example, portrays Burton, not out of vanity of the author but rather at the insistence of the printer, at least according to the amusing stanza 10.

This design is a very special information display. The title page and accompanying poem reflect the book's argument, organization, *and* intellectual method. That method—the cutting and pasting of images and words—is announced in the opening lines:

Ten distinct Squares here seene apart,
Are joyn'd in one by Cutters art.

Moreover, the confectionary design of the title page reproduces the intellectual architecture of *The Anatomy of Melancholy:* about one-third of the book consists of quotations and another third of paraphrases.[9] A busy cutter indeed, and Burton disingenuously comments:

Marke well: If't be not as't should be,
Blame the bad Cutter and not me.

Some confections represent subjects originating from a written text: examples include the title pages of *Rosa ursina sive sol, The Anatomy of Melancholy*, and Hobbes' *Leviathan.*[10] Confections can only sketch out complex texts, although the images may contribute fresh insights, and make visible what is textually invisible, obscure, or beyond words:

> If some illustrations of a text are extreme reductions of a complex narrative—a mere emblem of the story—others enlarge the text, adding details, figures, and a setting not given in the written source. Sometimes the text itself is not specific enough to determine a picture, even in the barest form. Where the book of Genesis tells that Cain killed Abel, one can hardly illustrate the story without showing how the murder was done.[11]

Confectionary images representing texts are also notably enriched by the context (labels, captions, surrounding text) and by the associations recollected by "instructed viewers." Meyer Schapiro writes:

> Seeing in a picture only a few elements from a known text, we are able to identify the story. The text is often so much fuller than the illustration that the latter seems a mere token, like a pictorial title; one or two figures or some attribute or accessory object, seen together, will evoke for the instructed viewer the whole chain of actions linked in that text with the few pictured elements, unless an incompatible detail arrests the interpretation. Examples are the paintings in the Christian catacombs of Rome where Noah stands in the ark, Daniel between the lions, and Susanna beside the elders. But the meaning of such reductive imagery may be rich in connotations and symbolized values not evident from the basic text itself; these were fixed for Christian viewers by what they had learned about the same themes from religious commentary and allusions in sermons, ritual, and prayer.[12]

Such connotations enhance the content derived from images, although information displays that rely on instructed viewers to provide detailed exegesis may only mystify those viewers from out of town.

8 9 Borage *and* Hellebor *fill two scenes,*
Soveraign plants to purge the veins
Of melancholy, and cheer the heart,
Of those black fumes which make it smart;
To clear the Brain of misty fogs,
Which dull our senses, and Soul clogs,
The best medicine that ere God made
For this malady, if well assaid.

10 *Now last of all to fill a place,*
Presented is the Authors *face;*
And in that habit which he wears,
His Image to the world appears.
His mind no art can well express,
That by his writings you may guess.
It was not pride, nor yet vain glory,
(Though others do it commonly)

Made him do this: if you must know,
The Printer would needs have it so.
Then do not frown or scoff at it,
Deride not, or detract a whit.
For surely as thou dost by him,
He will do the same again.
Then look upon't, behold and see,
As thou lik'st it, so it likes thee.

And I for it will stand in view,
Thine to command, Reader *Adieu.*

Robert Burton, *The Anatomy of Melancholy* (Oxford, 1638), title page and "The Argument of the Frontispiece."

[9] E. Patricia Vicari, *The View from Minerva's Tower: Learning and Imagination in The Anatomy of Melancholy* (Toronto, 1989), p. 4; Ruth A. Fox, *The Tangled Chain: The Structure of Disorder in the Anatomy of Melancholy* (Berkeley, 1976).

[10] Other intricate examples are Euclid, *The Elements of Geometrie* (London, 1570), preface by John Dee, translated by Henry Billingsley (the first English translation of Euclid); Marin Mersenne, *Harmonie Universelle* (Paris, 1636); John Bulwer, *Chirologia; or, The Naturall Language of the Hand* (London, 1644); and Giambattista Vico, *Scienza nuova* (Naples, 1744), with a confectionary frontispiece accompanied by 24 pages of detailed explanation.

[11] Meyer Schapiro, *Words and Pictures: On the Literal and the Symbolic in the Illustration of a Text* (The Hague, 1973), p. 11; also in Schapiro's *Words, Script, and Pictures: Semiotics of Visual Language* (New York, 1996).

[12] Schapiro, *Words and Pictures*, pp. 9–10.

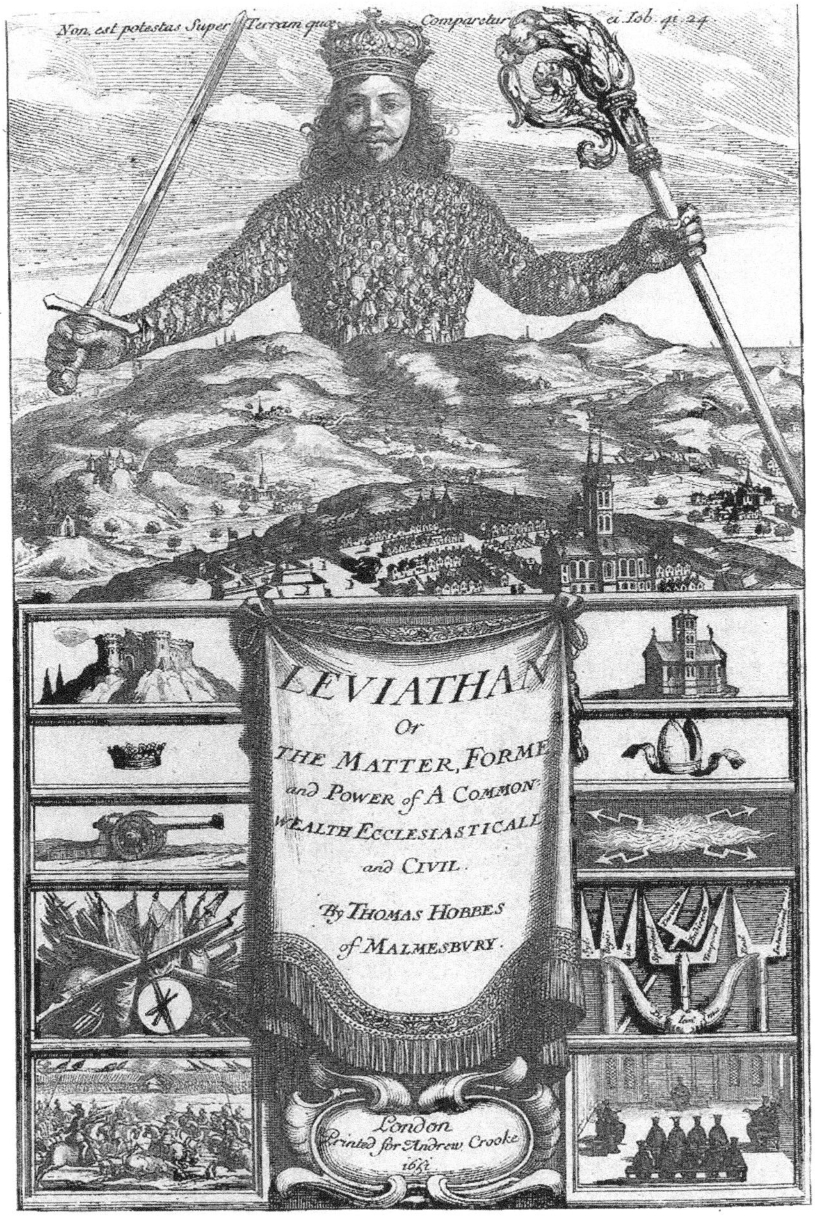

Thomas Hobbes, *Leviathan, Or the Matter, Forme and Power of a Commonwealth Ecclesiasticall and Civil* (London, 1651), title page.

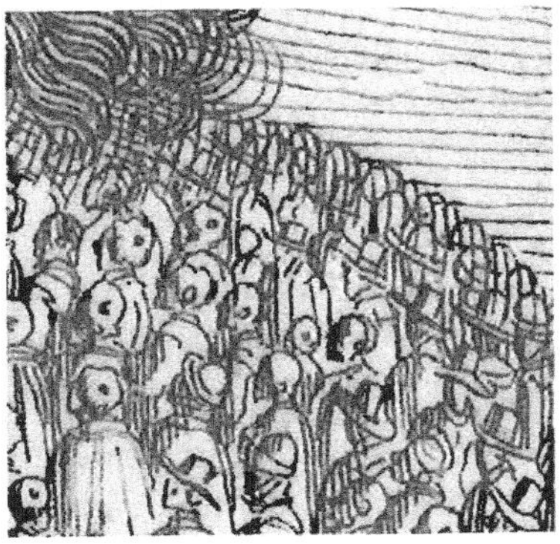

The elaborate and detailed title page of Thomas Hobbes' classic of political theory, *Leviathan*, combines both methods of organizing confections, the imagined scene (top half) and compartments (bottom). Reigning over the entire page is the artificial body constructed from a multitude of tiny citizens, described by Hobbes as a "great LEVIATHAN called a COMMONWEALTH OR STATE, in Latin CIVITAS, which is but an artificial man; though of greater stature and strength than the natural, for whose protection and defence it was intended. . ."[13]

[13] Thomas Hobbes, *Leviathan, Or the Matter, Forme and Power of a Commonwealth Ecclesiasticall and Civil* (London, 1651), edited by Michael Oakeshott (New York, 1962), p. 19.

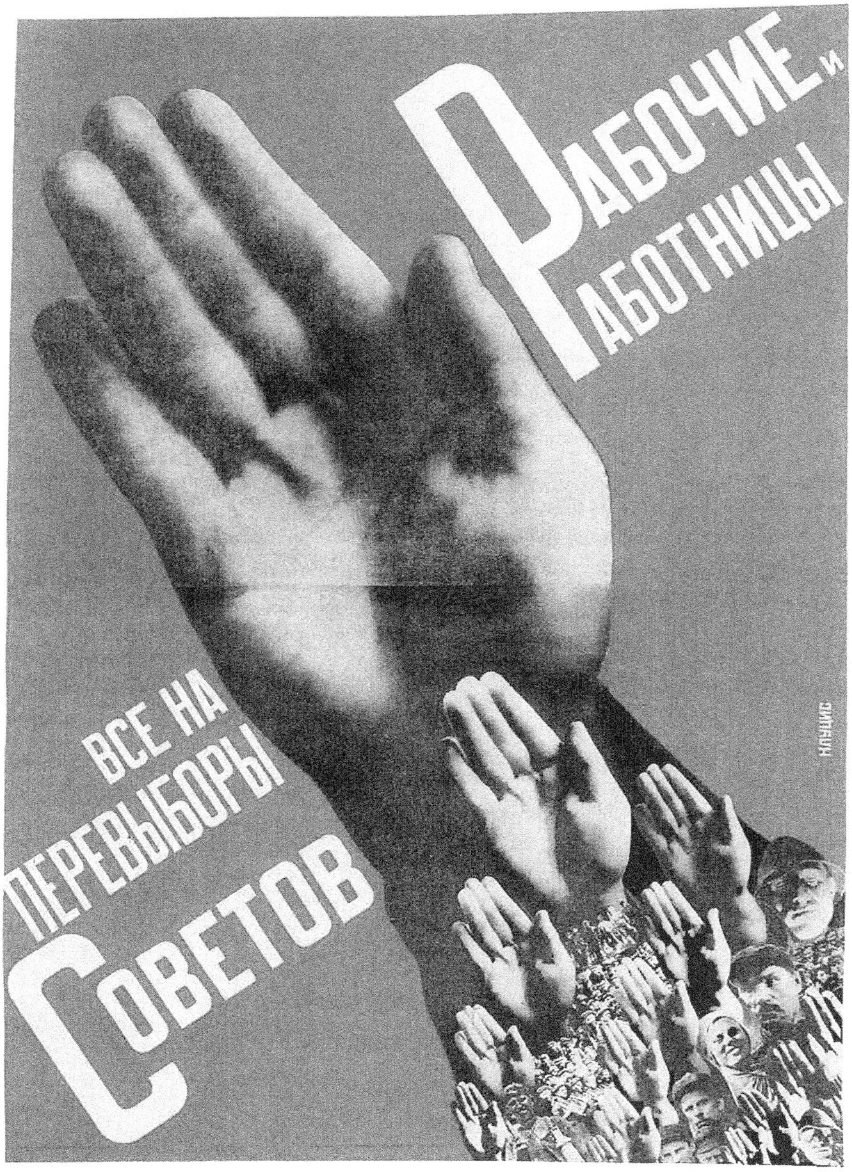

Gustav Klutsis, *Everyone to the Re-elections of the Soviets*, 1930, lithograph poster, 120 by 86 cm, 47¼ by 33¾ in.

A similar compositional analogy informs a 1930 poster by the Soviet graphic artist Gustav Klutsis. All citizens are urged to unite and vote for the Soviet candidates, the only ones running in the election. Both the title page and the poster reflect all-encompassing, statist doctrines. Above Leviathan is a line from The Book of Job, *Non est potestas Super Terram quae Comparetur ei*, "there is no power on earth which can be compared to him," a thought reinforced by the design:

> [Leviathan's] size, compared with the mountains, spires and fortresses beneath, implies a supreme power, an impression enhanced by the omission of a top border so that the tip of his sword is not so much cut off as lost in the skies. The sword is the emblem of the sovereign's temporal power. . . . The men who make up the

> body of Leviathan are portrayed in the act of making the covenant, of literally uniting themselves in the person of the sovereign. . . . The whole is fitted to Hobbes' theme since the citadel lies under the sword of Leviathan and the church under the crozier.[14]

The lower half of the title page is divided into a grid of compartments cleverly cross-linked by both format and content. Adding up to something more than a statement of themes and something less than an argument, the compilation of images reasons by analogy, metaphor, and visual and verbal parallelism:

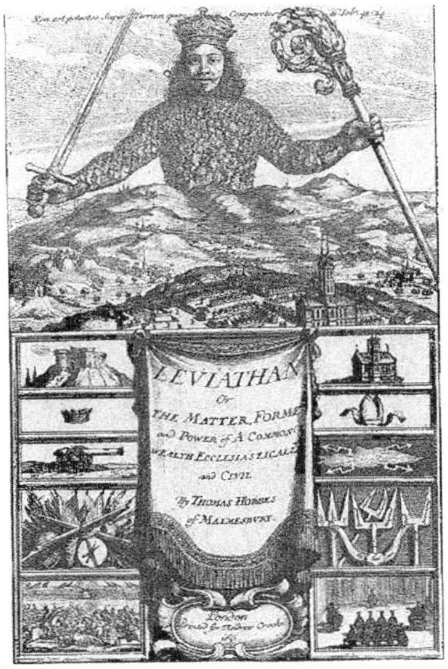

> Tabulated directly under the sword and the crozier, are further scenes and symbols showing the sovereign's exercise of temporal rule on the left and ecclesiastical rule on the right. They are meant to be read both downwards and across; this is indicated by the designer, who has made each compartment of a different size to that below and above but a pair to its opposite number. . . . At the top of the right side is the church . . . which matches the castle. The bishop's mitre matches the secular coronet. . . . The thunderbolt opposite the cannon signifies ecclesiastical punishment, that is excommunication. . . . The next compartment down shows the weapons of logic used in the discussion of ecclesiastical questions; they are placed parallel to the weapons of war. At the bottom the disputation shows the ecclesiastical way of settling a dispute in contrast to the battle opposite—the disputes of the schools. . . .[15]

In this dense, complex design, several elements double-function: little citizens add up to a larger body, compartments link both vertically and horizontally, and the head of Leviathan is a portrait of the author![16] The intensity of detail is quite astonishing; a comprehensive description of the visual elements of the title page required some 31,200 words.[17] Overall, the visualization, which Hobbes evidently helped to design,[18] may assist readers of *Leviathan* to appreciate its great scope and to recall its structure and argument.

LIKE Burton, Hobbes, and other confectioneers of 17th-century title pages who combine images to express their ideas in a second language, the American artist Joseph Cornell juxtaposes found objects in a grid of compartments (at right). Cornell's boxes, miniature theaters of reverie, assemble once-separate materials to create magical and cryptic architectures, three-dimensional collages.[19] For art, *collage* (French, *pasting*) combines images so as to create pleasing or provoking visual experiences, hardly expressible in words and rarely based on words; on the other hand, *confections* bring images together to display visual information, often expressible in words and often derived from words. Confection-makers cut, paste, construct, and manage miniature theaters of information—a cognitive art that serves to illustrate an argument, make a point, explain a task, show how something works, list possibilities, narrate a story.

[14] Margery Corbett and Ronald Lightbown, *The Comely Frontispiece: The Emblematic Title-page in England 1550–1660* (London, 1979), pp. 224–225.

[15] Corbett and Lightbown, pp. 225–229.

[16] Cornelis W. Schoneveld, "Some Features of the Seventeenth-Century Editions of Hobbes's *De Cive* Printed in Holland and Elsewhere," in J. G. van der Bend, ed., *Thomas Hobbes, His View of Man* (Amsterdam, 1982), 124–142; and Corbett and Lightbown, pp. 229–230. In a later edition of *Leviathan*, the face grew older!

[17] Corbett and Lightbown, pp. 218–230, This is an intensity of 91 words per square centimeter of the original *Leviathan* title-page, or 579 words per square inch.

[18] Corbett and Lightbown, pp. 221–222; but see also Keith Brown, "The Artist of the *Leviathan* Title-Page," *British Library Journal* 4 (1978), pp. 24–36.

[19] "I've read that Goethe, Hans Christian Andersen, and Lewis Carroll were managers of their own miniature theaters. There must have been many other such playhouses in the world. We study the history of literature of the period, but we know nothing about these plays that were being performed for an audience of one." Charles Simic, *Dime-Store Alchemy: The Art of Joseph Cornell* (New York, 1992), p. 48.

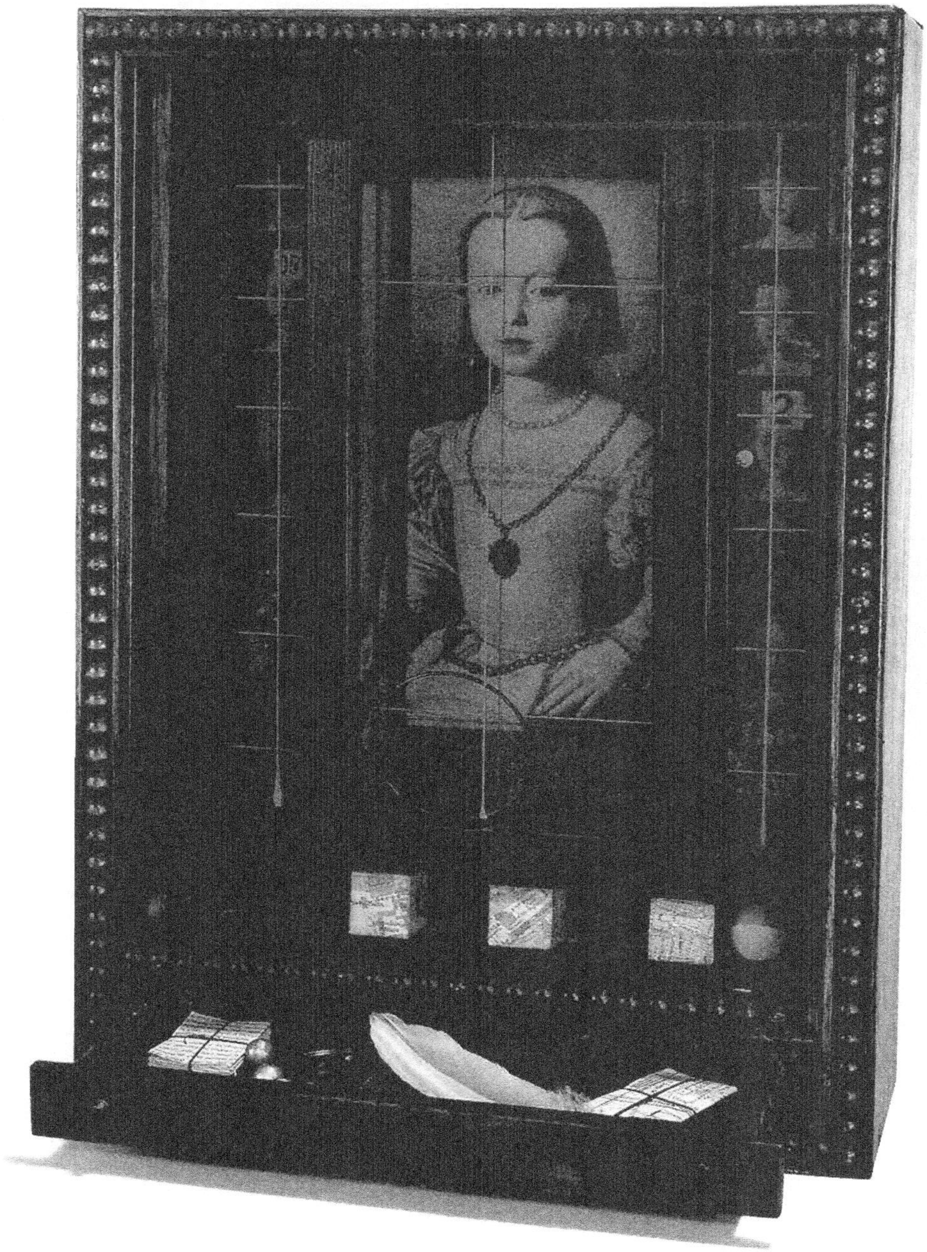

Joseph Cornell, *Medici Princess*, ca. 1952, box construction of painted wood, photomechanical reproductions, painted and colored glass, painted paper, string, photomechanical reproductions colored with ink, painted cork, metal rings, painted plastic balls, painted feather, tacks and screws mounted in painted wood shadow box. 44.5 by 31.1 by 12.1 cm, or 17⅝ by 12¼ by 4¾ in.

And accordingly, what collage is for art, confections are for the design of information:

> The collage technique, that art of reassembling fragments of pre-existing images in such a way as to form a new image, is the most important innovation in the art of this century. Found objects, chance creations, ready-mades (mass-produced items promoted into art objects) abolish the separation between art and life. The commonplace is miraculous if rightly seen, if recognized.[20]

[20] Charles Simic, *Dime-Store Alchemy: The Art of Joseph Cornell* (New York, 1992), p. 8. See also Christine Poggi, *In Defiance of Painting: Cubism, Futurism, and the Invention of Collage* (New Haven, 1992); and Clement Greenberg, *Art and Culture* (Boston, 1961), who writes, "Collage was a major turning point in the evolution of Cubism, and therefore a major turning point in the whole evolution of modernist art in this century." (p. 70).

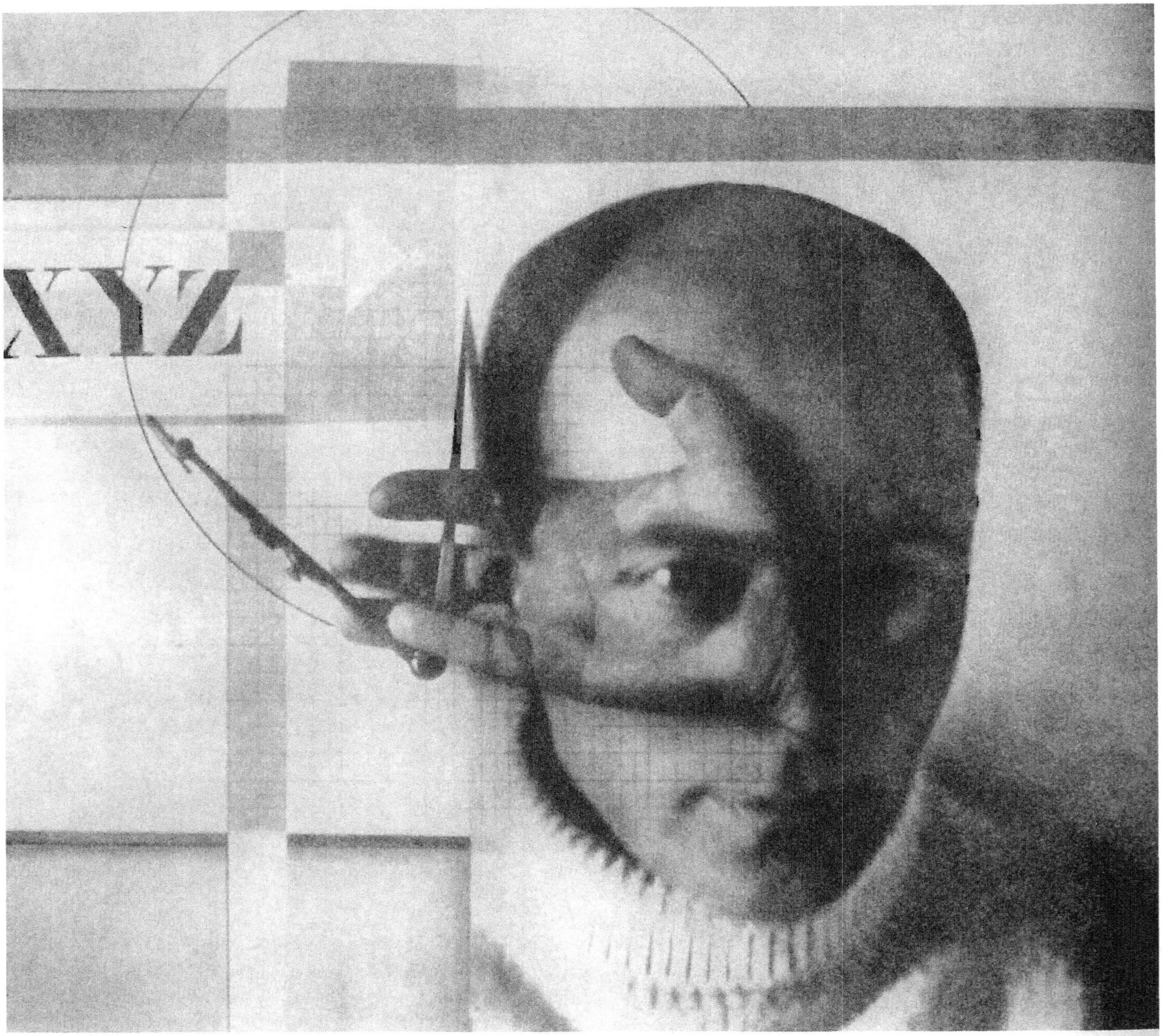

El Lissitzky, *Self Portrait: The Constructor,* 1924.

El Lissitzky's striking confection-photomontage, *The Constructor,* combines mind, eye, hand, tool which in turn arrange geometric forms, type, and line on an underlying grid. Overlapping images express a multiplicity of links and metaphors: the mind's eye, the hand of creation, the coordination of hand and eye, the hand and tool, the integration of person and work, the wholeness of artistic creation—and, possibly, even a halo for its saintly constructor.

By showing steps between the idea in the mind to the reality of the paper, Lissitzky illustrates the *process* of graphic thinking and creation. Each visual bridge acts as a verb to link up the nouns (mind, eye, hand, compass, image, type, grid, paper) of artistic work. That work on paper then reflects back (via the pointing arrow) to eye and thought. The grid of the graph paper orders both worlds.

The Constructor also points to the fundamental issue in representation: how do we go about depicting a world of three or more dimensions, the world our mind knows, on two-dimensional flatlands of paper?[21] In viewing the montage, our eye begins with the three-dimensional head, hand, and compass; then moves back toward the upper left to a two-dimensional world, exactly the translation required of art, perspective renderings, photographs, maps, multivariate statistical graphics, and many other displays of information. Appropriately, a tool (the compass) takes us from three-space to paper's two-space. Hand, mind, and eye intersect at a visual center of the montage; the centrality is enhanced by the strong contrast between the eye and dark shadow.

[21] For representational art, see, for example, John White, *The Birth and Rebirth of Pictorial Space* (London, 1957); and Martin Kemp, *The Science of Art* (New Haven, 1990). For contemporary art: Frank Stella, *Working Space* (Cambridge, 1986). For information design: Edward R. Tufte, *Envisioning Information* (Cheshire, Connecticut, 1990). For data graphics: William S. Cleveland and Marylyn E. McGill, eds., *Dynamic Graphics for Statistics* (Belmont, California, 1988).

This design is self-exemplifying. Lissitzky photographed himself; those are his hands holding the compass. The artist describes himself and his work, *The Constructor* by the constructor.

At the right, in ghastly contrast, we have another confected photomontage made up of human parts. This nightmare commenced soon after a design award was given to four people, who were then to appear on the cover of a design annual. The Creative Concept was slice-and-dice: cut up photographs of the four winners, then rearrange the bits and pieces into this stupendously unflattering composite, which, upon careful examination, only gets worse. An accompanying text describes the grotesque concoction: "Now here is the ultimate designer!" The exclamation point epitomizes the gushy witlessness of the effort, so contemptuous of its victim-subjects and its audience of readers.

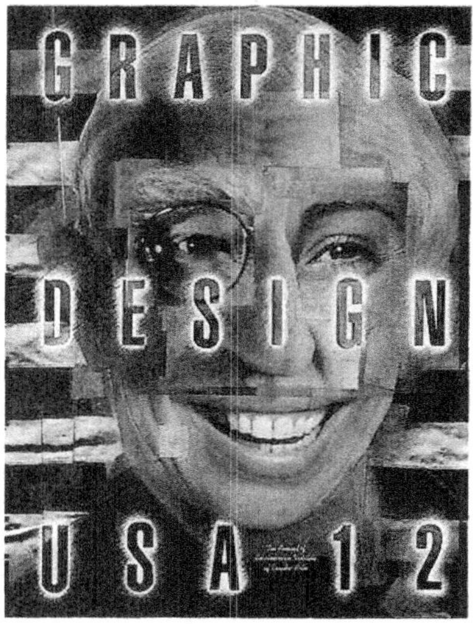

American Institute of Graphic Arts, *Graphic Design USA: 12* (New York, 1991), book jacket.

There are many differences between *The Constructor* and *The Ultimate Designer*—taste, subtlety, craft, skill. But most of all, it is a difference in the quality of the thought. Far from being a good idea, *The Ultimate Designer* is a terribly wrong guess. In contrast, *The Constructor* combines a richness of ideas with a complex analytic design that is thoroughly understandable.

The limits of confections arise from thinness of content, flimsy logic, poverty of annotating text, and heavy-handed arrangement of structure. And the "cutter's art" can tendentiously select evidence to make a point, to sell an argument, to win a debate. Confections stand or fall on how deeply they illuminate ideas and the relations among those ideas. At the heart of every intriguing confection, then, are intriguing concepts. Excellence in the display of information is a lot like clear thinking.

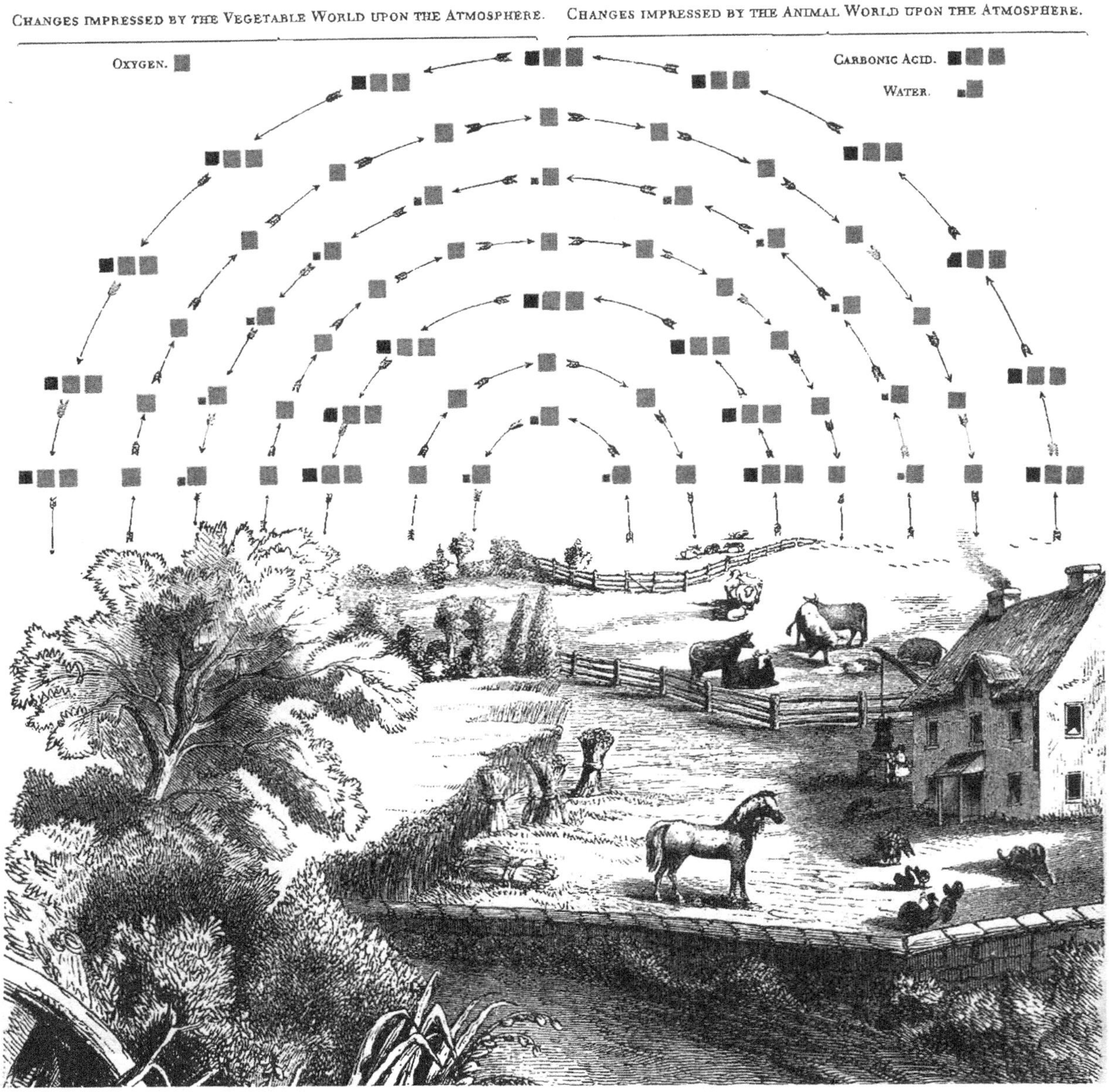

MERGING abstract color squares and barnyard particulars, this genial confection of the CO_2-O_2-H_2O cycle is accompanied by a hesitant and apologetic text that carries on about the possibility of unduly literal readings, as if diagrams are chronically threatened by misinterpretations:

> To fix distinctly in the mind the character of the changes wrought by growing vegetation upon the atmosphere, I have ventured again to resort to diagrams, which appeal to the eye. . . . The direction of the arrows shows carbonic acid and water, as it were, descending from the air, so as to enter the plant, at the same time that pure oxygen is set free, and rises, as it were, to take their place.

Edward L. Youmans, *Chemical Atlas; or, The Chemistry of Familiar Objects: Exhibiting the General Principles of the Science in a Series of Beautifully Colored Diagrams* . . . (New York, 1854), illustration at page 87.

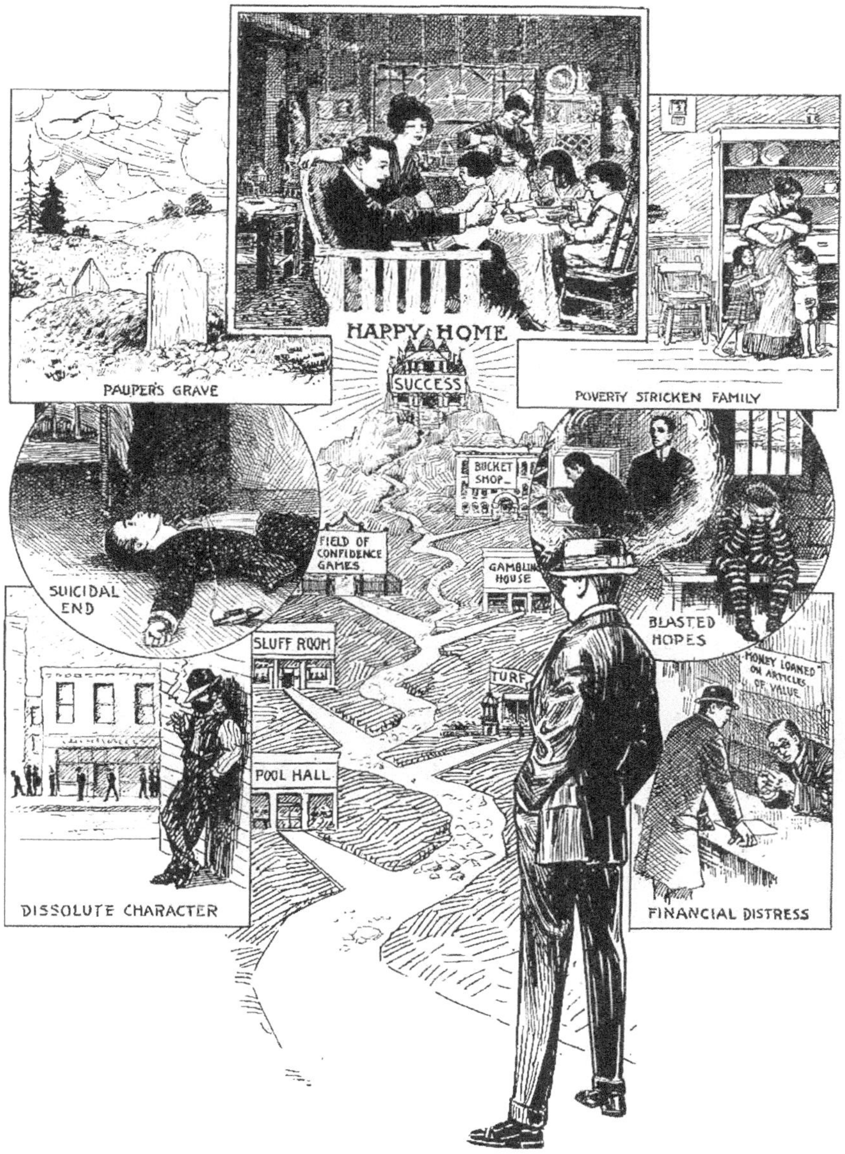

It is not to be supposed, as the picture might seem to show, that the plant has any power of attracting downward from a distance the carbonic acid and water particles. . . .[22]

Errors in reading, however, derive from specific, local explanatory failures or untruths. Diagrams do not suffer from some inherent defect that leads to confusion or misunderstanding.

Uncertainty and self-doubt did not appear to trouble the author of *Traps and Pitfalls to be Avoided in Order to Obtain Success,* this adventure-filled melodrama of personal character.[23] With nine distinct emblematic elements, including a memory within a scenario within the overall scenario, there is a sense of narrative, complexity, and even alternative—despite the one-dimensional analysis of success. In a clever maneuver with the timing of events, scenes are set as forward-looking flashbacks, a subjunctive visual voice. As in the *Leviathan* title page, an imagined scene is combined with compartments.

[22] Edward L. Youmans, *Chemical Atlas; or, The Chemistry of Familiar Objects: Exhibiting the General Principles of the Science in a Series of Beautifully Colored Diagrams . . .* (New York, 1854), illustration at page 87; quotation at page 86. Youmans' immensely successful *Chemical Atlas* is described in a note by Ralph E. Oesper, *Journal of Chemical Education*, 34 (August, 1957), p. 408.

[23] From a book with a title that is itself a verbal confection: H. K. James, *The Destruction of Mephisto's Greatest Web or, All Grafts Laid Bare, Being a Complete Exposure of All Gambling, Graft and Confidence Games with Stories Illustrating the Methods Employed by the Different "Operators"* (Salt Lake City, Utah, 1914), np, foldout, partially redrawn. Confectionary designs seem closely associated with long, very long, titles; such is the case for the dozens of titles and title-page confections of the 16th and 17th centuries, strikingly replicated in our present example from Salt Lake City in the early 20th century.

WHY IS THE POTOMAC RIVER SO DANGEROUS?

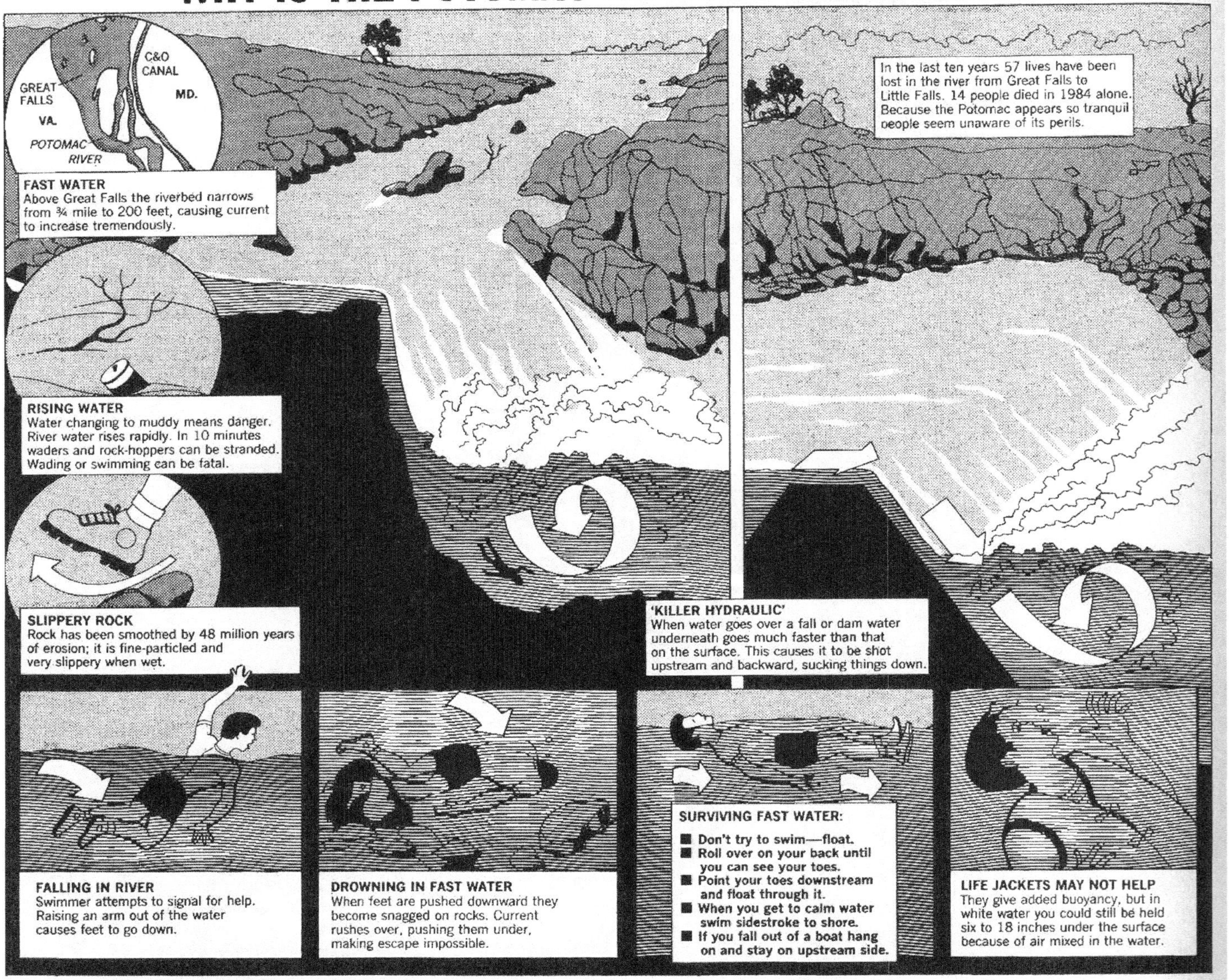

Great Falls Park Rangers Pray for Rain, to Save Lives

By Mary Jordan
Washington Post Staff Writer

Great Falls National Park rangers said they prayed it would rain today, not so much to keep people away but to keep them alive.

On each of the past two cloudless Sundays, a person who swam or slipped into the Potomac River near the park died.

If the sun shines as brilliantly as predicted today—drawing as many as 5,000 people to the park—authorities said, the chances that another person would drown would be as chilling as the cascading waterfalls themselves.

"There's a 1-in-11 chance that someone drowns [today]," said Howard E. McCurdy, an American University professor who has analyzed the 57 drownings that have occurred between Great Falls and Little Falls on the Potomac since 1975 for the National Park Service.

"A sunny, June Sunday when the water level is at a medium height makes the park service very nervous," McCurdy said Friday. "These tragedies aren't as random as we tend to think."

The study explains four factors contributing to a higher probability of drownings: weather, season, day of week and water level.

"Danger days" are what Joan Anzelmo, the park service site manager at Great Falls, calls warm, spring Sundays when the water level is between three and five feet.

On these days, when visitors sunbathe, climb rocks and picnic along the park's shoreline, Anzelmo said, the risk of drowning peaks, particularly because the water level is not high enough to alert people to the river's deadly undercurrents.

There are only five park rangers and two park police officers on each side of the 11-mile stretch of river between Great Falls and Little Falls in Virginia and Maryland.

For Earl V. Kittleman, the chief National Park spokesman, that means "I'm praying for clouds, drizzle or rain . . . , anything until we get past June weekends."

Anzelmo said that by July and August, news of the annual spring drownings scares more people away from the slippery rocks edging the Potomac, and fewer people visit Great Falls because many spend weekends at the beach or vacation elsewhere.

Yesterday, despite posted warnings and widespread news reports of the six drownings that have occurred this year, dozens of Great Falls patrons climbed perilously close to the river's edge.

Paul Galison, a 16-year-old Langley High School sophomore, stood a few yards from a sheer 50-foot drop into the Potomac yesterday. "I know it's dangerous," he said. "But the

See FALLS, C5, Col. 1

This news report and confectionary diagram are remarkably informative, describing a serious danger often fatally underestimated by park-goers. Note how the illustration explains *why* the river, with its dangers lurking beneath the surface, is so deceiving.[24] Drawings can present multiple and cut-away views, sequences of actions, focused annotation; in this case, it is better than any other method for explaining what is going on; it is certainly better than being there. Or imagine a television account of the same material: a murky Potomac River, a bereaved family, and mostly, an airhead announcer talking fast. Such a jumpy story—even if it went on for two minutes, an eternity in television time—would cover less than one-third of the news shown here (which takes six minutes to read aloud). Speech alone is sometimes an altogether inefficient, low-resolution method for communicating information, a point to be considered by teachers who rely on lectures, people running committees, and newscasters. Whenever possible, give your audience words and images written down on paper, even if only to supplement spoken words.

Although a television account would look much like any other disaster story (and thus contain little information), the printed report here is eloquent and memorable because of its specific and scary detail. Also the printed page allows *readers* to control the order and pace of the flow of information as well as the point of access, unlike the fixed one-dimensional ordering imposed by the rush of voice with video.

The illustrated narrative of disaster is right to the point, effectively showing dynamics and verbs and causes: slipping, falling, snagging of feet, gesturing, sinking, surviving. Thoughtful text-figure integration ties 20 to 50 words to each of the 9 separate but collaborating story-pictures. The typography is undistinguished; several captions have a clumsy right rag, partly the consequence of the short line-length.

The written news story below develops pretty much independently of the illustrations, with little repetition. However the major fact—57 drownings in 10 years—does not show up until the fourth paragraph, buried under something about hoping for rain, a catchy diversion which pretends to be *news* (for the deaths are *olds*, having happened for a long time).

Inclusion of 57 small photographs of those who died would add an individual and poignant quality to the general and analytical diagrams. And, on the map (at upper left), placing 57 dots to locate all the drownings would allow readers to particularize the danger by seeing what happened where *they* go walking. Fine detail activates viewers, as they search and edit, looking to turn a heap of data into a bit of relevant information.

Overall this is brilliant, all the more so because it was done in the rush of work at a daily newspaper.

The Washington Post, June 9, 1985, p. C1; the illustration was prepared by Johnstone Quinan of *The Washington Post*, based on information from The National Park Service.

[24] With the intensity of knowledge and passion so characteristic of the makers of excellent confections, Johnstone Quinan (letter, January 6, 1993) describes the origins of his illustration: "The Potomac River graphic came about because of a haunting memory. On a sunny, summer afternoon in the late 1970s, our family went to Great Falls National Park for a picnic. After lunch, we walked out on the rocks just below the falls. We heard shouting and as we watched, a young woman was washed downstream, over the edge of the falls and into the pool below. Within minutes rescuers came running with ropes, but she never surfaced. Her body was found much later. The experience stayed with me. We moved to Philadelphia where I worked for *The Philadelphia Inquirer.* Three years later I returned to Washington to do graphics for *The Washington Post.* The paper ran a story about yet another drowning at Great Falls. The picture of the young woman came again to mind and I began to wonder why that stretch of water was so dangerous. I did some research, made some rough sketches and showed them around. The editors liked the idea for a graphic, offered a half-page of space to it and assigned a reporter to do a separate story. Most of the facts came from the National Park Service people who worked at the site. The park rangers were trying hard to prevent deaths, but the water kept luring the unwary in. To test the power of the water, one ranger volunteered to be lowered into the 'killer hydraulic' with a rope tied to his waist. Even though he was a strong swimmer, the current sucked him under. They had to pull him up—there was no way he could get back to the surface by himself. After the piece ran, the Park Service had the graphic made into large, permanent, metal signs to display near the trail to the falls. The signs are still there."

By sorting through immense stockpiles of text and images, computers can quickly assemble and display one-time confections designed to serve immediate, local, unique purposes. For example, below is my interface for guiding museum-goers to exhibits and facilities. Right from the start, this opening panel shows the scope of information made available. Only a small part of the screen is devoted to computer administration (this is a touch-screen, these are the language options). Free of icons, decorative logotypes, and navigation apparatus, about 90% of the image is *substance*, a contextual overview describing the reservoir of data. In an architecture of content, the *information becomes the interface.* Rather than sequentially stacking up little bits of data to be unveiled gradually, this *flat interface* surfaces 45 options at once, distributing the information in space rather than in time. Museum-goers then touch the item that they wish to learn about (here, the location of Flemish paintings) and the next confection appears. Shown are a three-dimensional guide-map,

Touch any item for more information.

English | Español | Deutsch | Français | Italiano | 中文 | 日本語

INFORMATION

art information
bookstores
calendar
copyrights
film programs
gallery talks
guides
hours
photography
security
slide lectures
special programs
Sunday concerts
tours
wheelchairs/strollers

FACILITIES

cascade espresso bar
checkroom
concourse buffet
elevators
facility for disabled
first aid
garden cafe
lost and found
restrooms
stairways
telephones
terrace cafe

PERMANENT WORKS

American Painting
British Painting
Dutch Painting
European Sculpture and Decorative Arts, 14th–19th century
Flemish Painting
French Painting and Sculpture
German Painting
Information Design
Italian Painting and Sculpture
Netherlandish Painting
Spanish Painting
Twentieth-century Painting and Sculpture

SPECIAL EXHIBITIONS, NOVEMBER 2004

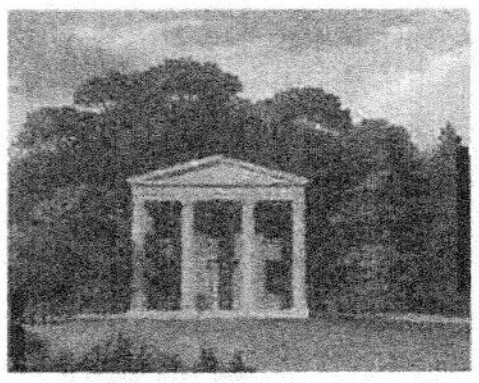
Architectural Designs of Humphry Repton

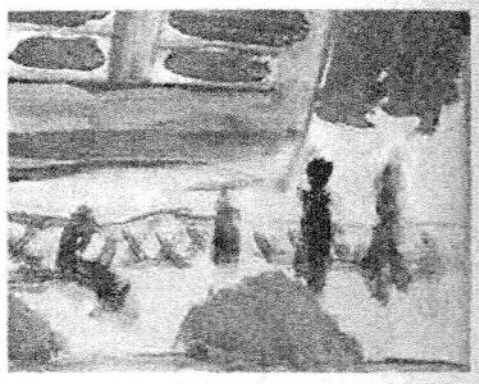
Henri Matisse: *Les periennes,* 1919

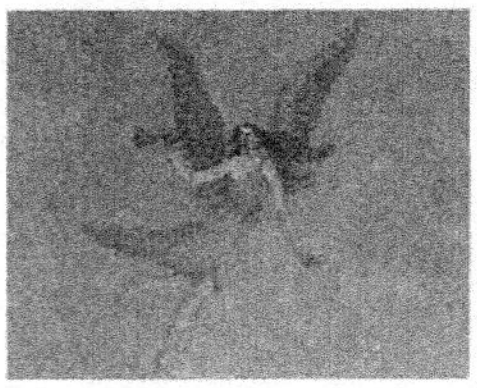
Henri Rousseau: French Winged Confections

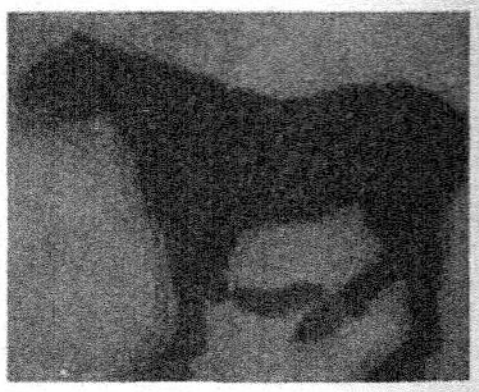
Susan Rothenberg: Recent Paintings

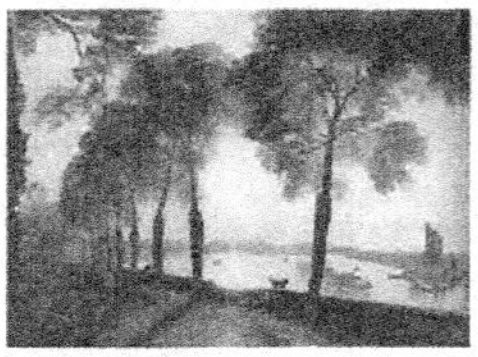
The Great Age of Tedious British Water-colors: 1750 to 1880

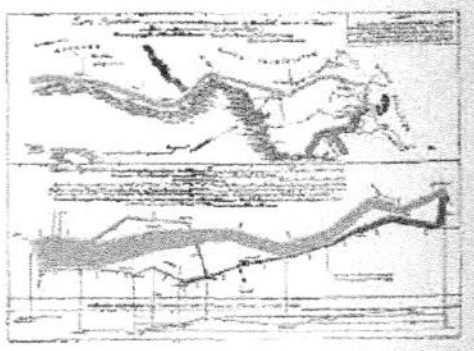
Information Designs of Charles Joseph Minard

written directions, and a live video image of museum-goers standing at the computer. Users will surely half turn and wave at the camera behind them. Again content dominates, with only two computer commands visible: (1) Return to the original table of contents, or (2) Touch the middle button to generate a sheet of paper reproducing what is on the screen: a map, written directions, *and* a video snapshot of the museum-goer at the computer kiosk! Emerging from a high-resolution printer, this paper serves as a portable and permanent memory, helping visitors navigate through a complex of buildings (shown here is the National Gallery in Washington). Indicating a route down the stairs, the red pointer on the video-image (linked to red line and footprint on the map) resembles the three-dimensional gesture made by someone giving directions, "Go around and down *that* way." Only a *printed* guide will lead people gracefully along a complicated route to Flemish paintings. The personal and entertaining photograph, combined with the map,

Concept and design by Edward Tufte; design and production by Bonnie Scranton, with Dmitry Krasny and Weilin Wu.

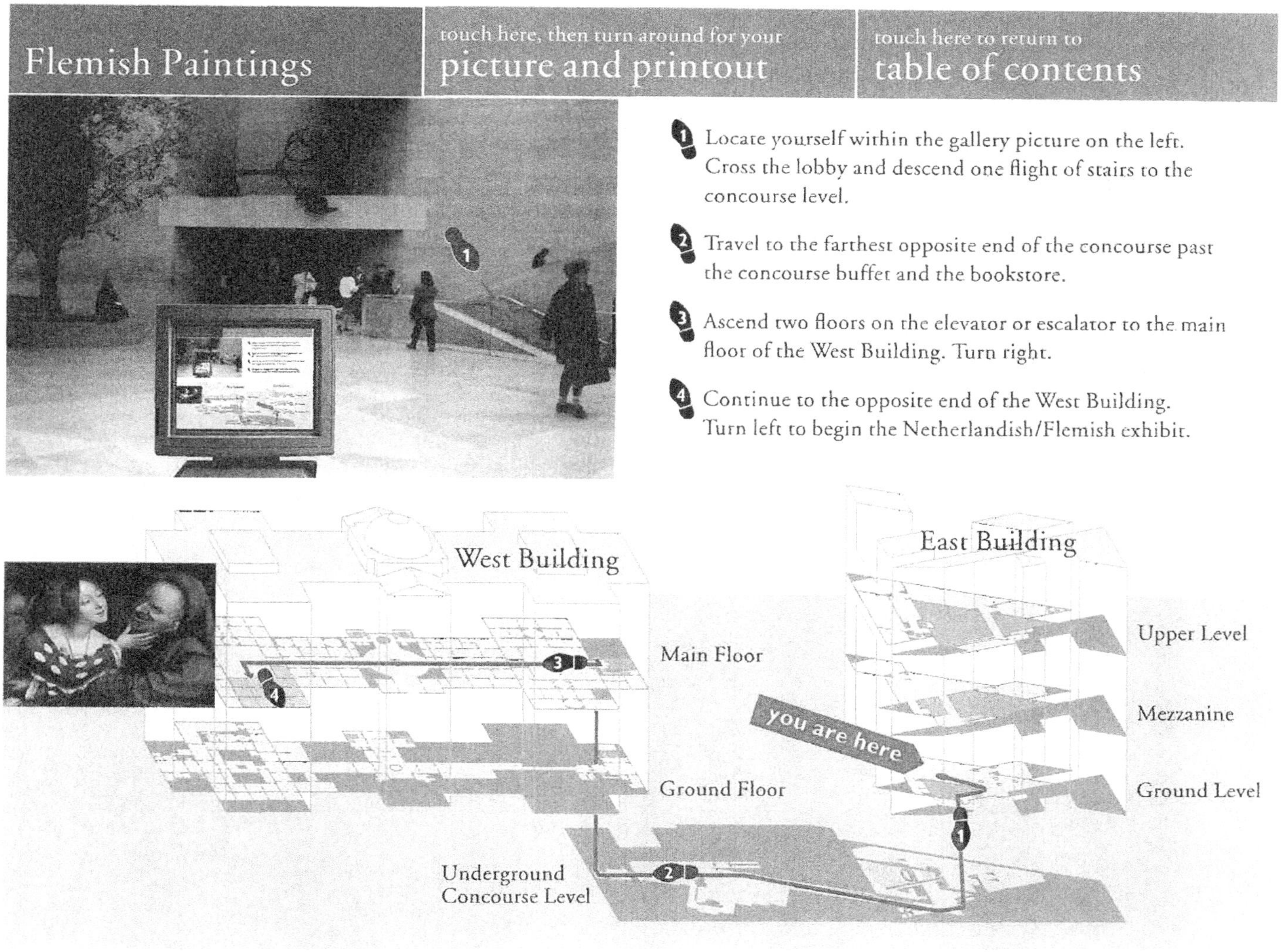

helps museum-goers orient themselves—in fact *see* themselves—within the three-space they are navigating. Each technology does what it is good at: the computer selects, organizes, customizes data; paper makes visible the high-resolution information in portable permanent form.

Information-sensitive designs are exacting and laborious, requiring a deep appreciation of the particular content at hand. More generic approaches to interface design are widespread.

For example, a news-broadcast method: as users approach the kiosk, the computer plays a 30-second video of the Director of the Museum welcoming the visitor, then a series of 20-second videos of curators of various galleries introducing their territory, and then the Vice President for Facilities Management pointing at the telephones and rest rooms. Besides resembling bad public television, such an approach commits a common error: the information architecture mimics the hierarchical structure of the bureaucracy producing the design. This also occurs in the design of magazines, as strongly colored frames delineate each sub-editor's turf. Those accented borders and running heads, sometimes the strongest visual statement on the page, are not there to help the reader but rather to replicate the organizational form.

Another way to design an interface such as the museum kiosk is to reason that people use computers all the time and so the design will simply follow standard computer practice. Thus the interface offers a sequence of binary choices, perhaps beginning as follows:

CHOOSE ONE (1) FROM THE LIST BELOW:

❑ **YOU LIKE ART?**

❑ **OR NOT?**

And so a museum-goer sequentially marches through a tedious decision tree in tiny irritating steps, as the logic of software is exposed to those who simply want to see some paintings or find a telephone. Context and overview are lost in this dopey approach. These poor designs are sometimes defended on the grounds that they conform to computer industry standards (for example, in a typical arranging-the-deckchairs-on-the-Titanic dictum: "Drop shadows on binary-choice boxes shall have the [pretend] light coming from upper left."). Ding-a-ling design is thus sanctified and institutionalized.

Another weak approach is to make the interface itself a conspicuous visual statement, with a great deal of creative effort going into styling a billboard that masks a data dump. Believed to be boring and in need of decorative spice, the content becomes trivialized and incidental. Too many interfaces for information compilations have suffered from television-disease: thin substance, contempt for the audience and the content, short attention span, and over-produced styling.[25]

[25] Printed publications and their readers have long been similar design-victims. Joseph Giovannini writes: "The effect of graphic design in many publications, then—even when it is handsome design—is the fragmentation or subordination of the text. The result affects no less than how we think: the broken page delivers impressions and even sensations, but it does not lead a reader into the depth that carefully elaborated ideas, crafted writing, and layered passages can create in quiet sequence. . . . The capitulation of text to layout can also be seen in books about the visual arts, in which texts are often treated as visual blocks that are subservient to pictures. In the most graphically 'painted' books each page is a design that may or may not have words, and texts are relegated to introductions that play a minor supporting role. Books about graphic design itself are notorious for having little or no text—they are simply compendia of full-page designs." Joseph Giovannini, "A Zero Degree of Graphics," in Mildred Friedman, ed., *Graphic Design in America: A Visual Language History* (Minneapolis, 1989), p. 204.

In addition to organizing information by means of analogies to television scripts, bureaucratic structures, software decision-trees, and music-television, interface designers have used a metaphor of the *book*, with viewers flipping through electronic pages. On the screen below, however, the metaphor has become the interface. Only 18% of the space depicts substantive information (photographers and their work); an astonishing 82% of the screen is devoted to computer administrative debris or to nothing at all. In a contrast symbolizing the priority of apparatus over information, compare the elaborately crafted system-icons (why won't just the words do?) with the distinctly clunky typography for the content, the names of the photographers. This spread from the book-parody shows only 53 typographic characters (last names and dates); real books display between 1,000 and 50,000 characters on a double-page spread.[26]

These quantitative measurements of the interface indicate how much the design itself has systematically reduced the already inherently low resolution of the 1990s computer screen (a resolution approximately

[26] The book metaphor used for this interface attracts unfortunate attention to the distorted and inconsistently rendered letterforms on the computer screen, so unlike the typography of well-designed books. Down the left part of the image, we have stamped-embossed sans serif,

Yearbook

then stamped-embossed serif,

Years

and, finally, a quirky system font—with an oversized x-height (presumably to improve legibility on the screen) resulting in cramped ascenders and descenders as well as a grotesque Y:

Yearbook

Yearbook page from *From Silver to Silica*, Interactive Media Group, The Minneapolis Institute of the Arts, 1991.

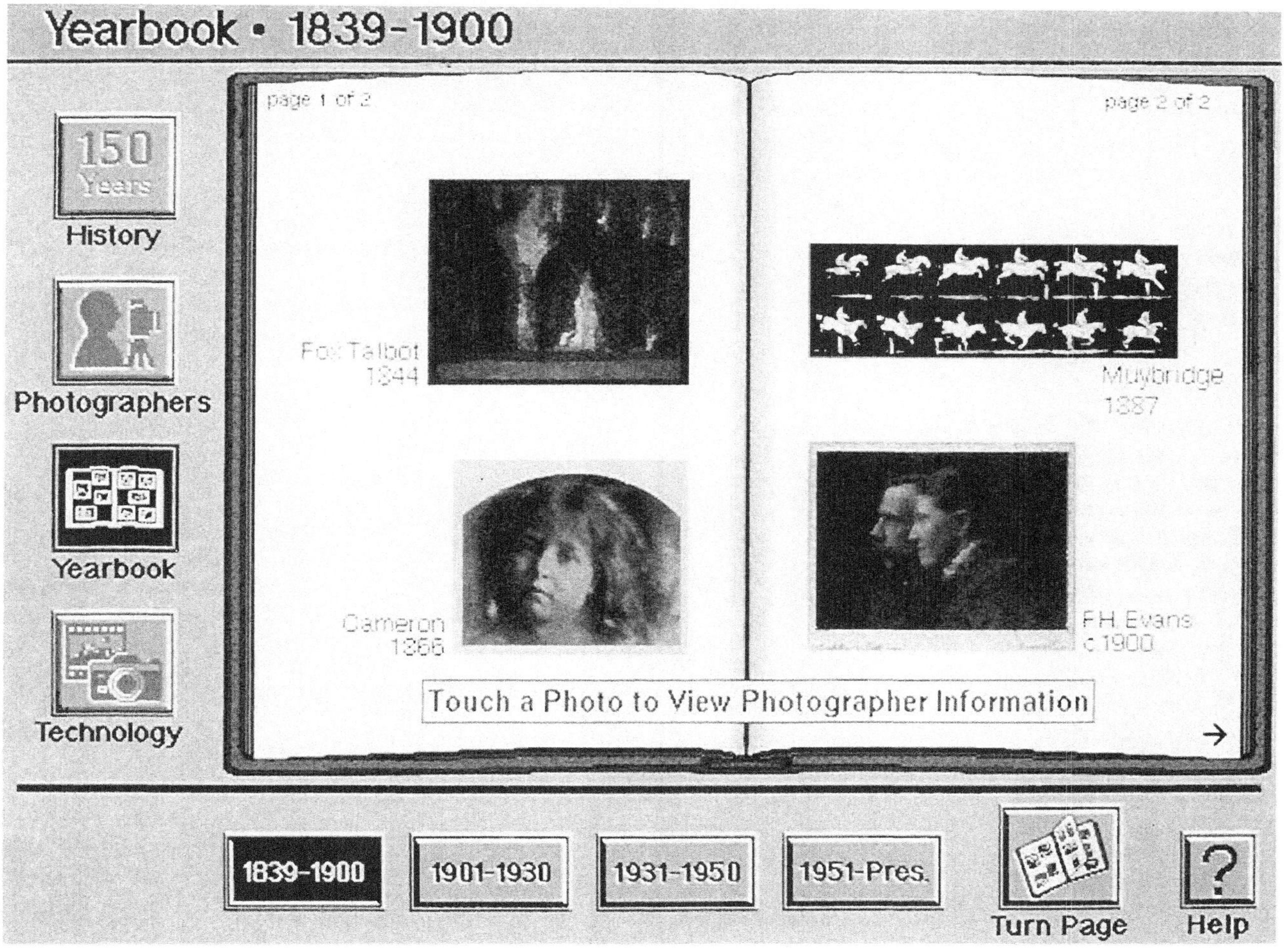

5% to 10% of a printed map). Direct measurement of content and non-content provides a quantitative assessment of an interface; these measures of the informational performance of a screen include:

- the proportion of space on the screen devoted to content, to computer administration, and to nothing at all;
- character counts and measures of typographic density (making comparisons with printed material as well as computer interfaces);
- the number of computer commands immediately available (more are better, if clearly but minimally displayed).

Applied thoughtfully, these measures may help to restrain the spatial imperialism of operating systems and of interface metaphors—and thereby enhance the richness of content displayed. Also such appraisals would make explicit a decision to devote only 18% of a computer screen to information, as we saw for the photographers' yearbook.

An eternal confection

THE first confection to leave the solar system was engraved on a 15 by 23 cm (6 by 9 in) gold-anodized aluminum plaque aboard the Pioneer 10 and 11 spacecraft launched in 1972 and 1973. After observing planets for 20 years, both Pioneer spacecraft have now left our solar system and have headed for the stars beyond, each carrying the plaque:

Hyperfine transition of neutral hydrogen, a basic unit of time and distance throughout the physical universe.

Outline drawings of humans (with prominent four fingers and opposing thumb), drawn in proportion to the Pioneer spacecraft in the background. Note the visual convention of the opacity of outline drawing as well as the lack of shadows.

Map of 14 pulsars locating the sun relative to pulsars and center of our galaxy. On the lines, binary digits denote pulse-*times* (deducible from their 10-decimal precision, an unlikely accuracy for stellar *distances*). With the hydrogen time-unit, an extraterrestrial analyst should realize that the times are about 0.1 second, a typical pulsar period. Since these periods decrease at known rates, pulsars serve as galactic clocks. Thus an advanced civilization could review its galactic database and identify the origin and time of launch, even if Pioneer is not discovered until several billion years from now.

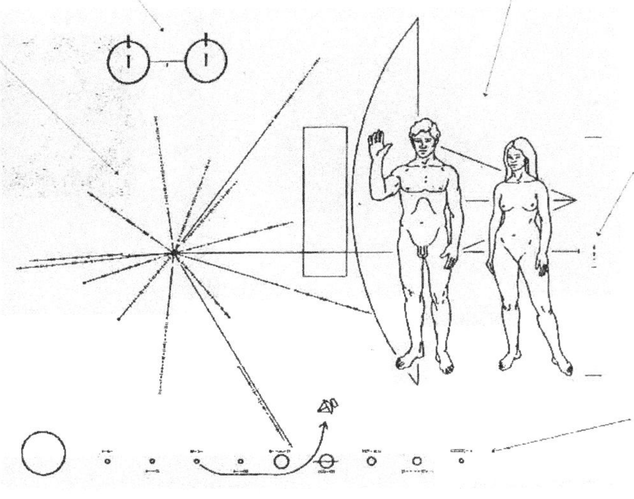

Binary equivalent of decimal 8, between tick marks indicating human heights. The hydrogen wavelength (21.11 cm) multiplied by 8 yields the woman's height (169 cm or 66 in).

Planets of solar system (note Saturn's rings), binary relative distances, and path indicating origin of Pioneer (which points back toward Earth).

This intensely quantified assembly brings together maps of pulsars and planets, scales for measuring time and distance through many orders of magnitude from atoms to galaxies, and outline drawings of humans and the spacecraft itself.[27] In one to ten billion years from now, perhaps long after our solar system has returned to dust, the Pioneer and its confection "may pass through the planetary system of a remote stellar neighbor, one of whose planets may have evolved intelligent life. If the spacecraft is detected and then inspected, Pioneer's message will reach across the eons"[28] and light-years of time and space, an eternal confection, a surviving memory of our Ocean of the Streams of Story.

[27] The annotation here of the Pioneer plaque is based on Richard O. Fimmel, James Van Allen, and Eric Burgess, *Pioneer: First to Jupiter, Saturn, and Beyond* (Washington, DC, 1980), pp. 248–250; and Roy R. Behrens, *Illustration as an Art* (Englewood Cliffs, New Jersey, 1986), p. 110.

[28] David Morrison and Jane Samz, *Voyage to Jupiter* (Washington, DC, 1980), p. 20.

THE development of perspective by Florentine architects during the 15th-century Italian Renaissance was a special gift to the world of visual thinking, for now people could see diverse objects located in a geometrically correct context. Confectionary designs are a similar gift to understanding. Like perspective, confections give the mind an eye. Confections place selected, diverse images into the narrative context of a coherent argument. And, by virtue of the architecture of their arguments, confections make reading and seeing and thinking identical.